French Fiction Today

FRENCH FICTION TODAY

A New Direction

LEON S. ROUDIEZ

RUTGERS UNIVERSITY PRESS

NEW BRUNSWICK, NEW JERSEY

Second Printing

Copyright © 1972 by Rutgers University,
The State University of New Jersey
Library of Congress Cataloging in Publication Data

Roudiez, Leon Samuel, 1917–
  French fiction today. A new direction.

  Bibliography: p.
  1. French fiction—20th century—History and
criticism. I. Title.
PQ671.R64   843'.03   70–185392
ISBN 0–8135–0724–3
Manufactured in the United States of America
By Rae Publishing Company, Cedar Grove, N.J.

for Jacqueline

Contents

French Fiction Today

Introduction

"I must Create a System or be enslav'd by another Man's," William Blake wrote in his *Jerusalem*, expressing a necessity that finds its echo in an admonition by Philippe Sollers, which figures as the last sentence of my concluding chapter. Blake is cited in Tony Tanner's introduction to his *City of Words* (New York: Harper & Row, 1971), a study in American fiction covering roughly the same period I am concerned with here—the one separating us from the second World War. If my final quotation echoes my first it also distorts it, as any echo must in its reverberating process, which takes place in this instance through the pages of my book. Echo and distortion: the two images aptly convey the impression one receives after setting contemporary French and American fiction side by side.

Basic assumptions and concerns are shared by the postwar generation of French and American writers. All realize that their work is primarily in language, and each of their works of fiction is a structure of words. Many of them also have a sense of being constricted, possibly determined, by the cultural, social, and linguistic patterns of the country in which they happen to have been born; escaping from such patterns is often at the core of their literary travails.

On the whole, however, French writers have shown a greater preoccupation with giving their work a social dimension, that is, with being socially or politically effective. There are of course exceptions on either side of the Atlantic. Still, I do not detect in French fiction writers that strong individualistic concern apparently characteristic of their American counterparts (verging on egomania in the case of Norman Mailer, even when he adopts a clearly political stance); nor does French fiction reflect with the same intensity the search for an illusive identity. As Richard Poirier recently noted, "We all see images of ourselves performing, on candid camera as well as on soap opera, until it is hard to know what is left in speech or gesture that can be truly claimed as one's own."[1] Philippe Sollers might have made that statement his own but for the final clause. To be free from the patterns imposed by society is certainly to be striven for; as to claiming any gesture or speech as truly one's own, he would probably ask, *Qu'est-ce que cela veut dire?*

Walter Kaufmann has written that France has, "more often than not, produced men who stand at the borderline of philosophy and literature."[2] It has become almost a cliché to accuse French writers of being overly interested in abstract theory. Today, however, except insofar as political theory is concerned, I am not sure that it would constitute an essential difference between them and American writers. Possibly they have at their disposal a larger body of continuously evolving source material produced by the speculations of French intellectuals, which are more widely disseminated than the books of American speculative thinkers. Perhaps French publishers have been (in the past at least) more receptive to the idea of bringing unorthodox, iconoclastic views into the open. Also, while French periodicals have more than their share of tradition-bound, myopic reviewers, there are enough intelligent critics writing for noncommercial publications who are willing to examine seriously new theories and new experiments in fiction.

If, then, there is a similar awareness of linguistic and cultural structures among fiction writers of both countries, eventual reaction to them varies considerably. The reasons for the difference appear to be in part political—and I shall return to that point briefly in my conclusion. As I see it, it lies in an unwillingness, on the part of a new generation of French writers, to separate literary (or linguistic) activities from any other human activity. Such an attitude goes hand-in-glove with the abandonment of old middle-class illusions about the "humanizing" effect of literature or the compelling values of "authentic" style. Richard Poirier marvels at the way Spiro T. Agnew (or his speech writer) illustrates an ability "to appropriate the language of one's enemies in the act of defeating them." That exemplifies the recourse to patterns in order to stimulate a reaction, a device constantly used in nearly all societies but to which our eyes had been closed for too long. Poirier continues, "Herein is a lesson for those who like to imagine the power of the word or of literature: power as a property, power of the kind at Agnew's command, can do what it wants with language, and language can do practically little to it."[3] Philippe Sollers' answer to that sort of abuse of power is clear: subvert the patterns by dismantling them from within, so to speak, making them ineffective by means of a conscious operation of language that changes the act of reading into a productive act. If I read him correctly, Poirier seems to be moving in the same direction, but without the imposing theoretical structure upon which Sollers and others of the review *Tel Quel* base their textual practice, when he urges that we acquire "a feeling for the power, still generating in those works [of literature], of the retraceable act of writing, composition, performance."[4] We shall indeed be encountering some of those very words in several chapters of this book.

In the spirit of what the writers themselves have been doing, those chapters will deal with works of fiction rather than with authors. No intentions, no biographies, no gossip. In discussing the fiction, I shall generally make no references to anything outside the fiction except in my final chapters; the reasons for doing so will be obvious enough. I should like to emphasize that I have no desire to sever the ties that bind a writer to his work; his active presence is what gives them a unity of sorts, and in all my essays but one(the last) a single writer is involved. That unity, however, is more important than what made it possible, and it is less so than the meaning that radiate from such an unified cluster. What goes into a work of literature or of art matters less to me than what comes out of it.

Having just used the term "literature," I should now like to dissociate myself from it to a certain degree. My quarrel is not so much with what has gone under that label; it is rather with the use to which it has been put. Too often, in what must surely be a degradation of its function, literature has been, in practice if not in theory, viewed as a delightful pastime for the idle rich. Some literature unfortunately lends itself to that only too well. Of course there should be pleasure in reading as well as in writing, but there are degrees in the quality of pleasure—of which Faust experienced the gamut. There is also a necessity, an urgency that drives a person to write (intransitively, as Roland Barthes says) and attracts others to his books. The shock of recognition, of which Melville spoke, where ordinary readers are involved, becomes the shock of discovery: the discovery of words used in a fashion not attempted before, of the new approach to reality that they afford, perhaps even the liberation of thought from an earlier linguistic confinement. It is a pleasure of the highest kind.

The writers whose works I examine here bear several common traits, which will become obvious along the way. They also exhibit differences, and the aggregate of their books does not reflect the doctrines of any school, nor does it illustrate the evolution of a genre. If anything, it shows that the concept of genre is not as useful as it was in the past. Actually, if the trend I discuss in my conclusion persists, the death of all literary categories may be at hand. For those reasons, I have avoided the use of the word "novel"; I can see no point in joining in the arguments of those who keep worrying whether this or that is "really" a novel. Likewise, I have eschewed the phrase "new novel" or *nouveau roman* as it is much too slippery and serves little purpose aside from fanning controversies. Some writers, such as Philippe Sollers, actually use the term *roman* with a subversive intent; others, like Jean Ricardou, favor the phrase *nouveau roman* precisely because of its provocative, exclusive possibilities.

While my concern is for those who have written the major portion of their fiction since the second World War, I nevertheless included an earlier writer. Raymond Roussel belongs here, in my opinion, since he was not really "discovered" until the fifties and many contemporary writers and critics refer to his works. Others might also have been included (and were, in an earlier draft) when their works, like those of Valery Larbaud or Jean Giraudoux, begin to reveal some of the concerns germane to contemporary fiction. I finally decided to omit them, for what is most interesting in French writing today is its revolutionary character, its desire to effect a break with the past. Although in my final essay I shall rapidly survey some of their antecedents, I do not wish to present today's writers as the latest link in a long chain in French literary tradition, into which they will eventually be assimilated. Theirs is not another instance of the romanticists' fight against classicism, of the Parnassians' against romanticism, of the symbolists' against Parnassus, and so on. This generation of writers is attempting to break away from literature.

Surrealism tried to do that very thing fifty years ago and failed. That there must be some connection between the two enterprises is obvious. That there is also a difference, giving today's writers some hope of success is also clear. As a matter of fact, the importance that surrealists have had for writers who came after them is no longer a topic for debate. Identifying the influence and tracing it, however, is another matter; it is a vast enough undertaking for at least a full-length study. I shall do no more than allude to it in several instances, particularly in the last two chapters.

Clearly, too, I have not presented a comprehensive picture of

present-day French fiction. A place might have been found for
texts by writers like Alain Badiou, Maurice Roche, Jean Thi-
baudeau, or Pierre Guyotat, for instance; or even better known
ones such as Julien Gracq, Raymond Queneau, or J. M. G. Le
Clézio. Yet, unwilling to compile an encyclopedia, I had to stop
somewhere, at an arbitrary point established by means of a
personal equation. Hence also some deliberate omissions—the
writings of Pierre Klossowski, among others, in spite of the
esteem in which they are held by intelligent French readers.

I began writing this study during the summer of 1967, in
Santa Monica, while teaching a summer course in French fiction
at U.C.L.A.; I finished the first draft late in the summer of 1968,
while helping to "restructure" the French Department at
Columbia after the revolt. Revisions then began; but the text
had reached something close to its present shape when books
by John Sturrock, *The French New Novel* (New York, Oxford
University Press, 1969), and Vivian Mercier, *The New Novel
from Queneau to Pinget* (New York, Farrar, Straus and Giroux,
1971), appeared. Sturrock discusses only Claude Simon, Michel
Butor, and Alain Robbe-Grillet, and his presentation is primarily intended for a British audience. Mercier, in addition to
Raymond Queneau, takes up six of the fourteen writers I
present here. In either case, as it was too late for me to benefit
from their pioneering work, I was relieved to note that the
critical viewpoint and the prejudices are not the same as mine.
These have changed since 1967, as so much around us has. I
have not written what I intended to then, nor have I done it in
the way I thought I might. For one thing, as my work progressed I became more and more attached to its object, gradually sharing more and more of the assumptions of the writers
I was studying. I believe now that what some of them are doing is of greater moment than anything that has been written
in the past.

Anything. If I have not succeeded in having others share that
feeling, that is of course due to my own shortcomings. As soon

as you can, go to a bookstore or a library and read these writers' texts. But do not look for a "thing of beauty"; look for yourself and for your role within them.

NOTES TO INTRODUCTION

References to works of fiction discussed in this book are to the original French texts. Translations are my own, except in the case of works by Samuel Beckett.

[1] Richard Poirier, *The Performing Self* (New York: Oxford University Press, 1971), pp. 6–7.

[2] Walter Kaufmann, *Existentialism from Dostoevsky to Sartre* (New York: Meridian, 1956), p. 41.

[3] Poirier, *Performing Self*, pp. 82–83.

[4] *Ibid.*, p. 84.

CHAPTER ONE

Raymond Roussel

Alain Robbe-Grillet, while working on *Le Voyeur*, had occasion to take a trip to the coast of Brittany. On the way, he decided that he was being given a fine opportunity to refresh his memory, to take a good look at the sea, the fishing ports, and the gulls—all of which might enter into the setting of his forthcoming book. "But no sooner had I glimpsed the first sea bird than I understood my mistake: on the one hand, the gulls that I now saw had only the vaguest connection with those I was describing in my book, and on the other, I could not have cared less."[1] He cared only for the gulls that soared out of the pages of his book. Several decades earlier, Jean Giraudoux had led one of his characters to the seashore, this time to the coast of Normandy. Simon, as Giraudoux called him, was about to leave Paris for extensive travel in continental Europe, but he had never experienced the ocean: "I should have been ashamed not to know the sea before plunging into Europe. . . . That was exactly it, at least as I imagined it, with its foam of gulls. All those who think of the sea know it. . . . I was delighted to have guessed right. Quite probably, I also knew beforehand what the glaciers were like, and the desert, and the void. From now on, there would be no point in checking such things too closely."[2] It is not difficult to detect a vague affinity with Oscar Wilde's remark about nature imitating art; in more apposite fashion, it implies that nature, or reality, assumes shape according to a model that language proposes. Relationship between language and reality lies ever at the core of the writer's care.

Rousel pointed out that he had travelled all over the world; he had seen the Near East and North Africa, India, China, Japan, Australia and New Zealand, the South Sea Islands, and most of Europe. For his creative activity, however, he claimed that such experience did not count: "Now I have not, from all my travels, ever used anything for my books . . . with me, imagination is everything."[3] A silly statement, if one were to take it at face value. Had Roussel not travelled all over Europe and the Orient, his works would have been different. What he probably meant was to establish a separation between the world as it appears and the fiction he invented. Along with Robbe-Grillet and other contemporary writers, he is interested in man's subjectivity and his will (or propensity) to distort, transform, or deny the outside universe. As a matter of fact, he was as much a victim of that propensity as an observer of it. What is so fascinating about Roussel is that nearly everything he wrote either rejects or ignores what most of us, by tacit consent, construe as reality—even when he appears to concentrate on a minute description of it. His was an inner world, conditioned by language just like ours, but where verbal creation feeds upon itself in the manner of a snowball. Replacing the "inner world" metaphor with a different one, the "world of language" for instance, would bring us very close to the concern of writers such as Philippe Sollers, whom I shall examine in my concluding chapters.

If Roussel was not led into the realm of surrealism (to which Giraudoux and Robbe-Grillet are also close), he occasionally skirted it and came near enough to be recognized and praised. André Breton himself was intrigued, proclaiming, "Roussel is, along with Lautréamont, the greatest magnetizer of modern times."[4] That Roussel had few readers until the 1960s is irrelevant in this context, for the magnetism Breton refers to has to do with the creative process—what he has called the alchemy

of words. Roussel, on the other hand, showed little interest in
the surrealists. His works are also lacking in two major surrealist preoccupations: the linking of surreality with reality and
the desire to change life. Nor is it clear if any portion of his
work could truly be interpreted in terms of a quest for the lost
paradise of childhood. He remembered his own with great fondness: "I have delightful memories of my childhood. I may say
that I then experienced several years of perfect happiness."[5]
It was possibly less urgent for him to seek such a paradise again,
for, in some ways, he carried it with him. Pierre Schneider has
distinguished his attitude from that of the surrealists by saying:
"His entire work is a kind of child's play . . . he plays while they
pretend to play."[6] Michel Butor was led by what he calls
Roussel's "salvaging of childhood" to mention Proust rather
than the surrealists.[7]

It is true that surrealists were attracted by his commonplace
descriptions of the fantastic. As J. H. Matthews puts it,
"Roussel's inventiveness catches the imagination and disturbs
most when, entirely without comment or interpretation, his
storyteller merely relates without sign of emotion what he says
he has witnessed."[8] But this does not so much imply an acceptance of the surrealists' *merveilleux quotidien* as it does an
exclusion of reality, a placing it within parentheses. What remains is a self-sustaining verbal universe, which Breton recognized as one of the very few created in his day. It is a complete
one, "a world re-created from scratch by a man fully set on
following only the bent of his own mind, insofar as such bent
might be unique."[9] This led Roussel along a one-way street,
beyond mere exclusion of reality, toward total denial. As he
shows no interest in transforming reality, it is tempting to call
him an escapist. Still, there are virtues in this escape into language, virtues of which he was in all likelihood unaware. His
contemporaries were equally blind and their judgment of him
was unduly harsh. If the variety of his more recent admirers
seems surprising, it could perhaps be explained by one feature

of his works: one could almost describe his creation as the establishment of a void. His logical, consequent, and seemingly matter-of-fact universe appears enchanted because of its availability. There is something in it for almost every reader.

As is often the case with writers, Roussel's first published work, *La Doublure* (1896), displays some of the basic characteristics that run through nearly everything he wrote. The narrative deals with an episode in the life of Gaspard Lenoir, a mediocre actor. After a humiliating failure on the stage, he and his mistress, Roberte, decide to put their savings together, leave Paris, and spend a few carefree weeks on the shores of the Mediterranean. All goes well at first; they have a grand time at the Carnival in Nice, but just before funds run dry Roberte walks out on Gaspard. He returns to Paris alone and in worse straits than before, for the only employment he can find is at a street fair in Neuilly. Such a plot outline reveals nothing startling or even original (although one might note its circularity). Some of the details are significant, but it is in the shaping and structuring of his material that Roussel displays some unusual features. Two of these strike the reader at once: the fiction is in verse, and two thirds of it consist of a meticulous description of the street scene—floats, costumes, and various incidents—during a few hours of the carnival. Were I to "judge" this verse according to traditional standards, I would surely be inclined to label it as doggerel of the worst sort. Actually, the word "verse" is somewhat misleading. A glance at the text gives one the impression that *La Doublure* is written in Alexandrine rhymed couplets, whereas it is really prose with pairs of rhymes every twelfth and twenty-fourth syllable. There is no rhythm; there are few of the pauses that characterize the French classical Alexandrine; and *enjambement* is the rule rather than the exception. If the text were printed as prose, there is a good chance that most readers would be unaware of the rhymes. Here, for an example, are the first three sentences of the book:

Le décor renaissance est une grande salle au château du vieux comte. Une portière sale sert d'entrée. Un vieillard, en beaux habits de deuil et l'air grave, est assis sur le bord d'un fauteuil à dossier haut.

(The Renaissance setting shows a large room in the castle of the old count. A soiled portiere serves as an entrance. An old man, wearing fine mourning clothes and a sober mien, is seated on the edge of a high-backed armchair.)

When the text is set in such fashion, its "verse" features are almost completely obliterated. Only a very astute reader would detect the rhymes *salle/sale* and *deuil/fauteuil*, even though they constitute a rhetorical generator in the composition. What matters is that the twenty-fourth syllable of the narration, as well as the word incorporating it, is determined by the twelfth syllable; the forty-eighth is then determined by the thirty-sixth, and so on, and objects, features, or incidents in the text are similarly determined. Such a process is not absolutely new: André Gide has remarked, for instance, that "The demands of versification have inspired Racine with some of his most subtle notations; these, as well as the most original and daring ones, were almost dictated to him."[10] With Roussel, however, the emphasis is obviously much greater.

In traditional writing, words generally are intended to express or convey some aspect or understanding of reality; here, in part at least, they are used to create that reality. One is again on the frontiers of surrealism, remembering Breton's "words that produce energy" and are able to command thought.[11] In later works, Roussel increases the creative role of words and their components, but in *La Doublure* they already serve to orient the progression of the narrative. It seems likely, for instance, that in the few lines I have quoted the count's mourning (*deuil*) required him to be seated in an armchair (*fauteuil*), and that later on a character's great sensitivity to the breeze (*souffle*) called forth a carnival float in the shape of a slipper (*pantoufle*)—or vice versa. More recently, writers such as Jean Ricardou have used purely verbal generators to produce most of the events in their fiction.

The carnival description occupies the entire third chapter

out of the six that make up the text, a disproportionately large one containing 116 pages of the Pauvert edition as against 13, 5, 7, 20, and 24 for the others. The length of that chapter is puzzling at first, and the purpose of the description is obscure. The book's slim plot is not advanced one bit: the episode seems a gratuitous parenthesis in the lives of Gaspard and Roberte. Then one realizes that the interruption is more important than the life, just as Roussel's inner world is more important than reality. Gaspard, a ham who thinks he can act, is limited to being an understudy. He is so mediocre that he himself begins to realize the impossibility of his ever breaking through; he has nowhere to go but down. Even his mistress is not all his: Roberte, who maintains herself a few rungs above the prostitute level, has been attracted to him through what the text calls "perverted love" after seeing him play the part of a shady underworld character. While she has been drawn to a mask that is worse than its wearer, he, ironically, thinks she is too good for him. Each one sees in the other a figment of his or her own imagination. Their love itself is a denial of reality. And when they leave Paris, it is to forget more than one bad performance on the stage. Gaspard wants to forget everything that he is, and the possibility of having Roberte all to himself during their spree represents another negation of reality. Thus he plunges into the carnival.

From the moment when we begin to follow him and Roberte through the streets of Nice, we enter a world of make-believe where every one is different from what he is in everyday life. All wear costumes and masks, and while we see everything through the eyes of Gaspard and Roberte, there is nothing in this chapter to contradict the impression that they are two lovers having the time of their lives. Even when Roberte runs into a friend of hers who is watching the excitement from a balcony, an actress whom Gaspard might logically be expected to know, he says the name means nothing to him; and Roberte, sensing that her friend is curious about her presence in Nice with Gaspard, says she will tell her all about it some other time. The refusal to let reality intrude upon the carnival could hardly be more explicit. A number of men accost Roberte as she and Gaspard walk along the streets, and they, too, are completely in the spirit of the carnival. They make up preposterous stories about themselves and their supposed love for Roberte, changing their lines shamelessly as occasion seems to warrant. On the whole, Gaspard takes it all with good grace—except when fantasy threatens to become reality. The most obvious illustration of this occurs when one of the amateur Don Juans pinches Roberte's waist. Gaspard intervenes and tells the intruder "in a curt and abrupt tone of voice" that he has had enough. He reacts in like manner to those whose disguises allude to the harshness of the world instead of contributing to the general atmosphere of harmless fantasy. A man made up as a beggar and displaying references to a financial scandal and a lame boy who pretends to be lamer than he really is likewise provoke his ire.

Some readers have found this section overlong and tedious, but in truth it could never be long enough, since the carnival suspends Gaspard's downfall. Comparing it with Victor Hugo's descriptions in *Notre Dame de Paris*, the anonymous reviewer for the *Times Literary Supplement* pointed out that, "What happens at the festival [in Hugo's work] carries the story a long way forward. In *La Doublure* the story is merely postponed."[12] Of course, but not "merely": this is essentially the way the meaning of the text is established. Ideally, the carnival and Roussel's description of it should go on for a thousand days and a day, for we know that when it ceases the final catastrophe will be close. In the end, at the Neuilly fair, as a barker drums up customers for the show that is about to begin, Gaspard cannot bring himself to be a part of the concomitant hustle and bustle. The last line of the book has him gazing at the stars in the sky and thinking, in all likelihood, of a more definitive way of escape.

Shorter works such as *La Vue* (1902), *Le Concert* (1903), and *La Source* (1904) effect the same sort of rejection, without even the pretext of a plot. Each one has a framework, in the guise of what one might call a brief introduction and conclusion, and that framework is precisely the reality that is being blanked out. Two dozen lines or so at the beginning of *La Vue* describe the narrator's pen, the tip of which contains a miniature photo mounted in a magnifying glass. He applies his right eye to the glass, closes his left to prevent his being distracted by anything taking place outside the window by which he is seated—and a sixty-two page description of the scene on the photo gets under way. A brief conclusion explains that he must stop because passing clouds have darkened the room and the photograph, and he muses on a period of the past that the picture has vividly resurrected but that is now "already dead, already far removed from me, swiftly carried away." Just as in *La Doublure* a realistic description of the carnival, that is of unreality, masked reality, in *La Vue* a meticulously realistic description of the impossible helps the narrator flee the present. The photograph represents an ocean-resort town seen from the sea. Among other patent impossibilities, the narrator depicts a thick vein on a hand resting on the handle of a cane, the hand belonging to an old man who is seated in a carriage being driven uphill on a road that is hidden from view by a row of houses in the background of the picture. In the terminology of Ferdinand de Saussure, in which the linguistic sign, made up of signifier (phonetic sound or written symbol) and signified (concept), points to a referent in reality, one might say that in this instance a sequence of signs have separated themselves from their referents (what can be seen on the miniature photo).[13]

Such discrepancies, which belong in the realm of literary plausibility, should not obscure an equally significant denial: in this story the aspect of reality that is most emphatically rejected is the passage of time. Naturally enough, it is happiness that is associated with time past, and the gathering clouds in the "real" landscape at the end of *La Vue* are an obvious enough correlative for present reality. The beginning of *Le Concert* is quite explicit about the same process: "Forgetting present time, I plunge again into old memories of happy bygone days." The narrator, at midnight (!), is rereading old letters; one was written from a hotel, and the letterhead has a picture of it and its immediate surroundings. Roussel needs a mere thirty-two pages to account for its details, completely obliterating the contents of the letter in the process. The pretext for *La Source* is much more trivial, but again it produces the same motion away from reality. The narrator is in a restaurant, the other customers are not pleasant to look at, his order is taking too long, and he is getting impatient. On his table, however, there is a bottle of mineral water. On the bottle, there is a label with a picture. About thirty pages take care of that.

The two works that have done most for Roussel's reputation are *Impressions d'Afrique* (1910) and *Locus solus* (1914). More ambitious than his earlier fiction, they exhibit, with a varying degree of emphasis, the same concerns or obsessions. Like *La Doublure, Impressions d'Afrique* is centered in the elaborate narration of a spectacle, this time quite an extraordinary one. It is presented to the reader as a series of what seem like outlandish and gratuitous happenings, the pretext for which is the coronation of Talou VII, emperor of a highly fictitious African realm. As the show goes on, he witnesses a number of elaborate, impossible performances and a display of contraptions that would have put Rube Goldberg to shame. Because of a flaw in one particularly difficult recital, the emperor rules that it must be repeated the following day. *Felix culpa*: the interval allows the narrator a long flashback (thus prolonging the literary feast) during which everything is explained in detail, everyone's background is thoroughly accounted for, and good and evil meet with their just rewards. Everything, from beginning to end, is totally unrealistic.

It appears that a shipwreck off the coast of Africa is what

made the narrative possible—just as a stage flop got things under way in *La Doublure*. A liner bound for South America is driven aground. All passengers come ashore safely (one assumes there were officers and crew aboard, but they are a realistic irrelevancy and therefore not mentioned),[14] only to be held captive by Talou. While waiting for ransom money to come from Europe, the stranded travellers prepare for a celebration that will mark both their liberation and the coronation of the African emperor, who has just added another kingdom to his possessions. To him, that latest victory represents freedom from a succession of hereditary wars, and for a number of individual participants the occasion also signifies various kinds of releases —from bondage, exile, or illness. In the end, the flawed performance is repeated, this time to the emperor's satisfaction, and the Europeans return home, thus completing a circle. *Impressions d'Afrique* is a fairy tale for adults written by an admirer of Jules Verne, hence a tale where supernatural magic has been displaced by science. In this instance, however, science, rather than serving life, liberates from it, just as it frees the emperor's son from the earth and allows him to soar into the air for a few brief moments. It also serves art, as in the case of rockets that reproduce paintings in the sky, for art itself, as Roussel appears to conceive it, effects the same kind of liberation. But freedom is a fleeting thing: the young man must soon come back to the ground, the pictures disappear into the night, the literary fantasy draws to a close.

The title lends itself to a pun: *Impressions d'Afrique* might be translated as "Printings of Africa," thereby stressing the verbal nature of the work. Clearly, the words of the text do not refer to any African reality or even to plausible events. As in the example I extracted from *La Vue*, signs are divorced from their referents. It might be possible to go one step further and suggest that if the narrative as a whole conveys a meaning (rejection of reality, for instance), its segments usually have no meaning beyond their necessary existence within the verbal framework of the text. While each performance that is described, as I have indicated, constitutes a microcosm of the pattern of the whole, the details and nature of any performance rarely signify anything beyond themselves. If one character has an affair with a woman named Flore in the Algerian city of Bougie, it is because (or in order that) another character has invented (or might invent) a vegetal candle (Flore=flora, and *bougie* is also a word for "candle").[15] Each episode is verbally dependent on every other one and signifies nothing beyond that dependence. Such a complex system of interdependence constitutes the unity of the text, a feature that, for reasons very different from Roussel's, will be of considerable interest to writers like Sollers or Ricardou.

In *Locus solus* we are also treated to a sequence of extraordinary performances. The difference here lies in the fiction that surrounds them. They are not created, so to speak, by a fictitious event that gives them a reason for being; nor, if they exist independently of that event, as in *La Doublure,* is the narration set in motion by it. The performances have been going on for some time, and some of them are to be repeated in the future, perhaps, as Michel Butor has suggested, in the hope of attaining a Kierkegaardian perfect, decisive repetition, "Liberating at the same time from death and from these vain, perpetual recurrences, but perpetually imperfect."[16] The story accounts for their existence but attempts no real justification for the narrator's becoming a spectator and then relating his experience: it simply happens that way.

Martial Canterel, a wealthy scientist, has transformed his country estate into a gigantic performing laboratory in which his discoveries are given spectacular, although not very practical, applications. A negation of time, similar to that implied in the earlier *La Vue,* may be detected in the sequence dealing with the refrigerated human bodies, frozen in the midst of a significant decor, that mechanically re-enact a crucial episode of their lives when set in motion by the scientist. The reader is told about these and other performances because the narrator, a friend of Canterel's, has been invited to visit the estate along with other intimates. I do not believe the lack of any sort of motivation for the withdrawal from reality is particularly significant, for there is nothing in the text to indicate a changed attitude towards life. At the end of the visit, the guests get together for a "gay dinner" in Canterel's country house, but this is part of the ceremonial of the visit.

What has taken place is a rhetorical shift through which the framework for the narrative has nearly been reduced to zero. Concomitantly, the author's indirect presence has switched from the framework to the main event. He was felt to be with Gaspard Lenoir in *La Doublure* and with the narrator of the subsequent works of fiction, but he seems here much closer to Martial Canterel, the organizer of the spectacle. The complicated machines Canterel has devised are analogous to the intricate fiction elaborated by Roussel. With each successive work (all were published at his own expense), he hoped to obliterate the failure of the preceding ones. As each one failed either to sell or to be noticed (let alone praised) by critics, with very few exceptions, his hopes for the next one must have grown more and more desperate and, in a form of defiance, caused him to emphasize its gratuitous, antirealistic aspects. Little excuse is thus provided for what is narrated in *Locus solus* and none whatsoever for the last fictional work Roussel published, *Nouvelles Impressions d'Afrique* (1928).

The compositional method used by Roussel in *Impressions d'Afrique* and *Locus solus* has much in common with the one he adopted for his other fiction. The process, which is also applied to his plays, was explained in detail in the posthumous *Comment j'ai écrit certains de mes livres*. Had Roussel remained silent about them, the chances are that these particular devices would have remained a secret for a very long time, if not forever. Revealing such a secret was perhaps hard to resist, especially for him, considering the compulsive way every detail in his fiction is accounted for. As a result, however, critics have tended to wallow in the revelations and forget that the elaborate explanations given in, say, the fiction of *Impressions d'Afrique* stop short of the final revelation, which must remain a mystery. Likewise, *Comment j'ai écrit certains de mes livres* gives only the preliminary steps of his compositional devices. The critics have also tended to take too literally his affirmation that the method he described had nothing to do with the composition of *La Doublure, La Vue, La Source,* or *Nouvelles Impressions d'Afrique.* Technically, he is right. But he himself has also pointed out that the method was related to verse composition: "It is essentially a poetic technique."[17] In both cases Roussel placed upon words, regardless of meaning, a large share of the creative burden. As the choice of words was sometimes arbitrary, this also has meant giving a greater role to chance. "In either case, there is unexpected creation due to phonic combinations."[18]

Roussel would take a sentence at random, say from a nursery rhyme or even from one of his own works and consider it exclusively from a phonetic point of view. As in a sort of extended pun, he would then try to think of other words that might approximate its phonetic scheme. "J'ai du bon tabac dans ma tabatière" thus becomes "Jade tube onde aubade en mat à basse tierce": the new words then serve to generate elements of a story, in this case a tale told in *Impressions d'Afrique* that involves a Persian who serenaded his beloved every morning, sitting by a basin where water spouted from a jade tube. Michel Butor has termed this "a sort of hallucinatory reading that consists in asking oneself, when faced with any kind of text, if it would not be possible to read it differently."[19] Marguerite Duras has done something similar, but only once, in passing as it were, when playing with the sounds of *la menthe anglaise.* Jean Ricardou, on the other hand, seems to do it as a matter of course. According to Michel Leiris, "Roussel has, much more than anyone else before him, drawn on the creative power of words. What is involved is a magical nominalism giving words the power to create things and enabling one to re-create the universe through the dislocation of a series of ordinary sentences."[20] One should remember, however, that this re-created universe negates the existing one.

Another aspect of the process involved taking two nouns, each of which could be given two different meanings, and linking them with a preposition. For instance, *palmier à restauration,* which might mean either a cookie for a meal or a palm tree for a restoration. The problem then was to work up a story around the ideas suggested by the two phrases as well as to utilize the words themselves. Such a problem is analogous to the one faced by the writer of a sonnet who must fit his statement into a given rhyme scheme and meter and a set number of lines. It is identical when the verse form actually suggests the statement. One recalls Paul Valéry's comment on his *Cimetière marin:* "It was born, like most of my poems, out of the unexpected presence in my mind of a given rhythm."[21] Nor is the problem unrelated to that of Martial Canterel in *Locus solus,* when, for instance, he is led to bring together two unrelated discoveries: an absolutely painless method for extracting teeth (without the use of anesthetics) on the one hand and a totally accurate formula for predicting the weather down to minute shifts in the wind and exact location and size of clouds on the other. The plight of the oversuccessful dentist faced with ever-growing mounds of extracted teeth he cannot dispose of could easily have developed into a hilarious situation. It is not hard to imagine what Marcel Aymé or Raymond Queneau might have done with such an idea, but Roussel had little sense of humor. Finally, the incongruous consequence of juxtaposing the two inventions results perhaps, as in the case of surrealist metaphor, in a work of art: a giant mosaic made of the thousands of variegated, discarded teeth, put together by a complicated machine activated by wind and sun. While this was already perceptible in *Impressions d'Afrique,* in *Locus solus,* just as the spectacle overshadows the framework, creation of the fiction and creation of the spectacle are brought closer together.

In *Nouvelles Impressions d'Afrique* the evolution is brought to a close; the fiction is the spectacle. Framework, narrator, fictional performances have completely vanished; there remains a 1276-line poem in four cantos that demanded seven years of Roussel's life. Like the mosaic in *Locus solus,* it strikes one at first as being a somewhat gratuitous tour de force. Africa, limited to Egypt, is present in the thematic headings of each canto: the house in Dumyat where Louis IX was kept prisoner, the scene of Napoleon's defeat of the Turks near the Pyramids, the mosque of Abul Ma'ateh, and the gardens of Rashid (Rosetta). The statement of the theme, however, occupies no more than a few lines at the beginning and a few more at the end of each canto (only one at the end of the third and the fourth). In two instances the statement is expressed in one sentence; but in all cases the sentence that ends the canto has begun on its first page—it has simply been interrupted by another parenthetical, associative statement. That statement, in turn, is interrupted by one enclosed in double parentheses. The latter is then broken up by one or more passages within triple parentheses. As one reads on, he encounters quadruple and quintuple parentheses and also footnotes that continue the rhyme- and verse-scheme of the text. A footnote to a line enclosed within quadruple parentheses also contains single, double, and triple parentheses and within the latter a sentence separated from the rest by a dash. It would take a mathematician working with a computer to figure out the precise relationship of that statement to the main theme of the fourth canto, in which it occurs.

In *Nouvelles Impressions d'Afrique* there are several instances of enumerations (more recent writers like Raymond Queneau or Michel Butor have also evidenced a fondness for catalogues). One in particular illustrates the device Roussel used elsewhere, but not in the composition of this last piece of fiction, as it lists a number of words with two distinct meanings. The final example of that series is the word *faute,* and its two meanings are not only distinct but opposite—negative, when it means "lack" and positive when it means "blemish." Roussel's obsession with verbal ambiguities might well be symbolic of a more general quest, analogous to André Breton's hope (expressed at the beginning of the second surrealist manifesto) of reaching a point from which opposites would no longer be perceived as such. Michel Foucault, without suggesting this analogy, has called *Nouvelles Impressions d'Afrique* a "treatise on lost identity" and a "cosmology of the Same."[22]

The line commenting on the word *faute*, with the meaning of "absence," is not far in the poem from the one that, given the system of parentheses around which this work is built, might be considered its center: "—De se taire, parfois, riche est l'occasion (There are sometimes great opportunities for silence)." That sentence contains the same kind of verbal antithesis that accompanied the mention of *faute*: the contrast between the profusion of *riche* and the emptiness of *taire*. At the same time, its immediate context displays a proliferation of words either suggesting or referring to fire (*feu, flambeau, grille, cendre, brûler,* and so on). It is a tantalizing statement, when we consider the role the concept of silence has assumed in contemporary criticism, such as Maurice Blanchot's, or the void that some commentators have discovered at the heart of much postwar fiction, burning away the fabric of conventional literature. It is also an ominous one when we realize that it was followed by Roussel's own silence. Some five years after the publication of *Nouvelles Impressions d'Afrique,* all his books having been written, his wealth dissipated and his health gone, drink or drugs no longer effective, literally burned out, he was found dead in Palermo under circumstances as mysterious as his life and as puzzling as his works.

NOTES FOR CHAPTER ONE (Roussel)

[1] Alain Robbe-Grillet, *Pour un nouveau roman* (Paris: Minuit, 1963), p. 139.

[2] Jean Giraudoux, *Simon le pathétique* (Paris: Grasset, 1918), pp. 31–32.

[3] Raymond Roussel, *Comment j'ai écrit certains de mes livres* (Paris: Pauvert, 1963), p. 27.

[4] André Breton, *Anthologie de l'humour noir* (Paris: Pauvert, 1966), p. 384.

[5] Roussel, *Comment j'ai écrit*, p. 28.

[6] Pierre Schneider, "La Fenêtre ou piège à Roussel," *Cahiers du Sud*, No. 306 (1951), p. 470.

[7] Michel Butor, "Sur les procédés de Raymond Roussel," in *Répertoire* (Paris: Minuit, 1960), p. 184.

[8] J. H. Matthews, *Surrealism and the Novel* (Ann Arbor: University of Michigan Press, 1966), p. 43.

[9] André Breton, "Fronton Virage," preface to Jean Ferry, *Une Etude sur Raymond Roussel* (Paris: Arcanes, 1953), p. 11.

[10] André Gide, *Divers* (Paris: Gallimard, 1931), p. 45.

[11] André Breton, "Les Mots sans rides," in *Las Pas perdus* (Paris: Nouvelle Revue Française, 1924), p. 169.

[12] "Revival of a Writer," *The Times Literary Supplement*, January 9, 1964, p. 18.

[13] Cf. Ferdinand de Saussure, *Cours de linguistique générale* (1916; rpt. Paris: Payot, 1968), pp. 97 ff.

[14] This is so from the point of view of the text; if I were to consider the author's point of view, I should have to say that, as a wealthy member of bourgeois society, he would not consider the crew worth mentioning.

[15] Cf. Christiane Veschambre, "Sur les impressions d'Afrique," *Poétique*, 2 (1970), 64–78.

[16] Butor, "Sur les procédés," p. 182.

[17] Roussel, *Comment j'ai écrit*, p. 23.

[18] *Ibid.*

[19] Butor, "Sur les procédés," p. 175.

[20] Michel Leiris, "*Comment j'ai écrit certains de mes livres,*" in *Brisées* (Paris: Mercure de France, 1966), pp. 58–59.

[21] Quoted by Jean Hytier in his notes to *Œuvres de Paul Valéry*, Bibliothèque de la Pléiade (Paris: Gallimard, 1957), I, 1674.

[22] Michel Foucault, *Raymond Roussel* (Paris: Gallimard, 1963), pp. 189, 186.

CHAPTER TWO

Nathalie Sarraute

By her own account, Nathalie Sarraute started writing in 1933, several years before Philippe Sollers was born. Within a span of three decades, from 1939 to 1968, she has published six works of fiction, a collection of essays, and two short plays. Quantitatively, that is not too impressive, and her audience has been a rather small one. The imprint she has left, however, is undeniable. Through her effective evocation of a new level of consciousness, she has, directly or indirectly, encouraged other writers to explore new directions in fiction, to bring forth statements of their own views or transformations of reality.

Out of the tightly knit pages of her narratives an inner world of gelatinous beings emerges under a pallid light. All anxiously groping for identical satisfactions, her creatures alternately experience pleasure and pain as tumorlike feelers either mingle with similar excrescences or become bruised by hostile reactions and are forced back into their own transparency and nakedness. Nathalie Sarraute is not primarily concerned with individualized characters, for these she sees as but fictions of the mind. She is not interested in molding a conventional plot into a perfect edifice; she agrees with Sartre that "adventures" lie outside authentic existence. She cares little for polite, rational discourse, for she believes what goes on beneath the surface of words is more genuine.

After quoting Katherine Mansfield's reference to "this terrible desire to establish contact," Nathalie Sarraute wrote in one of the essays of *L'Ere du soupçon* (1956), apropos of Dostoevsky's characters, that "their being continuously and madly in need of establishing contact . . . is what seizes them like a dizzy spell."[1] Dizziness might be experienced as one sways on the edge of a precipice—and, indeed, when in the same passage she alluded to Dostoevsky's statement concerning the "identical permanent stock" (p. 36) from which he had extracted the substance of all his works, she seemed to be playing on two meanings of the French word *fonds*, which (spelled without the *s*) also means depth. The implication is that only in the depth of his being does one reach the level where any authentic contact, either pleasing or painful, is possible. That is the level of truth, revealed when the protective coating of society's lacquer is removed, where the slightest impulse is registered, and the faintest perception is a scar. This level is well known by psychologists and also by traditional novelists; but Nathalie Sarraute has shunned psychological descriptions or analyses in favor of the events themselves, however minute they might be.

Her first book of fiction, *Tropismes* (1939), consists of a series of disconnected descriptions of that kind of event. According to biologists a tropism is the involuntary movement of an organism in response to outside stimuli such as light, heat, or chemical agents. Justin O'Brien has suggested that her title, in spite of its scientific tenor, might actually have a literary origin: the word appears, in a satirical context, in the early pages of André Gide's *Les Caves du Vatican*.[2] Be that as it may, Sarraute's tropisms, as she explained in *The Listener* some years ago, are those instinctive movements within one that are caused by other people or by the outside world: they "glide quickly round the border of our consciousness, they compose the small, rapid, and sometimes very complex dramas concealed beneath our actions, our gestures, the words we speak, our avowed and clear feelings."[3] At first sight, the twenty-four sketches that make up the revised edition (1957) are less "tropistic" than some of her subsequent texts. One can understand why Max Jacob, in 1939, wrote to her, "You are a profound poet, and I am placing your heavy volume (I say 'heavy volume' in the sense that one says a 'heavy heart') in a section with those poets that I reread."[4] They are prose poems, often tinged with melancholy or irony. The opening twenty-six-line sketch describes people walking in the streets, stopping in front of store windows, gazing, hardly capable of going any further, while their bored small children wait patiently for them to move on. Absorption of the individual into an aimless crowd, druglike effects of vulgar window displays, resignation of children in the face of an incomprehensible adult world—such might be the unexpressed reactions a reader could detect after giving the matter some thought. These, however, being passively observed, are apt to be overshadowed by active feelings of compassion.

Consider also the eighteenth sketch, framed in an English suburban setting. A dignified lady sits reading a magazine, knowing that "in a few moments they are going to ring the bell for tea," while in the kitchen the cook is peeling vegetables, knowing that "soon it will be time to roast the buns and ring the bell for tea." There is no outward activity of mind, for again it may be assumed that unconscious anticipation is the reaction provoked by the approach of a given time of day, by awareness of another person's presence. But it is hard not to read irony into the scene, to ignore the more delicate tropism in favor of social criticism. In the ninth sketch, on the other hand, there is no distracting interference. When "he" comes to visit "her" and begins at once to talk compulsively for fear that "she" might talk about herself, show her real hidden self, there is no difficulty in identifying the inner impulses of the psyche.

Constantly, Nathalie Sarraute has displayed signs of being wary of her readers: her next three works of fiction may be viewed in part as stages in an attempt to educate her audience as well as to master her own craft. As she has written in *L'Ere du soupçon*, "The reader, indeed even the most sophisticated one, as soon as he is left to his own devices, tends to create types; he simply cannot help it" (p. 70). Not only does he create types, corresponding to people or characters he thinks he knows, he also creates situations, plots, or themes. He will latch on to anything in order to mold the text he is reading into the stereotyped forms provided by his culture and education. As a tentative response to that sort of reader-aggressiveness, characterization, plot, and setting are reduced to a bare minimum in *Portrait d'un inconnu* (1948). One might call it naked fiction, for decor, social masks, and Sartrian "adventure" are stripped away, leaving us, presumably, with authentic reality. The title, which refers to a painting by an anonymous artist the narrator has seen in a museum, is a metaphor of the fiction. The anonymous "I" attempts a portrait of an unknown "he"—and both painting and text stare at the reader, sounding a call that is "pathetic, demanding" (PI, p. 86) and at the same time tragically silent.

In that silence lies a major theme of Nathalie Sarraute's entire work: the urgent need for true communication, which can be detected deep within every human being, is constantly being thwarted or crushed by falsehood, artifice, and social codes. The fronts people put up and the conventions they adhere to provide a semblance of security and communication, but they merely disguise the reality of human solitude. Silence and lies correspond to the two poles between which her texts oscillate: that for which there are no words and that which is described in clichés. Success is the adequation of language with elementary sensation; failure lies at either pole.

The opening pages of the book describe precisely such a failure experienced by the narrator with two different groups. With the one he encounters outright rejection, with the other a more complex misunderstanding. As a fictional device, the extremely sensitive, anonymous "I," whom we see from the inside, is pitted against characters, also nameless, who are seen only from without. Unable to break through their protective casing, the narrator has been forced back upon himself to a pathological degree. Throughout what I shall call the first part of *Portrait d'un inconnu*, up to and including the fifth chapter (actually, chapters in this and other fiction by Sarraute are unnumbered), the narrative stress is on him: everyone else, even the other two main characters, "elle" and "lui," are merely opportunities for him to display his sensitivity, and digressions give him occasion to present his views. (The latter naturally tend to give the work a slightly didactic tone.) Except for the "Portrait" in the title (also described in the text) and two references to Utrillo, cultural correlatives in this part belong to the most introspective of all arts, literature.

The fifth chapter, which takes the narrator to a Dutch city, amid evocations of Baudelaire's "Invitation au voyage," ends with his visit to the museum. There, the "Portrait of a man unknown," striking mainly because of its eyes ("his glance took hold of me"), perfects the false cure begun earlier by a psychiatrist: "I was free. My mooring lines were cut. I sailed, driven towards the open sea" (p. 87). Liberating him from an obsession with self, the painting opens his mind to others. Specifically, it causes him to identify with the unknown artist and attempt to understand the man unknown—"lui," who is the father of "elle." The second part lays stress on this other character. The cultural correlatives, with the one exception of Lewis Carroll, are painters. The woman of the story, who, at first reading, might appear to hold a central position, the object of the narrator's advances, stands revealed as a catalytic agent enabling both her father and the narrator to bare their more authentic selves—through the author's exposure of tropisms. All three are sensitive people; that is what, at this point, makes the revelation possible. A concluding chapter introduces a man named Louis Dumontet, who is engaged to "elle." He is all solid surface and shielded, as it were, by his name; no tropisms emanate from him.

In addition to stripping her main characters of names, backgrounds, and anything that might help the reader in "creating types," it also seems as though Sarraute occasionally tenders him misleading or contradictory clues. A group of my students reading the book for the first time were asked to give the narrator's age. Answers ranged all the way from "in his twenties" to "about fifty"—and there is some textual justification for each. Even Bernard Pingaud wrote that he was "young and sickly,"[5] which was also my first impression. In the next-to-last chapter, however, there are specific indications that he is beyond middle-age, balding, and with a bulging waistline. That uncertainty as to age, during the first part of the novel at least, might also encourage character-creating readers to miscast the woman and see a love-interest plot revolving about her. If they persist, it is really their own fault. On the other hand, those who think of her in terms of Eugénie Grandet are not completely to blame; and those who, when the narrator describes scenes he could not possibly have witnessed, begin to wonder how much of all this is "real" and how much "imaginary," can also more legitimately point to a slight hiatus between technique and apparent intent. Maurice Blanchot possibly had such matters in mind when he wrote: "And if something bothers us, it is rather the persistence of traditional elements, the outlines of a plot, the sketchy portraits, the need to justify this 'I' by giving him an external plausibility, some character traits, and even that pathological sensitivity that drives him to a psychiatrist."[6] For him, the fiction is obviously not "naked" enough.

Martereau, the character who has given his name to Sarraute's third work of fiction (1953), appears more solid and secure (like Louis Dumontet), especially when confronted with the delicate, nameless narrator and his equally nameless relatives. When his name is first mentioned, it suggests a "distant homeland" (M, p. 85), a "peaceful haven" (p. 86) from which the narrator has been banned. Gradually, that name is shown to be no more than a mask: the manner in which it

is associated with Holland in the text actually suggests a
trompe-l'œil quality. As it crumbles away, Martereau's uncertain gropings and ambiguous feelings are brought to light—
or, it may be better to say, into the twilight.

In addition to Martereau, about whom a plot of sorts evolves,
more than half a dozen episodic or referential characters are
also given names. Cultural correlatives, no longer exclusively
taken from the realm of art and literature as in *Portrait d'un
inconnu*, also come from history or legend. Both changes help
to anchor the book in the reader's familiar reality, even though
that may not have been intentional, and, at times, the anchor
seems to drag a bit. It is clear that Sarraute intended to reveal
Martereau as being as much the locus of tropisms as anyone
else: "He is as people are, not in traditional novels, but in
real life."[7] Somehow, she does not quite bring it off, and it is
hard to blame those who see Martereau as more "authentic"
than the narrator—precisely because he fits conventional reality
and appears unaffected by the wild fancies the latter's imagination indulges in.

The inadequacies of first-person narrative, here really a
modified interior monologue, are more obvious in Martereau
than in *Portrait d'un inconnu*. There we were dealing with a
set of relatively homogeneous characters. The problem as to
the reality of some of the descriptions is only a minor one:
other people's reactions, as supposed or imagined by the narrator, are always plausible within the atmosphere of the book.
But in *Martereau* two different worlds are involved, that of
"solid reality" (the masked people) and that of the semicon-
scious tropisms (the unmasked, hypersensitive people). To
penetrate Martereau's protective shell the reader needs an
intelligence other than the narrator's. Since the author does
not provide it, Martereau's inner reality and the narrator's
imagination become confused. What saves the book, ironically,
is the element of suspense and ambiguity contained in the
plot. Will Martereau, who has agreed to go along with a tax-

evasion scheme and bought a house in his own name but with money from the narrator's uncle, consent to relinquish the house? Such a question, however, is obviously irrelevant to Sarraute's concern.

In *Le Planétarium* (1959)—a false sky in which stars merely appear to be located—she has wisely adopted a stance halfway between omniscient author and recorder of different points of view and thus is able to enter the consciousness of a larger number of characters without creating confusion. Some of these are readily identifiable by name, and their activities seem to converge into a gossamer plot, which, metaphorically, is represented by the dome of the planetarium. The successful efforts of the main character, Alain Guimiez, to deprive his spinster aunt Berthe of a spacious apartment so that he and his wife might move into those more comfortable quarters make up the merely superficial sound and fury of life. Hidden to the naked eye like quasars in space, tropisms manifest their parallel existence as everyone responds or seeks a response, strives for approval or identification. On the plane of such movements it matters little which character is involved, for, as one of them says, "Everyone is alike, everyone resembles everyone else" (p. 34).

By now, one might hope, the reader has become aware of that—if he has kept up with the author's publications. He should be willing to accept the two levels of activities, allowing the masked characters to engage in pointless social pursuits but reserving the better part of his attention to the anonymous tropisms. Nevertheless, Henri Peyre, one of the most highly regarded academic critics of contemporary French literature, based his criticism of *Le Planétarium* on aspects of plot and characterization: "The story is certainly laid in stuffy claustration; never a touch of nature and never an intruder from the masses. Even in Proust, servants and elevator boys brought a touch of country life and appeared to be doing something with their hands."[8] To accuse Peyre of missing the intent of

Sarraute's work merely brings up the issue of intentional fallacy. The point is that intelligent readers have been unwilling to go along and progress with her from stage to stage in the process of audience-education. Whenever one of them is given the slightest chance, he slips back into his traditional reading habits—she knew it would happen, "he cannot help it."

In *Le Planétarium* there seldom is any lasting doubt as to which character is involved at any given moment; when there is, as in the case of the woman who bursts out laughing at the party given by Guimiez's in-laws, the uncertainty does not apply to any of those one has decided to call "principal." An excuse is thus provided for a gradual attempt at characterization, and the attention paid to such matters is easily diverted to the anecdotal dealings of characters with one another and thus to the elaboration of a significant plot. Richard N. Coe, in an excellent article to which I shall return later, describes the process as follows: "gradually the pronouns begin to germinate, the bones take flesh, the flayed psyches acquire expression, and, for one reader at least, the metamorphosis is complete. Immediately the whole novel slips into a new perspective: good, sound construction appears, faintly reminiscent of Angus Wilson, with a coherent plot . . . and characters!"[9]

Again it appears that Nathalie Sarraute was aware of the inadequacies of her fourth work of fiction (considering what she was attempting to convey). In *Les Fruits d'or* (1963) she gives evidence of having acquired an even greater degree of control over her technique and material. This work has very little extraneous decor, and, with its successor, *Entre la vie et la mort*, it is the most accomplished from the point of view of her esthetic aims. The slender plot involves the rise and fall of a novel's reputation. Tropisms within an indeterminate numbers of characters and presented, as in *Le Planétarium*, from as many different points of view, grow in intensity as the imaginary work, "Les Fruits d'or," becomes quite the rage among members of the Paris literary set. As the opinion-makers impose their views those tropisms reach their highest level of intensity and then recede as the novelty wears off and a new fad takes its place, eventually pushing the book into oblivion. If such a plot can be called slender, however, it is also a serious one. It does not seem, as in the previous fiction, a mere pretext allowing the author to deal with what she is really interested in. The door knob and plate of *Le Planétarium* could have been a mirror or a chandelier; the apartment could have been any other valuable possession; and the book would have remained essentially the same.

The making and unmaking of a novel's image as contrasted with its intrinsic nature and merit raise questions as to what constitutes a literary masterpiece (assuming that the term still has meaning, as it does within the framework of this book) or, in more general fashion, as to what criteria may be used to assign value to any given text. Such matters must be of considerable concern to a writer as dedicated as Nathalie Sarraute, even more so after the publication of several controversial works, when comments from admirers may well have been as embarrassing as attacks by detractors were exasperating. These matters should also be of great interest to readers who expect more from a book than a temporary diversion.

In *Les Fruits d'or* the anecdote can no longer be called trifling, for it has reached a plane of significance that is comparable to the new aspect of human reality revealed through tropisms. These now take place within characters that are not always named and are seldom identified; readers are thus frustrated in their desire to create a set of characters and link them along in the chain of a linear story. Three unnamed individuals, two men and a woman, are clearly involved in the first ten pages of the book. Others (but are they really "others"?) named Marcel, Lucien, and Jacques appear in subsequent pages. A man named Bréhier is obviously the author of "Les Fruits d'or." Brulé, Orthis, and Mettetal are critics. Their interrelationship and who speaks or reacts to whom at any given moment could possibly be determined by painstaking analysis —but that would no longer constitute creative reading; it would amount to sheer pedantry.

Entre la vie et la mort (1968) gives one the other side of the picture: no longer concerned, as in *Les Fruits d'or*, with the fate of a novel after it has been published, Sarraute turns the spotlight on the creative process. In the words of Mary McCarthy, "Nothing of the sort—a rending of the veil—has been attempted before, and one would have said in advance that it was impossible, short of demonstration, to show how an author composes, that is, to create with words a sort of program music imitating the action of other words as they assemble on a page."[10] Somehow Sarraute succeeds, perhaps because, to her, creation is the most interesting side of the literary phenomenon, just as hidden tropisms fascinate her more than outward gestures—and there is a definite link between tropisms and creativity. As Yvon Belaval wrote with reference to the earlier volume, *Tropismes*, "Nathalie Sarraute has chosen as her subject creation as it comes to life."[11]

The setting of *Entre la vie et la mort* is absolutely barren except for metaphors expressing inner psychological states or actions that transport one to a king's court or a military encampment. The technique is as effective, if not more so, than in *Les Fruits d'or*. Surnames are few and even less conspicuous than in the preceding work. There is Régier, a famous writer, Frémiot, the publisher, and Burel, his editor; the rest are utilities. All play inconsequential parts compared to the anonymous writer, whose creation the book is about, his family, friends of prepublication days, and the new ones he has made after the work he has been struggling with has appeared. Each provides a stage for the manifestation of tropisms. Broad outlines of a narrative can be detected: the writer, whose book has given him notoriety, explains to his admirers how he works; then a series of flashbacks reveal his developing sensitivity as a boy, encouragements from his mother, his efforts at writing, literary discussions with friends, acceptance of manuscript by the publisher, his mother's and father's reactions, and the book's success; again explanations of himself and the way he composes. Of course, my suggested outline becomes rather blurred when one actually reads the book, and chronology is not faithfully adhered to.

The title refers to the precarious state of the writer in the presence of the deep, essential fountainhead within himself, out of which his creation flows. His sensitivity leads him to that spring, and the problem is to remain with it, for if he loses it or it runs dry, the creative artist in him dies. Such preoccupation with the background of the work and stress on sensitivity to the material world place Sarraute apart from many of the leading writers of the postwar generation. *Entre la vie et la mort* affirms her independence from the most recent trends. Even more than in *Les Fruits d'or*, she relies on irony to define her position. Towards the end of that work, after the noise made by fashionable fakers has subsided, one reader manages to establish an authentic rapport with "Les Fruits d'or," and his attitude is conveyed in straightforward fashion. But here, such positive statements as exist are dispersed throughout the text and presented in tentative manner: "everything here should assist in the unfolding, the asserting of— what should I call it? This activity of a fragment of living substance?" (EVM, p. 104). On the negative side of her position, the third chapter, with its list of homonyms, suggests a parody of Raymond Roussel: "Hérault, héraut, héros, aire haut, erre haut, R. O." (pp. 28 ff.). Elsewhere she appears to be directing her irony at Maurice Blanchot, as when a critic explains to the writer that his work has a central pivot: "But consider: that center is a hollow. It is a silence. It is a gap in the continuum of time." (p. 142). Or at Philippe Sollers and the group identified with the review *Tel Quel*, when she presents this exchange: "You were telling stories to yourself . . . No. It wasn't anything. Just words" (EVM, p. 38). The writer, as the romanticists had already decided, suffers more than other people. *Entre la vie et la mort* might well be subtitled, "Portrait of the Artist as a Young Martyr."

Tropisms, which Nathalie Sarraute views as the major ingredient of her texts, take place, according to her own definition, beneath the level of actions, gestures, and words. Words, on the other hand, whatever the main character of *Entre la vie et la mort* may say, are the basic components of fiction. The problem of expressing those wordless events is perhaps no greater than that involved in rendering violent emotions that transcend normal powers of expression. One might even say, with Yvon Belaval, that "a word is no more profound if it has been uttered silently rather than articulated aloud; when a novelist or a poet uses it to depict feelings, its nature does not change whether it refers to the shadow cast by a post on a terrace or the shadow of a doubt, whether it conveys a truism or a subtle remark."[12] Nevertheless, though the nature of words is not affected, difficulties are increased when a writer endeavors, as Sarraute does, to have readers participate in the activity rather than to give them a description of it. In all cases of course, the choice of words must be appropriate and effective. Where tropisms are concerned, the choice of imagery can also pose a number of problems.

I have already alluded, in the case of Martereau, to the fictional link Sarraute establishes between a person's name and the social masks he dons. Direct, conventional use of the word "mask" also occurs, as when it is defined as "that individual, artificial, fixed expression people often assume when they look at themselves in a mirror" (PI, p. 63). It is also a "heavy, hard cast" (M, p. 32) that they fashion in order to portray others, like the "grotesque and outmoded mask of a musical-comedy mother-in-law" (P, p. 52) that Alain has placed on Gisèle's mother. The use of a name as a metaphor for such masks, fairly obvious in *Portrait d'un inconnu* and *Martereau*, is somewhat more complex in *Le Planétarium*. There, most characters bear only one name, with the exception of Alain Guimiez, Germaine Lemaire, and a minor personage, professor Adrien Lebat. Germaine Lemaire's protégé, René Montalais, Alain's wife, Gisèle Guimiez, and his father, Pierre Guimiez, also have full names, but their first and last names are never associated. We know Alain's mother only by her maiden name, Delarue; his aunt is Tante Berthe, his late uncle, Henri; Gisèle's father and mother are merely Robert and Madeleine; Germaine Lemaire's other disciples appear as Jean-Luc, Lucette, and Jacques. Secondary characters appear only as names, that is, as masks or silhouettes that enter fleetingly the main characters' range of perception. Major characters (whose names are, on the whole, infrequently mentioned) carry their names as they might an artificial excrescence that is either emphasized or not, according to the needs of the fiction. It would appear that, for instance, "Germaine Lemaire" and "Maine," her nickname, are two very different masks; or that "Alain Guimiez," "Alain," "he," "son," "nephew," and "son-in-law" correspond to different levels of authenticity or reality. A similar, although simpler device is used in *Les Fruits d'or*, where characters evolve on three separate levels: they are anonymous (authentic), bearers of Christian names (semiauthentic), or bearers of last names (masked). Even though *Les Fruits d'or* appears more effective in this respect, the device is not carried to *Entre la vie et la mort*, in which the reader is not allowed behind the masks of named characters.

Ordinary words, too, are but the proper names for objects, actions, or thoughts; like them, they can be bearers of masks. Frequently, one finds Nathalie Sarraute skillfully shifting back and forth between stereotypes and what she deems authentic language. As with characters, the device is more obvious in the first two works of fiction following *Tropismes*. Stereotyped words or phrases are occasionally found in quotation marks or even capitalized in *Portrait d'un inconnu* and *Martereau*: "We

have entered the Sacred Domain of 'Life,' as they call it, of
'Practical Matters,' of 'Hard Facts,' as they say with a sigh"
(PI, p. 58); "Money that I have earned 'by the sweat of my
brow,' just imagine" (M, p. 23). In *Le Planétarium*, however,
a comment like "such fine workmen who know their job thoroughly, who love it, too, one should always patronize the better
stores" (P, p. 10) bears no sign of emphasis—no more than its
opposite number, "idiots, big brutes, without an ounce of initiative, no interest in what they are doing, not the slightest indication of good taste" (P, p. 13), made, of course, by the same
person about the same workmen who have come to install a
new door. Stereotyped words and phrases are both protective,
in that they help to establish a character in his accustomed
role, and harmless because they have no more significance
than what happens in the course of a parlor game: "Happy
smiles . . . sympathetic glances . . . exquisite scene .. . delightful comedy perfectly cast, with well-matched actors" (P, p.
149). What takes place on the authentic level, on the other
hand, is likened at times to the "bloody games of the Roman
circus" (M, p. 75); or to a bullfight when "a bull, dripping
with blood, lowers its head and confronts the matador" (P, p.
143); or to the experiences of early Christians in the cata-
combs—"they are surrounded by pagans, hunted down, they
will be martyred, humiliated" (FO, p. 110); or to scenes of
torture, with "a sadist relentlessly torturing his victim" (EVM,
p. 55). In all such instances, words are no longer harmless;
they harbor pernicious germs (M, p. 133). As the narrator in
Martereau expresses it, "There are no harmless words between
us, there are no longer any harmless words" (p. 283).

The metaphor of protective shell is but a short conceptual
step from that of mask. There are, in Sarraute's first three full-
length works of fiction, at least forty specific references to a
"shell" (either *coquille* or *carapace*, depending on the connotation desired). We witness characters who "struggle, forehead against forehead, clumsily ensconced in their shells, their

heavy suits of armor: 'I am the Father, the Daughter, my Rights'" (PI, p. 48). The analogy between the two groups of metaphors is made obvious through juxtaposition. In addition, there are even more numerous uses of such related adjectives as "hard," "smooth," "solid," and the like, applied to characters when their guard is up and they have taken refuge behind society's props. Louis Dumontet is thus represented as "Extremely sure of himself. Impassive. Imposing. A reef. A rock that has withstood all of the ocean's onslaughts. Unassailable. A compact block. All smooth and hard" (PI, p. 222). Even the syntax is adapted to the metaphor of rocky solidity. There is also a kind of shell that protects not only the wearer but others as well, the uniform. Related to stereotyped phrases, it enables everyone to play his part and identify others in unthinking security. "He is undressed, they give him his underwear to put on, it is part of the prescribed dress. They have him don his uniform" (EVM, p. 25). The issuing of a uniform is a sort of exorcism. Opposed to hardness and relative safety, there is softness and vulnerability. Correspondingly, one finds many adjectives describing such a state, as in the following example: "at his feet, she was there before him, thoroughly soft, at his mercy, always within reach" (PI, p. 196).

Earlier, when quoting a passage from *L'Ere du soupçon*, I suggested the image of a precipice to express the feelings of those about to establish contact on an authentic level. As a character totters on the edge of the abyss (there are about fifty references to "bottom," "hole," "void," and so forth), he is overcome by dizziness and then usually sinks into the chasm. The process is a slow one, and characters are agonizingly conscious of it: "That time, as it almost always happens when things have gone a bit too far, I had the impression of 'hitting bottom'" (PI, p. 25). They do not fall precipitously, rather they slide (the verb *glisser* alone appears about sixty times), as the old man and his daughter do in *Portrait d'un inconnu*: "their shells, their armor are splitting up all over, they are naked, without protection, they slide downward, hugging each other, they go down as if to the bottom of a well" (p. 185). On their way down, some occasionally manage to catch hold of something solid and chin themselves up to the surface again. More than fifty instances of verbs expressing the idea of clinging to, holding on to, testify to their reluctance to leave their accustomed level. What they most want is security, not authenticity. There are thus many references to the verb "to cuddle up" (*se blottir*) in a warm, safe place, often in a "nest"—a word having similarly cute, stereotyped overtones in French as in English.

Unwillingness to let go of a solid, artificial world is also conveyed by the usually unfavorable connotations of the words used to describe what is found beneath. Fearful characters find that level markedly suspicious (as evidenced by the frequent appearance of the word *louche*). They picture it as an amorphous world of undefinable, slightly repulsive motions (*remous* and *grouillements*), where all things are soft and gluey (*gluant*), where living entities are reduced to the condition of larvae. Ironically, one of the literati praising the fictitious novel in *Les Fruits d'or* emphasized that it contained "no swarming of larvae, no floundering in some miry depths or other emitting asphyxiating miasma, in some undefinable slimy ooze where one sinks in" (FO, p. 60).

Such uneasy sensations as characters experience when viewing the depths of their being lend a mysterious, almost magical, aura to the nether regions. Those are the primitive areas of men, where our artificial civilization has not penetrated, and strange, terrifying powers appear to reign. Their demoniacal nature is implied by Nathalie Sarraute's occasional use of the verb "to exorcise". One instance occurs when she is speaking of Dumontet's use of clichés, "Those words he seems to reel off mechanically must eventually have the soothing, exorcising effect that simple, monotonous words of prayers have upon non-believers" (PI, p. 236); and another, when a disappointed

Alain returns from the apartment of Germaine Lemaire and invokes his masks, "Gisèle . . . my love, my wife . . . Gisèle . . . That name exorcises"'" (P, p. 111). Waiting to be exorcised, so that they might enter the Sacred Domain of a previous quotation, are several ghouls, vampires, dragons, and a sorceress. Complementing this exorcistic process, one might expect a certain amount of religious imagery; there are hints of it, as when Martereau's cordial handshake and backslap have a soothing effect on the narrator, like "the imposition of hands, exorcism, the sign of the cross that causes the Evil One to flee" (M, p. 91); but it becomes significant mainly in *Les Fruits d'or*. I shall return to that point presently.

Once they have reached the realm of authenticity, characters can truly communicate. They do so either through a devious utilization of words that become like "tiny safety valves releasing heavy gases, unhealthy emanations" M, p. 283), when something about the tone, the sound of a person's voice, even the pauses between utterances suggests suspicion or hatred. They can also confide more directly, through a mysterious, instantaneous process. Here we reach the crux of Nathalie Sarraute's problem, for, as I indicated earlier, and as the narrator in *Martereau* makes clear, "All this and even more is expressed not through words, of course, as I must express it now, lacking other means" (p. 34). She too, as supernarrator, must use words. Her answer, in the composition of her fiction up to and including *Le Planétarium* and again in *Entre la vie et la mort*, seems to have resided in extensive recourse to animal imagery. Basic, semiconsciousness actions and reactions taking place below the polished level of civilized life are thus pictured as analogous to the instinctive comportment of animals.

Animal metaphors occur in instances that numbers in the hundreds. Some thirty-odd references are to animals in general (*bête* or *animal* with an appropriate qualifying phrase). There are in addition at least one boar, two toads, two horses,

four tigers and hyenas, four mice, four bulls, five pigs or pig-
lets, six foxes, six monkeys, seven cats, seven wolves, a dozen
snakes, a flock of sheep, and forty-odd references to dogs or
packs of dogs! One also detects half-a-dozen larvae, a dozen
or so more developed underwater creatures, forty birds, and
close to fifty insects of various description. All that in addition
to the reference to animals in common sayings or proverbs
such as *il n'y a pas de quoi fouetter un chat*, which occurs
several times.

To that enumeration one should add a list of spare parts:
animal attributes mentioned either in conjunction with a specific animal reference or alone—as in the description of the
uncle's attempt, in *Martereau*, to free himself from his partners
in abysmal communion. He tries to "erase, as with a sponge,
with his mushy voice, what he has imprinted in her, in me,
the indelible scars left by his claws, his teeth, his spurts of
hatred that burn, disfigure as sulfuric acid doses" (M, p. 56).
"Claws" and "tentacles" are probably the most typical of such
attributes. Less easily pinned down because of the subjective
element involved, there are close to two hundred and fifty
instances of verbs or nouns describing actions or conditions
either exclusively associated with animals or, within the context, readily suggestive of animal life. Over thirty occurrences
of "biting" illustrate such implicit references, as in the following
example: "What a treat to watch him stagger out, blinking
in the light, and finally see in broad daylight his ornery, sneaky,
scornful, down-trodden appearance, and, repressed by fear,
his desire to bite" (M, p. 23). They are closely followed, in
terms of frequency, by such verbs as to wriggle (*frétiller*),
crawl (*ramper*), snort (*s'ébrouer*), and various descriptions of
sounds produced by birds.

Closely related to the preceding category, numerous implicit or explicit appeals to the sense of smell catch the reader's
attention. These do, in a way, belong to the group of animal
actions, beasts commonly being credited with acutely devel-

oped olfactory abilities; but human beings, too, register scents with varying degrees of intensity. It is also more difficult here to draw the line between an obviously intentional use of an animal characteristic and the perhaps unconscious use of a figure of speech. When, for instance, does *flair* really mean scent, and when does it mean something like "instinctive feeling"? What matters, in the final analysis, is the effect on the reader. Because of the sheer number of references involved, it is quite likely that many of the clichés in Sarraute's fiction have been contaminated, so to speak, and reactivated by proximity to live metaphors. At any rate, smells are linked to the more primitive, uncivilized activities of man, and it is significant to find about one hundred fairly specific references to smells or to the act of smelling, in addition to or associated with some fifty references to "emanations" that may or may not be perceived with the nose, ranging all the way from an "exquisite, cool scent" (M, p. 51) to "the miasmas that emanate from us" (EVM, p. 24) and a "vague carrionlike stench" (M, p. 175).

The olfactory appeal is dominant although far from exclusive; but when made in combination with appeals to other senses, it would seem to make the most lasting impression. For instance, in *Martereau*, the uncle on his way home thinks of his wife and pictures her as "silky and pink, wearing perfume" (*soyeuse et rose, parfumée*, p. 55). The words convey tactile, visual, and olfactory impressions, and all three adjectives are general in nature. *Soyeuse* has connotations that tend to make it overlap into areas of sight (silk is shiny, and the metaphorical connotation of "radiance" may well be aided in French by the near homonym *soyeuse/joyeuse*) and hearing (silk swishes). *Rose* is not a particularly original or distinguishing attribute, especially considering that the human eye has the ability to register phenomena with great precision. *Parfumée* is pleasantly vague, but olfactory perceptions in man are rather imprecise. The scent, however, is amplified by a nearly automatic throwback to *rose*, now perceived not as a color but as a fragrant flower—the net result being that the third adjective seems the most effective, the most likely to be remembered. Stylistically less subtle but perhaps more typical of the undertow that occasionally catches the reader off balance is the description of Pierre in *Le Planétarium* as he approaches his sister: "He gives off a kind of radiation, like a fluid, it flows out toward people, out of his narrow eyes, out of his Buddha-like smile, out of his silence" (P, p. 136).

Visual elements are present throughout the fiction, although less strikingly, and visual imagery as such is relatively rare. There is an obvious connection here with the world of appearances, the nonauthentic level. More visual references appear in *Le Planétarium*, where the surface of life is given greater emphasis than in the previous fiction and also in *Les Fruits d'or*. Very little can actually be *seen* in *Portrait d'un inconnu* or *Martereau*. Characteristically, visual sense impressions are most precise and frequent in those pages of *Portrait d'un inconnu* that deal with the narrator's travels, after he says he has been exorcised (p. 81); and a number of them are directly inspired by Baudelaire's "Invitation au voyage" (the references to Holland and to painting are significant in this respect). In *Martereau*, they are more noticeable wherever Martereau and his wife are involved. In *Les Fruits d'or*, the metaphorical connection between sight and mask is illustrated in the "recognition" scene: "We are, after all, among people of our class . . . Same flower in the buttonhole, same spats and satin vest, same eyeglass" (p. 12). A visual picture emerges; one sees a kind of masquerade. That is in contrast to the unusual instance of a technically visual image that leaves practically no visual impression, such as "the semidarkness of what is poetically called 'the inner landscape'" (PI, p. 25).

Finally, tactile references also appear in noticeable numbers in Sarraute's fiction. This is consistent with what we have seen so far, since, like olfactory ones, they correspond to a more primitive means of perception and communication. If there are fewer tactile than olfactory references, it is probably because actual contact may be considered a metaphorical representation of Sarraute's supposed goal for her characters. A tactile metaphor conveys the satisfaction felt during one of those rarely achieved moments: "The two of us are there, as we used to be, huddled together, isolated from all others. I experience the delightful, comfortable feeling one has upon plunging into a lukewarm bath" (PI, p. 46).

Many of the metaphors either suggest violence or are explicitly linked with it. Roman circuses and bullfights have already been mentioned. The contemporary circus provides an image of mental torture as characters are made to play the clown, and they make themselves ridiculous under the floodlights, before a crowd of spectators (M, p. 259; EVM, p. 234). Military imagery and an accompanying array of wounds, humiliations, and conquests, within contexts ranging from the Turkish conquest of Byzantium to attacks by American Indians and armored tanks prowling through a conquered city, serve to render the feeling of psychological torture that people experience in confrontations with others. Animals, in many instances, are preying upon other animals, fleeing before them or fighting. The vocabulary of the hunt provides a ritualistic element, enabling related metaphors to mirror the complexity of human relationships, those hardly perceptible but sudden shifts from the supposedly authentic to the nonauthentic. All that violence is, in the main, essentially negative: it is almost invariably depicted from the point of view of the victim or of someone in sympathy with him or her. The aggressor is essentially the Other. Nearly everyone of Sarraute's main characters could exclaim with Alain Guimiez, "There is only one victim here, myself" (P, p. 86)—and in *Entre la vie et la mort* that becomes the author's own cry.

None of Sarraute's imagery is unusual per se. The emphasis on certain image categories is perhaps more so, but even in that respect there are precedents. A striking analogy exists between the imagery of her fiction and François Mauriac's. Martin Turnell has noted the elder Mauriac's preoccupation with the sense of smell, his "use of the language of violence," his frequent references to mud, squalor, and decay, his predilection for animal and insect metaphors.[13] It is not too important that the two writers were probably drawn to those categories for analogous reasons: a portrayal of the base nature of man when unaided by God on the one hand, a description of instinctive, preconscious phenomena on the other. In each case, a very different value judgment is implied. What may be more significant is the effect upon the reader of types of images that he is made to absorb in greater proportion than usual. Timorous Catholics have denounced François Mauriac for being obsessed with sin, perhaps even enjoying it, and attracting perverse readers to his books. One critic has accused Nathalie Sarraute of defining human relationships through her insect comparisons.[14] Ludovic Janvier has referred to her "sadism" and characterized her view of human relations as being "at the same time a gluey aggression and a somewhat vile collusion."[15] It is likely that she herself sensed the danger in her use of imagery.

While Sarraute's stress was already more attenuated in *Le Planétarium*, in *Les Fruits d'or*, she tilted the scales away from her menagerie, and in *Entre la vie et la mort* she achieved a balance that is far more effective. In *Les Fruits d'or*, the Sacred Domain conjures up visions of religious rites, ecstacies, and persecutions. Literature, or rather its false front embodied in Parisian literary cliques, has become "a sacred abode" (p. 48). Sarraute presents one with visions of an orthodox, dogmatic church hierarchy, supplemented with well-meaning innocents to whom the kingdom of heaven belongs (p. 108), who are shaken by heretics who roam the streets in their bare feet, beating their breasts, calling for repentance, and preaching the gospel of Christ (p. 124). Establishment critics and their *salon* henchmen are the high priests of a hollow religion in which the faithful are concerned only with being in step with the authorities: the work of art is far less important than one's attitude towards it. The critic is the one who allows the crowd of worshippers to "file silently through the sacred halls filled with the relics that [he] has presented for their veneration, that [he] has offered, imposed upon them as objects of their piety" (p. 52). The religion is not necessarily Christian, and one of the opinion-makers exhibits the "smile of a Hindu deity" (p. 92). Other categories have not completely disappeared, and they will come to the fore again in *Entre la vie et la mort.* Monkey cages at the zoo, shepherd dogs, scorpions, and circus horses compete with olfactory, tactile, and visual imagery, visions of military operations, court and church rituals.

The relative emphasis on religious imagery in *Les Fruits d'or* led Dominique Aury to observe that "Literature has assumed the sacred character of Religion or Party, it harbors Inquisitors and Stalinists."[16] This was perhaps placing too much stress on inauthentic moments in the text and disregarding Sarraute's irony. It again illustrates the danger inherent in an unbalanced use of imagery. In this instance, the emotional impact of a series of related images obliterated the appeal directed by irony at the intellect. The spread of imagery in *Entre la vie et la mort*, in my opinion, does better justice to the subject matter. Religious imagery is present, but more subdued than in the previous book, as when the writer exclaims: "Flaubert . . . Baudelaire . . . just like them . . . you understand nothing . . . I take upon myself all the sins of the world" (EVM, p. 83). Nathalie Sarraute's control is at its peak. Indeed, Dominique Aury had previously reproached her with being too much a master of her subject, too much a master of her craft.[17] I believe readers notice craftsmanship to the extent that they are unable to enter into the writer's fictional structure. In the case of Sarraute, a sizeable part of her potential literary audience was apparently left outside. The perceptive readers she has had are found, in the main, among fellow novelists and a number of critics.

In her essays Sarraute has accurately diagnosed the reader's tendency to create characters, even when given the slightest of clues, as an obstacle to the understanding of a text based on tropisms. Creating characters, however, is but one particular aspect of the reader's creative potential, which writers recently have encouraged rather than hindered. It is, after all, even in its more limited, traditional scope, such creativity that makes reading an active, fruitful pursuit. But somehow she has felt the compulsion to structure her fiction so that the reader does not create. I quite agree with Richard N. Coe that her wariness is often felt by the reader as a form of aggressiveness: "For Madame Sarraute, the reader is the enemy; he is there to be ambushed, demoralized, ultimately brain-washed."[18] It might have been better to take advantage of the reader's ability, guiding it in order to lead him to the discovery of her "truth." He might have been more willing to accept one that he had partly created. Even had he distorted it to some extent, the consequences would not have been catastrophic. At this point one might well recall Proust's remarks concerning distortion in literature: "Fine books are written in a kind of foreign tongue. Each one of us, over the words of a text, places a meaning, or at least an image, which is often a misinterpretation. But in fine books, all such misinterpretations are beautiful."[19]

As things stand, with the reader as enemy, Nathalie Sarraute is at the mercy of her own errors and weaknesses, which can lose her a battle or even the war. Success depends on her maintaining him constantly within her grasp, fighting on her own terms. As Coe sees it, a book of hers "attacks us where we are most vulnerable: not in the rational regions of the mind, but somewhere beyond, or on the very fringes of consciousness, destroying our assumptions and beliefs before they are so much as formulated; and we have no defense."[20] People who are attacked have a tendency to fight back. The reader is bound to assume traits imputed to him. He will move back to the rational plane and, like the masked Dumontet, "exorcise" the work of the writer. "If only, somehow, out of this faceless nightmare, he could create a sane, familiar world, he might perhaps escape." The monsters, seen as characters, might be driven away. Finally, "Suppose in desperation he should . . . start creating *people*? At once, of course, the hallucinatory power of the novel is lost."[21] The reader must, indeed, be kept in a state of hallucination, literally fascinated, thus hardly capable of active participation. No writer, of course, can achieve that for any great length of time. Sarraute's evident, although limited, success is testimony to her own creative ability. (One should also note that Coe's strictures antedate the publication of her two most recent and most accomplished works, to which they are less pertinent.) But what contributes to her fiction's hold is not only the strange power that permeates it; it may also be an occasional tension between theory and practice, such as the one discussed by Maurice Blanchot.

It is idle to speculate on the kind of fiction Nathalie Sarraute might have written had her esthetics been more open to reader participation. Her books are as they are. Seen within the context of those written by younger writers, they appear to have performed the necessary, albeit negative, function of helping to clear fiction of some of its superficial, culture-bound paraphernalia. Perhaps all they need, in order fully to come into their own, is a new generation of readers with a different creative bent. Innocent of today's prejudices, they will not need to be indoctrinated by her essays. A few decades from now, her theories on fiction-writing might matter as little to those readers as those of, say, Emile Zola, matter to people today.

NOTES FOR CHAPTER TWO (Sarraute)

[1] Nathalie Sarraute, *L'Ere du Soupçon*, p. 33. Within this chapter, all references to Nathalie Sarraute's works appear in the text with the following abbreviations: *Tropismes*, T; *Portrait d'un inconnu*, PI; *Mar-*

tereau, M; *L'Ere du soupçon*, ES; *Le Planétarium*, P; *Les Fruits d'or*, FO; *Entre la vie et la mort*, EVM. See Bibliography for complete references.

[2] Justin O'Brien, "Sarraute: 'Tropismes,'" in *The French Literary Horizon* (New Brunswick: Rutgers University Press, 1967), p. 333.

[3] Sarraute, "New Movements in French Literature," *The Listener*, March 9, 1961, pp. 428–429.

[4] Quoted in Mimica Cranaki and Yvon Belaval, *Nathalie Sarraute* (Paris: Gallimard, 1965), pp. 96–97.

[5] Bernard Pingaud, "Le Personnage dans l'œuvre de Nathalie Sarraute," *Preuves*, No. 154 (December 1963), p. 24.

[6] Maurice Blanchot, "D'un art sans avenir," *Nouvelle Revue Française*, No. 51 (March 1957), p. 492.

[7] Sarraute, "New Movements," p. 429.

[8] Henri Peyre, *French Novelists of Today* (New York: Oxford University Press, 1967), p. 367.

[9] Richard N. Coe, "The Anti-Reader Novel," *Time & Tide*, March 29, 1962, p. 28.

[10] Mary McCarthy, "Hanging by a Thread," *The New York Review of Books*, July 31, 1969, p. 6.

[11] Yvon Belaval, "Nathalie Sarraute: *Tropismes*," *Nouvelle Revue Française*, No. 62 (February 1958), p. 337.

[12] *Ibid.*, p. 336.

[13] Martin Turnell, *The Art of French Fiction* (New York: New Directions, 1959), pp. 348 ff.

[14] Georges Anex, "Nathalie Sarraute: *Portrait d'un inconnu*," *Nouvelle Revue Française*, No. 54 (June 1957), p. 1115.

[15] Ludovic Janvier, "Nathalie Sarraute ou l'intimité cruelle," in *Une Parole exigeante* (Paris: Minuit, 1964), p. 78.

[16] Dominique Aury, "La Communication," *Nouvelle Revue Française*, No. 127 (July 1963), pp. 96–97.

[17] *Ibid.*, p. 97.

[18] Coe, "The Anti-Reader Novel," p. 28.

[19] Marcel Proust, *Contre Sainte-Beuve* (Paris: Gallimard, 1954), p. 303.

[20] Coe, The Anti-Reader Novel, p. 27.

[21] *Ibid.*, p. 28.

CHAPTER THREE

Maurice Blanchot

Between the fiction of Maurice Blanchot and that of his con-temporaries, Beckett and Sarraute, there are noticeable bonds. Like Molloy, Malone, and their various synonyms, the char-acters of Blanchot's early narratives wander about in an incom-prehensible world, find themselves victims of unjustifiable circumstances, and deteriorate physically without apparent reason, attempting all the while to communicate with others. Like the semianonymous beings of Sarraute, they seek to ex-teriorize what lies beneath the surface in the twilight zone that either precedes language or lies beyond it, using words in a desperate attempt to verbalize that for which there are no words. Differences are no less perceptible. Blanchot's writings do not emphasize the grotesque, and his attitude towards language is far more complex than either Sarraute's or Beck-ett's. He does not punctuate the failures of his characters with humor ranging from slapstick to scatology, nor is he concerned with the somewhat instinctive nature of tropisms.

A struggle with language, not as an inadequate tool, but as an element both distinct from and distinctive of human reality, capable of endowing the literary work with generative qualities, actually brings Blanchot closer to the surrealists and writers such as Raymond Roussel and, especially, Mallarmé. The lat-ter's efforts to remove words from too close an adhesion to the material objects they designate, that is, to free signs from their referents, interested Blanchot very much. Of the many state-

ments Mallarmé had made concerning language, he thought
that "the most remarkable pertained to the impersonal aspect,
the kind of independent and absolute existence" the poet
attributed to it.[1] According to Blanchot, the surrealists went
one step further: they "understood, in addition, that [language]
is not an inert object: it has a life of its own and a latent power
that we do not control."[2] These and many other remarks scattered through his critical essays clearly indicate that Blanchot
has pondered at length over the nature of language, as have
contemporary linguisticians with whose works he is presumably
acquainted. He is well versed in philosophy, as his references
to Hegel and Heidegger attest. He is also a critic and a theorist
of literature. But we need not at this point investigate that
background material in depth, important as it may be to an
understanding of his thought.[3] His fiction must stand as fiction
and be examined for what it might yield to the steady gaze of
a receptive reader, with only occasional references to Blanchot's
critical texts.

Of the ten volumes of fiction he has published so far, two
offer promising paths of investigation to the critic, for they are
openly presented as different structures of the same material.
The first one, *Thomas l'obscur*, published in 1941, was again
offered to the public in 1950 under the same title, to which
were added the words "new version" and a prefatory note
explaining that "the present version adds nothing, but as it
omits a great deal it can be called other and even quite new."
An author may keep writing the same book over and over
again, using different materials to state the same theme or
express (a word that is viewed with increasing disfavor by
the younger generation of writers) the same truth, which he
believes his previous work has not adequately portrayed—or
he may unconsciously be getting rid of an obsession. Here the
process is a conscious one; the material of the new book was
all contained in the old, and the architecture is roughly the
same. The reader's attention is no longer directed towards

examining the different ways in which a truth might be "expressed." He is led to focus on the different meaning suggested by a new arrangement of words. Even though one might argue that the theme is identical in the two versions, the effect upon the reader must needs be different.

The original *Thomas l'obscur* was followed by two other works of fiction, *Aminadab* (1942) and *Le Très-haut* (1948), that quite obviously belong to the same rhetorical system. Also in 1948, *L'Arrêt de mort* appeared, which marks a change of direction, confirmed by the new version of *Thomas l'obscur* as well as by four more recent texts. It appears as if Blanchot had sensed he had been on the wrong track and by publishing a reworked version of his early fiction wanted to stress that the switch was less radical than one might think, while at the same time enabling one to see precisely what differences there were between the two approaches.

In its original state, *Thomas l'obscur* was over 100,000 words in length while the new version has less than 30,000. Cutting out more than two thirds of a narrative's basic ingredients cannot fail to have a pronounced effect. Gauging that effect is more difficult if one reads the two versions in their chronological order, for referents of the words that have been left out will almost inevitably remain as a halo in the mind, affecting the structure of what one is reading. I shall therefore use the second version as a point of departure.

From the standpoint of the narrative, which is told in the third person, there are two characters, Thomas and Anne, their developing relationship, the death of Anne, and the effect of that death upon Thomas. Other characters are mere utilities; the setting is vague and nameless—a beach, woods, a hotel dining room, the countryside, various rooms; the time is unspecified. At the beginning we find Thomas alone, sitting on the beach. He decides to go in for a swim that lasts the length of the first chapter. As Thomas swims out to sea, in a direction he had not taken before, fog hides the coast from him; he feels alone with the sea, then alone in "an absence of sea,"[4] and such a phrase is characteristic of Blanchot. As sudden gusts of wind stir up the ocean, Thomas struggles and has the sensation of actually becoming the sea. Eventually, he strives to reach a special region, "something like a sacred spot, to himself so well suited that it was enough for him to be there in order to be; it was like an imaginary hollow into which he sank, because before being there his shape had already been imprinted into it" (TO-2, p. 13). After that he returns to the beach, and stares at the sea and at a distant swimmer. He contemplates the expanse of ocean with a kind of sorrow, as if he had felt "a freedom that was too great, a freedom obtained by breaking all bonds" (TO-2, p. 15). The experience has been an unusual one, to say the least, bearing the earmarks of an initiation.

From the outset, emphasis has been laid on the exceptional; but what distinguishes this narrative from other related accounts (for instance, Tchen's murder, in the first chapter of Malraux's *La Condition humaine*, which is also an initiation), is that the esthetic experience is as unusual for the reader as the physical one is for the fictional character. The well-known process of "identifying" with the protagonist of a fictional text can give birth to considerable émotional response, perhaps even involvement. Rarely does it constitute, strictly speaking, an experience, that is, rarely does the reader feel as though he himself had gone through an ordeal in the character's stead, so to speak. In order to achieve such a transfer, Blanchot omits all references that would tie the event to any specific time or place and thus prevents one from projecting it into a familiar aspect of reality, hence away from himself. In addition to abstracting it from reality, Blanchot also removes the action from the commonplace. Finally, he gives key words a denotation that is different from the one we normally give him. As with Mallarmé, this means loosening the bonds that link signs to their referents and also introducing some play into the rigid association between signifier and signified.

There is, strictly speaking, nothing revolutionary about that
to be sure. He himself has pointed out, within the context of
an essay on Kafka, that "a narrative written in the most simple
prose already assumes an important change in the nature of
language";[5] and the innumerable consequences and controversies resulting from Aristotle's having written that the personages
of Homer and of tragedy were better (that is, other) than we
are need no further stress. What is new here is the intensity
with which language is removed from its utilitarian use and
the direction taken by the removal from the commonplace.
Swimming in a river or in the ocean is a fairly ordinary activity.
As described by Jean Giono, for instance, at the beginning of
the second chapter of *Le Chant du monde*, it departs from the
commonplace. Because of the character's outstanding physical
characteristics, his sensitivity to the river, the account takes
on epic quality. There is, however, nothing fantastic about it,
nor are any supernatural forces involved. Not only is Blanchot's
account out of the ordinary, but one is tempted to say that it
enters the domain of the fantastic.

I call this a temptation, as it is a reaction of the analytical
mind, looking back at the text from outside and considering
the point of view of the story and its degree of plausibility,
after the reading has been completed. The temptation needs
to be resisted, for it is the textual experience that matters rather
than any rational examination coming after the fact—an irrelevant procedure on account of the way the narrated event has
been abstracted from everyday reality. When calm seas, fog,
high wind, and turbulent waters are presented in very close
succession, one might first marvel at the kind of "reality" that
has thus been described, but one soon senses that no real description is involved: the words in this text are not the usual
signs pointing to referents of everyday experience. "The water
revolved as in a whirlpool. Was it really water?" (TO-2, p. 11).
Statements appear self-contradictory and, as Jean Starobinsky
has pointed out, abstract and concrete terms, objective and

subjective approaches, central and peripheral points of view, active and passive verbs are all used almost interchangeably.[6] Language is as much unsettled as "reality" is. In a way, it becomes the reality of fiction. Since readers tend to be more affected by the language of a narrative than by its subject-matter, this is what can make the reading of *Thomas l'obscur* a profound experience.

The second chapter takes Thomas into a wooded area and down into a cave. His underground sojourn seems even more fantastic than his stay in the water. Trapped for hours in darkness and solid rock, he nevertheless is able to proceed forward and perceive things with his eyes; but what he sees appear to be materializations of his own thoughts, and as he moves ahead a whole world of matter penetrates him physically. His thought becomes exterior to himself, and he finds he is inhabited by his own cadaver, which he attempts to vomit. At the end, Thomas' thoughts reintegrate a body that has been bereft of its senses. The word "sacred," which appeared in an earlier quotation from the first chapter, does not figure in the text of the second. While the first experience might be termed a purification, the second is literally a descent into hell. An integral part of initiation procedures, it also prefigures the events to follow.

The reader, too, has been initiated. He has been transported into a world utterly different from his own. A few comparisons between corresponding portions of the two versions of *Thomas l'obscur* should illustrate this.

On the whole, the physical setting of the first chapter in the second version is barely noticeable—it has been abstracted into nonexistence. In the earlier 1941 version, it is apparent (in addition to a more elaborate style, a point to which I shall return presently) that the setting had some importance. There is another swimmer, to whom Thomas calls out who does not respond. There is also an empty boat that drifts by. Both incidents occur before Thomas' stranger experiences, and their eerie flavor adumbrates what is to follow. The setting thus plays an introductory role. It contains, to use Julien Gracq's phrase, "warning signals" similar to the Gothic novel trappings of *Au château d'Argol*. Remembering André Breton's praise of "Monk" Lewis in the first surrealist manifesto, I believe such details may properly be interpreted as a first, albeit superficial, indication of surrealist presence in Blanchot's work. The original version of the underground journey contains analogous signals, with odd-looking trees and strange-sounding birds contributing to the atmosphere; and, as the main portion of the narrative unfolds, differences between the two renditions become more obvious.

In the 1950 edition, Thomas and Anne are not only the main characters, but statements by them or about them dominate the book almost exclusively. Where other characters appear, they are usually nameless and their role is minimal. The anecdote becomes thinner and thinner, and even such simple actions as swimming (except, of course, Thomas' initiatory experience in the sea), walking in the woods, or sitting down with others at a hotel dining-room table are eliminated from the structure. The major event of the work, Anne's illness and death, also occurs in the abstract. She is found asleep on a garden bench (which garden and by whom are irrelevant questions); she lies ill in her room, is visited by friends and by her mother (only one friend bears a name, Louise, and she is only mentioned once); and eventually she dies without doctor or priest having been summoned, without any material cause of her death having been suggested. In the 1941 version of *Thomas l'obscur*, we see anecdotes and characters playing a much larger role.

The first half of the book is set in a resort town, the second half in a large city—and it is clear that the trip between one and the other was made by train. In the city, such mundane places as restaurants and museums are easily identified. Another major character is involved in the action, a woman called Irène, and something close to a love triangle appears to take shape. As in more conventional writing, all this is meta-

phorical, incidents and minor characters being vehicles of a
single tenor—the meaning toward which the fiction is structured. With Blanchot, however, their metaphorical nature is
emphasized by his keeping them at a greater distance from
everyday reality. Many "warning signals" are instrumental to
that effect: when Irène first meets Thomas, for instance, she
is described as having "faithfully kept, for the first time, the
date set by destiny and, moreover, by Anne that very morning" (TO-1, p. 121). Words and phrases such as "destiny" or
"for the first time" are of the kind that normally lead the
reader to expect some extraordinary transformation in the narrative. In more extended fashion, when Irène walks in the city
streets, she is presented as being so obsessed with Thomas that
she sees his likeness, or part of it, in every person she encounters; but Blanchot, as does Robbe-Grillet more than a decade
later, offers such fancies as if they were real, refusing to intrude
upon the text with an extraneous message to the effect that a
switch from the plausible to the implausible (or imaginary)
has taken place; as a result, when Irène sees Thomas in a restaurant, one is no longer sure at what level the encounter takes
place (TO-1, pp. 148 ff.). The subsequent meeting between
Irène and Thomas at the museum is hardly questionable, upon
reflection, but it follows the other one so closely that its fanciful treatment tends to appear realistic by contrast. Something
close to a fusion of the real and the marvelous has been accomplished, when one considers the level of the story.

On the verbal level, I am reminded not so much of surrealism
as of Jean Gireaudoux, nor am I the first to associate the latter's
name with Blanchot's. Claude-Edmonde Magny, in her book
on Giraudoux, had detected similarities between *Thomas
l'obscur* and *Aventures de Jérôme Bardini* (1930).[7] Although
she does not refer to them, those pages dealing with the museum visit offer most striking analogies. Metaphors and conceits
are perhaps not handled with as much agility, but every now
and then a sentence crops up that, with a change in pronoun,

might not have been out of place in *Suzanne et le pacifique*
(1921). The suggestion that art-minded museum attendants
wax floors with greater ardor in front of anonymous paintings
in order to slow down visitors—that is almost worthy of
Giraudoux. The same might be said of a statement concerning
the unique nature of a work of art (in this instance a painting
by Titian): "Anything that might be used to seduce plants,
to flatter stars, such as magic words or metaphors, left the
picture unmoved; even more, it became radiant, and it obsti-
nately refused, at least in a figurative sense, to be a picture"
(TO-1, p. 156). The very phrase, "magic words," belongs to
Suzanne.[8] She, however, refusing, as she puts it, the outlook
of a German or a Russian, will not lend a tragic note to her
situation, stranded as she might be on her deserted Pacific
island. Blanchot's characters show no such compunction. A
kind fate, in the shape of a group of wandering Englishmen,
restores Suzanne, virtually intact, to her native land, while the
destiny of Blanchot's Anne is to experience solitude, illness,
and death.

Both the museum passage and the three excerpts quoted by
Claude-Edmonde Magny have disappeared from the revised
version of *Thomas l'obscur*—and with them those obviously
"precious" aspects of style that suggest Giraudoux. In the example just quoted, the verbs "to seduce" and "to flatter" as well
as the parenthetical phrase "at least in a figurative sense" would
almost certainly, had the episode not been deleted, been replaced or suppressed. On the other hand, the unqualified
statement about the picture that "refused to be a picture"
remains characteristic of Blanchot, as an illustration of his
removal of language from its utilitarian function. As with elements of the narration, actual stylistic changes made in the
revised version point towards a greater economy of means and
a more considerable break between fictional reality and the
reader's reality.

In the following sequence, taken from the episode of Anne's

illness, those words maintained in the second version appear in italics (and within brackets if added or changed), all others having been deleted:

Elle seule vit s'approcher, à la vitesse d'un bolide [*d'une étoile*], *ce moment* idéal, le dernier peut-être, *où* elle allait reprendre [*reprenant*] *contact avec la terre* [*elle ressaisirait*], avec *l'existence banale*, où elle *ne verrait rien* [*ne sentirait rien*], seule existence véritable. *A travers des nuées rapidement chassées au-dessus d'elle,* elle prit tragiquement conscience de l'instant unique où elle embrasserait son frère qui ensuite cesserait d'être son frère, *où elle pourrait vivre, vivre enfin,*—rien n'était perdu—se marier, finir son écharpe à l'aiguille, *et peut-être même mourir,* mourir d'une mort imprévue, *épisode merveilleux.* (TO-1, pp. 195–196; TO-2, p. 106)

(*She alone saw this* ideal *moment approaching with the speed* of a fire-ball [*of a star*]; it might well be the last, *during which* she would resume [*resuming*] *contact with the earth* [*she would again hold on to*], with *commonplace existence,* where she *would see nothing* [*would feel nothing*], the only genuine existence. *Through fast-driven clouds above her,* she became tragically conscious of the unique instant when she would kiss her brother, who would then cease being her brother, *when she might live, live at last*—the situation was not desperate—get married, finish her knitted scarf, *and perhaps even die,* die of an unexpected death, *marvellous occurrence.*)

Furthermore, in the revised text, the phrase that begins the second sentence has been transferred to the beginning of the first, which now reads: "*Elle seule, à travers des nuées rapidement chassées au-dessus d'elle, à la vitesse d'une étoile, vit s'approcher (She alone, through fast-driven clouds above her, saw approaching with the speed of a star).*" Originally, the two sentences each contained one image that complemented the other. Merging the two sentences into one caused a fusion of the images, while replacing "fire-ball" (*bolide*) with "star" (*étoile*) added an element of unreality to the vague mystery suggested by "clouds" (*nuées* traditionally signals poetic connotations, as opposed to the prosaic *nuages*). *Bolide* is no longer a live metaphor; it is a cliché applied to almost any fast-moving object, a racing-car for instance. *Etoile,* on the other hand, gives

the image an unusual quality of the sort one so often finds in
Blanchot. Intellectually, we know that stars move at incredible
rates of speed, but our experience suggests that they are stationary. As a result, *vitesse d'une étoile* produces tension. De-
leting a few explanatory words or phrases, particularly the
qualifier *idéal*, again emphasizes the unique nature of the
approaching moment and also divorces it from the more traditional realm of the ideal. References to an existence in which
basic attributes of of life, such as seeing and feeling, are absent
contributes to the same effect, and this renders the phrase
instant unique superfluous. Finally, by removing concrete
illustrations, the words *vivre* and *mourir* are not only restored
to an abstract level, they are brought close to juxtaposition
within that moment the sentence describes. Such a time, when
speed and immobility, life and death, appear to coincide, is
at the end of the sequence characterized by the word *merveilleux*. Again one is reminded of surrealism, but this time at a
deeper level, and of the emphasis André Breton has placed
upon that word in the surrealist manifesto.

A sentence from the previous paragraph of the text of *Thomas
l'obscur*, identical in both versions, reinforces the analogy:
"Dark night where there were no more contradictory terms,
where those who suffered were happy, where white and black
shared a common substance" (TO1, p. 194; TO-2, pp. 104–
105). That sentence, in turn, may be matched with a statement
from Breton's second manifesto: "Everything leads me to believe that there is a given viewpoint in the mind, from which
life and death, the real and the imaginary, past and future,
what is communicable and what is not, high and low, cease
to be perceived as contradictory terms."[9] Anne's "moment,"
the approach of which she perceives, is very much like Breton's
hypothetical "viewpoint in the mind." The annihilation of
being that he professes to seek has its metaphorical counterpart
in Blanchot's fiction: Anne's death, through which Thomas is
able to attain a higher level of existence. The situation resem-

bles that described by Breton in his *Nadja* (1928). Nadja disappears into an asylum while Anne vanishes in a more radical fashion, but each woman acts as intercessor for her narrator and protagonist. In each instance there is an effort to transcend the limitations of conventional reality and traditional behavior (in the broadest sense of the term). Anne's death results in illumination for Thomas (Breton had associated annihilation with brillance),[10] in his becoming aware of the presence, within himself, of another Thomas "whose genuine existence would consist in not being" (TO-1, p. 216). In other words, he, too, will partake of an aspect of death. Just as dream and reality may be said to fuse into the "surreal," Thomas will attempt to integrate light and darkness, to assimilate that obscure part of himself; "the more the shadow of my thought receded, the more I conceived of myself, in this flawless light, as a possible host, full of desire, of that obscure Thomas" (TO-1, p. 217; TO-2, p. 144). He then adds that, in the fullness of reality, he believes he can come into contact with the unreal, and that is what surrealism was essentially about. As Breton sought to explore the deeper recesses of the mind, *Thomas l'obscur* represents a quest for the obscure regions of the self.

As those observations indicate, and I feel confident a more detailed comparison between the two texts of *Thomas l'obscur* would confirm this, rhetorical changes evident in Blanchot's work do not manifest a rejection of surrealism after an early infatuation. Quite the contrary, his later fiction reveals an affirmation of its more basic tenets. What one finds in the two works that follow the original *Thomas l'obscur*, *Aminadab*, and *Le Très-haut*, is a stress on the more obvious aspects of surrealism, on the sign posts calling attention to its domain, rather than on the domain itself. This, however, has not resulted in a kind of Gothic novel similar to the first one by Julien Gracq. The writer that readers of *Aminadab* were reminded of was Franz Kafka. Sartre, one of the first to make the connection, was also quick to point out that Blanchot had not read Kafka at the time. Instead of having been influenced by him, he was probably led to the Czech writer through the devices of *Aminadab*.

A man named Thomas is again the main character. A discussion as to whether this is the same Thomas as before seems hardly relevant. Neither one is given background, family, friends, or even a home. Beckett's Molloy at least had a mother, to whose room he at last returned. Thomas first appeared on a beach, as we have seen, out of nowhere, is transformed by an extraordinary experience, and is last seen on the shores of the ocean. In *Aminadab*, he or another Thomas arrives alone in a small town where he is obviously a stranger. No reason is given for his being there, no indication as to where he has come from, and, even more than in *Thomas l'obscur*, the events that follow appear to be determined almost exclusively by chance. Thomas allows himself to be chosen, somewhat as Breton, the narrator of *Nadja*, did in the streets and movie theaters of Paris, letting people and programs come as they might.[11] Nevertheless, he does not answer a call unless there is some element of mystery involved. When a man issues a straightforward invitation, Thomas is not interested. When a woman in a fourth- or fifth-floor window across the street makes an ambiguous sign, he is intrigued. Not knowing if he should interpret it as a summons, a friendly wave, or a dismissal, he hesitates. When he makes up his mind and crosses the street, he has unknowingly embarked upon a quest that will fill the 240-odd pages of the book. Perhaps he finds the woman eventually, but what he found and what meaning it might have for him the reader is not told, for the narrative ends as Thomas asks her who she is.

The inception of the narrative in *Aminadab* suggests an analogy with the individual as he is about to write, as Blanchot conceives of his position. He is a stranger, because he does not use language as others do, in a utilitarian way, and when he begins to write he does so without motivation or purpose.[12]

When Thomas enters the house in answer to something he does not know how to interpret, he finds himself caught in an endless series of frustrating, Kafka-like experiences. He gets lost in hallways, cannot communicate in any satisfactory fashion with the people he meets, becomes a tenant in the building, is manacled to another man whom he drags along in his wanderings (he is not sure whether he is prisoner or captor), befriends another woman (perhaps a servant), is told contradictory things about the occupants of the house and their relationship to one another, cannot decide whether his fate is to be judged for an unknown crime or to judge others in equal ignorance of what they may have done, and eventually becomes ill. As in the 1941 version of *Thomas l'obscur*, two women are involved, one subservient to the other, who guide the main character toward a kind of salvation. Again, illness plays a crucial role; it is because of that illness that he is able to reach a region hitherto unattainable. After he recovers, he penetrates into the room of the woman named Lucie, who, he thinks, is the one who beckoned from the window. She, bearing a name suggestive of light, prepares him for the annihilation of his being, for a darkness in which everything will become clear—metaphors similar to those I quoted in connection with *Thomas l'obscur*. Here the protagonist hesitates, and his last question "Who are you?" may represent an ultimate effort, perhaps futile, perhaps not, to reject such an arcane form of understanding. The answer to his question is of course not given, nor would it seem to matter much, for the text concludes, "It was as though that question might allow him to clear up everything." We shall never know whether it was the right question or not.

Aminadab, in its general outline, even more than *Thomas l'obscur*, lends itself to allegorical interpretation. Sartre considered that to be true of a number of episodes and proceeded to give his own interpretation of them.[13] While they are quite plausible, they are not those that first occurred to me, nor are they identical with those proposed by Georges Poulet.[14] One probably tends to see allegories to the extent that one remains exterior to the fiction and fails to participate fully in the textual experience. I am inclined to blame Blanchot himself for the reader's failure, for in multiplying incidents that, although decidedly strange, are specific, sequential, and certain—therefore constituting a narration that may readily be retold or summarized—he gives the reader no opportunity to participate. The reader listens to the narrator and interprets what he hears.

With *Le Très-haut* the narration moves into slightly more recognizable surroundings, and the narrative shifts from third to first person. The events described are probably no more implausible than those of Albert Camus' *La Peste* (1947); they exude nightmarish qualities because accepted laws of causality, progress, and transformation do not apply. The atmosphere is much less Kafka-like than in *Aminadab*, and this may well be the result of a conscious effort on Blanchot's part to achieve a distinctive manner. The first-person narrative also helps to bring the action closer to home. *Aminadab* described another world, which could be interpreted either as the distorted image of the reader's or as being Other in an absolute sense; but *Le Très-haut* shows one's own world gone awry.

The easiest way to account for this third work is to call it the story of a plague in a large city. The theme of illness is thus once again restated, but it is treated more extensively than before. Already in *Aminadab* there were illness among the tenants and rumors of an epidemic in the mysterious upper stories of the house. A distance was nevertheless maintained between those incidents and Thomas's own experience, while in *Le Très-haut* the epidemic is more like a maelstrom that engulfs everything, including the narrator. Individual illness, here that of the narrator, is no longer the central element of the narrative: when the story begins, it is already a thing of the past. The action moves from the individual to the collective, ending with the annihilation of the narrator. It begins with a

brief affirmation and a rhetorical question: "I was not alone,
I was an ordinary man. How could I forget such a phrase?"

Reminiscent of attempts by traditional novelists to suggest
that the unusual or shocking experiences of their characters
might well have been those of the reader, as with Duhamel's
Salavin or Camus' Meursault, that statement, by being placed
at the outset of the narrative, acquires ironic overtones, for
what obviously stands out at first is the narrator's strangeness,
even though mitigated by the first-person point of view. He
is called Henri Sorge; the family name does not have a French
ring to it. One thinks, rather, of the German word meaning
"anxiety" or "concern." That connection has led Pierre Klossowski, in an interesting but abstruse essay, to a possible
interpretation of the book's title (to appreciate it one should
remember that "le très-haut" is the French equivalent of "the
Almighty"): "God, deprived of his name, or existence deprived
of being because it is deprived of God's name, would become
'anxiety.' "[15] The narrator has become the metaphor of God,
whose creation has become his illness or perhaps his sin, and
whose disappearance is suggested at the end.

A resident of the city, Sorge seems as new to it and its inhabitants as Thomas was in the fantastic house of *Aminadab*.
That is partly due to his illness. He himself speaks of the
"revelation" it has afforded him: "Until recently, men were
only fragments, and they projected their dreams toward heaven.
. . . But now, man exists. That is what I have discovered" (TH,
p. 29). It is perhaps such existence that spells the death of
God. A series of encounters or conversations serves to establish Sorge's distance from those who have not risen to his own
level of awareness. They also point to a converging pattern of
ills of various sorts. Like the beggar who, according to Sorge,
exists only in order to "give the impression that things are not
really going like clockwork" (TH, p. 17), they might be in-
dicative of a concern (*Sorge*) that literature is meant to communicate and simultaneously of the distance between the

language of literature and that of the marketplace. Eventually, the plague emerges as a possible metaphor for the condition of this world.

In addition to the epidemic, disastrous fires break out in several sections of the city, and there is also evidence of considerable political and social unrest if not of actual uprisings. Social or political matters, however, are not, in my opinion, the focus of the book. Like the plague and the fires, they, too, are metaphors for something else. Vague and unsatisfactory as the phrase might sound, the book seems essentially a statement about the human condition—or, to refine this a bit more, it represents a writer's attempt to speak the human condition (rather than speak about it). The narrator's affirmation concerning the existence of man is one of several pieces of evidence - pointing in that direction. Not that politics is unimportant; rather it is a symptom or consequence of more fundamental things.

Connected with the theme of social unrest is that of the underground (the book was published soon enough after the German occupation of France for this concept to have been highly suggestive at the time) and of darkness. Again we meet with a recurrent motif: previously there had been the descent into the cave, in *Thomas l'obscur*, and the concluding episode in *Aminadab* when Thomas was told that the path toward salvation lay in a direction that would have led him gently but deeply into the caves of the earth. His mistake had been to seek the upper regions of the house, projecting, as Sorge confesses to have done, his dreams toward heaven. The myth of Orpheus, a favorite of Blanchot's, is not very far in the background, along with his perpetual return with, and loss of, Eurydice; and also close is André Breton's "depth of the mind," where there are "strange forces capable either of joining with those that exist on the surface or struggle victoriously against them."[16] Jacques Lacan, starting from Freud's remark that dreams are organized like picture-puzzles, has asserted that the structure of the unconscious was the structure of language.[17] If true, this would make the probing of language, which is the concern of so many contemporary writers, analogous to an exploration of the unconscious. Maurice Blanchot sees Orpheus as the writer whose skill enables him to undertake his voyage to Hades, that is, into the unconscious regions of his being. His supreme accomplishment would consist in bringing back Eurydice to the light of day. For him, she represents a state akin to Breton's "viewpoint of the mind," which the writer necessarily strives to reach and contemplate—at which point Eurydice vanishes. "The sacred night encloses Eurydice within its shadows, it encloses within the song [of Orpheus] all that transcends his song."[18] His is a necessary failure, one that ensures the integrity of his quest, for, had he succeeded, his "masterpiece" would have resembled an Eurydice stripped of her meaning, of her nocturnal essence.

L'Arrêt de mort (1948) appeared almost simultaneously with *Le Très-haut*. A two-part narrative, each one corresponding to a different reading of the title—the stopping of death or the death sentence—it marks the rhetorical change that prompted a revision of *Thomas l'obscur*. Like *Le Très-haut*, it is told in the first person, as are the three books of fiction following the second version of *Thomas l'obscur*. The narrator is nameless; one usually thinks of this as a means of removing part of the literary screen between author and reader. Other characters are occasionally referred to by the initial letter of their names— a traditional device, it would seem, to give fiction a semblance of reality. The book is a short one, the two stories extremely simple, and the more spectacular aspects of the previous works have been discarded. What remains is again in the spirit of Breton's *Nadja*, with one important difference: the reader is very specifically made aware of the book's being a product of language. Whatever his first impressions might have been, he soon realizes that the narrator's anonymity is but a correlative to his nonexistence; if the characters' names are reduced to their initial letters, it is because they do not have enough substance to carry more than that. The existence of characters as human beings, except perhaps in the beginning of *Le Très-haut*, has never been convincingly affirmed in Blanchot's fiction. That is especially true of the women, who have a function to perform rather than an identity to display. In *L'Arrêt de mort*, the distance between created character and creating thought (that is, language) is reduced to a minimum. While maintaining at one point that "a thought is not quite like a person, even when it acts and lives like one" (AM, p. 62), the narrator notes, some time later, referring to a friend, "She behaved in my presence as freely as a thought" (AM, p. 112).

Once more, illness and death permeate the narrative. The first part describes the circumstances of the death of a relatively young woman, a close friend of the narrator's, his staying away during her critical illness, and how her death is seemingly postponed so that he might spend one last day with her. The second relates his strange, accidental encounters with two other women, the eery days he spends with one, ending with her literally fatal decision to have a cast made of her hands and face. The framework is quite ordinary, and so are the words that carry the story. What gives the book its strength is the manner in which commonplace words are placed in juxtaposition and unusual connotations abstracted from reality. Thus, describing how, in his overheated room, the temperature at night comes down to the low seventies, he adds: "But even in the most trying moments, when there was warmth only in ice, I have never again experienced that feeling of absolute cold resulting from a temperature of seventy-three degrees" (AM, p. 88). Although metaphorically attributing warmth to ice is something of a cliché, the conceit acquires renewed vigor through use of the phrase "absolute cold" and its suggestion of absolute zero—a state considered to be beyond practical reality.

Throughout *L'Arrêt de mort*, death as the end of physical

life is viewed intellectually rather than emotionally, even on
the superficial level of the anecdote—a tale that could be said
to belong, like the earlier ones, to the realm of the fantastic.
One might also view death as correlative to the writer's involvement with language (in traditional terms, Orpheus did venture
into the kingdom of the dead), during which language ceases
to be a practical function, and the writer himself refuses a
world in which objects and people alike have become com-
modities and ventures into a realm that is absolutely Other.

L'Arrêt de mort and the second version of *Thomas l'obscur*
constitute the pivots of Blanchot's evolving rhetoric. With *Au
moment voulu* (1951), we enter his privileged domain without
the benefit—or the hindrance—of warning devices, sign posts,
or semblances of conventional plot. What action there is takes
place in a small apartment, presumably in Paris, shared by two
young women. A man, the narrator, a friend of one of them,
appears at the door of the apartment as the narrative unfolds;
it then goes on to describe what may be their changing relationships. The setting for *Celui qui ne m'accompagnait pas*
(1953) is a house in the country, surrounded by a garden of
sorts. The narrator is alone with someone else, perhaps. In
Le Dernier Homme (1957) we are transported to what appears
to be a large resort hotel, close to or on the seashore. There are
hallways, doors, individual rooms, lounges, and a gambling
room. The existence of two other characters appears reasonably well established: a woman friend of the narrator and
another man, probably older. It may well be that *L'Attente
l'oubli* (1962) has the same setting, but only hallways and a
room remain identifiable. While the earlier fiction bore a label,
either *roman* or *récit*, this story carries none. It might be called
a poem. Comprised of two parts followed by what could pass
as epilogue, it is subdivided into stanzas or sequences varying
in length from a single sentence to several pages. The larger
portion of the text constitutes a dialogue between a man and
a woman—the only characters involved, if that term may be

applied. In this dialogue, they use either the *tu* or *vous* forms; in the first part, the man is mostly designated by *il*, sometimes by *je* or *tu*, but in the second part he is always *il*. This interchangeability of pronouns seems to reflect the disappearance of the narrator. There remain anonymity, waiting and forgetting, words that are both necessary and futile.

The reader cannot help feeling disoriented, and, as Blanchot himself argues in another context, he may be forced to become actively involved in the text. "Without a fulcrum, deprived of the pleasure of reading, he can no longer view matters from afar, maintaining between himself and the narration the distance that goes with the act of observing, for remote elements, in their presence without presence, are available neither at a distance nor at hand, and they cannot be objects of observation. Henceforth we can no longer talk of sight. The narrative ceases to be what may be seen by means of a chosen actor-spectator and from a given point of view."[19] Younger writers like Sollers or Ricardou would say that the "pleasure of reading" should make way for the collective activity of writing.

The movement that carries Blanchot's fiction forward is similar to that evidenced in the work of Samuel Beckett, especially the French trilogy—from the towns, countryside, seashore, and forest of *Molloy* to the eery nothingness of *L'Innommable*. Beyond what I have indicated above—and I may well have superimposed my own fables on his texts—to identify a plot or simply a coherent, sustained narrative in those books by Blanchot is just not possible. Paraphrasing them would be harder and even more pointless than paraphrasing a poem by Mallarmé. Characters gradually lose what little fabric they had. Names are discarded first; the last narrator to be named was Thomas, in the second version of *Thomas l'obscur*. Other characters retain them in *L'Arrêt de mort* and *Au moment voulu*, although, in the latter, Judith is a name that is given a woman by each of the other two characters in turn—it is not actually hers, it exists only to establish transitory relationships as suggested by the Biblical connotations of that name. After that, one finds merely pronouns.

One of the women in *Au moment voulu* tells the narrator after a long discussion, "I hardly believe in you" (p. 118). The other character of *Celui qui ne m'accompagnait pas* affirms, "You know, there is no one" (p. 65). In that instance, the reference appears to be to a third person the narrator thinks he has seen in the house, but in the more general context of this text the statement reverberates *ad infinitum*. It comes as no surprise, later on, to read the narrator's questions regarding his hypothetical companion: "would he still hear me? Where is he now? Perhaps very close by? Perhaps he is at hand? Perhaps it is he that my hand slowly pushes back, thrusts aside once more?" (CAP, p. 173); or to be confronted with the book's final statement, "everything had already disappeared, disappeared with the day" (p. 174). The reader's right to generalize the questionable aspect of characters is implicitly given in *L'Attente l'oubli*: " 'Don't you have faith in me?' She meant her truthfulness, her words, her behavior. But I was thinking in terms of a greater disbelief" (AO, p. 37). In another conversation, the man will profess that he has no doubts as to the woman's "presence"—and she then reproaches him for preferring that presence to herself. It would seem that his attitude at this point is analogous to that of a reader who believes in characters: he clutches at every possible straw that appearances present to him in order to force a strange reality into more comfortable, familiar structures.

Two thirds of the way into *L'Attente l'oubli*, one detects an attempt to organize the "events" into some kind of linear, coherent story. Towards the end, it is clear that the endeavor has not been very productive: "What point have we reached in the story?—There probably is not much of the story left right now" (AO, p. 153). Such groping for a "story" is a correlative to the quest characters engage in. Male protagonists or narrators throughout Blanchot's fiction are the seekers, the unsure, the stumblers, reaching for a light (or a darkness), to which female intercessors might lead them. The surrealist cult of woman as standard-bearer of the irrational seems in evidence here, in addition to Blanchot's own modified myth of Eurydice. Whether it is Thomas or one of the subsequent nameless ones, from the ambiguous signal in *Aminadab* to the "words that were also perhaps intended for him" of *L'Attente l'oubli* (p. 7), the protagonist encounters an interruption, a call away from complacency or routine. (It is true that in *L'Attente l'oubli* the man signals first; but his is a commonplace action, and it is she who irritatedly rushes into his room, asking for "the meaning of a gesture about which there is obviously nothing to say" [p. 117].) Thomas cannot be persuaded that the hard road upward is not the right way. The narrator of *Au moment voulu* has to be warned that "No one here wishes to tie himself to a story" (p. 108), and although that affirmation makes a strong impression on him, his successor, the man of *L'Attente l'oubli*, while he repeats it verbatim (p. 22), has to be persuaded all over again. The earlier narrator had come to realize that "One who wants to live needs to relax within the illusion of a story, but such relaxation is not allowed to me" (AMV, p. 156); the protagonist of *L'Attente l'oubli* has to experience the same truth on his own until it can finally be said of him, "He is no longer protected by the hidden aspect of things" (AO, p. 136). The life referred to is the same *vie réelle* of which Breton spoke so sarcastically in his first manifesto, and *histoire* may be equated with adventure (in the Sartrian sense of the word), myth, quest, or anything that attempts to impose a satisfying, linear, logical, and therefore artificial explanation on a complex reality. The comfort it provides is a false security that isolates one from true existence.

I suppose it is a sense of that existence that Blanchot tries both to experience and to have his readers experience. His repeated efforts have their corollary in those of his characters as they attempt to communicate with one another. The means of communication that is at their disposal, language, is on a par with story and characters: it is a part of the fiction and a conventional counterpart of reality, but it is not reality. Hence the peculiar nature of Blanchot's texts, since he must at the same time use language and distrust it. If story and language sometimes appear as vehicles in a metaphor of which reality is the tenor, that situation is complicated by the former's being dependent upon the latter for their existence: "If things were divided between things that are seen and things that are said, language might endeavor to erase that division, to make it deeper, to leave it intact while giving it speech, to disappear within it. But that division upon which language is operative is still only a division in language" (AO, p. 143).

Language appears to betray reality, and it also betrays the speaker. At the outset of *L'Attente l'oubli*, the man reads back to the woman those notes he has taken while she was speaking. She listens, but fails to recognize herself: " 'Who speaks?' she would say. 'Who speaks, anyway?' " (p. 7). It is the same question that is asked in a number of works of fiction today, particularly at the end of Michel Butor's *Degrés*, with similar implications as to literary creation. Instead of emphasizing authentic communication between individuals, as did Nathalie Sarraute, Maurice Blanchot appears to be carried beyond that to a question about, and a questioning of, man's being. In so doing, because of the intimate relationship between man and his language, he faces a similar problem in finding words for what cannot be put into words. If he conceives of himself as being in the same situation as the narrator of *Au moment voulu*, "And what was I really, if not the reflection of an appearance that did not speak and to whom no one spoke, only capable of (relying on the endless quiet of what was outside) questioning the world, silently, beyond a window pane?" (AMV, p. 94)—he must nevertheless translate his silence into writing.

This brings us back to an observation by Blanchot, quoted earlier in this chapter, concerning the essential difference between the language of fiction and everyday language. One step further, if one remembers that ordinary language exists for the purpose of communication, one might say that, the opposite of communication being silence, the language of fiction is a form of silence. "At the outset, I do not speak in order to say something, but there is something that needs to speak."[20] Such a need is analogous to a compulsion. "I cannot describe the misfortune that befalls the man who once has begun to speak" says the narrator of *L'Arrêt de mort*, adding nevertheless, "I must speak" (p. 65). Like Beckett's *L'Innommable*, whose last words are "you must go on, I can't go on, I'll go on," Henri Sorge, the narrator of *Le Très-haut*, a gun pointed at him, his back against the wall, forever poised between life and death, closes that book by shouting, "Now, it is now that I speak." If we can, however, imagine Beckett's character in the act of continuing, Sorge's speech is beyond the range of normal perception. He has come close to that hypothetical point in space and time of which I have already spoken, and, like Thomas in the preceding books, he has done so through a series of fantastic and horrible experiences. In the *récits* that follow, the mood shifts to a calm from which joy is not excluded. The "point" is ever present: witness the emphasis on a unique moment implied in the very title of *Au moment voulu*. In *L'Attente l'oubli* characters grope for a condition in which they would experience expectancy of past time and oblivion of the future. As with surrealists, there are intimations of a lost paradise, and if it is more abstract than that of childhood it is that more difficult to conceive. Blanchot demands a great deal from the reader.

NOTES FOR CHAPTER THREE (Blanchot)

[1] Maurice Blanchot, "Le Mythe de Mallarmé," in *La Part du feu* (Paris: Gallimard, 1949), p. 48.

[2] Blanchot, "Réflexions sur le Surréalisme," in *La Part du feu*, p. 95.

80   FRENCH FICTION TODAY

³ For a different approach, cf. Geoffrey Hartman, "Maurice Blanchot," in *The Novelist as Philosopher*, ed. John Cruickshank (London: Oxford University Press, 1962), pp. 147–165.

⁴ Blanchot, *Thomas l'obscur*, deuxième version, p. 12. In this chapter, references to Blanchot's fiction henceforth appear in the text with the following abbreviations: *Thomas l'obscur*, TO-1 and TO-2; *Aminadab*, A; *Le Très-haut*, TH; *L'Arrêt de mort*, AM; *Au moment voulu*, AMV; *Celui qui ne m'accompagnait pas*, CAP; *L'Attente l'oubli*, AO. See Bibliography for complete references.

⁵ Blanchot, "Le Langage de la fiction," in *La Part du feu*, p. 80.

⁶ Cf. Jean Starobinsky, "Thomas l'obscur, chapitre premier," *Critique*, No. 229 (June 1966), pp. 498–513.

⁷ Claude-Edmonde Magny, *Précieux Giraudoux* (Paris: Seuil, 1945), p. 13.

⁸ Jean Giraudoux, *Suzanne et le Pacifique* (Paris: E. Paul, 1921), p. 120.

⁹ André Breton, Second Manifeste du Surréalisme (1930; rpt. in *Manifestes du Surréalisme* [Paris: J.-J. Pauvert, 1962], p. 154.

¹⁰ Breton, *Second Manifeste*, p. 154.

¹¹ Breton, *Nadja* (Paris: Gallimard, 1928), pp. 38 ff.

¹² Blanchot, "La Littérature et le droit à la mort," in *La Part du feu*, p. 308.

¹³ Jean-Paul Sartre, *"Aminadab* ou du fantastique considéré comme un langage," in *Situations I* (Paris: Gallimard, 1947), pp. 122–142.

¹⁴ Georges Poulet, "Maurice Blanchot, critique et romancier," *Critique*, No. 229 (June 1926), pp. 485–497.

¹⁵ Pierre Klossowski, "Sur Maurice Blanchot," *Les Temps Modernes* No. 40 (February 1949), pp. 306–307.

¹⁶ Breton, *Manifestes*, p. 23.

¹⁷ Jacques Lacan, *Ecrits* (Paris: Seuil, 1966), pp. 267 & 495.

¹⁸ Blanchot, "Le Regard d'Orphée," in *L'Espace littéraire* (Paris: Gallimard, 1955), p. 183.

¹⁹ Blanchot, "La Voix narrative," in *L'Entretien infini* (Paris: Gallimard, 1969), p. 563.

²⁰ Blanchot, "La littérature et le droit à la mort," p. 327.

CHAPTER FOUR

Samuel Beckett

It has been said of Raymond Queneau that, in spite of the hilarious aspects of some of his works, he was, at heart, a melancholy clown. Of Samuel Beckett on the other hand, and although his fiction crawls with hopelessly alienated bums whose view of the condition of men is almost exclusively bleak, it might well be said that he is basically a humorist. However much his characters suffer (or seem to suffer), the reader's first reaction more often than not is one of laughter. Of course, his humor is far from gentle (Beckett has been likened to Swift), but its presence is undeniable; it is perhaps the only thing that makes his texts emotionally bearable. One may, possibly, feel nothing but revulsion for the "love" that exists between Macmann and Moll, in *Malone meurt*, but the sample of one of her letters to him is a comic delight, as is the analogy drawn between his doggerel verse and the texts of religious mystics.

The publication of Beckett's French trilogy, as *Molloy*, *Malone meurt*, and *L'Innommable* are often called, was preceded by the translation into French of his prewar *Murphy* and followed, after some years, by *Comment c'est*, which could be read as an epilogue—and which also opens the way for further developments that I shall not go into. *Murphy* caused a small ripple in London in 1938, being favorably reviewed, but it was greeted with total silence when the translation appeared in Paris in 1947. Nevertheless, because it is his first major publication in French, because the translation is his own, and, more importantly, because of what links it to the trilogy, it needs to be considered along with those three works of fiction that were written in French. If *Comment c'est* is the epilogue, *Murphy* represents the overture to the trilogy, an overture in which a number of subsequently developed patterns and themes are clearly stated. Appearing in Paris within a span of six years, *Murphy* and the trilogy constitute the corpus of Beckett texts that has conveyed his significance to a French audience. Michel Butor, for instance, was encouraged, after reading *Molloy*, to submit his first piece of fiction to the same publisher. Had he not done so, the publication of *Passage de Milan* might have been delayed several years. After the trilogy, with *En attendant Godot*, Beckett entered the international literary scene.

Murphy is much more comical and more traditional than the books that follow. Hugh Kenner has even written that "it is not a typical Beckett book."[1] That may be true, but perhaps only on the surface. It is certainly cluttered up with elements that are not present in the trilogy—realistic setting and conspicuous learned allusions, for instance. Once these have been cleared away, permanent patterns emerge. The setting of *Murphy* is stated explicitly: Cork, Dublin, and, principally, London. Within London, a number of streets and landmarks are readily identifiable. French readers have no difficulty in finding their bearings because Beckett has taken the trouble to set up the analogy, King's Cross Station—Caledonian Road/Gare Saint-Lazare—Rue d'Amsterdam. Within this familiar world, six major characters and about a dozen minor ones, not counting several who do not appear directly, perform a grotesque kind of ballet. Such characters, however, are not to be taken as real people, for they are, in the text, referred to as puppets, nor are they reflections of people of one's own world. Their idiosyncracies are much more startling, and their learning is, on occasion, impressive or disconcerting. They refer to Hippasus of Metapontum, Oswald Kulpe, Guillaume de Champeaux, and Arnold Geulincx in what seems like the most outlandish context; the names of Descartes and Leibnitz are casually dropped. All that has a flavor reminiscent of Queneau's *Le Chiendent* (1933), which Beckett could well have read. Yet Queneau's erudition, probably as extensive as Beckett's, is more discreet. Both attempt to disguise it, Queneau by omitting references, Beckett by throwing in invented names along with the authentic ones. Because of the relative obscurity of some of those, the results, to the reader, is one of ridicule; as in Rabelais, scorn is heaped upon a certain kind of learning. That is part of the humor in *Murphy*, accentuated by the protagonist's being characterized as a nonreader. Whatever his intentions, Beckett may have felt that this aspect attracted too much notice, perhaps misleading some to view his work as satirical, therefore eventually possitive in nature. He is, to my mind, thoroughly negative: Murphy's remove from books is more important than Neary's foolish esoteric learning.

Leaving the clutter aside, one thing stands out. As all commentators have remarked, this fiction is about a quest—or a hunt, as Hugh Kenner suggests.[2] Some add that it is a double quest, that of Murphy for himself, that of Neary and company for Murphy. I should prefer to say that Neary and his cohorts are performing the parody of a quest. Murphy, on the other hand, is no seeker but a wanderer. His main concern is to protect himself from the world. He is a nonseeker as much as he is a nonreader. The reluctant, almost negative way in which he goes about looking for a job is rather typical of him. A reference to Celia as a Penelope without suitors suggests a parallel between Murphy and Odysseus, a wanderer *par excellence* who longs to return to that small island lying toward the gloom of darkness—his Ithaca. As Murphy plods along, crafty as the Greek when he deals with Vera, the waitress, and with Rosie Dew, he, too, longs for that time when he can go home, and even beyond that to being "more and more and more in the dark, in the will-lessness, a mote in its absolute freedom."[3] Molloy recalls his own wanderings, but he has come to a place of rest, and so have Malone and the narrator of *L'Innommable*; more about them later. Neary is the counterpart of a courtly knight, its negative image, who sets out on a series of adventures in order to win the heart of his beloved lady—Miss Counihan. Actually, he is concerned with things more sexually satisfying than the heart, and her own purity is no more than a mask. As the price of her favors, she assigns him the task of bringing back evidence that Murphy (her true love, she says) is dead, or unfaithful, or financially in bad straits. All she really sees in Murphy is a good provider. The quest Neary embarks upon is a rather absurd parody, serving as pretext for a number of comic incidents, such as Cooper's barging in on the amorous scene between Wylie and Miss Counihan, or mock philosophical discussions, like the one between Neary and Wylie about the universe as being a closed system. Having several oddly assorted beings engaged in such a quest, each one for a different reason, encourages shenanigans. But incidents and characters' attributes, grotesque as they often seem, have not been chosen without a deeper purpose, unfathomable though it may be, and they keep on reverberating through the trilogy.

Murphy himself does not yet epitomize the bum, typical of Beckett's later imaginations. Most characteristics, however, are already present, dispersed throughout the book. Molloy explains that during his wanderings, "there were only two postures for me any more, the vertical, drooping between my crutches, sleeping on my feet, and the horizontal, down on the ground" (p. 31). He inherited that from Cooper, who could likewise only stand or lie—never sit down (at least not until Murphy is found). The latter, too, wears a bowler, another trademark, which he can never remove, perhaps to compensate for Murphy, who never wears a hat. Molloy jams down his hat on his own head "with such violence that I couldn't get it off again" (p. 138). Earlier in his fictional life, Molloy confided, "I quite liked getting drunk" (p. 54), while Cooper's "only humane characteristic was a morbid craving for alcoholic depressant" (Mu, p. 44). In describing Macmann's attire, Malone remarks that his coat is too long but his hat too small. Kelly is dressed in the same fashion when he is wheeled out to fly his kite in the final chapter of *Murphy*.

Murphy rests by a flock of sheep in Hyde Park and encounters Rosie Dew and her dog, Nelly. Molloy, as he wakes up in the country, sees a shepherd, his dog and his sheep, and later, in the town, he meets with Sophie Loy (frequently referred to as Lousse) and her dog, Teddy. When he sees the sheep, he wonder if they are being taken to be slaughtered. After Murphy is forced to leave West Brompton, Celia finds a place for both of them not far from a slaughterhouse; Molloy's mother lives in the neighborhood of slaughterhouses; Moran, approaching a flock of sheep, likens himself to a butcher about to make his selection; old Louis, one of Malone's creations, who is an expert at slaughtering pigs, buys a mule that was being taken away to be slaughtered; and the celebrated jar of *L'Innommable* also rests near the slaughterhouse. Perhaps these characters and their creator sense an affinity between the condition of men and that of cattle being led to slaughter. The link is nearly made explicit by Molloy, who finds safety in sleep because he believes a hunter never shoots a sleeping beast. Murphy is also interested in human slaughter, euphemistically called executions, at the nearby prison. When leaving Celia he asks, "Wasn't there to be an execution this morning?" But he is disappointed: " 'Never on Sunday,' said Celia" (Mu, p. 105). Men's lot is a sad one. As the omniscient author of *Murphy* remarks, "All the puppets in this book whinge sooner or later" (Mu, p. 92).

In the last book of the trilogy, the Unnamable is sure of very few things, but among them are his tears, ceaselessly streaming down his face. The reader, on the other hand, is not inclined to shed any more tears than when reading, say, Voltaire's *Candide*, for seldom is he allowed to lose sight of the puppetlike nature

of the characters. The Unnamable, speaking of those creations
he plans to bring forth, uses the word "puppets," just as the
author of *Murphy* did; in that work, we are told that all except
Murphy himself are puppets. It is clear that Murphy is the
author's surrogate: he is the center of things, and all other
characters exist for him(if not by him). In the last two works
of the trilogy, the narrator creates everyone else, or they think
they do, and in the end he has perhaps created himself. As the
reader realizes, he has actually been created by language. The
situation is not so clear with respect to *Molloy*, where Molloy
and Moran, in their respective halves, occupy a stage intermediate between that of Murphy and that of Malone. The
general pattern is one of gradual shift from main character
surrounded by author-created puppets, to main character who
produces his own puppets, to the flow of language that creates
them all. There is also a kind of circular transformation involved,
for on the one hand Murphy, having been created by the
author-narrator, is closer in kind to Neary and the rest than
Malone is to Macmann, and on the other the Unnamable seems
so far removed from one's own everyday reality that it is hard,
both for the reader and for himself, to distinguish him from his
creations. It is he who refers to Murphy as a bag of sawdust,
thus implying he is a puppet, and who occasionally thinks
he is Mahood instead of himself—whatever that is.

As the gap that separates Murphy from Celia does not seem
so great, there have been hesitations as to what her nature is.
Ruby Cohn, for instance, is reluctant to abandon her to the
realm of puppetry.[4] John Fletcher calls her "the most subtly-
drawn secondary character in the whole novel."[5] Nevertheless,
she is the kind-hearted, lovable prostitute, a hackneyed character in European fiction if there ever was one. What partially
saves her is that the reader tends to forget that essence of hers
as she gets immersed in the language of the fiction. The comic
effect of Celia's declaration, "I am a prostitute" (Mu, p. 167)—
which is more effective in the French version, because of the

word *putain* (whore)—is largely due to her situation's having slipped into the background. In the meantime, she has become something of a mother-image. In addition to her wise, worldly advice, her urging Murphy to get himself a job (of him she wished to "make a man," Mu, p. 52), here she is in their Brewery Road home, sitting in the rocking chair, patiently waiting for his return. That, of course, is Murphy's precious rocker, which he abandons to Celia temporarily and later reclaims. Capable of motion, like a bicycle, but stationary, like a bed, it exists halfway between the two. Molloy, as readers of the fiction will recall, abandons his bicycle to Lousse and later reclaims the bed from his mother.

As Neary pursues Murphy for the sake of Miss Counihan, his interest in the latter eventually vanishes while his concern for Murphy increases: he sees in him "the Friend at last" (Mu, p. 145). In the end, after Murphy's death, Neary acts more and more like a close relative. It is he who reads Murphy's will— and who takes it upon himself to authorize Cooper to disregard it. As fate would have it, the authorization was superfluous, and a barroom brawl provokes the dispersion of Murphy's ashes among "the sand, the beer, the butts, the glass, the matches, the spits, the vomit" (Mu, p. 196). Before Neary disappears, he conspicuously avoids Miss Counihan, as apparently Murphy had much earlier. He is not unlike Moran, who embarks upon his quest for Molloy under orders from Youdi but eventually loses interest in his mission and in Youdi, changing either into Molloy or at least into someone (or something) very much like him.

While not yet a bum, Murphy surely is no dandy. With his old jacket, "a tube in its own right," which descended clear of the body as far as mid-thigh" (p. 57), his crumpled trousers, both items originally black but now a peculiar shade of green, rather "aeruginous", his celluloid shirt-front ornamented with a lemon-colored bow tie, he suggests a clown. Critics have amply substantiated Beckett's permanent fascination with clowns and also their behavior. To pick only one example of the latter, there is something thoroughly clownish about Molloy's attempt to ride a bicycle. The sight of Murphy walking down the street is extraordinary: "His figure so excited the derision of a group of boys playing football in the road that they stopped their game" (p. 105). He was at one time interested in the stars, and when Celia first saw him he was standing on a London street corner contemplating the sky; now his life is dominated by astrology. Molloy undergoes a similar change of interest; he points out that he used to concern himself with astronomy, but now that everything within him is crumbling his main preoccupation is with magic. Malone also was curious about the stars and, one evening, as he gazed at them, he imagined he was back in London. He appears to be identifying himself with Murphy on his street corner. Such a speculation is made even more tempting when one recalls that Murphy had dropped a paper on which he had been making calculations concerning the stars. Malone, in describing his notebook, says that the first few pages are covered with figures and symbols. They obviously mean nothing to him any more, but he thinks they must have been related to astronomy or else astrology.

Figuring the motions of celestial bodies is not the only kind of calculation that fascinates Murphy. Before he is approached by Rosie Dew, as he thinks about eating the five assorted cookies he has bought from Vera and wonders about the order in which they might be eaten, he is entranced by the thought that one hundred and twenty possibilities are open to him—but Rosie's dog soon disposes of them all. The situation is analogous to that of Molloy confronted with his sixteen pebbles and four pockets to put them in: his problem is to find a way to insure that all sixteen will be sucked sequentially, none of them twice. After much cogitation he arrives at a satisfactory solution, although not a perfect one; but rather than wait for someone to ruin it, he tosses all but one pebble away, thus eliminating the problem.

Molloy, Malone, and the Unnamable all tell stories. Malone, thinking of the characters he has created and disposed of, remembers an old man in London—at least he thinks it was in London—whose throat he cut with a razor. That brings us back to Murphy, his Brewery Road flat, and the old recluse who lived on the floor above. His situation is developed into the ones in the trilogy, except that, even though death constantly preys on their minds, the protagonists do not actually commit suicide. The incident, along with a few others, also suggests the intriguing possibility that Malone is the author of *Murphy*. Murphy himself, being no narrator, tells no stories; the work does, however, contain a number of secondary narratives— those by Celia, Neary, and Cooper that have been "expurgated, accelerated, improved, and reduced" (Mu, pp. 15, 40, 90). A compulsion to babble away is thus clearly stated, although in less satisfactory fashion than in his subsequent fiction—which will not be expurgated to the same extent.

Toward the conclusion of the narrative, Murphy, whose commitment to life is far from enthusiastic, does not commit suicide: he is killed accidentally in his faithful rocking chair by a gas explosion, shortly after he has vaguely thought of the possibility of going back to Celia. After his body has been cremated, we are informed that "the parcel of ash must have weighed well on four pounds, [the average weight of a seven-month foetus]" (p. 195).[6] The circle is now complete, with Murphy weighing the same amount as when he was in his mother's womb. This is much like the circle travelled by Molloy, who eventually returns to his mother's room, wishing it were his mother's womb (in Freudian dream interpretation, a room is often a woman). Perhaps the same could be said of Malone and the Unnamable, and the latter possibly never left it. The most obvious example of narrative circularity can be found in the second part of *Molloy*, which ends precisely at the point where it began. The fiction could go on forever. Circles are far from rare in Beckett's work.

The greatest link between *Murphy* and the trilogy, what allows one to speak of it as an overture, is that it contains the seed of the development of those three subsequent works. When describing the three zones of Murphy's mind, in the explanatory sixth chapter, the narrator is also defining the three zones in which the trilogy functions: "There were the three zones, light, half-light, dark, each with its specialty" (p. 84).

In the first zone we have "the forms with parallel, a radiant abstract of the dog's life, the elements of physical experience available for a new arrangement" (Mu, p. 84). That is the realm of *Molloy*. It represents the first stage of a journey into the mind, which develops into a journey into language, since that is what the mind is made of. It represents a completion of, and elaboration on, the one undertaken by Murphy when lying in the grass or tied to his rocking chair. In *Molloy*, there still is a correspondence, or parallel, between the world of the mind and the outside world, between language and things, between signs and their referents. Metaphorically it is expressed by the correspondence between the two parts that make up the book; within the narration, it is expressed by the survival of a certain amount of realism. On a more restricted level, it is stated on the first two introductory pages by linking the activity of the mind to the production of a book: "So many pages, so much money" (p. 7). The creative act, in this instance, appears to constitute the means of communicating between the two worlds—something that was quite a mystery to Murphy. Not that Molloy understands the process any better: "The truth is I don't know much" (Mo, p. 7). Writing in his mother's room, he is in the world of the mind, where language reigns supreme, and he tells of an earlier period of his life when he lived almost exclusively in what Murphy would have called the exterior universe, a physical world in which sense perceptions were not verbalized. The difficulty he has in recalling his own name or that of the town in which his mother lived illustrates this perfectly: "I had been living so far from words so long, you understand . . . Yes, even then . . . there could be no things but nameless things, no names but thingless names" (pp. 45-46). He later elaborates, "Yes, the words I heard, and heard distinctly, having quite a sensitive ear, were heard a first time, then a second, and often even a third, as pure sounds, free of all meaning" (p. 74).

Language is something that goes on outside of his real self, even though he hears it in his mind, independently of his own volition. One is reminded of the autonomous, craggy existence of language Michel Foucault sees as emerging in our times.[7] That is also why words could not hurt him: "Insults, abuse, these I can easily bear, but I could never get used to blows. It's strange. Even spits still pain me" (Mo, p. 30). He reacts mainly to the physical. Hence also the importance accorded to material possessions, especially if they have no meaning, that is, if they cannot be rationally accounted for in the world of the mind. The most nearly perfect of these is the object he has taken from Lousse and for which he knows neither name nor purpose. A French reader would easily identify it as a knife rest, but to Molloy it has the characteristic that things have in the early essays of Robbe-Grillet—it is there and nothing more. His notions about death or, as he himself rephrases it, about being put to death are likewise purely physical: "Oh they weren't notions like yours, they were notions like mine, all spasm, sweat, and trembling, without an atom of common sense or lucidity" (Mo, p. 103). Molloy's physical life is not controlled by reason.

The sequence of events in the first part, the wanderings of Molloy, hardly satisfy the rational mind; discontinuity is the rule. The Lousse episode is typical. Riding in the street he runs over her dog, which was on the sidewalk. Lousse saves him from an angry mob (why should anyone have been upset?) for a preposterous reason. She asks him into her home so he can help bury the dog—a task of which he is incapable. He stays for an undetermined length of time, wandering through the house and grounds. One day he leaves, without warning or good-bye, abandoning his bicycle, which was useful, but stealing a few small articles of silverware, which are useless to him. The next major episode is set at the seashore, without any indication as to why he went there, how he got there, or how long it took. A sentence by Georges Bataille seems to describe that technique: "The narrative is based on a device according to which one represents without coherence patently incomplete aspects of reality."[8] That, however, located in a footnote to an enthusiastic review of *Molloy*, was written with reference to *Murphy* and not intended as a compliment. It expressed Bataille's disappointment with the earlier work, read after the discovery of *Molloy*. It also shows that Molloy was truly a stranger, even more than Camus' Meursault had shown himself to be, a decade earlier. Seen through Molloy's eyes, reality was no longer recognizable as such, and Bataille wrote in the third line of his review: "Everything in it is fantastic." Yet, in contrast to the writings of Blanchot for instance, there is nothing fantastic about this book of Beckett's. It represents, to go back to the statement found in *Murphy*, elements of experience that are used for the sake of a different organization—that of a literary text, the exact workings of which Molloy does not understand, but the meaning of which the reader might grasp. One reason why that experience no longer seems recognizable is obviously that the absence of mind has deprived it of so-called "human" quality.

Molloy's disjointed account of his wanderings is, to go back to *Murphy* once more, "a radiant abstract of the dog's life." Quite early in the narrative Molloy reveals his sympathy for dogs when he speaks of "one of those stray dogs that you pick up and take in your arms, from compassion or because you have long been straying with no other company than the endless roads." (Mo, p. 15). Repetition of the similar words, "stray" and "straying," applied both to man and dog, emphasizes the relationship. Lousse understands that; she explains the life she has organized for him at her home, and he sums it up by saying, "I would as it were take the place of the dog I had killed, as it for her had taken the place of a child" (Mo, p. 70). The Lousse episode, however, is the turning point in the first part of the story. When she buries her dog, Molloy merely stands by, partly because of his physical handicaps, but also for a more significant reason: "On the whole I was a mere spectator, I contributed my presence. As if it had been my own burial. And it was" (p. 54). Neither Lousse nor Molloy had planned it that way; nor is he, in spite of his statement (which is attributable to Beckett as author more than to Molloy as narrator), completely aware of what is taking place. Of course, the entire physical side of Molloy will not disappear at once; rather it will cease to dominate his life. As he himself describes his stay at Lousse's, he mentions those moments when his experience is completely physical, like that of an animal, in total communion with nature; then he adds, "But that did not happen to me often" (p. 73). Most of the time he retires into what, in the French version, he calls his closed box, impervious to weather and to nature, where questions are being raised. It is the equivalent of Murphy's "large hollow sphere, hermetically closed to the universe without" (Mu, p. 81). It is the inquiring human mind.

Because he can less and less be at one with nature, because the "dog's life" is more and more a thing of the past, he can no longer stay with Lousse, who bases her relationship with him on a vanishing condition. He leaves her abruptly. Lousse apparently would like to maintain him in a doglike state, as Circe tried to keep Ulysses and his companions transformed into swine. Ironically, Molloy accuses Lousse of giving him moly, which is what Hermes gave Ulysses as an antidote to Circe's spells. When he leaves Lousse, he notes that she did nothing to try to prevent him—except perhaps by spells. As in *Murphy*, such random and inconsistent references serve to conjure up thoughts of the wandering Ulysses in the reader's mind. They also indicate that, although both Molloy and Ulysses are wanderers who eventually return home, Beckett is not attempting to retell Homer's epic in modern dress. Nor, I hasten to add, has he written a sort of medieval allegory that could be deciphered minutely, statement by statement. There is a general underlying pattern that gives meaning to the work, in and out of which Beckett is apt to meander, as humor moves him—or language.

The meditating reader can usually forge some order out of apparent chaos, fitting elements of the narrative into his own "new arrangement"; yet he must take care, lest it become a forgery. After making some sense out of that key episode at Lousse's house, during which the Old Molloy was buried, he might well decide that the journey to the sea was a most apposite symbol to herald the birth of a New Molloy. There Molloy will linger for a while, close to the source of all living things. He even wonders if, at one time, he did not put out to sea. On the beach, he encounters women gathering driftwood, and one of them even tries to approach him. This is vaguely reminiscent of the meeting between Ulysses and Nausicaa, but Beckett makes a mockery of it, perhaps teasing the reader, perhaps simply enjoying himself. More important, it is on the beach that Molloy faces the problem of determining the proper sucking order for his sixteen pebbles. There, truly, is a concern most worthy of the human mind; no calculating dog ever devoted its time to such weighty matters. Molloy has verily entered into the life of the mind. Concomitantly, the life of his body deteriorates.

One must grant that even before the Lousse episode Molloy was a sad sight to behold; now, however, his body seems on the verge of falling apart. He had expected to grow steadily worse with age, on account of his many weak spots, "But what was not to be expected was the speed at which their weakness had increased, since my departure from the seaside" (Mo, p. 122). His better leg gets worse than his bad one, a number of his toes drop off, and furthermore, "my true weak points were elsewhere" (p. 123). As he proceeds through the forest, walking becomes more and more difficult for him and is replaced with creeping. As the body becomes close to inoperative, the mind becomes more resourceful. Molloy beats and kicks the charcoal burner he meets, displaying ingeniousness, sadism, and esthetic passion for symmetry, none of which a dog could ever do. Finally, as he reaches the edge of the forest, his body rolls helplessly into a ditch; his mind comments, "Molloy could stay, where he happened to be" (p. 141). But that is not just the account of one man's journey. There is an epic quality to the first part of *Molloy* that is quite unrelated to the mock-epic incidents I have mentioned. There is a timelessness about it, created by Molloy's vagueness concerning time intervals, his inability to state whether he has spent days or months or even years in this or that locale. There arises a feeling that the wandering has been going on practically forever, produced for instance by Molloy's remembering a time when "[railroads were still on the drawing board]" (pp. 116–117). It is almost the story of mankind's evolution from a simian stage to present achievements of the intellect. Calling that progress is something of a joke. Like the one Murphy tells Celia before going to the M.M.M., as the Magdalen Mental Mercyseat is referred to, it produces hysterical laughter in some, but others, like Celia, are not amused. (Women in Beckett's fiction take things rather seriously: Martha does not appreciate Moran's humor either.)

Part two of *Molloy* is the account of a parallel journey undertaken by Moran at the behest of his mysterious employer. His mission is to find Molloy. He fails to do so, yet he becomes somewhat like him in the end. Actually, the resemblance appears greater than it is because Moran changes much more than Molloy did in the course of events. The Molloy we abandon at the end of part one is to some extent like the one we encountered at the beginning, only much worse, but Moran undergoes a real metamorphosis. He is introduced as a man of some standing, albeit modest, the owner of a small house where he lives with his son and a housekeeper. Assured of a steady job, he is fastidiously rational and calculating about everything down to the most trifling acts of existence. He describes himself as being "a sensible man, cold as crystal and as free from spurious depth" (p. 174). He is a well-adjusted person in a civilized society. He also lives outside of what Murphy called a sphere and Molloy a box. During his afternoon nap, "Far from the world, its clamours, frenzies, bitterness, and dingy light, I pass judgement on it and on those, like me, who are plunged in it beyond recall, and on him who has need of me to be delivered, who cannot deliver myself" (p. 171). Although an integral part of the exterior universe, there are moments when he is able to judge it, and it is thanks to such moments that a transformation takes place. Molloy had started from a more authentic position, for the world of nature is real. Moran's universe is inauthentic, being isolated from reality by a screen that protects him from it. Such a screen has been perfected by the human mind, but to the extent that it shields one from inner reality as well as from outer reality it represents perversion. Throughout this second part of *Molloy*, one witnesses a destruction of that screen, "a frenzied collapsing of all that had always protected me from all I was always condemned to be" (p. 230).

Critics have argued whether events of the second part of *Molloy* take place at the same time or after those of the first. Ruby Cohn even suggests that the order of the two parts should be inverted. I simply believe that the two parts are presented in the order in which they were intended to be read. When Moran is directed to search for Molloy, he is not so much supposed to seek another individual as he is to probe the nature of his own existence. That is a transposition of Neary's quest, which was begun with an ulterior purpose. Moran's mission is not to find Molloy but to carry on the investigation begun by the latter. Clues to that effect are the gong that Molloy hears in the forest and that is sounded in Moran's house and the voice that Molloy hears in the morning, as he lies in the ditch: "Don't fret, Molloy, we're coming" (p. 140). But indeed, the very existence of both

Molloy and Moran is problematic. The narrator of part one makes reference to the things he may have invented "in the interests of the narrative" (p. 84). Has he also invented Molloy for the sake of giving cohesion to that narrative? Moran never gives a direct quotation of Gaber's original instructions, aside from the order to leave the same day accompanied by his son. The only mention of Molloy's name is made by Moran, when talking to himself, nor can he think of anyone who might have spoken to him of Molloy. Still, his supposed quarry is not unknown to him. As to his actual existence, "Perhaps I have invented him, I mean found him ready made in my head" (p. 173). Had he invented Molloy, Moran could then be identified as the narrator of part one; the qualification suggests that the narrator of part two is also the narrator of part one. Moran and Molloy are two facets of his mind, that is, of the language that determines its organization—they represent two linguistic structures that could not be fused into one.

That leads me to speculate that one of the two parts might have existed in embryo form, either simply in Beckett's mind or in rough drafts or notes in the English language, the other having developed in French from the very start. As to the conjectures concerning Molloy and Moran's existence, we all know it is a game, as both were clearly "invented" by Beckett. Nevertheless, our being led to such exercises is significant, for it shows that the text itself actively promotes the destruction of traditional "characters" in fiction, something I shall be coming back to time and again in these essays. That should encourage us to free ourselves from considerations of plausibility in the narrations. As we examine the relationship between parts one and two, it might be more productive to note their contrapuntal aspects rather than their chronological ones. I have in mind details such as these: while Molloy has considerable difficulty remembering his name, Moran affirms his in the second paragraph of his "report"; Molloy rides a bicycle in spite of his disabilities, but Moran goes along on the baggage-rack of his son's machine; Molloy accidentally kills a dog and attends its funeral, while Moran intentionally kills a man wearing city clothes whose face resembles his own and hides his body under some branches—the former disposing of his past "dog's life," and latter renouncing the complacency of civilized life. A list of such contrasts could be extensive.

Leaving Molloy wherever "he happens to be," I move on to the second zone of Murphy's mind, which is that of "forms without parallel. Here the pleasure was contemplation. This system had no other mode in which to be out of joint and therefore did not need to be put right in this" (Mu, p. 84). That is the realm of *Malone meurt,* and, as the French text of *Murphy* makes clear, the "other mode" is that of the "real" world. The French version continues with the observation that this is where Belacqua's vision unfolded. Of course, Belacqua is too permanent a fixture in Beckett's works to be identified exclusively with any one work. The word "vision" is a crucial one as it clarifies the vaguer "bliss" of the English text. What Belacqua sees in the fourth canto of Dante's *Purgatory* is a portion of the intermediate journey, the one leading from Hell to Paradise. *Malone meurt* describes an intermediate stage between light and darkness. That the narrative is meant to continue the one from *Molloy* is clear from the identification of the narrator as a crippled old man, alone in a room, in bed; from his identical statement as to how he got there (Malone says he does not remember, Molloy says he does not know, but both add, "Perhaps in an ambulance, certainly a vehicle of some kind"—Mo, p. 7 and Ma, p. 15); and from a vague remembrance of having wandered in a forest. The reader is with him in that room from beginning to end. There is no need for anything "to be put right" and be made to conform to requirements of the outside world, pretending that the narrator is Molloy, Moran, or someone else, and the stories he tells about Saposcat or Macmann are presented as pure fiction. In announcing the several kinds of stories he plans to tell, he refers to himself as an artist. In organizing his activities, he plans to take inventory of his possessions as soon as he has finished telling his stories. On second thought, he decides to precede the stories with an account of his present state, thus balancing the inventory: "Aesthetics are therefore on my side, at least a certain kind of aesthetics" (Ma, p. 13). Again, the French version of Murphy makes the link more obvious, for instead of the pleasure being defined as "contemplation" it is called *esthétique*. Malone's beautiful plan will come to naught, but the esthetic preoccupation is there—he is the artist at work. He is within Murphy's "large hollow sphere," out of which his fictions spring forth, and he has identified with his mind, specifically stating that he has taken refuge within it (Ma, p. 112). Obviously, Raymond Roussel would have approved. Malone, however, appears disappointed to notice that what he takes out of himself is very much like himself: "I wonder if I am not talking yet again about myself. Shall I be incapable, to the end, of lying on any other subject?" (pp. 25–26). One might recall Jean Cocteau's saying that he was a lie that told the truth. It would be unlike Beckett to deal only with the serious aspects of literary creation, and a goodly portion of *Malone meurt* is parody: parody of the old-fashioned novel, especially in the Saposcat-Louis episodes ("What tedium!"), parody of the writer at work. Later, as the young Sapo (or someone else) reappears in the shape of old Macmann, the parodic element is less emphasized, while the tone and humor are more like that in *Molloy*. Malone, who calls himself a nonagenerian, contemplates imminent death but also enjoys imagining his past life. "It was pleasant to lie dreaming on the shelf beside Belacqua, watching the dawn break crooked" (Mu, p. 85).

The third zone of Murphy's mind is "a flux of forms, a perpetual coming together and falling asunder of forms" (Mu, p. 84). This is a dark region in which he conceives himself as motionless, something like a projectile without origin and without destination, "caught up in a tumult of non-Newtonian motion" (p. 85). That is most readily recognizable as the realm of *L'Innommable*. The narrator begins in utter confusion as to location, time, and identity. His disorientation is such that he cannot find appropriate words to describe the condition of the surrounding area; the connotation of words constantly betrays his intentions—a problem that will also come up in Claude Ollier's texts. There are no days where he is, but still he says, "Here all is clear" (I, p. 13). When he speaks of the world of men, he calls it the domain of light, but he soon affirms, "Nothing nocturnal here" (I, p. 26). Perhaps "grey" is the word that might best describe his environment. Although he seems to settle for that compromise, he must finally reject it: "black is what I should have said" (I, p. 33). Molloy and Malone had previously been beset by similar difficulties, which reflect the tendency of language to absorb anything into its preset structure, thereby encouraging clichés, facilitating everyday communication, but opposing its force of inertia to the new and the unknown. Maurice Blanchot, in his writings, is concerned with the same negative aspects of language, the curse it pronounces on authenticity, virtually destroying it at the same time it expresses it. To name something old is to describe it; to name something new is to falsify it. The narrator of the third piece in the trilogy is the truest of all of Beckett's narrators because he remains nameless. To reach out from the "large hollow sphere" of his mind into the outside world, he has appointed surrogates, Murphy, Molloy, Malone, who represented and misrepresented him. Through intertextual effect (I shall be returning to that concept in later chapters), he may now be viewed as the narrator of the two other works in the trilogy, dissolving their narratives as he dissolves himself.

Earlier protagonists are summoned, becoming shapes that circulate about him in the dark, in his strange, non-Newtonian world. Puppets, all of them. But he can only produce more, for all the mind can do, almost by definition, is to generate words: "I am obliged to speak. I shall never be silent. Never" (I, p. 9). So he invents more stories and more characters: Basile, who becomes so interesting that the Unnamable changes the name to

Mahood (adopting him into the family, so to speak), and Worm. Somewhere along the line, he finds himself in a further quandary; he thinks he has invented all these beings, but the possibility emerges that they have actually invented him. Language and the mind are so inseparable that the question of which came first is as unanswerable as the one about the chicken and the egg. Did he invent Mahood, or did Mahood invent him? Or perhaps Mahood, Malone, Molloy, and Murphy are collectively responsible for his existence. A mysterious "they" have determined what he is, just as Western culture has determined us, and Geulincx, Dante, Swift, Descartes, and Joyce (among others) have molded Beckett. "Do they believe I believe it is I who am speaking? That's theirs too" (I, p. 120). It may be that the solipsistic *Amor intellectualis* that led Murphy to his rocking chair and incidentally to his death corresponds to nothing real. Communication between the inner sphere of the mind and the outer universe, which Murphy assumed but could not explain and Molloy expressed through the creative act, is rejected as a lie in *Malone meurt* and *L'Innommable*. The life of mind goes on forever, describing beautiful circumvolutions while the world outside goes to pot. Conversely, Marguerite's customers in *L'Innommable* come and consult the menu outside her restaurant without ever seeing, hearing, or smelling Mahood in his jar. The only thing the mind can do, when the pain is not too sharp, is laugh at the world and at itself, and keep adding words to words without end: "you must go on, I can't go on, I'll go on" (I, p. 262). And so do readers and especially critics, who, in more than a score of full-length books and countless articles, have grafted thousands of words upon Beckett's own thousand. And there is no end in sight.[9]

As the Unnamable felt compelled to go on, Beckett himself was unable to stop, even though his narrator(s) had been pushed into nothingness. Another fiction eventually followed what could have been looked upon as a dead end. Eight years after the publication of *L'Innommable, Comment c'est* (1961) provided the trilogy with a conclusion. It is a somewhat bitter one. Humor, which verged on the slapstick variety in *Molloy*, and became more Swiftian in the latter two volumes is now almost exclusively of the blackest kind. Lyricism, on the other hand, which appeared as early as *Molloy* in episodic fashion and seemed incongruous or parodic when it did, is sustained throughout the whole length of *Comment c'est*. Brief descriptive touches, with normal colors added, take us away from Beckett's bums. Specific details like "the emerald grass . . . white rails a grandstand color of old rose" (C, p. 35) help conjure up the image of a race track in April or May. A mother, a mistress, love are alluded to; also, more extensively, suffering and torture, companionship and solitude. In other words, feelings and passions are reintroduced and complete the picture given in the trilogy.

Love and friendship had not been absent from Murphy. "What is my life now but Celia?" (Mu, p. 18) is Murphy's own rhetorical question. "He writhed on his back in the bed, yearning for Murphy as though he had never yearned for anything or anyone before" (Mu, p. 145) expresses Neary's feelings. Murphy and Celia drift apart, and Murphy is dead when Neary catches up with him. In the trilogy, love is reduced to sex and made a mockery of; friendship is nonexistent. In *Comment c'est* the birth of love, young love, is described in lyrical, even moving terms, despite the customary details Beckett can never withhold. Love, however, leads not to happiness: a wife is loved less and less, jumps out of the window, spends the entire winter in the hospital before dying. Friendship is depicted as a relationship in which the roles of victim and executioner alternate, producing only an exchange of suffering. That is expanded into a dismal picture of human solidarity, a vision of a great circular chain of beings through which torture and pain go their eternal rounds, "and these same couples that eternally form and form again all along this immense circuit that the millionth time that's conceivable is as the inconceivable first and always two strangers uniting in the interests of torment"

(C, pp. 146–147). (The image is basically similar to the one used in the brief 1971 work *Le Dépeupleur,* with its two hundred naked bodies locked into a vast cylinder.) Religious themes are introduced in a less casual way than in the trilogy. Rather than being dismissed out of hand, God is at one point envisaged as a possibility. Soon enough, however, doubt covers everything. There still is someone or something that says "I," but it is hardly a narrator, not even a dismembered one. One could call it a voice, the voice of the text in which particulars of the narrative are generated for its own convenience—as we were led to suspect in *Molloy*—and it all amounts to little more than words. Only solitude remains, and the certainty of death, and the obsessive presence of that voice in the text—but whose text?

NOTES TO CHAPTER FOUR (Beckett)

[1] Hugh Kenner, *Samuel Beckett: A Critical Study* (New York: Grove Press, 1961), p. 52.

[2] *Ibid.,* p. 57.

[3] Samuel Beckett, *Murphy,* p. 85. Subsequent references to Beckett's fiction appear in the body of the text with the following abbreviations: *Murphy,* Mu; *Molloy,* Mo; *Malone meurt,* Ma; *L'Innommable,* I; *Comment c'est,* C. Translations are those of the New York editions published by Grove Press, Inc.; the references, however, are always to the French editions. See Bibliography for complete references.

[4] Cf. Ruby Cohn, *Samuel Beckett: The Comic Gamut* (New Brunswick: Rutgers University Press, 1962), p. 47.

[5] John Fletcher, *The Novels of Samuel Beckett* (London: Chatto & Windus, 1964), p. 47.

[6] Words within brackets, in this and one other instance, have been translated by myself, as they were omitted from the Grove Press editions.

[7] Cf. Michel Foucault, *Les Mots et les choses* (Paris: Gallimard, 1966), p. 313.

[8] Georges Bataille, "Le Silence de Molloy," *Critique,* No. 48 (May 1951), p. 389.

[9] Cf. Raymond Federman and John Fletcher, *Samuel Beckett: His Works and His Critics* (Berkeley: University of California Press, 1970).

CHAPTER FIVE

Marguerite Duras

The work of Marguerite Duras came to the attention of critics, especially outside of France, at the time of the publication of her sixth book, *Le Square* (the translation of which was closely followed by the release of her first movie, *Hiroshima mon amour*). An unusual text, it seemed related in some mysterious way to the works of Sarraute and Robbe-Grillet. It also appeared to break the continuity of style and technique with her previous ones. As more of her fiction was published, the link with those writers who were receiving considerable attention throughout the fifties grew more and more tenuous. As a result, she now finds herself somewhat isolated from "literary" trends or circles. She herself has become very reluctant to discuss literature or even her own works. Critics, in turn, have not given her the attention she deserves.

A definite evolution can be detected in her fiction, with two turning points identifiable: *Le Marin de Gibraltar* (rather than *Le Square*) and *Le Ravissement de Lol V. Stein*. The early works tended to be dictatorial in their rhetoric. They were also diffuse and contained many descriptions in the conventional mode, as that of the picturesque "père Bart," the tavern keeper, in *Un Barrage contre le Pacifique*, together with much analysis and explanation. The opening paragraph of the same book, stating what meaning the purchase of a horse had had for the three main characters ("And they felt less isolated, now that they were linked by that horse to the outside world") and the prediction made on the second page that "they were about to meet someone, and that meeting would change the lives of all three," are typical of what she would later eschew. In her attempt to keep a tight rein on the reader's imagination, she revealed a probably unconscious acceptance of traditional esthetics. Nevertheless, some of the themes and preoccupations that run through her better-known works were already present from the beginning.

The three works of her early period, *Les Impudents* (1943), *La Vie tranquille* (1944), and *Un Barrage contre le Pacifique* (1950), are essentially analytical. The latter two might even be viewed as allegory and parable, respectively. Like those that follow, they present the reader with an identical predominant condition that generates incidents of the narrative: a stifling, nearly unbearable situation from which characters cannot escape on their own. (In early works they receive outside help. In later ones they often learn to assume their condition rather than attempt escape, but even in the most recent one, *Abahn Sabana David*, it takes the arrival of a fourth character to enable Sabana and David to begin the process that will lead to their salvation.) Here, especially in the first two, Marguerite Duras is concerned with the condition of the young who are imprisoned within the family group, which attracts them and repels them at the same time. Maud, the twenty-year-old daughter in *Les Impudents*, is rescued from her family by a stranger, but even after she has become pregnant she feels compelled to return to the family cell. Only when she seizes the initiative and breaks her bondage by denouncing an older brother to the police does her mother reject her, liberating her so to speak. This work, in which freedom is obtained partly through an impulse coming from within, is unique. It contrasts sharply with *L'Amante anglaise*, written almost a quarter of a century later, where a similar impulse inspires a murder, dooming the character instead of liberating her.

Maud was the central intelligence of *Les Impudents*, a third-person narrative. *La Vie tranquille*, with its view of hard, un-rewarding life on an isolated farm, presents a picture of the human condition as seen through the consciousness of a first-person narrator, Francine. Neither she nor her immediate family is responsible for the plight they find themselves in. The culprit is an uncle who, through some misdeed, caused a scandal, forcing the family to flee the town, where they were well-to-do and respected. The evil having come from without, she is led to expect a savior from without—and he does indeed show up, somewhat enigmatically, in the person of a man named Tiène, who seeks work at the farm. In contrast to what happened in *Les Impudents*, her unaided attempts to save her-self have indirectly and unintentionally caused the death of her uncle, to whom she was indifferent, and the suicide of her young brother, whom she loved. Tiène, who appears midway between the two deaths helps her to find herself and perhaps save herself. When the two first meet and become acquainted, their talk expresses much more than the words they use would indicate. Duras, however, does not attempt to "show" the di-alogue—she describes it: "That conversation was not actually a conversation. . . . He seemed absent-minded and I, too, would answer him absent-mindedly."[1] Later, he questions her in-tensely in order to discover the underlying motives for her first act, to reach her own truth, which he knows to be "pure and coherent" (VT, p. 85)—but it is he who says so; the reader is not made to sense it. After her brother's suicide, she is sent to the seashore by Tiène. She engages in much self-analysis and has a pointless encounter with a mediocre man that prefigures the meeting of *Le Square*, although here, her indifference re-sults in the man's drowning. The entire episode enables her to discover who she was, and she then discourses at length on what has happened. Shortly after her return to the farm, her en-gagement to Tiène is announced. They will be married soon, because he must leave before winter comes. Having played his role, the savior disappears as unaccountably as he had come.

The allegory might be reconciled both with Christian myth and with existentialism, but while Marguerite Duras is undoubtedly acquainted with the writings of Sartre, she surely is no Christian believer.

In *Un Barrage contre le Pacifique* metaphysical overtones are laid to rest and replaced with social ones; the atmosphere in this book has reminded critics such as Armand Hoog of the works of Erskine Caldwell.[2] While an oppressive family situation is still the cause for individual misery, the economic ruin that befalls the mother and her two children is directly traceable to the corrupt colonial administration of prewar French Indochina. The mother continues madly to wage a losing battle both against the all-powerful administration and the Pacific Ocean, but the children know that they cannot fight. They wait for someone to rescue them and take them away. The girl turns down a rich suitor, but her brother meets a wealthy married woman who will be the "savior" of both. The escapist theme is not abandoned until *Les Petits Chevaux de Tarquinia* (1953). Love between brother and sister is important, as in the previous work, whereas the mother-child relationship is given greater emphasis in some of the later works, as it already was in *Les Impudents*. Special meeting places and dances serve the narrative, but no crystallization takes effect. A picnic in *La Vie tranquille* acquired ceremonial aspects because it was so unusual and because, at one point, Francine and Tiène consciously repeated the words they had used when they first met. In *Un Barrage contre le Pacifique* the ritualistic value of dancing is not fully realized as several couples are involved in a number of different places and circumstances. A tendency towards proliferation is evident here. It, too, will be checked in *Les Petits Chevaux de Tarquinia*. Only afterwards do we get the remarkable economy of plot that characterizes the four works of her middle period, to which two later ones must be added, *Détruire dit-elle* (1969) and *Abahn Sabana David* (1970).

A man and a woman meet in a public square. They talk at

length, and we learn of their helplessness, of their longing for
a love and a freedom they have never known. At last they part
company, perhaps to meet again, perhaps not (*Le Square*,
1955). A lonesome mother accompanies her child to his piano
lessons. During that lesson a crime is committed in a café
nearby, and for the rest of the narrative the mother tries to
understand why a man murdered his mistress, wishing that she,
too, could be loved by a man passionate enough to kill her
(*Moderato cantabile*, 1958). Three French tourists in Spain,
a married couple (with a small child) and their woman friend,
are forced by a storm to spend the night in a small town where
a man has just shot his wife and her lover. The murderer is at
large but the French wife, who is as lonesome as the protagonist
of the previous story, finds him by chance and tries to save
him. She fails, losing her husband to the other woman as well
(*Dix Heures et demie du soir en été*, 1960). An old man waits
for a contractor outside the house he has bought for his
daughter. The contractor's child comes to warn him that her
father will be late. The old man continues to wait, and the contractor's wife comes to say that he will be later still. They both
wait and despairingly talk about his daughter and her husband,
whose love they sense they are losing (*L'Après-midi de
Monsieur Andesmas*, 1962). As Germaine Brée put it in her introduction to the American edition of those four works. "Each
novel concentrates on one central relationship that gives it its
dramatic cogency, but it is not an isolated relationship, for im-
placably it draws all other relationships into its orbit, mod-
ulating them as it were."[3]

The man in *Le Square* is a peddler, travelling from town to
town, hawking small articles in public markets; he is perhaps
thirty years old, and he has accepted mediocrity as his lot. She
is twenty; she is maid and governess for a bourgeois household
that live not far from the square. Unlike him, she finds her lot
intolerable and lives only for the day when she can cast it away.
The dialogue between the two nameless characters develops

then as a dialogue between two attitudes toward life, between two situations, both oppressive. Ironically, it is the man, to whom our culture has assigned an active role, who has adopted a pessimistic, passive outlook. His partner, predisposed by temperament toward positive action against the social injustice of which she is a victim, is forced into passivity by her situation as a woman. Like Maud, Francine, and others she, too, is pushed into the seemingly unrealistic position of waiting for a savior from abroad.

As fiction, *Le Square* offers the unusual feature of being written almost exclusively in dialogue form—something no major writer had attempted since Roger Martin du Gard's *Jean Barois* (1913). Brief descriptive sections provide a framework for each of the three parts into which the work is divided. Within the descriptive pages, a child appears—also a recurrent motif in much of Duras' fiction. This child, a boy, is the one the girl is supervising in the public square. He is the pretext for bringing her and the man together. The boy also embodies nature's elementary urges and its indifference to human problems. Concerned only with his own desires, he plays, expresses hunger, thirst, and exhaustion, thus punctuating the dialogue and marking the passage of time between four-thirty in the afternoon and dusk. As the man and the woman become acquainted and tell each other about their jobs, one soon notices the unrealistic features of their language. No ordinary Frenchmen of their social status, meeting on a bench in a *jardin public*, ever talked in such a manner. The words themselves are commonplace (although there is no slang), but they are seldom specific. Describing the objects he sells, the peddler says they are varied and small, the kind one always needs but usually forgets to buy (S, p. 12). Later he speaks of a trip he has taken to a city in a foreign country, but without ever mentioning names (pp. 34 ff.). On the other hand, a specific reference is occasionally made where either none or many more would have been expected. Asked if any qualifications are necessary

for his job, the man suggests literacy, although he says that is
not indispensable—but one should be able to read the name of
the town when arriving at a railroad station! The girl notes that,
because of her employment, she always has enough to eat. At
the place where she works they often eat very good things,
sometimes leg of lamb.

This device, which on occasion borders on the humorous
(more so, of course, when quoted out of context, that is, out of
style), gives enough implicit particularization to preserve
some semblance of individuality for the book's two characters,
thus balancing the effect of the first device. It can also give
symbolic value to a specific detail. The peddler remarks that
although he travels a lot he keeps returning to the same towns,
but sometimes he notices that a change has taken place: in
spring, for instance, there are cherries in the marketplace (p.
27). Those splotches of red keep cropping up throughout *Le
Square*, acting as correlatives to the feeling of hope one traditionally associates with spring, but also to the memories of
a lost paradise of childhood. Both man and woman have vivid
memories of the days when they used to steal cherries from
orchards. In the foreign city described by the man, even though
he himself emphasizes the honey-colored light that impregnated
the atmosphere, his references to the setting sun and words such
as *feu* (fire) and *incendie* (conflagration) are likely to bring
back the color "red" in the reader's mind. Because of the
emotional charge contained in that description, there is no
strain involved in linking such redness to that of the cherries—
they, too, have acquired symbolic value. The recurrence of red
underlines the intense passion felt by the girl, a passion that
loses none of its fire for being repressed. It corresponds to the
inner wounds she has suffered, but the life-giving principle
it symbolizes might well be what sustains her. The objects that
give off the color, through the ambiguous directions they suggest, convey a feeling that might be termed oppressive when
one thinks of the characters' lives (the fiction generated in the

reader's mind) or circular if one considers the book's structure (the text itself). Setting sun and childhood cherries, however, do not completely cancel out the cherries of spring and the radiance of the foreign city, nor can a reader be blamed for thinking of that color's political connotations.

The peddler's visit to that city has had for him the effect of a quasi-mystical experience. He has been deeply marked, and he shares that complexion with many other protagonists of Duras' writings. Their experience might be active or passive; in either event it constitutes a trauma that affects them permanently. Early works suggest the trauma caused by what Marguerite Duras has called the absolute injustice of childhood.[4] The murder scene at the outset of *Moderato cantabile* and the jilting of Lol V. Stein in the story that bears her name are perhaps the most striking cases. In his strange city, the man of *Le Square* had undergone a sense of being at one with the world, of being as worthy as other men. He felt a sort of happiness that he cannot describe and also the welling up in him of a strength that could not find its object. The girl identifies it with hope; he adds that it is the hope of hope. In other words, as the context of the story bears out, it is undistinguishable from despair. As the girl says, immediately after he recounts the foreign city experience, "If there were only people like you, we would never succeed" (p. 57).

The pattern of his travels suggest the circular mold impressed upon his life, from which he is unable to break loose. The stable routine of her existence filled with periodic events also connotes circularity. The child evokes circular motion as he appears at the beginning of each division of the fiction and then disappears from sight. The two main characters' tendency to touch upon a subject and then wander off before coming back to it again and again brings the same figure to mind. While his own traumatic experience is a thing of the past, the man envisions the girl as having one in the future. It will be hers on that day when she opens the living-room door and tells her employer that she is leaving. "And you will always remember that moment as I remember my trip" (p. 68). For him it has had a disabling effect. He recalls it as one does a dream and imagines hers will have similar consequences. Repetition of the event once more brings forth the image of a circle; this time, however, it contains the seeds of its destruction. The concept of repetition emerges out of the man's point of view, but the reader need not accept it. The mere fact that the event will be repeated in another person's life implies discontinuity. Actually, the whole story is structured toward a breaking away from the circle. In order to break away from something one must, of course, first be aware of its presence and of its constrictive effect.

Circularity of dialogue is especially noticeable in part one; its linear progression is more evident in the two other parts. Not only do the characters reveal more and more about themselves, they also begin to understand each other. Their talk becomes oriented, if ever so slightly, toward the future. What the peddler terms his cowardice is more fully assumed by him, and there is a possibility that he can transcend it. What he calls her courage, even her heroism (p. 61), is on the verge of losing its uncompromising tone. The child, in the third part, does not vanish as previously: he sits at the girl's feet and sporadically calls attention to himself. At the end of this third section, there are indications that, on the coming Saturday, she might for the last time be going to the popular ballroom she had been visiting every week, hoping to be picked out by the man who might set her free. In spite of the conflicting temperaments and outlooks evidenced between the peddler and the maid, he might well turn out to be the "savior" she has been waiting for. Perhaps she has succeeded in breaking the spell of his passivity.

The book has three characters and three parts. One might recall that if, in geometry, three points define a circle, emblematically the figure three stands for the resolution of a dualistic dilemma. The answer, of course, lies outside the scope of this particular work, for when the two part company the reader is left with nothing more tangible than a possibility of the man's going to that Saturday dance. The dance is given more and more emphasis as the text reaches its conclusion. The significance it carries for Marguerite Duras might well reside in its being a ritual that requires active participation by an indeterminate number of people, involves a minimum of set rules, is accompanied by music and drink, and brings together man and woman in a culturally accepted communion of erotic gesture. All of that transforms public dancing into a celebration that temporarily eradicates drabness and suffering. The ballroom or dance motif is also one that runs through Duras' work from *Les Impudents* to *Le Vice-consul*.

What the two characters in *Le Square* actually say strikes one at first as being as insignificant as their station in life. But the tone that is given to their utterances, the serious consequences they deduce from matter-of-fact statements, the emotions they arouse—all conspire to channel the reader's imagination into his own psychological storehouse, enabling him to create two human beings that far transcend the particularities of those given by the author. The characters talk and talk, seemingly saying nothing, while laying bare the most secret recesses of their being. Referring to the girl's part in the dialogue, Maurice Blanchot remarks: "In everything she says with such extreme reserve and restraint, one detects the impossibility that lies at the core of human lives and that her own position impresses upon her every moment of the day: that job of being a domestic, which is not even a job, which is like a disease, a lower form of slavery, preventing her from having a bond with anyone, not even the slave's bondage to his master, not even one with herself."[5] After the girl describes how unpleasant it is to take care of a senile, eighty-two-year-old woman, weighing about two hundred pounds, the reader is moved rather than surprised by her saying, "And please note that I haven't mur-

dered her, even two years ago when I came back from a visit
to the union local . . . and that I still don't murder her, still
not, although it would be easier and easier to do" (p. 105).
That does not surprise the reader because such an expression
of feeling comes after he has read two-thirds of the way through
the book and it has been adequately prepared by considerable
implied feeling that was left to be developed by his imagination.

The characters themselves are aware of the revelatory nature of their statements. As I see it, this is made quite clear by
their extraordinary politeness to one another. They know that
their questions or their comments can inflict serious moral
wounds, and they handle their words with extreme caution.
(That suggests an obvious analogy with Nathalie Sarraute's
tropisms on the level of the anecdote, but not on that of the
text.) Such unrealistic precautions also constitute a signal to
the reader. His sensitivity alerted, he is in a better position to
pick up the overtones. Another indication is a character's (almost always the woman's) occasionally urging the other to
speak, to talk some more—rather than asking a specific question (*dites voir*, p. 27; *Et encore? . . . Et encore?*, p. 86; *dites-
moi encore*, p. 134; *encore une fois, vous, vous?*, p. 138). She
seems to imply that he will reveal important matters, regardless
of what he talks about. The analogy with psychiatry comes to
mind, but I do not believe it should be pushed much further,
at least not in a conventional fashion. It, too, is primarily a signal. One might conceivably argue that it calls for the applica-
tion of psychoanalysis to textual interpretation, as practiced by
Julia Kristeva of the *Tel Quel* group, or by Hélène Cixous, following a reading of Freud that is advocated by Jacques Lacan.[6]

The idea that banal words and even silence could be a means
of communication was not new to Duras at the time of *Le
Square*. More than twelve years earlier, when describing a
scene between the two lovers of *Les Impudents*, she had
affirmed that possibility: "From now on, they understood each
other completely. As soon as they outlined a gesture, which

need not be completed, through the most ordinary words, which they no longer felt obliged to speak. Silence, charmingly pregnant, began to be possible. They had ceased being two" (I, p. 132). In *Le Square*, however, such a process is no longer explained by a narrator and rendered somewhat trite by that explanation—the reader experiences it.

Much of that invites comparison with a more recent book, *Détruire dit-elle* (1969). Both pieces of fictions demonstrate the same narrative concision, the same emphasis on elliptic, disturbing dialogue. In the later of the two, the social milieu is that of most of her other fiction, the middle class, and the locale is a resort hotel patronized mainly by the ill or the convalescing. It is the milieu of those who, in *Le Square*, were the unseen oppressors, mirrored in the mind of the maid. *Détruire dit-elle* could be said to represent the other half of the picture, with revolutionary ferment introduced into the midst of a sick and frightened bourgeoisie by Alissa, an eighteen-year-old woman, who speaks the words of the title (p. 34). Other characters are much older. One is her husband, Max, a professor of history—of future history, a time when there will be nothing left. He is therefore silent, and his students sleep (p. 122). There are also Stein, an acquaintance who, like Max, is trying to become a writer, and Elizabeth, a convalescing guest at the hotel, who fascinates Max in the fullest sense of the word. The narrative line could, I suppose, be interpreted on the level of purely personal, emotional, and sexual relationships, a tale of eroticism and madness; but a sense of impending revolution can also be read into it. The latter is far from obvious, but nothing is ever obvious in Marguerite Duras' writings. There is no allegory to be deciphered; rather, a mood is to be felt. Thus, the tennis games that are being played in the background, although not by hotel guests, do not "stand" for any struggle or riot threatening the establishment. Nevertheless, the words that are used to describe the sound of the balls (especially in French, where the same word *balle* is used both for "ball" and for "bullet") lend an ominous tone to what the reader imagines, and in his mind the tennis court itself could benefit from an unconscious association with the *Jeu de Paume* hall, where the so-called Tennis-Court Oath of 1789 was sworn. The surrounding forest, which is dangerous "because" the guests are afraid of walking into it (D, p. 34), a cracking sound heard in the air (p. 133), and the final surge of music that shatters trees and strikes down walls permit the initiated reader to elaborate his own political or social creation out of the strands, both subtle and corrosive, tendered by the author.

If one examines an earlier work such as *Le Marin de Gibraltar* (1952), it is not hard to see in it a prefiguration of the books of the middle period and indeed a turning point in Duras' concept of fiction. One is confronted with two main characters who show some resemblance to those in *Le Square*. The man, who in this instance is the narrator, is a petty government clerk; basically passive, he nevertheless triggers the events of the story. The woman, eldest of five children, whose father owned a small-town café, is an activist who realizes that she must be chosen by a male savior. She therefore institutes what might be termed a negative search wherein the apparent seeker offers herself as a quarry. Anna has run away from home at nineteen; at twenty, she has taken a job as bartender on an American millionaire's yacht. Eventually she marries him and still later inherits the yacht. When she enters the story, she is imbued with a legendary aura. She is a beautiful, wealthy American who sails the seven seas looking for a man she used to know. It is as though a spell had been cast on her, for she is unable to abandon her search for the elusive being she calls the sailor from Gibraltar. How could such a romantic impersonation fail to attract a savior? He turns up in the guise of the narrator, a most unlikely candidate for the part, as Anna's yacht is anchored off the beach of a small Italian resort. He has been vacationing with his mistress (also an employee at the ministry where he works). He neither likes his job nor loves his mistress, but he lacks the will power to walk out on either one. When he encounters Anna, however, something happens within him, and he does exactly that—not that he acquires any special power; rather his mistress and his job drop off like ripe fruit from a tree. He then sails off with Anna, in pursuit of the sailor.

This is Duras' longest work of fiction and probably the richest, but in art, wealth is not necessarily an asset. *Le Marin de Gibraltar* is structured on dialogues, an important change in technique from that used in *Barrage contre le Pacifique*. The trouble stems from having to rely on too many different contributing dialogues in order to establish the book's meaning. Often, too, the dialogues are overburdened with material that tends to generate minor disgressions, hence distracting the reader. As the story develops, one overhears successively a series of dialogues between the narrator and a truck driver, an Italian girl, a innkeeper, and the narrator's mistress as well as several involving the narrator with Anna and a number of minor characters, sometimes individually, sometimes in a more general conversation. In one of the latter instances, a man relates a story that requires several thousand words. Anna herself, in a more controlled dialogue, is twice allowed to speak some eight hundred words without being interrupted (MG, pp. 141–42, 144–46). At the same time, the reader is aware that all that is not "just talk," no more than it is in *Le Square*. Conversation is a process by which people disclose what they are, not only to others but to themselves as well. Within the framework of the narrative, characters become what they are through subjection to such a process (which, it should be clear, goes beyond the traditional process of characterization by means of dialogue, often a mere revelation of essence rather than a becoming). Significantly, there are already some instances of one person's urging another to "say something," no matter what (for example, MG, p. 158). At the outset of *Le Marin de Gibraltar,* the narrator is a nonentity. He talks very little. Of his fellow employees at the ministry we learn that he feels more

like killing them than speaking with them (p. 24). It is the
narrator's conversation with the truck driver that makes him
realize that he must leave both his job and his mistress. Each
succeeding conversation gives him a bit more substance, and
in the end he has become the sailor that Anna has been seeking.

The first dialogue between Anna and the narrator takes place
at a popular outdoor dance. There, he does what the girl of *Le
Square* hopes the peddler will do—he chooses her. Ironically,
he becomes her "savior" by displaying a signal of distress (p.
121) in a narrative metaphor of what the mythical sailor "actually" did when, adrift in a small boat off Gibraltar, he was
taken aboard the yacht. He does that quite simply, by describing
his own life. But as he casts his lot with Anna's he soon understands that he must join her in the mysterious chase even
though they have become lovers and their love is genuine. Late
in the narrative, when she asks him, "And what if I had made
up the whole thing?" (p. 275), he answers that it would not
change things much. The search has been revealed as a ritualistic quest, and, without such a ritual, love between Anna and
the narrator could not endure. For it is what characters in this
book refer to as *un grand amour*, but it does not possess the
characteristics lovers normally associate with it—it is not a
secure, long-lasting state. As one character comments, a state
like that "is something sad to behold" (p. 320). The protagonists of *Le Marin de Gibraltar* are in a dynamic situation;
their love is not guaranteed, it must be tested continuously.
The men who preceded the narrator on Anna's yacht failed the
test, partly because they did not take it seriously. Some embarked as if going on an ordinary cruise, bringing books,
cameras, and so on; one tried to convert Anna; another was
foolish enough to suggest that she forget the sailor from
Gibraltar. The narrator has left everything behind, pursuing
the legendary sailor, first near Marseilles, then in Central Africa,
in all seriousness. When the narrative is about to close, they are
off to the West Indies. As Anna remarks, it is a gay life. It will

remain so only as long as the two lovers are seriously playing their dangerous and fanciful game. Another evolution in Duras' works is thus in evidence, as the theme wavers between escape and acceptance.

While the motif of the "savior" appears with great constancy throughout Duras' fiction, ritual connected with intense erotic experience, an embryo of which was noticed in *La Vie tranquille*, is dealt with at length in only two of her later works: *Moderato cantabile* and *Le Ravissement de Lol V. Stein*. In the first of these, Anne Desbaresdes, who is "happily" (if conventionally) married to a successful manufacturer, has the revelation of a love so great or so unusual that it could only be fulfilled in death. This is similar to Anna's experience in *Le Marin de Gibraltar* (the similarity of the two names could be more than coincidental, and one might note that the main characters of *Dix Heures et demie du soir en été* and *Le Vice-consul* are respectively Maria and Anne-Marie, the latter being once referred to as Anna Maria), except that in *Moderato cantabile* the event is objectively presented by the author. Of Anna's discovery of love we know only what she herself is willing to tell—and she is inclined to mythify.

The contact, even though accidental, with a love that leads to crime opens up an entire new world for Anne Desbaresdes. She symbolically deserts the fashionable section of town where she lives in favor of the proletarian café where the crime was committed. She engages in conversation with a former employee in her husband's manufacturing concern. With his assistance, through a series of revelatory dialogues, she attempts a ritual identification with the slain woman. He tells her about the woman, she tells him about herself (it is he who uses the characteristic *Parlez-moi*, see M.C., p. 55, or *Inventez*, p. 79). She drinks a lot, as do characters in *Le Marin de Gibraltar* and those of several other texts, in part because drinking is good, but also, here especially, because of the underlying analogy with a Dionysiac ritual. As suggested by a reference to her *ventre de sorcière* (p. 137), Anne is a sorceress who partakes of the blood of the god. With it she will acquire some of that natural power that he wields, from which civilization, culture, and social status have estranged her. It enables her to penetrate into a region where reason is of no avail: "There is no point in trying to understand. One cannot understand to such an extent as that" (p. 150). Eventually the lives of the two women—Anne and the victim—merge in a "ritual of death" (p. 153). When the man says to her, "I wish you were dead," Anne answers, "It has been done" (p. 155), and walks away into the setting sun.

Le Ravissement de Lol V. Stein, the second of the two ritualistic love stories, is far more complex. Lol has been so severely affected by the public rejection she suffered at the hands of her fiancé, Michael Richardson, that she sinks into vegetative life for about ten years. Even though she marries and has children, she barely exists. Then, through a casual encounter with the narrator, she is given a chance of coming back to life. It may be possible to see the recovery from her trauma as being effected by her stealing Jacques Hold, the narrator, away from his mistress, Tatiana: she would be cured by the realization that she could do to others what had been done to her, that she is not insignificant compared to other women.

But the process might well be more complicated than that. Lol had been discarded, so to speak, in the most casual fashion. Her love story had not been brought to its ritual conclusion. While she has been rejected at a public dance, it is the woman her fiancé walks away with who is presumably involved in the ceremony of love. Lol dreams of a conclusion in which her fiancé would begin to undress her. As her clothes were removed, her body would gradually be replaced with that of the other woman; a "velvet-like annihilation of herself" would occur (R, p. 56). When, after ten years, Lol looks up her childhood friend, Tatiana, and meets Hold, she somehow senses that with

their help she can bring her story to a satisfactory end. Lying
in a field of rye she watches the lighted hotel room where
Tatiana and her lover meet, and she identifies with her friend—
for that, in her world of fantasy, is the indispensable first step.
Only from such an annihilated position in another woman's
body can she cry out to her fiancé and beg him to take her back.
The narrator, like the one in *Le Marin de Gibraltar*, is aware of
the game being played, and he accepts his role within it. He and
Lol go back to the scene of her shattering experience. They
become lovers, and that night the identification is perfected:
"And there no longer was any difference between her and
Tatiana Karl, except for her remorse-free eyes and for the way
she referred to herself . . . the two names she used: Tatiana
Karl and Lol V. Stein" (p. 219). All is over between Hold and
Tatiana, but they will meet one last time at the hotel to bring
their own story to a conclusion. When they arrive, Lol is out-
side, sleeping in the rye.

The end of Marguerite Duras' narrative is left open. Lol may
well have destroyed herself or, more likely, have succeeded in
destroying the ghost that had been haunting her. The role of
Jacques Hold (he is a doctor) has perhaps been played out,
and a reborn Lol will be given back to her husband. Perhaps
not. Because of the psychological implications of this work,
one of Jacques Lacan's comments is worth noting: "We should
remember with Freud that in his subject the artist always precedes us and that we are not called upon to play the psycholo-
gist where the artist has cleared the way. That is precisely
what I acknowledge in the ravishing of Lol V. Stein, where
Marguerite Duras reveals, without being acquainted with my
work, a knowledge of what I teach."[7]

In another respect, *Le Ravissement de Lol V. Stein* marks a
turning point in that problems inherent to the very nature of
fiction are now being emphasized. Generally speaking, in the
novels published before *Le Marin de Gibraltar*, the fiction was
both closed and certain—closed in the sense that the reader's

contribution did not significantly affect its meaning, certain in the sense that the reader's willing suspension of disbelief was expected. *Le Marin de Gibraltar* and the five works that followed could be characterized as open but certain. *Le Ravissement de Lol V. Stein* is both open and questionable. Such divisions cannot, of course, be considered rigorous, for there are questionable as well as open aspects to *Le Marin de Gibraltar*. Contrariwise, the oppressive circularity of *Les Petits Chevaux de Tarquinia* is relieved by the characters' existential assumption of their situation, which is explicitly conveyed to the reader: "As to love, one has to live it completely with its boredom and everything, there is no possible escape from that" (P, p. 258). The way the characters reach that conclusion and the manner in which their lives are affected by it are not analyzed. Otherwise, the reader's freedom is restricted by the author. The questionable portion of *Le Marin de Gibraltar* pertains to what is narrated by Anna rather than to the fiction presented by Duras: although one might not believe what Anna says, one accepts the existence of that character in the story and believes that she speaks the words that are reported as hers. Obviously, what is open results from the ambiguity of Anna herself. In *Le Ravissement de Lol V. Stein*, on the other hand, such questionable aspects are an integral part of the structure.

As in *Le Marin de Gibraltar* the story is presented from the point of view of a first-person narrator. When the narrative begins and for a long time afterwards, the connection between narrator and narration is uncertain. It is not until more than a third of the story has been told, when Lol comes to visit Tatiana after ten years of silence and is introduced to Jacques Hold, that the latter identifies himself as the narrator. He had begun by giving a few facts concerning Lol's youth, stating, on the second page of the book, that those were things he knew—and implying that he knew little more. On the fourth page he confesses, "I no longer believe anything of what Tatiana says, I am not convinced of anything." He then prefaces the next narrative sequence with this warning: "Here are, in full, intermingled, simultaneously, the fabrication told by Tatiana Karl and what I invent." (p. 12). As one continues to read, he finds an expression of uncertainty constantly maintained. At the start of the fourth (unnumbered) chapter, the still unidentified narrator explains the kind of approach he has selected in order to deal with his subject, "since I must invent the missing links in the story of Lol V. Stein" (p. 41).

But must he? As a character, he is under no compulsion. As the author's surrogate, he must indeed reveal the story of Lol. Can the author make a distinction in her invented material between fictional reality and fictional falsehood? Later on, the narrator, who is apparently able to differentiate between the one and the other, prefaces some of his remarks with the statement, "I see this," others with, "I invent" (pp. 62, 64) or with the combination, "I see, I invent" (p. 64). After Jacques Hold has identified himself, he relates only those events to which he has been a witness. One readily accepts his observation, when transcribing Lol's words in a conversation, "This woman lies" (p. 124), or when giving the presumed thoughts of Tatiana, "I invent" (p. 178). On the other hand, it is disturbing to have him admit, "I am lying" (p. 140), or, "I want to avoid going to the Hotel des Bois, I am going there" (p. 147). At one point, Tatiana herself shouts at Jacques Hold, "Liar, liar" (p. 185). When the narrator and Lol are together, toward the end of the story, he places the whole narrative in questionable perspective: "I deny the ending that will probably come to separate us, its ease, its desolating simplicity, for since I deny that one I accept the other, the one that needs to be invented, the one I don't know, that no one has yet invented: the ending without an end, the beginning without end of Lol V. Stein" (p. 214).

With that statement the author's surrogate withdraws, expressing a willingness to play the role of a mere character. He relinquishes all his powers to the reader, who must now in-

vent what "no one has yet invented." Lol now belongs to him—
she has been his, of course, from the beginning, but the ritual of
reading, of her being turned over to him, has been completed.
At the same time, the title acquires its full meaning. The secondary sense of *ravissement* fits Lol's ecstatic states and her
contemplative attitudes outside the hotel, but she has never
been forcefully abducted, not even by Jacques Hold, whom she
chose as her "savior," as other female characters in Duras'
fiction had done. The narrative stands in part as metaphor of
the act of literary creation: Lol V. Stein has been abducted from
the author's domain by the reader.

In *Le Vice-consul* we are confronted with an even more complicated affair, for two narrations are involved instead of one. A
character, Peter Morgan, tells one story, but he does not do so
as the author's surrogate: she has a very different story to tell.
The scene is set in Calcutta. Peter Morgan is one of several
English friends the wife of the French ambassador has gathered
about her. He has been obsessed by the sight of an insane
female beggar, presumably from Cambodia, who shares the life
of Indian lepers, eating scraps from the embassy garbage cans.
Spurred by an anecdote the ambassadress has told him, Morgan
invents a background for the woman, depicting a miserable
chain of injustice and suffering extended along a ten-year
journey, on foot, from Battambang to Calcutta. To him, as to
the other Europeans in Calcutta, she is an object of scandal.
It is, however, relatively easy to keep her at a safe distance:
fences and armed guards protect the *vie tranquille* of the well-
to-do.

But there is another cause for scandal, and this is the subject
of Marguerite Duras' own tale, so to speak. The French vice-
consul at Lahore has been recalled to Calcutta, pending further
investigation, because of his shocking behavior. Matters are not
very clear: at night, he would shoot at lepers and dogs from
the windows of his residence; he would cry out in the dark and
also fire his gun inside the house. As in the case of the mad

beggar, a search for antecedents gets under way. Begun on the two opposite sides of the earth, one following the course of abject poverty and the other a privileged existence, two lives follow different paths to Calcutta where they explode in madness and scandal. Both biographies represent tales from the outside. The sanctuary they disturb, which constitutes the reality of the book, is the European colony of that Indian city or, at any rate, of the portion that gravitates about the French embassy. At its center, there is a woman—the ambassadress.

Someone asks Peter Morgan if the begger from Battambang is to be the only character in his book. He answers no, there will also be Anne-Marie Stretter (V, p. 183). That was the name of the woman for whose sake Lol V. Stein's fiancé walked out on her. That is now the name of the wife of the French ambassador, and at a formal embassy party she wears the same dress that the other woman wore when she appeared at the fateful dance. The halls of the embassy are like "those of a casino in a seaside resort town, in France" (p. 93)—that describes the place where Lol was abandoned by Michael Richardson. In *Le Vice-consul*, Michael Richard had been one of Anne-Marie's lovers. This, however, does not in my opinion represent a belated effort on Duras' part to build a fictional world of recurrent characters and places in the manner of Robert Pinget. The change from Richardson to Richard is probably the tip-off. In *Le Ravissement de Lol V. Stein*, Anne-Marie replaces Lol in Michael's affection. In the subsequent work she replaces Lol from a functional point of view—she is not the same woman, she plays the same role. Like Lol, she may also be said to belong to the reader, and she is truly at the center of the narrative. In the light of a changing esthetics, one might call her a transfigured Jamesian central intelligence. As Peter Morgan has related her to the beggar, someone else relates her to the vice-consul: "By the way, the vice-consul at Lahore, whom does he resemble? . . . He hears the answer: me, says Anne-Marie Stretter" (p. 204). Without her, the book would fall apart, leaving only two disconnected narratives, but she is a void at the center of things: "At the club, other women talk about her. What goes on in that life of hers? Where can one find her? One does not know" (p. 109). She needs no protection from the two Calcutta scandals, for she is, morally speaking, an outsider. Characteristically enough, her final position is left ambiguous. When one of her close friends suggests that they must all forget about the vice-consul lest they lose their image of Anne-Marie, another friend says, "Here, someone is lying" (p. 193), but he does not specify who.

The story of the beggar is an outright fabrication. As was the story of Anna in *Le Marin de Gibraltar*, it is told by one of the characters. The story of the vice-consul is a puzzle, with many pieces missing. The story of Anne-Marie will be as true as the reader is able to make it. The author contributes her truth, the reader his. If the two can become part of a harmony, the book succeeds. The author, however, cannot directly attain a truth that is not within herself (or himself). An awareness of such a limitation goes hand in hand with the development of an esthetics that shifts a sizeable part of the creative burden over to the reader. Unless there is some intuitive resonance, as in the many dialogues scattered throughout Duras' fiction, from those in *Le Marin de Gibraltar* to the one between the vice-consul and Anne-Marie Stretter, people can understand one another only up to a point. All this is explicitly brought forward in *L'Amante anglaise* (1967).

A modified version of an earlier play entitled *Les Viaducs de la Seine-et-Oise* and later readapted for the stage under the title *L'Amante anglaise*, the narrative bearing this title, like the original play, takes its point of departure from a rather ghastly crime actually committed in France in 1954. The culprits were found; they confessed; they were brought to trial and sentenced; but no one, including the criminals themselves, could give an adequate motive for the crime—and thus, in Duras' view, it remained "unsolved." In the narrative of *L'Amante anglaise* the criminal is reduced to one, for better focus; she is a woman named Claire. The story consists of a series of three interrogations, conducted by a narrator who says he intends to write a book about Claire. (Contrary to what happens in a few other works, the book a character is writing or plans to write is not the book we are reading.) He has a tape-recording of the scene in a café that led to Claire's admission of guilt and her arrest. He plays it back in the presence of the café owner and questions him about the people involved, especially about Claire. He then talks to Claire's husband and finally he sees Claire herself.

At the very outset, the café owner raises the question of truthfulness: "The difference between what I know and what I shall tell you, what are you going to do about it?" The narrator does not answer within the context of the narration but within that of the reader's act: *"That constitutes the share of the book the reader must contribute. It is always present."* (A, pp. 9–10). As one progresses through the three narratives, one notices not only discrepancies between the characters' memories or interpretations concerning the same fact, but also the different views they have of one another and themselves. When Claire is reached, she turns out to be very different from what one expected, almost likable in spite of her crime. But the narrator eventually reaches a stage beyond which he cannot go: his truth and hers are no longer compatible. She suggests that she might tell him some of the things she had concealed or that she might even succeed in explaining why she committed murder but he is no longer interested (A, p. 193). She keeps talking, practically to herself. Her last lines, also the last lines of the story, constitute an appeal to the reader disguised as an admonition to the narrator: "If I were you, I would listen. Listen to me" (p. 195). The main character is thus abandoned to the reader, as had been the characters of the two previous works. The title comes from the plant grown in the garden, where Claire was fond of staying. It is *la menthe anglaise* (peppermint), but her spelling was poor, and she had various ways of transcribing that phrase. Sometimes it would come out as *l'amante anglaise* (the English mistress), which produces the title. One transcription she did not think of would have come out in English as "the clay mistress" (*l'amante en glaise*): to be abducted and fashioned by the reader.

For reasons about which one can only speculate, Marguerite Duras did not pursue her experiments in that same direction. After *L'Amante anglaise* came *Détruire dit-elle*, upon which I have already commented, and *Abahn Sabana David* (1970). Because of its concision, its emphasis on dialogue, the unrealistic nature of characters and setting, it might also not have been out of place among the writings of Duras' middle period. On the other hand, the very stress that is placed on symbolism, a nearly extreme refusal to allow the text to be contaminated by "literary" style and the more explicit references to politics place the book in a category somewhat apart from everything that preceded it. Actually, calling the references explicit is somewhat of an overstatement. At first, the book seems to deal with the condition of Jews. Abahn, who lives in an isolated house outside the city and is known as Abahn the Jew or Abahn the dog, has been sentenced to die. Sabana and David come to stand guard over him until Gringo, his executioner, arrives. The howling of dogs outside is heard intermittently. Soon another man, also named Abahn, joins the group. From there on, there is nothing but talk.

At this point, I hardly need to stress the importance of "talk" in a text by Duras. The device operates as before, only the dosage is much heavier. But what about the Jews? One does not have to read far into the book before noticing the symbolism. Then, to me at least, it seems that while some of the references fit the Jewish situation, others do not. Suddenly everything becomes clear, and the text reads like an amplification of the retort made by students in Paris in 1968 to the accusation levelled at Daniel Cohn-Bendit. When authorities, delighted at the opportunity to blame an "outside agitator," said that Cohn-Bendit was a foreigner on two counts, the students chanted, "We are all German Jews!" As I read it, *Abahn Sabana David* turns out in effect to be a prose poem in praise of the *gauchistes* ("New Left," perhaps), of all those who proclaimed solidarity with a German Jew (at first Sabana, then David, through a series of dialogues that are often highly ritualistic, go over to the side of the two Abahns), of all who refuse the "establishment," whether communist or capitalist. "On his body, says Sabana, on his arm, there is something written . . . It is the word NO, says Abahn" (ASD, p. 123). The references that allude to the persecution of Jews are those to the Nazi gas chambers and to the Russian salt mines (pp. 22–23). It is, nevertheless, the transparent allusion to a Nazi concentration camp, that of Auschwitz, that transforms the Jew into a broader symbol. When Sabana has gone over to Abahn's side, David accuses her, "People say that she is Jewish, that she comes from far away." Abahn then adds, "From German Judea . . . From the city of Auschstaadt" (p. 101). It is then explained that Auschstaadt is everywhere. "We all come from the city of Auschstaadt, says Abahn." That is very similar to the students' chant. It might also be a way of saying that a new kind of political consciousness arose when the atrocities of the concentration camps were disclosed, one that demanded solidarity with the victims.

The three names that Duras uses in her title move in the same direction. All three, to a non-Jew, leave a vague impression of being Jewish, but upon investigation neither Abahn nor Sabana reveals a Semitic etymology. There is of course no question concerning David but, ironically, he is the last to identify with Abahn the Jew. The name David is doubly ironic as it means "the beloved" and he has come as agent for a killer. The executioner is Gringo, a name that, on this continent, is applied by Mexicans and others to foreigners, who are usually seen as oppressors or exploiters, from the United States. In the context,

however, Gringo is a communist party official. He gives speeches
at the *Maison du Peuple*—even speaking all night at the
twenty-second congress (p. 79). His name is Gringo because,
in the point of view from which this text was written, the communist establishment is no longer distinguishable from the capitalist one. The party, the businessmen (*les marchands*, pp.
14–15), the *Société Immobilière* (p. 82—probably meaning the
big international combines), are all united in their fear of those
who will not fit into the system. They are the "others," and
they are called Jews (p. 20). Abahn is (or are) conscious of it,
even to the point of assuming that position: "Do you come to
shatter unity? David asks . . . / Yes. / To divide? To inject confusion into unity? / Yes. / To sow doubt into people's minds?
/ Yes" (p. 104). He is (or they are) also willing to take the consequences: "It is normal that they kill you, that they seek you
out like a plague. / Yes, says the Jew" (p. 104). Men such as
Abahn, who cannot live with the establishment, used to be
communists: "You used to belong to Gringo's party before this?
/ Yes" (p. 45). But now they are thoroughly disillusioned.
Their attitude is epitomized by that of the Jew; he once spoke of
freedom, then of despair, and now he has lost all certainty. "He
is a different man, says Abahn. He is a communist who believes
communism is impossible; he adds, Gringo thinks it is?" The
question is addressed to David, who came to the isolated house
as Gringo's man; he answers, "Well, yes" (p. 94). They do not
have any positive values to propose, nor do they know where
their actions are leading them. They do know that the existing
system must go: "Look carefully about you: destroy!" (p. 136).
That is an obvious echo from the preceding *Détruire dit-elle*.
Love, nevertheless, is what unites them. The final exhortation
given to the group, at last joined by David, is paradoxically one
implying unity: "REMAIN TOGETHER . . . DO NOT LEAVE
ONE ANOTHER ANY MORE" (p. 149).

Lucien Goldmann once told me that there were two major
romantic writers in France today, one on the right, the other on

the left. To the right stands Henry de Montherlant, to the left, Marguerite Duras, and it is hard to believe that either one would be pleased to be associated with the other in this or any other way. I do not know whether or not Goldmann was able to read *Abahn Sabana David*, which appeared shortly before he died. If he did, he must have been amply fortified in his belief.

NOTES TO CHAPTER FIVE (Duras)

[1] Marguerite Duras, *La Vie tranquille*, p. 74. Henceforth, all references to the works of Marguerite Duras appear in the body of the text with the following abbreviations: *Les Impudents*, I; *La Vie tranquille*, VT; *Le Marin de Gibraltar*, MG; *Les Petits Chevaux de Tarquinia*, P; *Le Square*, S; *Moderato cantabile*, MC; *Le Ravissement de Lol V. Stein*, R; *Le Vice-consul*, V; *L'Amante anglaise*, A; *Détruire dit-elle*, D; *Abahn Sabana David*, ASD. See Bibliography for complete references.

[2] Armand Hoog, "The Itinerary of Marguerite Duras," *Yale French Studies*, No. 24 (Summer 1959), pp. 68–73.

[3] Germaine Brée, Introduction to Marguerite Duras, *Four Novels* (New York: Grove Press, 1965), p. viii.

[4] Cf. Pierre Hahn, "Marguerite Duras: 'Les hommes de 1963 ne sont pas assez féminins,'" *Paris-Théâtre*, No. 198 (1963), p. 34.

[5] Maurice Blanchot, "La Douleur du dialogue," in *Le Livre à venir* (Paris: Gallimard, 1959), p. 192.

[6] Cf. Jacques Lacan, *Ecrits* (Paris: Seuil, 1966); Julia Kristeva, *Recherches pour une sémanalyse* (Paris: Seuil, 1969); and the September, 1971, issue of *Littérature* devoted to "Littérature et psychanalyse."

[7] Jacques Lacan, "Hommage fait à Marguerite Duras du ravissement de Lol V. Stein," *Cahiers Renaud Barrault*, No. 52 (1965), p. 9.

CHAPTER SIX

Claude Mauriac

In the course of an interview, Claude Mauriac explained that the specific characters he had introduced into his fictional works were not indispensable per se—another set might have done just as well for his purposes. "All people are the same: scared stiff at the thought of death and obsessed with sex . . . It is an obvious fact: we are all interchangeable. That's what we call togetherness."[1] Such a statement identifies François Mauriac's son as the literary heir to Nathalie Sarraute on two counts. First, we have the belief in a basic identity of people beneath a veneer of superficial differences; then there is the emphasis on factual evidence provided by reality—his characters are interchangeable because people are. Sarraute was more subtle in this respect, and nearly all her psychological observations involve characters as created by writers of fiction. But the hypothetical author she discusses at one point in *L'Ere du soupçon* is concerned with "Those men that he would so much like to know and enable others to know";[2] and when she remarks, not unfavorably, on the modern reader's supposed preference for nonfiction, she adds, "What fictional story could possibly compete with that of the Poitiers recluse, or with the accounts of concentration camps or of the battle of Stalingrad?"[3] Still, her arguments are used to discredit not fiction but a certain kind of fiction. Claude Mauriac goes one step further and gradually casts a pall of suspicion upon the very notion of fictional literature. At age seventy-five, François Mauriac, then an essayist, no longer fired by the creative urge that had brought Thérèse Desqueyroux to life (this was before he was seized with a final surge of fictional writing), made these melancholy comments: "What can I say, I no longer have sufficient faith in the novel . . . Truth is so much superior to fiction. I am now, I am quite willing to admit, amazed at the importance I used to attach, many years ago, to all those stories that I told. Now, I consider that a bit childish . . ."[4] Claude reached such a disenchanted stage much faster.

As much dominated by rigorous intellect as his father's books were by violent, instinctive passion, his first piece of fiction, *Toutes les Femmes sont fatales* (1957), is meticulously composed, full of scrupulous correspondences and subtle balances—"A true mind-teaser for careful readers."[5] The words are from the book itself, for Claude Mauriac likes to have his narrator, who discusses a work he is planning to write, provide the key to the one being read: "One could begin reading my book anywhere, reading and rereading it in any order one might choose. An essay more than a novel. Fictional essay, perhaps, a genre that needs to be invented" (T, p. 219). That sort of thing makes for a fascinating game of patience, but there is another side to the coin—what fascinates a reader's rational intellect might not attract one with a creative mind.

Told in the first person by Bertrand Carnéjoux, the character who provides the major link between this and the three subsequent books, *Toutes les Femmes sont fatales* consists of four separate interior monologues, each one covering a brief period of time, but the entire set spans about fifteen years. Through his eyes and mind one also meets, among a host of others, most of the characters who will figure prominently in the later fiction, but one is not much affected by what is hardly more than a succession of names. That, at any rate, is all they represented to me. There is little rapport between them and the narrator who ruminates on his anxieties in Rio, Paris, New York, and prewar France—little rapport, it seems, beyond matters of sexual involvement. Within the text's frame of reference, this is as it should be. Carnéjoux, who is just past forty and still a bachelor at the end of the third sequence (chronologically the last), notes that all women are interchangeable. As for himself, "Who am I, if not a male animal just like all others?" (T, p. 130).

Constantly thinking of the women he has slept with or is about to seduce, he is, in Rio and in Paris, haunted by the memory of one, Marie-Prune, whom he respected. Then, somewhere between the Paris and the New York sections, she has become his mistress. We are then treated to a version of the male-oriented cliché concerning the woman who has accepted sexual intercourse, a reflection of the double standard accepted in middle-class culture, without evidence of any ironic distance separating Mauriac from his narrator. When the newspaper the latter works for gives him an assignment in the United States, "Marie-Prune was then so little like the young woman who had been so dear to me for so long, that I was relieved to go off on this business trip" (p. 142). The fourth and final section accounts for a night Carnéjoux spent with his first mistress. After living together for three years, the two have separated but they come back to each other every now and then, between other affairs, and this is one such night. It is a rather extraordinary sexual encounter, during which he thinks of other women, impending war (the year is 1939), death, and literature more than of his mistress, against whom he lies. A presentation that is somewhat traditional makes the setting seem much more incongruous than a similar one in Claude Simon's *La Route des Flandres*. Here and throughout the earlier monologues, his obsessive enumeration of women and sexual encounters, while giving a rather primitive or even bestial representation of the well-to-do, produces nothing lewd. What informs all four sections, saving them from being merely the record of a retarded adolescent's search for personal gratification, is Carnéjoux's constant preoccupation with death, his realization that he will grow old and die without the world's being the poorer for it. Flitting from one woman to the next, he seeks, beyond physical pleasure, what he calls "the frontiers of death" (T, p. 276).

While Claude Mauriac makes use of some relatively new techniques introduced by other writers, among them Dujardin, Gide, and Joyce, his first novel is not exactly revolutionary. Carnéjoux's literary and sensual quest is sparked by an epiphany. As a young man, he had thought himself unique, irreplaceable; but at dawn one day, looking out of a window towards the steeple of Saint-Germain-des-Prés, he realized that he had been wrong. "One morning in my nineteenth year, at the break of dawn, in the month of August, the emptiness of my life was revealed to me" (T, p. 22). More than twenty years after that experience, in New York, he again refers to "the revelation of that pale and pure morning" (p. 192). Later still, in Mauriac's second work, *Le Dîner en ville,* Carnéjoux speaks again of the truth he had known, "such as had been taught me by a quiet and radiant dawn, in Saint-Germain-des-Prés, many years ago" (p. 281). Contrasting with the peacefulness of that dawn, another image, from farther back in time, keeps emerging into his consciousness: it is that of a small railroad station in the country where a little girl is sharpening a pencil with an open pair of scissors. Cutting the umbilical cord or cutting the thread of life: the ambiguous symbol appears unexpectedly as Carnéjoux watches the girls on the beach at Rio and again in the story's next to last paragraph, followed by the statement, "and I am scared" (p. 276). In *Le Dîner en ville,* Carnéjoux is reminded of the girl and her scissors and the dawn at Saint-Germain-des-Prés within the same moment of conscious reflection, and again in *La Marquise sortit à cinq heures* he reflects on the "forsaken peasant girl . . . sharpening a pencil with a blade of her scissors shaped like a cross" (p. 178). Only once in *Toutes les Femmes* do we catch a glimpse of what will distinguish the two subsequent books—what Mauriac himself has termed the interior dialogue:"When, between man and woman, there is a clash of aggressive glances that size up each other without disappointment . . . they have taken possession of each other more decisively perhaps than if they had made love, and they have traded their most intimate secrets" (p. 44). That, however, is merely a description of what happens; for a demonstration of the silent exchange one must wait for a couple of years.

Le Dîner en ville (1959) showed far greater originality. The setting is a snobbish apartment on the Ile-Saint-Louis in Paris during a formal dinner party. The book opens with the guests' entrance into the dining room and closes as they leave the table to go back to the salon for coffee. Plot is characteristically nonexistent. The apartment is that of Bertrand Carnéjoux, now married to Martine, the daughter of one of his former mistresses. Six guests have been invited, and they are either single or have come alone, for a variety of reasons engineered for the sake of providing more revealing material. With the same aim, Mauriac also arranged for an unlikely combination of age groups, including a young student and an ancient, although hardly respectable, woman. There is no narrator involved, and the book consists exclusively of a supposed transcription of the conversation and thoughts of those eight people seated around the table. But the lack of descriptions or narrative statements is not its main originality. Marguerite Duras' Le Square, published four years earlier, one remembers, was almost entirely in dialogue form. Le Dîner en ville includes not only conventional dialogues and interior monologues but also interior or "silent" dialogues. Ironically, the disappearance of the narrator is somewhat illusory, for he has been resurrected in the guise of an omniscient transcriber who records not only the dinner conversation but the thoughts of each and every guest. First-person narration, third-person narration with central intelligence, interior monologue—all had a vague claim to realism. Mauriac's technique, in theory, has none. In practice though, it affords a greater illusion of reality, partly because of its newness, partly because the reader has been granted godlike powers to see (or hear) things "as they really are." Such aggravating problems dealing with fictional realism are not laid to rest until writers of the next generation, like Sollers, Ricardou, and others, reject the concept of literature as mimesis.

Claude Mauriac's "recording" technique is endowed with one additional feature, which might have been considered a drawback but actually fitted his purpose quite well: as the transcription is supposed to be authentic, with no editorial matter added, there is no external way of identifying the person who thinks or speaks. Since, according to Mauriac's postulate, all men and women are basically alike, the anonymity of the guests conforms to reality. There are, nevertheless, distinguishing characteristics, superficial as they might be, that permit identification in many if not all cases—manner of speech, obsessions, professional competence, and so forth. Such features also prevent the reader from getting lost among the eight table talkers and transforms the text from the puzzle it might have become into something eminently readable. Mauriac here parts company from Nathalie Sarraute, who, in some of her works, seemed to take pleasure in confusing the reader who might be trying to identify an anonymous character. Phrases like *Ah! mais alors* or *c'est sensationnel*, familiarity with Balzac's works, erudite knowledge of the Orléans dynasty, preoccupation with techniques of the novel, concern for one's children, interest in sun bathing or in dresses—all act as effective identifiers, less artificial than proper names.

There are two outsiders at the table. The student is only a temporary one, since he is a cousin of Martine's and will eventually take his place within the group. He knows that he will and that gives him a *mauvaise conscience*, but in the meantime he can still judge its members and condemn them. The real outsider is a young Canadian woman who wants a career in the movies and is presently Carnéjoux's mistress. A country girl, she was raped when she was in her teens, and her mind keeps going back to that event. She despises the group but intends to use the men in it to obtain fame and money. Taken together, the presence of these younger people begins to give the book something like a social dimension, which has completely lacking in *Toutes les Femmes sont fatales*. Removing Carnéjoux from his former position as narrator also adds to the dimension of *Le Dîner en ville*. Previously, his obsession with sex and death had an egotistical tinge. He said that all men were like him, but in the text he was the only one to say so. Here, the obsessions are shared, emerging clearly out of the several interior monologues. Preoccupation with sex runs through the length of the book. Fear of death is revealed first when someone mentions the year 1925, enabling the other guests to situate themselves in relation to it. Even the student, who was not born until 1939, must confess (to himself) to sharing the obsession: "And yet I am already acquainted, indeed I am, with the anxiety of growing old; what suffering it gives me" (D, p. 85).

In *La Marquise sortit à cinq heures* (1961) the setting shifts to the Carrefour de Buci, a busy Paris intersection on the left bank, filled with detailed and confused activity. It is between the hours of five and six on a warm afternoon, late in the summer of 1960. Once more there is no conventional narrator, only what appear to be transcriptions of dialogues, interior dialogues, and interior monologues. Bertrand Carnéjoux is still the central character, and he spends the hour watching the street scene from his balcony. But something has happened to him. He is separated from his wife, has renounced his mistresses, and resigned from his editorial positions to devote himself to the writing of his next book, which one is now reading. He has apparently become fully aware of the futility that characterizes human activity, including his own, and in contrast with the attitude of his earlier representations he has become reconciled to it. "I am conscious of my nonexistence at the same time as I realize theirs. I am detached from our ephemeral lives. Ever since, I have left women, children, newspaper, and relative wealth in order to devote myself, no longer to my pleasures, but to the understanding of what my pleasures meant" (M, p. 15). He has taken over the role of outsider that belonged to the student in *Le Dîner en ville*.

The situation, however, is a bit more complicated, for Claude Mauriac is becoming more and more self-conscious in his own role as author and needs to have Carnéjoux's thoughts focus on problems of the writer. The main character becomes split: Carnéjoux's *alter ego* Desprez, an erudite historian, who is watching from a balcony on the other side of the intersection, assumes the part of commentator that Carnéjoux, in his statement, has led the reader to expect. The link between the two is made clear by their identical physical stance above the Carrefour de Buci as well as by their sharing the same cleaning woman. If the name "Carnéjoux" suggests the idea of toying with flesh, "Desprez" is close enough to *dépris* and its connotation of being freed from a bond or a habit. He could be said to represent Carnéjoux's new self, one who fully accepted the Saint-Germain-des-Prés revelation, for the name also echoes the last two words in the name of the church. Carnéjoux watches the people in the street, thinking of his future book, which becomes present through one's act of reading. Desprez watches the same people, thinking of those who had lived and died there in the past, which becomes present through his own reading of the many books and documents he has collected. The whole of time collapses into the present of the human mind.

Such a concentration of time into the fictional hour during which the action of the book takes place is what expands the scope and interest of *La Marquise sortit à cinq heures* far beyond what had been attempted in *Le Dîner en ville*. Desprez can account for "at least eight centuries of Paris life, at this precise spot" (p. 15), and he discloses a frightening record of crime and injustice throughout those centuries. Everything that is read by a character is of course reproduced in the text. Interspersed among the various monologues or dialogues one is thus confronted with, among others, a text by Jean Juvenal des Ursins describing the massacre of the Armagnacs in 1418 when the Burgundians captured Paris: *"Throughout the very city much killing took place . . . Not only were men being killed, but women and children too"* (p. 55). There are a number of texts by Pierre de L'Estoile describing how heretics were murdered (p. 65) or how Henri IV captured a small town near Paris. *"He gained control of it after having killed nearly one thousand burghers in the place"* (p. 82). A text by Edmond-Jean-François Barbier gives an account of the execution of a murderer in 1738 (p. 181), and so forth. At the same time, *Les Temps Modernes* is also being read, and testimony relative to torture during the Algerian war (which was still going on in 1960) extends the story in space as well as in time. A passer-by is obsessed with the thought of what he may have failed to do to prevent children from being sent to concentration camps at the time of the German occupation of France during the Second World War. The historian comments, "all those murders in the name of God or King or Right, century after century, always, *just as today, just as today"* (p. 67); and again, "And God knows that people kill and torture, legally or not, in Paris, almost everywhere, and for little reason, *just as today, just as today"* (p. 84). His thoughts, his old texts, the magazine items, are read within the context of news reports dealing with the sexual involvements of movie stars, trivial conversations, and monologues ranging all the way from the ridiculous to the pathetic. The process constitutes a form of "intertextuality" that was used more and more in the 1960s, particularly by Michel Butor in *Mobile*, in a spirit resembling Mauriac's, and by Philippe Sollers in *Nombres*, embodying a very different esthetics.

What emerges is of course a strong indictment of Western

civilization. Such a condemnation, intellectual in origin, is given an emotional hue by the pervasive presence of children, both on the Carrefour de Buci and in the literature of the past. Carnéjoux's daughter, Rachel, whom Martine has brought to visit her father, serves as catalyst for the reader's feelings. The process is sparked by Martine's mute observations, as she and her daughter walk away: "Those eyes that are so trusting, so much fervor and happiness. That wonderful, that blessed trust of childhood—betrayed for thousands upon thousands of years . . . Those generations upon generations of deceived children, condemned everywhere and always" (p. 31). Her remarks are given even more poignancy some one hundred and fifty pages later when they are echoed by the man who cannot keep his mind off concentration camps: "What they have killed in each one of those small beings was first of all trust, tenderness, innocence . . . How can one forget those hundreds of thousands of battered souls within their thin, hungry bodies" (p. 189).

These devices are much the same that Michel Butor had used in *Degrés*, which appeared a year before *La Marquise sortit à cinq heures*, in a very different context, but with essentially the same effect of arousing the reader. There is also a difference in the handling of the episodes. Butor is more discreet, less prone to call attention to what he is doing, while Mauriac cannot help explaining everything, constantly tugging at the reader's elbow. (In similar fashion, there is hardly an interior dialogue, in this or the preceding work, during which Mauriac does not emphasize the nature of that dialogue and what it accomplishes.) The uncertainty that characterizes the narrator's identity in *Degrés* has its echo in the split between Carnéjoux and Desprez, to which one must add Mauriac's own intervention at the end. The breakdown of Vernier, Butor's major character in *Degrés*, has a pale counterpart in the confusion of the final pages of *La Marquise sortit à cinq heures* and in the narrator's discouragement—whoever that narrator might be. "I shall no longer check any date, any fact, what's the use?" (M, p. 303). It is also reflected in the historian's despair of gathering all the pertinent information. "What a mad quest! My poor, sated mind is loosing its bearing" (p. 268). The story of Bonini's grief, in *Degrés*, has its parallel in Loubert's "great sorrow"—both have lost their wives. It matters little whether this is influence or coincidence: resemblances help to isolate the distinctive qualities of each. In the case of Mauriac's texts, these seem to be anxiety and self-consciousness.

The themes of injustice and suffering subsume the theme of death that has been carried over from the previous works. Many more characters from different walks of life help to express the universal fear of death posited by Claude Mauriac. The anxiety of one person is so strong that he practically obliterates the life of the four-year-old Rachel, musing, as he sees her walk by: "Talking about that little girl, still so small, someone who will not be born until many years from now . . . will say, one day, a day that is not so far away, to another little girl: 'You don't remember your poor grandmother . . .' " (M, p. 111). Newspapers headline an airplane crash in which everyone was killed. A woman is dying in a hotel near the intersection. A man who has an apartment next door has just died in Lyons on a trip; his wife has gone to bring back his body and his small son sits silently on the street curb, staring at the buildings across the way. An old woman has died recently, and her husband, Loubert, nurses his sorrow. It is he who helps to draw the reader's attention to the egotistical nature of our feelings about death. His son-in-law is the one who has died in Lyons, but Loubert resents having to care for his grandson in his daughter's absence—"As if I were in a condition to do that, with my great sorrow" (p. 287)—and insists on giving all the details of his wife's death to a bored visitor. When he finally reads him her last will, his voice becomes "quivering, happy, jubilant" (she has left him everything, her daughter nothing), a witness to his "ferociously egotistical love" (pp. 307–308).

Earlier in the book, a young man shopping with his grandmother constantly watches her, for he fears she might die. At one moment, as she closes her eyes, he imagines that she may be dead, but this only starts a train of thought in which he envisions all the activities that death will necessitate. Her eyes open suddenly: "I feel a tinge of something like disappointment, and yet I love her so deeply" (p. 76). Mauriac's characters like to think of themselves as full of love and sorrow for others: "Me, such a noble heart!" (M, p. 253) exclaims a woman poet. The young man's concern for his grandmother's health probably translates no more than a feeling that the longer she lives, the longer his own lease on life. The anxieties of all these people are not limited to their fear of death. They are all wrapped up in themselves. Some are ingenuously so, like the repulsive set of girls who play practical jokes via the telephone or like the more attractive red-head in tight slacks, who, to the reader's delight, runs across the setting between pages 87 and 130, leaving behind a trail of envy, jealousy, and sexual desire. Others are much more self-conscious. The *lycée* student, on his way to his girl friend's home, worries about "My tall, thin body, my yellow complexion, my pimples" (p. 29). A maid contrasts her condition with that of movie actresses she is reading about, saying, "I, who am so pretty" (p. 69). A young woman with a voluptuous figure admonishes herself, "Don't ever run. Walk in a composed manner, in my fine, raw-silk dress, like a well-brought-up young lady" (p. 128). A café waiter convinces himself of his own superiority over his customers and his colleagues (p. 148). The middle-aged homosexual, who calls himself "la marquise," thinks of himself in the third person and seems to concentrate in himself anxiety over old age and death and the egocentric vanities human beings are capable of. Such anxieties, as they were in *Toutes les Femmes sont fatales,* are usually translated into sexual terms, only they are now applied to a host of characters instead of being nearly monopolized by Carnéjoux, who, in this book, appears strangely ascetic.

His main task is to express himself on the techniques of fic-

tion. He does this first, as in the previous work, as a writer
thinking and dropping hints about the book he is writing and
about fiction writing in general. But earlier, Carnéjoux was a
character who was also a writer, and his other activities were
in the foreground; now he is a writer and nothing else. What
he had to say in the past about the book he was planning threw
light on the one being read. In *Le Dîner en ville*, when he
talked about "Le Plaisir grave," one had the impression that
it resembled *Toutes les Femmes sont fatales*, and one feels that
"Le Déjeuner au bistro" has much in common with *Le Dîner
en ville*. In *Marquise sortit à cinq heures*, however, it becomes
increasingly obvious as one progresses through the book that
it is precisely the one Carnéjoux is working on. The far greater
frequency of his reflections on his craft are partly the cause
of that impression. How the convention that forms the basis of
this work is gradually exploded becomes a more important consideration.

In *Le Dîner en ville* an identical convention was strictly adhered to. Here, Mauriac begins by respecting the framework
of his *carrefour* and of his hours. Then, a first, plausible exception is made for historical texts, and next, texts about Algeria
are brought in. What goes on in the street is supplemented by
what happens inside the various houses. Historical persons
who have lived on the spot are followed by others who merely
passed by. These are succeeded by fictional characters who
could be connected with the *carrefour* (the eighteenth-century
Manon Lescaut, for one) and by real persons who simply might
have passed by, "Anonymously and without leaving any evidence," for it is reasonable to assume that "they *all* have one
day or another passed through this intersection . . . Voltaire,
Bonaparte, Hugo" (p. 273). Finally, a fictional character is
introduced who lives somewhere overseas and happens to be
thinking about the *carrefour*, the name of which he can no
longer remember.

The process is not without analogy to one Butor used in

Degrés when, by introducing the concept of negative relationships, he managed to integrate all the students and teachers of
a *lycée* into his system of family relationship groups. That is,
of course, quite legitimate, but one of its consequences can
be, as it is here, to call attention to the fiction *qua* fiction and
to the close connection between what Carnéjoux is thinking
and what is actually taking place, that is, to his creating the
events that he pretends to be recording. The impression is
completely confirmed by the instance in which he notes what
another character has thought, in an interior monologue that
has just been transcribed with the obvious intent of using it
in his book—which he has just done (p. 221). What is clearly
meant by Carnéjoux's being the author of the book we are
reading is that he has now become Mauriac—a harmless sup-
position, since he has, early in the text, divested himself of
nearly everything that made him the fictional character of
the two other works. He has become the omniscient narrator
and Claude Mauriac's surrogate. In the last few pages, Mauriac
gives the show away by stepping into the text himself: "Novelist
brought to life by a novelist that, as novelist, I have myself
placed in a novel where, nevertheless, nothing has been invented" (p. 311). As usual, he must carefully explain what was
becoming evident.

This explanation does not really mar the ending of the book.
It matches the tone of this and previous works and brings matters to their logical conclusion. At one point Carnéjoux admonishes himself, "I must carefully avoid adding commentaries,
no matter how short, to my quotations" (M, p. 271), but
Mauriac does precisely the opposite by means of Carnéjoux's
remarks on fiction writing. In another respect, he is like
Nathalie Sarraute: not only does he want to control carefully
what goes into his work, he also wishes to restrain the reader
and make sure he does not take out of the work more than
was intended. As he intervenes in *La Marquise sortit à cinq
heures*, he stresses what he considers to be the link between

the fiction and the reality. Carnéjoux had explained that the
dead woman of the novel was "really" the wife of an older
cousin of his, whose name was not Mathilde but Agnès, and
Mauriac takes it from there: "As for me, I do indeed know
that the real name of that dying woman was no more Agnès
than Mathilde" (M, p. 311). Those are logical statements
within the framework of an esthetics that considers the work
of art mainly as an end product. Everything it contains has
been carefully placed there by an author who, in turn, has
selected his material from reality, within or outside of himself.
Analysis of the work should then, almost inevitably, lead back
to the author and his world. Such art invites the criticism of a
Sainte-Beuve.

The title of this third work refers of course to Paul Valéry's
saying that he would never write such a preposterous sentence
as "La marquise sortit à cinq heures," which had been pub-
licized by André Breton in his surrealist manifesto. Its context
is given in the epigraph; it is discussed in the body of the
work (pp. 89–90); and it provides the first and last (with a
variant) sentences in the book. Because the marquise is a
middle-aged, male homosexual, it acquires an ironic twist,
but that is a minor point. Valéry, in attacking that kind of
narrative statement, was condemning what he thought was
trivial and traditional in the mass of contemporary fiction, but
in effect he was attacking a symptom rather than a disease.
The judgment weighed heavily in the minds of writers during
the thirties and forties, and Claude Mauriac deserves some
credit for reversing it, so to speak—showing that even such
a statement as "la marquise sortit à cinq heures" might be used
in a serious work. Indeed, commonplace narrative or descriptive segments can be found in *L'Attente l'oubli*, one of Blanchot's most esoteric and abstract works. Sentences such as "He
would watch her stealthily," and "Two windows allowed light
into the room and, separated by a few steps, cut obliquely into
the wall" might be found in almost any work of fiction.[6] But

in a degraded work, they constitute its entire texture; its stuff is reduced to the story alone. In traditional esthetics, however, plot and story have their place, no matter how subservient they may be to theme, myth, pattern, or symbol. As Mauriac writes, in the guise of Carnéjoux: "In the present as in the past, the anecdotes to which my fictional essay will be boiled down will have no importance at all. And yet, they will make up my only reliable asset" (p. 192).

He undoubtedly shared the apprehensiveness of many older novelists when faced with Valéry's dictum. Even though he used the anathematized statement to show that the poet had been mistaken, his last sentence, "The marquise did not go out at five," is an unwitting justification of Valéry's distrust. In emphasizing the reality that lies at the source of his fiction, he not only refuses to recognize the creative power of language but, by laying bare the mechanisms of his work, he has in one sense retreated from the position assumed by traditional novelists, who, like Balzac, might have considered their fiction more important than reality. "Thus the novel has gradually faded away during its next-to-last pages, disappearing, with neither sham nor mask, for the benefit of the novelist who, if he directly inserted himself into his book, has in the end purified it of its last traces of fiction by having it reach a truth where literal exactness was preferred to literature" (M, p. 313). While some writers of the postwar period might well consider that a step backward, many share his uneasiness with "literature." The alternative, however, might not necessarily be "fact."

L'Agrandissement (1963),[7] the final volume of the series featuring Bertrand Carnéjoux, is something of a letdown. As the title suggests, this work is an enlargement of a detail of the preceding one, and it consists of a long interior monologue attributable either to Carnéjoux or to Mauriac himself, spun in the length of time required by the Carrefour de Buci traffic light to turn from amber to red, green, and amber again. In his monologue, Carnéjoux (let us suppose it is he) creates and expands on what he had previously pretended to record, to the extent, for instance, of projecting the lives of passing *lycée* students forward to the time when they have become old *lycée* professors. He also reminisces about aspects of his own life, and he thinks, as usual, about the art of fiction. If it does not provide an exciting esthetic experience, it certainly is not uninteresting. I might even say that it generates considerable intellectual enjoyment. A work of this sort would have pleased Julien Benda, who once wrote: "Esthetic emotion is typical of intellectually based emotion."[8] In a 1945 pamphlet directed against Benda, Claude Mauriac had stated what he believed to be the truth about fictional characters: "It would indeed appear that the finest moments in the finest novels are those where the creator loses control of his characters."[9] His echoing such a long-standing platitude shows that, before he began publishing fiction, his esthetics was, like that of Nathalie Sarraute, rather conservative. Assuming that it underwent no radical change, at least as far as characters were concerned, the assertion made by Mauriac the critic remained for Mauriac the creator an unattainable ideal. For a true intellectual, and he is one without doubt, it must be extremely difficult to relinquish control over the activities of the mind. The well-known statement Paul Valéry attributed to his Monsieur Teste applies to the creator of the Carnéjoux novels: "I am both being and seeing myself; seeing myself see myself, and so forth."[10] Claude Mauriac appears to be sitting in an ideal hall of mirrors— observing himself watching himself writing fiction.

The handling of time in this tetralogy is both logical and fascinating in its progression. From an extended time sequence involving a narrow subject, Mauriac moved on to a more restricted framework in time (one evening) and a broadened subject. Next, by limiting the time to one hour, he extended his scope tremendously. In the fourth fictional work, reducing the framework to approximately two minutes might have permitted an enlargement encompassing the infinite depth of the human psyche. But if that does not take place—perhaps because Mauriac lacked genius, perhaps because the human psyche lacks depth—the experiment was well worth undertaking. In any case, it marks a point beyond which the Carnéjoux series could not logically be continued.

Claude Mauriac broke the cycle with *L'Oubli* (1966), which was greeted by several enthusiastic reviews but in my opinion had best be forgotten.[11] The mock detective-story plot that holds things together, involving cliques of novelists, was probably meant to be taken as light satire and high-level amusement. Actually, it is more grotesque than burlesque and somewhat embarrassing in its inanity. Too bad, because an excellent idea lies at the center of the narrative. A boy of twelve and a girl of seven play together in spite of their parents' forbidding them to, and during their play they discover something very important. Both are obsessed with the incident throughout their lives, although neither one can remember what was discovered and said or who the other one was. When they meet again much later, both, separately, think of the incident but do not connect it with each other, and they part never to meet again.

Ideas, however, are not sufficient to make a work of art, and this one gets lost among the nonsense. It does serve to remind us that most of Mauriac's characters have had a traumatic experience in their childhood or youth that haunts them from then on. That, and other obsessive elements as yet unnoticed, will perhaps emerge more clearly when his fictional work is complete—assuming that he does pursue it—giving it a greater dimension than his intellect had allowed. What is clear is that his esthetics remains traditional. He emphasizes this once more through the fictional writer in *L'Oubli*: "I do not like what I see in some of today's novels, the indetermination purposefully planned by the author who accepts, ahead of time, all explanations of his work; who takes advantage of all analyses, without having deserved them, of all investigations. I shall not, any more than they do, furnish answers to the enigma, to the series of enigmas that will make up my novel, but I shall arrange things in such wise that one explanation, and only one, will be possible for each mysterious aspect; any reader, with a modicum of intelligence and attentiveness will be able to solve the problem if he reads me carefully and takes my cues into account" (O, p. 38). It is generally unwise to attribute to an author the statement made by one of his characters. In this instance, however, the evolution of Mauriac's fiction, what he has said about "fictional essays," and the general congruence between the theories expressed by earlier characters and those he has propounded himself should help in removing any compunction one might have on that score. This is the author speaking, the man who wishes to remain in complete control; to him, the writer is all-important, the reader follows.

Bringing together this and other remarks I have quoted in this chapter and examining them from the point of view of more recent esthetics, one might say that Mauriac's attitude can be traced to individualistic bourgeois pride. Seen in that light, his affirmation concerning the sameness of all human beings becomes ironical. There certainly is a conflict here and a source of tension for Mauriac. It appears that he cannot bring himself to abandon the myth of the individual creator, perhaps even the genius, with inspiration manifesting itself in some gifted individuals. Nor does he like to think that the writer might not be responsible for what he writes, that he might be conveying the realities of his culture, civilization, or class more than anything really his own. One should also add, with respect to another prejudice manifested in this last quotation, that the wealth of meaning a reader might extract from an aleatory work of art does not reflect credit on the author— that, again, is an individualistic fallacy. It enriches the reader and, if that reader is a critic, many other readers as well. For Mauriac, however, the reader's function is less to create than to decipher.

NOTES FOR CHAPTER SIX (Mauriac)

[1] André Bourin, "Techniciens du roman—Claude Mauriac," *Nouvelles Littéraires*, June 4, 1959.

[2] Nathalie Sarraute, *L'Ere du soupçon* (Paris: Gallimard, 1956), p. 88.

[3] Sarraute, *L'Ere*, p. 66. The first reference is to the factual story that André Gide was instrumental in making widely known through his *La Sequestrée de Poitiers* (Paris: Gallimard, 1930).

[4] Quoted in Pierre Audinet, "*Thérèse Desqueyroux:* Théâtre? Non! Cinéma? Oui!," *Nouvelles Littéraires*, March 23, 1961.

[5] Claude Mauriac, *Toutes les femmes sont fatales*, p. 219. Henceforth, all references to Mauriac's books in this chapter appear in the body of the text with the following abbreviations: *Toutes les femmes sont fatales*, T; *Le Dîner en ville*, D; *La Marquise sortit à cinq heures*, M; *L'Oubli*, O. See Bibliography for full references.

[6] Maurice Blanchot, *L'Attente l'oubli* (Paris: Gallimard, 1962), pp. 21, 29. One might note that in the same year that *La Marquise sortit à cinq heures* appeared Françoise Mallet-Joris published *Les Personnages* (Paris: Julliard, 1961), where she inserted the same statement about *la marquise* at the center (p. 142) of her book, as the first sentence of a brief section—less obtrusively but just as pointedly as Claude Mauriac had done.

[7] Paris: Albin Michel, 1963.

[8] Julien Benda, *Belphégor* (Paris: Emile Paul, 1918, rpt. 1947), p. 58.

[9] Claude Mauriac, *La Trahison d'un clerc* (Paris: La Table Ronde, 1945), p. 76.

[10] Paul Valéry, *Œuvres*, Bibliothèque de la Pléiade (Paris: Gallimard, 1960), II, 25.

[11] Vivian Mercier, in his *The New Novel from Queneau to Pinget* (New York: Farrar, Straus and Giroux, 1971), does not think much of *L'Oubli* either, but he still devotes more than a half-dozen pages to it. Curious readers are hereby referred to his book.

CHAPTER SEVEN

Claude Simon

Surveying the ten works of fiction Claude Simon has published so far, one becomes aware of several stages in his esthetic development. In his earliest work, which is relatively conventional, from *Le Tricheur* (1945) to *Le Sacre du printemps* (1954), he appears to be searching for the right focus and style to give to his work. With *Le Vent* (1957) he seems to have found it, at least temporarily, and the next three books, through *Le Palace* (1962), reveal a highly disciplined concentration on a single character, theme, or setting, and a distinctive style. Meanwhile, *La Route des Flandres* (1960) had begun to evidence a preoccupation with textual matters. *Histoire* (1967), which came out after a five-year silence, shows a confident and relaxed Simon—he knows he can allow his fiction to become more complex, letting textual and thematic developments intermingle, without having to fear its getting out of focus. Finally, *La Bataille de Pharsale* (1969), with its emphasis on textual operations, was the sign of yet another renewal, as it aligned itself with the most recent trends in French writing.

Critical recognition came to Simon only after *Le Vent*. While feeling no compulsion to attempt a rehabilitation of his previous works, some of which read like dry runs for later ones, I believe they are well worth examining, both in the context of their author's developing craft and in the context of their times. Of the writers who have found eminence after the end of the Second World War, he is almost alone in allowing history as such to intrude into his fiction. Jean Pierre Faye is another, but he belongs to a more recent literary generation. Claude Ollier and Marc Saporta allow the reader's consciousness to be affected by a specific aspect of contemporary events, such as the French colonial problem or the German occupation. Michel Butor maintains a general sense of history as an oppressive presence. But in some of Claude Simon's books historical events, like the Spanish civil war, function as they did in Malraux's a generation earlier—and not at all as they do in Sartre's fiction and drama. In spite of chronology, Malraux actually might be said to stand at mid-point between Sartre and Simon in this respect. Sartre is interested in a man's "project," his existential choice when confronted with an historical situation; Malraux is more concerned with using the situation in order to give meaning to a person's life; and Simon emphasizes the situation mainly as it fills one's consciousness.

During Claude Simon's first two stages, his fiction could be characterized as being structured by time. But in the time-space equation, it is the spatial element that receives the most attention. Rather than progressing in linear fashion, gathering experience as they go, his characters seem more like giant, interlocking receptacles: time fills them relentlessly, and there comes a moment when they can take no more. A balance is destroyed and they come crashing down, carrying others with them or, at the very least, damaging the equilibrium of the structure of which they are part. The past is felt as a material presence that can be inventoried. There is no need to go in search of lost time, for it weighs on characters only too heavily.

Seen in retrospect, it is no gratuitous impulse that triggers the very first act of the main character in *Le Tricheur*:[1] he throws his watch away. A denial of conventional chronology, characteristic of all of Simon's work, is already in evidence in the jumbled narrative sequences of that text. The protagonist is a man who refuses to be governed by chance. He takes matters involving life and death into his own hands, and that can be described as a form of cheating—hence the title. There is much that is traditional here, especially in the handling of both narrative and descriptive sequences, much also that is typical of the later Simon, although sometimes only in embryonic form. Thematically, of course, it cannot be separated from what follows. But while the performance is a creditable one, such that a lesser writer might justifiably be proud of, the master's imprint is not sufficiently strong to make a detailed examination as rewarding as it will be in the case of *Gulliver*.

The setting of *Gulliver* (1952) is postliberation France. Its mood is one of disillusionment and cynicism, reflecting the mood that prevailed in the country after the initial euphoria had subsided. It is a mood that had already been expressed in Marcel Aymé's *Uranus* (1948)—except that Aymé, because of a different political orientation, sensed the mood earlier and sympathized with it. Not sympathy but bitterness pervades Simon's book, and its title refers to the tone of Swiftian satire, not, as I see it, to any particular detail of the fiction. While he has given two of his main characters strikingly large bodies, their physical traits seem only a reminder of satirical intent. The giants are twin brothers. One collaborated with the Germans, the other joined the Free French Forces in London as a pilot—but neither one is respected back home. Both are involved with a group of peculiar individuals, and one of the major events of the narrative consists in their going to a party that ends up with what might be described as gangland murder, followed by the suicide of the principal character, known as "le beau Max." (The theme of suicide was also present in *Le Tricheur*.) A number of other characters are thrust into the limelight, each in his or her turn, and all are morally demolished when the narrative ends. What, in part, turns this book into such a scathing satire is the manner in which the various subplots and individual biographies are linked to, and made dependent on, the story of Max. He is somewhat despicable, and this negative value infects everything else.

The events that constitute the more immediate action take place during two successive days and nights; others cover a number of years; the longest sequence deals with the life of Max since his childhood. There is, however, no narrative distinction between the various episodes. Nearly always, the same verb tenses are used—imperfect and past definite, as required by conventional syntax. This in itself is an indication of Claude Simon's individual concern with time. His placing the several sequences on the same syntactical level implies a denial of chronology similar to the one found at the outset of *Le Tricheur* but expressed by different means. The two exceptions to an otherwise consistent verb usage, although barely noticeable, actually reinforce that denial. Three paragraphs (totalling less than a page), dealing with Max as a small child, the most remote time period in the book, are dominated by verbs in the present tense, with a sprinkling of past indefinites and one future (pp. 236–237). Later, some eight pages, involving a significant moment in his life, are also told in the present (pp. 248–256). Strictly speaking, the only events taking place in what what might be called the reader's present are those of the first and last chapters.

Chapter one begins late in the afternoon of the second day and continues into the night, for less than thirty pages, ending with the first violent death—chronologically the third and last. The time perspective is given on the second page: "during the previous night . . . a man had died, perhaps murdered, another had killed himself. They did not know that yet another was going to die." After the end of that chapter, almost everything is a flashback: main flashback for what I have termed the immediate action, secondary flashbacks for biographies of the principal characters, or at least for those elements of their past that converge on the present locale, and, in the case of Max, tertiary flashbacks presented from his own point of view. The final chapter, balancing the initial one, provides the reader with a sense of relief—at first: "It was a quiet, silent, and halcyon day" (G, p. 374). Such a mood, however, is merely a vehicle for irony. Gradually dissipated, it is replaced with feelings of antagonism among the characters, and the novel ends with an expression of hatred.

Between the first and last chapters, the flashbacks are quite orderly. The main one proceeds in strict chronological fashion, interrupted only by the secondary narratives that are necessary to account for the accumulation of events within a character's spatial consciousness, when they have welled up to the point of making violent action inescapable. Just before the shooting begins, Max realizes that there is no point in asking himself questions, for he clearly sees himself "proceeding now towards the logical, unescapable consequence of a series of actions that had not begun merely a few hours earlier in the locker room at the soccer field, nor even the previous day, nor the month, nor the year; as a result, it was useless to wonder what had driven him to follow Bobby tonight, what was driving him now as, in complete and scornful ignorance of what he was going to do, he once again turned his steps toward the silent house squatting in the hollow of the dell" (G, p. 170). The present time implied by "tonight" (*ce soir*) is possibly a slip, but it is a significant one. Coupled with the present participle, "proceeding," which governs most of this sentence, it affirms the permanence of past within present. Critics have expatiated upon the proliferation of the present participle in Simon's more recent fiction; the tense appears infrequently in *Gulliver*, but when it does it is so closely associated with a major theme as to make its subsequent development appear absolutely organic. This same passage, while showing the vitality of the past and the character's being conscious of its force within himself, also makes it clear that the same character is blind as far as future consequences are concerned.

Looking forward to Simon's utilization of the myth of blind Orion, one is tempted to see here a prefiguration, in all likelihood an unconscious one, of his present view of the writer who, when he begins to write, has no inkling of the direction in which his writing might lead him, but knows that something within him urges him to write on. His character's blindness justifies another device characteristic of Claude Simon, the withholding of information from the reader. Aside from providing an element of suspense, this lessens what has come to be considered the artificiality in third-person narrative technique, in that the author's omniscience is not so obvious. There is also the possibility that, in this instance, the author is not omniscient. As early as this, he may have allowed words some initiative in shaping the narration. Or else the concealment was dictated by problems related to theme and characterization. Not only does he have to step back in order to inform the reader that Max is ignorant of the future that his past has built up for him, but his characters' lack of awareness makes it difficult for them to conduct their own flashbacks. If they were able to do so, this would amount to giving them the power of introspection and self-analysis in a moment of crisis, something of which they are not capable. The result is that Simon removes himself from his characters even more than François Mauriac did in his own flashbacks (in *Thérèse Desqueyroux*, for instance). Thus the long flashback of Max's life is inserted between the shooting scene and his suicide a few hours later, at a moment when "he could feel pressing on him the steady weight of that thing, its odor of darkness." He can no more analyze the "thing" than he can fight it, and the examination of his past must be done from without. Even the point of view is not consistently his, shifting from Max to several episodic characters. Nevertheless, the impression of being very close to Max is given the reader at the end of this episode, when feelings and gestures immediately before suicide are described in detail and then cut off without any intimation of intent or consequences. Skillfully as such incidents are handled, the fact remains that the devices used are traditional tricks of the trade.

The opening lines of *Gulliver*, "At *apéritif* time, on Monday evening, in a small café in the neighborhood of the station, three regular customers were seated," are as old-fashioned as anything that could be found in a novel by Paul Bourget. When the first few sentences of *Le Vent* (1957)—a work that owes a great deal to *Gulliver*—are compared with them they provide a most striking contrast: "A fool. That's all. And nothing else. And everything people have been able to tell or invent, or try to deduce or explain, that can only confirm what anything could see at first glance. Just a plain fool." We are not only plunged *in medias res*, a commonplace in fiction today, but we are given no immediate indication as to the identity of the speaker. We know neither about whom or to whom he is talking. The words pour out, almost compulsively, breathlessly, and continue to do so with minor variations in intensity, carrying with them images of people and events, until the end of the book some 230 pages later. They are like the wind, which gives its title to the book, blowing fiercely through the southern French town where the action takes place, "an unleashed force, aimless, condemned to exhaust itself endlessly, with no hope of ending" (V, p. 241). The style of *Le Vent*, developed in the fiction of the middle period and emphasizing continuity and accumulation, is one of the techniques Simon was searching for. Like the symbol of the unrelenting wind, it is part of a structure that aims at creating within the reader a sense of the past's dynamic pressure. But this style did not originate in *Le Vent*. There are many pages in *Gulliver*, especially those describing the more significant episodes, that show Simon's ability to write in such a manner, almost, one might say, naturally. His problem was one of unity. In *Le Vent*, it was solved by having the story told in the first person by a narrator who has put together information gathered from the main character and a number of others with whom he happened to be acquainted. Claude Simon pays his respects to conventional verisimilitude, for the author's surrogate teaches in a *lycée* and is doing research on Romanesque churches in the region. He is well qualified to assemble the various pieces of the puzzle created by the sudden appearance and strange behavior of the protagonist in the town.

Le Vent bears a curious subtitle: "Attempted Restoration of a Baroque Altarpiece." It is of course linked to the narrator's profession. The first two words offer no difficulty; the reference to a "Baroque Altarpiece" becomes clear only in the context of Simon's spatial concept of the past. An altarpiece usually depicts, through painting or sculpture, an assemblage of characters and scenes that represent the culmination of a tradition, that is, of a past, without which they could have no meaning for the viewer—legends dealing with the lives of Christ and of the saints, for instance. That tradition, with all its details, has irrevocably solidified them as well as divorced them from chronology, by juxtaposing the Crucifixion, the Last Supper, and knights in medieval armor, thus joining the realism of details to the fantasy of the aggregate. The attitude toward reality implied here is specifically set forth on the opening page of *Le Vent*. What we know of reality is "merely that fragmentary, incomplete knowledge, made up of a sum of brief images, themselves incompletely apprehended by the eyes, of sayings, themselves poorly grasped, of sense perceptions, themselves poorly defined, and all of it vague, full of holes, of blanks, which imagination and something like logic attempted to correct with a series of risky deductions." That is the problem of the narrator, one that did not exist for the omniscient author of *Gulliver*, and he is thereby, along with the reader, brought into closer intimacy with the characters, who retain the relative blindness they had in *Gulliver*. Instead of blindness, one might well say innocence. The religious undercurrent of the subtitle becomes even clearer when one realizes that Antoine Montès, the protagonist of *Le Vent*, comes rather close to being a Christ figure.

The relationship between this work and the earlier one becomes apparent. *Le Vent* represents a refining, perhaps even a sublimation of a pattern encountered in *Gulliver*. At first a variation on the theme of the prodigal son, it now appears as a veiled allusion to the life of Christ. Set in the context of Simon's other works, however, the value of such cultural references diminishes to a large extent. At least a change of emphasis should take place. The absence of the prodigal son, Christ's stay in Egypt and Galilee, both serve to establish a distance. Translated into Claude Simon's fiction, it becomes the distance between generations, between youth and old age, promise and fulfillment, innocence and corruption. The cry of Christ on the cross, "Why hast thou forsaken me?" could be uttered by any number of Simon's characters, especially by older ones addressing their former selves.

The reappearance of the son in *Gulliver* and *Le Vent* reflects the same theme as the confrontation between son and stepfather in *Le Sacre du printemps* or between the protagonist and his younger self in *Le Palace*. It is expressed again in capsule form in the description of an old photograph in *L'Herbe*, contrasting "the well-behaved child with gnarled knees . . . and the old man, overrun, crushed, smothered" (H, p. 226). In *Gulliver*, Max cut himself loose early from his wealthy, presumably corrupt family. He volunteered (and was wounded) in the First World War, after assuming both the name and the place of someone who did not want to fight. He showed up again in his home town only after his father's death. Dissatisfied, alienated, he has transformed his life from an affirmation of innocence into a corrupted quest for value and satisfaction, and he now acts as a magnet for catastrophes. Antoine Montès disappeared even earlier in life than Max did (he was still *en ventre sa mère!*) and comes back likewise after his father's death; but although giving him similar catalytic powers to trigger disasters, Simon shows him while he still possesses an innocence rather like that of Parsifal. To the reader, if not to the townspeople, he is more understandable than Max, because he is less complex. As Max had returned about six years before the main action in the story took place, he had had a chance to become a part of the town's life again and to appear as one of several intriguing characters—this, of course, from the standpoint of plausibility, which is still a valid one as far as these books are concerned. Montès, on the other hand, is as strange to the townspeople as he is to the reader. His appearance on the scene coincides with the beginning of the narration (even though the narrative is a flashback). As far as knowledge of the town and its inhabitants is concerned, he is as innocent of it as the reader is. The latter can readily sympathize with his troubles.

In *Le Vent*, the reader's present time is posterior to the narrated events, as the narrator reminisces. First, one is in a lawyer's office, and it is the lawyer who makes the first statement, but he soon fades away, and one concentrates on Montès as seen through the narrator's consciousness. In a number of instances, the narrator dissolves into omniscient author as he relates what only Montès himself could have seen or experienced. The device of inserting brief statements like "as Montès told me later" only calls attention to the implausibilities. That is particularly noticeable in those moments of emerging awareness, after some shock or trauma, when the outside world impresses itself gradually upon the character's consciousness: "It was only after a while that Montès felt the priest's hand upon his arm, saw quite close by a mass of flabby, grayish flesh that seemed to flow around the nose and mouth, forming a series of meandering, flaccid folds, studded with gray hair." At this point Simon throws in a protective statement, "He told me it took him a moment to realize it was a face." (p. 192). That does not actually spoil the paragraph that follows, but it does not help either. Simon, when writing *Le Vent*, was apparently not fully convinced that superficial matters of verisimilitude could and indeed must be subordinated to the organic, esthetic necessities of the work of art. That he was at least partly aware of the precedence that should be given the latter is evident from his treatment of dialogue.

Not at all concerned by Nathalie Sarraute's condemnation

of "the monotonous, clumsy, 'said Jeanne,' 'answered Paul,' with which dialogue is usually strewn,"[2] he keeps the device and modifies it for greater effectiveness. He uses it not only in run-in dialogues, as Faulkner does, where it is perhaps less noticeable, but also in indented forms, where he appears to flaunt it at the reader. Using no verb, only a conjunction and a pronoun, Simon appears to consider them substitutes for the traditional French dash that precedes indented fragments of conversation. But since he also uses the dash on occasion, it would seem that the sequence "And he: . . ./ And she: . . ." serves an emphatic purpose, characterizing those exchanges in which there is opposition or a momentary emotional clash between two characters. The device is both unrealistic and effective. Another feature of Claude Simon's dialogues is that they are often interrupted, not merely in the middle of a sentence, but also in the middle of a word. While it could be argued that this realistically reflects what happens in rapid-fire conversation, at least for the first kind of interruption, such a chopping-off process relates to the refusal to accept a linear concept of time. It is in harmony with the "breathless" impression created by Simon's style in this group of works and mirrors the constant accumulation of experience within a consciousness, ever increasing and ever present.

Neither of these aspects of dialogue originated with *Le Vent*. Fragmentation was already present in *Gulliver* and, in one instance, in *Le Tricheur*; emphatic dialogue-identification appeared in *Le Sacre du printemps*, which embodies a different approach to the problem Simon was attempting to solve. It is also the forerunner of *Le Palace* (1962), for in both instances we are dealing with a Spanish civil war experience confronted with a much later situation. Simon must have sensed that a temporary esthetic salvation lay in the direction of the first-person narrative, but perhaps he did not realize that the traditional, plausible first-person narrative was only one of several possibilities. He was still, in part, a victim of the realistic fallacy.

Le Sacre du printemps focusses on the early fifties and a young man named Bernard. In the background loom his stepfather and the Spanish war. Essentially, the book describes a confrontation between the two men, a clash between two receptacles of experiences. Simon handles the situation by dividing his narrative into two parts of two chapters each. Chapter one, part one, is told by Bernard himself; in chapter two, a shift to the third-person narrative presents a more detached view of Bernard. Chapter one, part two, begins in the third person, but only to introduce the stepfather as a secondary narrator, who relates his Spanish experience to his new wife, in the first person of course. The final chapter, again in the third person, brings Bernard and his stepfather together. Unity is achieved by means of family relationship, involvement of both Bernard and his stepfather with the same girl, and, even more artificially, with a coincidence of dates. "Contemporary" events take place on December 10, 11, and 12, 1952, Spanish war events take place on December 10, 11, and 12, 1936. Obviously, this is not organic unity, nor is it good collage, for no great spark leaps forth from the juxtaposition of the various elements. What interest there is in this book emerges from the situation created by Bernard, that is, by the sum of his experiences, even more so by his lack of them (for, in some ways, he, too, prefigures Montès), when confronted by a no-longer so innocent outside world. The Spanish experience appears to obsess Simon. To him, it may be a necessary ingredient of consciousness, but in the story it is esthetically superfluous. Or else, Bernard's experience was superfluous: each one obliterated the other. In *Le Palace*, the conflict is resolved by fusing the two consciousnesses into one, and the same person confronts his own civil war experience in Spain with the total experience of what he has become many years later.

The narrative elements in *Le Palace* are more closely woven together. A Frenchman goes to Barcelona, has a glass of beer

in a café across the street from a modernistic bank building.
Where the bank now stands there used to be a luxury hotel,
the "palace" of the title, which burned down during the final
stages of the Spanish war. As he looks at the bank and thinks
back to the few days he had spent in the hotel, apparently
as a volunteer for the loyalists, when it was requisitioned by
the republican forces, he re-experiences both the events and
the material objects of that particular past. Central to his recollections is the hotel room where he had been with four other
men during most of a sweltering summer afternoon in 1936.
With him were a talkative American, a gun-toting Italian, a
man who looked like a school teacher, and one who was wearing what resembled a policeman's uniform. Outwardly, it would
seem that five men of different backgrounds were accidentally
brought together, then scattered in various directions, each to
his own life or death, but the reader is viewing things from
within the mind of the Frenchman, then a student at the
university. Even though none of the four others has left a name
in the Frenchman's memory, thus ceasing to exist as a "real"
person, each has become a quasi-material component of his
consciousness.

It is therefore his own past of which he is taking stock as
he contemplates the building that has replaced the hotel. The
narrative proceeds from an initial chapter called "Inventaire"
to a final one entitled "Le Bureau des objets perdus," where
the possibilities that might have changed his life have been
lost, overwhelmed by the accumulation of events that followed
his Spanish experience, thus leaving him only with a minor
modification of his being. It is within himself that the encounter
between the all too innocent and the all too wise takes place,
and in the process his inner perspective is changed. At first he
considers his former self as "this remnant of himself, or rather
this trace, this blotch (this excrement as it were) that had
been left behind: a derisive character seen to stir about, ridiculous and presumptuous" (P, p. 20). The last lines of the book,

however, suggest a similar concept by means of a very different image, as the boxes of the shoeshine attendants are likened to "ancient and mysterious little chests, tiny and ridiculous child coffins" (p. 230). That ending conveys a taste of ashes, and it is tempting to see in the ruins of his former self both a thematic adumbration of the narrator's eventual distegration (as a concept in fiction) and an inner correspondence to the now destroyed palace, itself an objective correlative to the Spanish Republic. That might tend, thematically, to place the civil war in the forefront—instead of where it belongs, in the background of the protagonist's consciousness. The palace is both a correlative to the war and to his consciousness. The narrative is so structured as to make of the war not an outside reality, an absolute that might be used as a standard by which past actions might be evaluated, but a fragmented series of events, of which several become the components of an inner reality.

In similar fashion, *La Route des Flandres* (1960) is not about the French army retreat in 1940; rather, it describes the attempt by one participant to make some sense out of the life and death of another (a death that occurred during the military rout of 1940, a time of intense psychological stress). As in *Le Palace*, the historical event is viewed from a later point in time, on the occasion of a purely personal experience that releases a previously repressed trauma. What in the later piece of fiction triggers an inventory of the past is an emotional shock, but also a somewhat arbitrary one: the Frenchman did not have to return to Barcelona. The catalytic event of *La Route des Flandres* is deliberately sought by George, who is the central consciousness of this story. He thinks sleeping with Corinne, the dead man's widow, will provide him with certain clues he is looking for—although he does not realize how much his own memory will yield on that occasion. From that point of view, it is almost a necessary event and one to which the narration comes back regularly. That is one of several reasons that leads me to place this book a few rungs above *Le Palace*, which follows chronologically. Others reasons include the emphasis placed in *Le Palace* on the funeral of the slain republican leader and the long narration of how the Italian eliminated a political enemy in a Paris restaurant (which takes up an entire chapter, over one fifth of the book)—both of which, in spite of their being closely related to the main character's experience in Barcelona, captivate the reader's attention and prevent the book from being as sharply in focus as it might have been. What may have happened is that Simon was becoming gradually more and more interested in textual motifs but had not yet found an effective way of weaving them into the fictional architecture, as he later succeeded in doing in *Les Corps conducteurs*.

The success of *La Route des Flandres* is in large part the result of Simon's having built a very rigorous architecture for his narrative. He was thus able to achieve a more complex interweaving of thematic elements than the fundamental plot of *Le Palace* allowed. An episode of the 1940 retreat provides the framework: remnants of a battered cavalry unit roam the countryside amid corpses, burning trucks, and carcasses of horses; the unit commander, Captain de Reixach, gets killed, and George is eventually taken prisoner. In the meantime, the men are lost and keep returning to the same place in spite of themselves; each time they recognize the same dead horse. Such wandering is correlative to the processes of George's imagination, some years later, as he spends the night with Reixach's widow, Corinne, and tells his tale. Within the narration, horses, dead on the battlefield, alive in Reixach's peacetime stables, or metaphorical in relation to George's and his captain's common ancestor, are the verbal (textual) means that give his imagination unity. What obsesses George is the manner in which Reixach died (so peculiar as to suggest a form of suicide) and the sort of life that made that death necessary. The captain is thus as much the central character of the fiction as George is. The latter is the consciousness through which the events of the captain's life acquire significance. The real disaster in *La Route des Flandres* (Simon had considered subtitling it "Description fragmentaire d'un désastre") is that of Reixach's life. Looming historically larger is the French army's disaster in Flanders—esthetically a mere objective correlative —and the catalytic agent that helps in bringing everything into focus is George's erotic disaster with Corinne. Just as the cavalrymen keep encountering the dead horse, George's narrative keeps wandering back to Corinne.

George enjoys a peculiar position in this story, part narrator (but much more integrated into the narration than his predecessor in *Le Vent*), part protagonist (but somehow subordinated to Reixach). It is he who speaks at the outset of the narrative, but less than twenty pages later he is replaced by an anonymous narrator who refers to George in the third person. From then on, the narrative shifts back and forth between first and third persons, sometimes in traditional fashion with the opening or closing of quotation marks, at other times with no typographical indication that a change has taken place. In the second section the ambiguity is compounded when part of the narrative is taken over by Blum, another member of Reixach's unit, who has also been taken prisoner. (In at least one instance the anonymous narrator intervenes to explain that there is no way of telling whether George or Blum is speaking.) There is also some uncertainty as to the person George is talking to. One supposes at first that he is either reminiscing silently or talking to Reixach's widow, but near the end of the first part everything is put into question. "Then he stopped. It was not to his father that he wanted to speak. It was not even to the woman who lay unseen next to him, perhaps it was not even to Blum that he was explaining, whispering in the dark, that if the sun had not been hidden they might have known on which side their shadows travelled. Now they no longer rode through the green countryside, or rather the green country path had suddenly vanished and they (Iglésia and he) stood there, stunned, stopped" (RF, pp. 100–101). George, of course, whatever he is, is talking to the reader; or better, the text addresses itself to the reader as text rather than as communication. This heralds the beginning of the evolution that leads to Simon's third manner.

In the passage just quoted, four separate scenes are fused, all centered upon George: the basic scene with Corinne, always implied when not specifically mentioned; one with Blum in a freight car on his way to prison camp; a third one with his father; and a fourth with Iglésia, another cavalryman (and former jockey), as they are about to come upon the dead horse. *La Route des Flandres* thus exhibits a tripartite confusion affecting narrator, narration, and listener, destroying the three indispensable elements of traditional story-telling. What remains is no longer a story, properly speaking, but something that one might conveniently call a text—an assemblage of words that functions according to linguistic laws. As Bernard Pingaud wrote about one of its features, "transition from fictitious scene to real scene (and vice versa) is in most instances effected by surprise, the narrative turning not on a fact, not even on an analogy (thereby giving up all logical links), but on a word, as in music a simple chord is enough to indicate modulation."[3] Going one step further, Jean Ricardou gave such pivotal words the designation of "structural metaphors," since what enables the transition to take place is often the shift from one meaning of that word to another. The most striking example he gives concerns the references to *traditions ancestralement conservées comme qui dirait dans la Saumur* ("traditions ancestorially preserved as if they had been soaked in brine"), where the meaning "brine" immediately gives way before "French officers' cavalry school," located in the town of Saumur (which lacks the final "e" of *saumure*, meaning "brine").[4]

Claude Simon had previously published *L'Herbe* (1958), not as accomplished as *La Route des Flandres* but a text in which his concept of time is given clear emphasis. Aspects of style, dialogue, and narrative technique previously noted are present here to the extent and quality one might expect, considering the chronological position of this work in relation to others. The central consciousness is Louise, who, along with her husband, lives with her in-laws. The main character is Marie, her aunt by marriage, who is in a coma and near death. Necessarily, then, the greater part of the narrative consists of a series of flashbacks. One also encounters familiar patterns: variations on the theme of confrontation between young and old (Louise's husband and his father, Louise and Marie, her husband as he is now and his former self), and attempted restoration of the past. The instrument of this attempt is a small tin box, given by the dying Marie to Louise during a scene that has definite mystical overtones. This box contains "the very webb of her existence" (H, p. 123), it is all that is left of her, it is Marie—and it is also Louise. The box, an old cookie tin, is decorated with the picture of "a young woman clad in a long white dress, partially reclining in the grass" (p. 11). At the beginning of the book, Louise is standing in the grass, talking to her lover, ready to elope with him. At the end, she is lying in the grass, again talking with her lover, but now a defeated woman, unable to leave. She has become the image on the box, she is tied to it, as Marie was tied to its contents.

The tin box is Marie's "pyramid," her "monument," and what it contains has spatial quality. Inside, there are items of inexpensive jewelry and a number of notebooks. These notebooks, however, do not constitute a diary, a linear record of spent time; they are much closer to an inventory, a record of objects and money acquired or surrendered. The acquisition of canned goods balances the loss of a sister, and the sale of walnuts is compensated by the purchase of an umbrella. Undoubtedly this is, in part, a commentary on bourgeois life analogous to the satire found in such works as François Mauriac's *Genitrix*—with a bit more compassion on Simon's part.

More generally, though, it expresses time as a "frightful accumulation" (p. 140) of matter that stifles not only innocence but life itself. In a pointed paraphrase of what old Gisors says in Malraux's *La Condition humaine* about the fifty years it takes to make a man, Louise reflects "on all that is needed not to make a man or a woman, but a corpse—one of those things one wraps up in air-tight boxes" (p. 140). The actual coffins that are buried in the ground are but objective correlatives to the more significant ones. Marie's real coffin, her "mausoleum" (p. 141), is her tin box. Louise's father-in-law's is his own body, bloated with food and self-indulgence. Perhaps Simon would say that we all have the coffins we deserve. We build our mausoleums very gradually, no one can see them grow—not even ourselves—any more than one can watch the growth of a blade of grass.

The epigraph of *L'Herbe*, a statement by Boris Pasternak ("No one makes history, one cannot see it any more than one can see the grass grow"), extends the analogy beyond the life (or death) of a person, making of each one an imperceptible part of history. This specifically broadens the significance of the dying Marie: "If to endure History . . . is to make it, then the drab existence of an old lady is History itself, the very stuff of History" (H, p. 36). It also points towards Claude Simon's more recent work, *Histoire* (1967), which stands as a remarkable synthesis of several previous themes and achievements. The tin box of *L'Herbe* is with us again—metamorphosed into a chest of drawers full of old postcards. Its role in the work remains similar from a thematic standpoint. Textually speaking, it is a generative element. Within the framework of the story, it is more effective since, belonging to the narrator's grandmother, its falling into his hands can be taken for granted, and it reinforces a natural link instead of creating a seemingly artificial one.

The entire emphasis of *Histoire* is on integrating the architecture of the narrative into a natural framework, something

CLAUDE SIMON   **171**

La Route des Flandres had already attempted and partially
accomplished. The basic unit here is a day in the narrator's
later years, from early morning until after midnight. Both his
parents and the relatives of their generation are dead. He has
been married, and the marriage has just broken up. The account
of his day is divided into twelve chapters, although there is not,
as in Butor's *Passage de Milan,* any precise correspondence
between chapters and time of day. They are unnumbered,
possibly to avoid such a suggestion, and untitled, for there is
no theme, image, or event each one might be tied to exclusively. (The device, used in *Le Palace,* of having a sentence
begin at the end of one chapter and continue at the outset of
the next is again in evidence.) If we consider the day of the
narrative to constitute the present time of the fiction, the first
and last chapters then belong outside of time and serve a purpose similar to the corresponding chapters in *Gulliver.* The
second chapter starts with the awakening of the narrator; the
eleventh chapter closes as he watches the stars from his bedroom window. In the meantime he has gone out into the street,
encountered a former beau of his mother's, visited his bank, had
lunch in a restaurant, returned home for an appointment with
an antique dealer, driven out to the shore to get a cousin's sig-
nature on a legal document, driven back to the city, had a
sandwich in a café, and taken a stroll before going home to
bed. A completely uninteresting day, a mere canvas on which
to weave the drama of a single person against the backdrop
of history. Colonialism, two world wars, the Russian revolution, and the Spanish civil war are inescapably present throughout the pages of *Histoire.*

What sets things in motion is the narrator's decision to sell
a chest of drawers and the ensuing necessity to empty it of
its contents—the mass of postcards. They are sent by various
members of the family, but those that spur his memory most
were mailed to his mother from all over the world by his father
before their marriage. Much of his life is resurrected in the

process, modified by present obsessions. That, at least, is how things appear to the reader; but if one looks at this work with the insight gained from reading subsequent ones, he sees a need to modify the order of those events. If one will refrain from allegorizing, from attempting to fit matters into a plausible story, and remain on the textual level, he should realize that the postcards are at the very source of the fiction. Their aggregate has generated the chest of drawers and the reason for its being where it is. Each individual card has generated an incident or series of incidents that eventually create the narrator's life and all the aspects of the fiction.

To go back to the narration and the fable it allows readers to elaborate, one does not get the impression of a series of flashbacks as in the preceding books; the narrative seems closer to an interior monologue. It even includes something like a parody of Joyce's *Ulysses* as the narrator, remembering indecent transliterations of Latin responses a schoolboy friend used to make at Mass, says when approaching his washbasin in the morning, "Introibo in lavabo" (HS, p. 43). Buck Mulligan is not far behind. (Not too close, either, and this could be no more than a tongue-in-cheek device to establish a distance from Faulkner, with whom Simon must have become tired of being compared.) As the day of the narrative unfolds, the narrator's life is spread out before us, some of it in chronological order. There are actually three planes of development: the present time, the narrator's life, and incidental forays into the past. The first two constitute the fixed, arbitrary elements of the architecture, which nevertheless corresponds to biological realities. The third is, esthetically speaking, a chance element; it is the one more obviously determined by the reality of the thought process, that is, by the nature of language. That sort of freedom under a close-fitting harness is an essential virtue of this book.

As in previous works, the theme of *Histoire* is the accumulation of time, its accelerating encroachment upon innocence and life, the increasing weight it places upon a person until it eventually destroys him. A concomitant theme is that of decay. The selling of a chest of drawers, together with the indication that other items in the narrator's house will be sold in the future, is related to his obtaining a mortgage on another piece of property. All are objective correlatives for something that is constantly implied but never specifically mentioned: his whole life is breaking up. The narrative is motivated by a sense of catastrophe and the need, compulsive and partially subconscious, to determine its causes. That was also the reason for the flashback account of Max's life in *Gulliver* and for other subsequent narratives as well. But with the exception of *Le Palace*, all were conducted from the outside or, as in the case of the stepfather in *Le Sacre du printemps*, presented as a formal, conscious recollection. The recourse to interior monologue or to what gives the illusion of being one (for the narrator as subject leads a precarious existence here) permits greater involvement on the reader's part, as he lives the story instead of merely listening to it, and gives more plausibility to Claude's Simon's withholding of information. It is no longer simply an effective technique that creates suspense. It is, as in Robbe-Grillet's *Le Voyeur* or in Ollier's *La Mise en scène*, an integral part of a person's tendency to suppress undesirable events from his conscious thought. The void that lies at the center of *Histoire* and keeps sucking everything else in its direction is the fate of the narrator's wife, her probable suicide. That such a suicide is indeed the hidden *histoire* the title alludes to in one of its connotations is suggested not only by the narrator's fascination with a newspaper headline about a woman who jumped to her death, but by frequent references to Reixach's death on the battlefield of *La Route des Flandres* and the implication that the latter allowed himself to be killed because of his wife's infidelities. Furthermore, he suppresses until the last chapter the memory of a very suggestive sleeping-pill scene. Thus the list of suicides in Claude Simon's work grows longer.

Reixach's reappearance is symptomatic of his creator's assur-

ance, the new-found ease with which he roams over the texts
of his fictional works. George, in *La Route des Flandres*, was
a distant cousin of Reixach's. The narrator of *Histoire* refers
to an old "tante de Reixach" (p. 12), but Corinne, Reixach's
wife, is also the narrator's first cousin, and they were brought
up together. He also seems identical with the narrator of *Le
Palace*, for an incident that took place in Barcelona during the
civil war comes to the surface again. His sacrilegious friend,
Lambert, who goes through a communist phase, recalls Abel
(all the letters of that name are in "Lambert"), the communist
student in *Le Sacre du printemps*; the locale is Pau, a southern
city, as in *Le Vent*. The situation does recall that of the traditional fictional universe, of which Balzac's is typical. In it,
characters (seen as people), their preoccupations, and the setting in which they carry out their activities constitute the
ingredients of a familiar world, spread out over a number of
fictional works. On the other hand, one is also reminded of
what has more recently been called intertextual activity, where
"quotations" from other works, considered as "texts" rather
than "stories," increase the creative potential (the productivity)
of those into which they are inserted. The narrator of *Histoire*
is also placed in a curiously ambiguous position. As the author's
surrogate, he has created the world that is presented to us,
but he has also inventoried it and thus discovered himself as
the product of the past he has described. More accurately, he
is the product of his language, the result of everything he has
written. The last word of the book, "me?", toward which everything has been building up, expresses the astonishment, or
perhaps the horror, at such a discovery.

Histoire seemed such a felicitous culmination of Simon's
writings, it restated and related so many of the earlier themes,
that it was hard to visualize the work that might follow. This
is *La Bataille de Pharsale* (1969), a text that heralds the appearance of a third stage in his fictional development. One of
a number of factors that apparently prompted the change was

Simon's first visit to the United States, especially to New York, which he made in the fall of 1968. There he was struck by the kaleidoscopic variety of the metropolitan area—lower Manhattan, Brooklyn Heights, industrial areas of New Jersey, fall colors in Bear Mountain Park and in Westchester, various lookout points and bridges over the Hudson and other waterways, which he saw in quick succession and also telescoped together from the top of the Empire State building. Another factor has been a growing interest in the thought process that Claude Lévi-Strauss has called *bricolage* (the act of pottering, of making objects with whatever materials are at hand), a term that, I have been told, had also been previously applied to language at the Linguistic Circle of Prague. The term might actually be superfluous, for Lévi-Strauss himself has remarked that "the intermittent interest in 'collages,' which arose at a time when craftmanship was dying out, might well be no more than a transposition of 'bricolage' to the plane of speculative ends."[5] As the interest in collage has been more than a passing one, that term might well suffice for our needs. Be that as it may, it is still useful to remember the comparison Lévi-Strauss has made between *bricolage* and mythic thought, which operates by means of analogy and proximity, and constitutes "an intellectual aspect of 'bricolage.' "[6]

The new manner revealed in *La Bataille de Pharsale* does not signify a complete break with his previous fiction, for one of its important features was already noted in connection with *La Route des Flandres*. The work is a text, not a linear narrative but an assemblage of words ruled by linguistic laws rather than by those of plausibility and everyday logic. An indication of the evolution that has taken place since *Le Palace* may be conveyed in the contrast between "Inventaire," a chapter heading from that book and "Lexique," the title of the second chapter of *La Bataille de Pharsale*. The shift is from representation of an objective exterior reality as absorbed by a subjective consciousness to a display of the reality of language as constituting the subjective world of an individual. That aspect of the book has been dwelt upon by Jean Ricardou, who presents it almost as if it embodied characteristics of his own texts. Noticing that "Pharsale" is an anagram of "la Phrase," he entitled his essay on Simon's book "La Bataille de la Phrase."[7] One is naturally reminded of Ricardou's own *La Prise de Constantinople*, in which the back cover is an exact duplicate of the front one, except for the substitution of one letter in the title, "La Prose de Constantinople." What Ricardou says is generally true, but, in my opinion, his own interests have led him to overemphasize the purely linguistic features of Simon's book.

As the logic of the fiction is removed from the domain of reality (involving, say, considerations of psychological plausibility) to the linguistic one, generative elements become more noticeable. Ricardou has shown, for instance, how words in Paul Valéry's stanza (taken from *Le Cimetière marin*), which Simon uses as an epigraph for the first part of *La Bataille de Pharsale*, are picked up in the first few paragraphs of the narrative and then allowed to reverberate throughout the fiction; how the first word of the book, *jaune* (yellow), is disseminated, not only as a color (that is, as signified, also summoning words such as *safran, bananes, urine, soleil*, and the like) but by means of anagrammatic or homonymic processes (generating, for instance, words such as *nuage* [cloud] and *Jeanne*); or how the shooting of an arrow into an adversary's mouth (*pénétrant dans sa bouche ouverte*) calls forth, because of one connotation of *bouche*, a description of people emerging from a subway entrance (*la bouche du métro*).

Nevertheless, while agreeing with Ricardou that one should not restrict Simon's work to purely lyrical and sensorial aspects, I am reluctant to see the latter ignored. Indeed, a section of the second chapter entitled "Le Guerrier" (The Warrior) shows the presence of such aspects. Here, the narrator describes a cavalryman gone berserk in a military barracks; when the soldier takes his sword out of the racks, one hears "a metallic, icy rustling sound" (BP, p. 138). The narrator recalls a similar auditory sense impression received when, as a child at the circus, he watched a magician unsheath the swords with which he would pierce the box in which a beautiful girl was locked. This second scene has been activated by a sensory stimulus coupled with an emotional response. The sound has caused the narrator to feel a "shudder" similar to the one he felt as a child. A sword is involved in both scenes, but the word "sword" alone, either as signifier or as signified, was not sufficient to bring the second scene to light. The link between "rustling" and "shudder" is phonetically closer in French, *froissement/frisson*, but neither is that linguistic analogy enough to conjure up the earlier scene. It is actually the (involuntary) memory of the first shudder experienced at the circus and associated with an identical sound that produces that scene. Articulation might also be thematic or conceptual, that is, taking place at the level of the signified alone. For instance, as in standard interior monologue, a thick blob of white and pink paint on a painter's brush might suggest the gooey confections sold at outdoor fairs that are held during All Soul's Day. This in turn suggests the gloom surrounding that time of the year, the odor of acetylene lamps, and cheap baubles sold in fair booths, including porcelain statutes of Buddha with white stomachs—which brings up the painter's model, half naked in her kimono, together with the realization that the atmosphere of her love was the same as that of the fair, cheap and gaudy, that it reeked of "guilt and disaster." From there one is led to a remembrance of youth, of being so late coming home that no plausible lie could possibly account for it, and of the anguish that resulted (BP, pp. 48–51).

There are several major narratives in *La Bataille de Pharsale*. One describes war episodes that could have been inserted in *La Route des Flandres* without startling the reader. Another centers in an affair with a painter's model named Odette (the Proustian overtone is surely not accidental). A third tells of an auto trip to Greece and the site of the battle of Pharsalus. A fourth depicts a boy struggling with his Latin homework dealing with that same battle. A fifth involves a train trip through Italy. There are also detailed descriptions of love-making and battle scenes evidently based on sculptures and paintings. Narratives and descriptions are broken up and their fragments juxtaposed, sometimes even interwoven. In the process, images of intense jealousy and death are set up against a foil of indifference on the part of those not directly involved. Various references, such as the one to "Uncle Charles," might lead one to assume that there is a narrator who is identical with the one in *Histoire*, but even more than in that work this text acquires an autonomy of its own and tends to push such an imagined narrator into the background if it does not destroy him utterly. He is no longer the actor; he is the stage upon which the action takes place. He is also the observer (of which there may well be more than one). As we learn in the last section of the second chapter, he is designated by the letter O, which is also the symbol for zero, that is, nonexistence. The initial O designates not only the observer but also the object being observed (a duality already hinted at in *Histoire*). In addition, O is the first letter of the name Odette, the model whose representation in the text could perhaps be seen as correlative to that of ancient Rome, for whom Caesar and Pompey were fighting (as two men appear to be currying favor with Odette)—a struggle culminating in Pompey's defeat during the battle of Pharsalus.

If *Histoire* ends with a word that challenges the identity of the author of *Le Tricheur*, thus completing a rather wide circle, *La Bataille de Pharsale* achieves another kind of circularity, not unique in postwar fiction, by ending with the very sentence that set it in motion. This recalls a statement from the diary of Maurice Merleau-Ponty, in connection with the language of both Simon and Butor: "Such uses of language may be understood only if language is conceived as a being, a world, and if Speech [*la Parole*] is thought of as the circle."[8]

Claude Simon's most recent book, *Les Corps conducteurs* (1971), has a history that enables one to grasp in more concrete fashion the writing process characteristic of his third manner. He had been asked to contribute a text to the Skira collection called "The Paths of Creation." That text, published as *Orion aveugle*, came with a preface in which he explained how he writes. "From my point of view, there are no paths of creation other than those one clears step by step, that is, word after word, through the treading of the pen itself" (p. 6). To which he added: "Before I start setting down signs on paper, there is nothing—aside from a formless mass of more or less confused sensations, of more or less precise memories; and a vague, a very vague project." The painting by Nicolas Poussin, "Paysage avec Orion aveugle," serves as a metaphor for the writing activity, which has become, at this stage of Simon's evolution, nearly identical with the one described by Blanchot.[9] The writer is blind to the extent that, having nothing to communicate, driven by a need to say "something," he proceeds without knowing whither such a need might take him.

In the case of *Orion aveugle*, it began with the desire to put "something" together (*bricoler*), using as a point of departure a few paintings that he liked—in particular, "Charlene," by Robert Rauschenberg—which brought forth other images or representations of the American continent. Reference to the Poussin painting might have come either as the source or the aftermath of a sequence in *La Bataille de Pharsale*, the one I have mentioned in a different context, which describes the cavalryman gone berserk in "the barracks-room in the middle of which such a Goliath, or rather Orion, reeled about like a blind man" (p. 140). It was then added, I suppose, to the construction being put together; the idea was to unify it within the theme suggested by the title of the Skira collection. It must have seemed wondrously apposite, blindness having been, ever since Homer, a likely symbolic attribute of the writer. The text of *Orion aveugle* was then published, lavishly illustrated with reproductions of many of the generators that set it in motion, and itself standing as an illustration of a specific approach to fiction writing. The initial purpose having been fulfilled, Simon felt he needed to pursue his work. "And it now seems as though the path cleared by *Orion aveugle* should lead somewhere" (O, p. 13). That "somewhere," however, does not designate the traditional kind of ending one expects in a narration, for the emphasis is on the text rather than the anecdote. Consequently, the path followed by the writer "can have no other end than the exhaustion of a traveller exploring that inexhaustible landscape." The landscape he has in mind is that of man's language. At such a time of "exhaustion," a piece of fiction comes into being, "which will not tell the exemplary story of some hero or heroine, but that very different story constituted by the singular adventure of the narrator who never abandons his quest, discovering the world gropingly, in and through the written language" (O, pp. 14–15).

"Pottering" might be basic, but it is not sufficient for Claude Simon. He needs to weld things together within a unifying architecture. What Poussin's painting and the resulting symbolism did for *Orion aveugle* is not enough for the organization of this developing fiction. The basic generative elements being linked with the American continent, it seemed natural enough to center the various textual products of such elements describing the brief stay of a traveller in a large American city. (The city is easily identifiable as New York, in spite of the insertion of a number of European items that emerged out of the writer's consciousness.) The parallel between physical travel and a writer's "adventure" in language is obvious enough.

Plastic representations by Rauschenberg, Fernandez Arman, George Brecht, Picasso, Brassaï, Jean Dubuffet, Poussin, Louise Nevelson, and Andy Warhol, photographs of the Amazon river and a public telephone, engravings and illustrations of various sorts, pertaining to man's anatomy, a cigar box, Christopher Columbus in America, signs of the Zodiac, and an anarchist's bomb in the French parliaments first produce a series of texts, which resemble descriptions, generated by those objects. The texts are then ordered into a sequence involving the consciousness of the traveller, who has attended a writers' conference in South America, has flown over the Amazon, becomes ill in New York, tries to phone a woman with whom he has had an affair, and so on. As far as the reader is concerned, the impression produced might well be that of a story centered in the consciousness of a main character. The circumstances and timing of his illness, acting upon his sensitivity, cause him to reflect on or to remember a series of incidents, which are then described. I believe it is an indication of Simon's success in giving *Les Corps conducteurs* an organic architecture that such a fable can arise. But from a textual point of view it is nonetheless apparent that the character has been created out of the sequence of textual descriptions (inscriptions might be a better term) generated by the objects I have enumerated. Indeed, the story of the traveller is neither particularly significant or interesting. What is fascinating is the way things happen to him in the world of language.

All the generators for this text having been framed in one way or another (by the sides of the canvas, the sides of the cigar box, and the like), one begins to understand why an excerpt from this work, when it was published by *Tel Quel*, was entitled "Propriétés des rectangles"[10] and why Simon thought a possible subtitle for the book might be "Propriétés de quelques figures géométriques ou non." The allusion is not only to the way paintings, engravings, or photographs usually appear, but also to the painter's awareness of the size and proportions of the canvas whenever he draws a line or inserts a colored surface. Simon, having been a painter before he became a writer, perhaps felt that awareness more acutely than other writers and transposed it to his writing, where it becomes sensitive to the demands of the fictional framework when organizing groups of those "signs on paper" that he has blindly set down.

The "conductive bodies" of the title are first and foremost the words in the text, and the appearance of extracts in *Tel Quel* is an indication of the close relationship that exists between that group's literary theories and Simon's practice. Those "bodies" are also human bodies—those of the main character, of women, of crowds in the street, of the participants at the writers' gathering—all conductive of sexual impulses, emotions of various kinds, and political passions. *Les Corps conducteurs* integrates sensual and textual activities to a remarkably successful degree.

NOTES TO CHAPTER SEVEN (Simon)

¹ Henceforth, all references to works by Simon appear in the body of the text with the following abbreviations: *Gulliver,* G; *Le Vent,* V; *L'Herbe,* H; *La Route des Flandres,* RF; *Le Palace,* P; *Histoire,* HS; *La Bataille de Pharsale,* BP; *Orion aveugle,* O. See Bibliography for complete references to Simon's works.

² Nathalie Sarraute, *L'Ere du soupçon* (Paris: Gallimard, 1956), p. 105.

³ Bernard Pingaud, "Sur la route des Flandres," *Temps Modernes,* No. 178 (February 1961), p. 1029.

⁴ Jean Ricardou, "Un Ordre dans la débâcle," in *Problèmes du nouveau roman* (Paris: Seuil, 1967), p. 48.

⁵ Claude Lévi-Strauss, *La Pensée sauvage* (Paris: Plon, 1962), pp. 43–44. Roman Jakobson confirmed to me that the term was used in discussions in Prague in the thirties, but he does not remember when and by whom it was launched.

⁶ Lévi-Strauss, *La Pensée,* p. 32.

⁷ Jean Ricardou, "La Bataille de la phrase," in *Pour une théorie du nouveau roman* (Paris: Seuil, 1971), pp. 118–158.

⁸ Maurice Merleau-Ponty, "Cinq Notes sur Claude Simon," *Médiations,* No. 4 (1961), p. 6.

⁹ Cf. above, p. 67.

¹⁰ Simon, "Propriétés des rectangles," *Tel Quel,* No. 44 (Winter 1971), pp. 3–16.

CHAPTER EIGHT

Robert Pinget

Quelqu'un, the 1965 work by Robert Pinget, immediately invites comparison with Claude Simon's *Histoire* (1967). They both have roughly the same architecture, in that they are based on the activities of one man's life from morning till night on an ordinary day. In both, thoughts of the first-person narrator are stimulated by present actions and perceptions and directed elsewhere, in time or in space. In the end, each one has unwittingly revealed a great deal about himself. In both, much is made about material possessions. In Pinget's book, however, objects and records, in addition to being clues or correlatives, are really the generators of the character's existence. Also, instead of being a receptacle of the past that determines his present (a major feature of some of Michel Butor's characters, too), that character is a voice that builds a façade of words, in which he represents himself. Such is also his present, one of his own creation.

The narrator of *Quelqu'un* may be the co-owner of a small rooming house in the outskirts of Agapa in traditional Pinget country, where the Manu River flows. The way he tells his story, it all began some ten years earlier (Pinget characters have a tendency to think in terms of ten-year periods) when he ran into a friend he had not seen for a long time. Hoping to break away from their humdrum lives, the two decide to put their savings together and start afresh with a business of their own. As anyone might have guessed, they are now steeped in as much mediocrity as before, but that is merely a minor aspect of the tale. The narrator is an inveterate mythomaniac. Part of what he says is obviously false, and the rest is doubtful. On top of that he has a very poor memory, so that even when he is sincere he cannot be sure he has got the facts straight. On the day the text describes, he has lost a piece of paper he thinks important—although he later realizes that it is not. He says he is working on a manuscript ("Anyway, what I call my manuscript"),[1] a treatise on botany, and the missing paper contains important observations. He starts searching for it, but he soon decides that the only way to find it is to pretend he is not looking for it. Consequently, he attempts to account for all his actions since he got up that morning. In order to make things clear (and this almost reads like a parody of Butor's *L'Emploi du temps*) he must throw in a bit of background. One thing leads to another, and before one knows it his life is laid bare, all because of a lost scrap of paper. Or is he only pretending to look for his notes in an attempt to tell something about his life?

At any rate, he has a miserable day, fails to find anything, and is convinced he has flubbed the account of his life. For the reader, on the other hand, it is a moving and often hilarious experience. Gingerly treading his way among dangerous creatures —the maid (who doubles as cook during the summer), the co-owner, the two remaining spinster boarders (the others are away on vacation)—the narrator nearly always manages to say the wrong thing, arousing their ire or their scorn. Objects are untrustworthy. The one person more vulnerable than he is, a retarded boy who "helps" around the house, he cannot protect. There is also a neighbor whom he has never met. Something about the design of his weathervane convinces him that the two men could have nothing in common. But his need for someone (*quelqu'un*) is such that he keeps imagining his going over to the neighbor on some pretext or other and discovering that they do have a great deal in common after all. Even in those imaginary events he commits blunders. Finally the only suc-

cessful meeting they have is the one in which he imagines
assisting his neighbor on his deathbed—then inheriting his
manuscripts. Manuscripts and letters are recurrent motifs
throughout Pinget's work, correlatives to the desire to communicate. The narrator of *Quelqu'un* says at one point, clarifying the title: "If only one would understand me, put himself
in my place. I wonder if someone would want to. Someone"
(p. 52).

Pinget succeeds in transforming the reader into that "someone," and I, for one, was able to identify with the poor wretch,
more than with Samuel Beckett's bums. I am inclined to accept
the latter as images, located in a fantasy world truer than the
one we call real—but still a world that is quite other. The
horror world of Pinget's characters is much closer to the
reader's. On occasion, though, its people reverberate faint
echoes of Beckett. When the narrator of *Quelqu'un*, trying to
remember whether or not he talked to anyone after breakfast
and if so, to whom, suddenly exclaims, "But of course, it all
comes back to me," one is reminded of Molloy's similar statement when he remembers his name at the police station. When
the narrator of *Quelqu'un* expresses boredom with what he is
relating, when he says "What rot!" (*misère*), one recalls Malone's boredom with the story of Sapo and his identical exclamation. To Beckett's crude bag or sack corresponds Pinget's
more civilized valise: "One's existence in a valise, neatly packed,
properly labelled, so as to have what might be needed, just in
case. So, people are continuously preparing their valise, they are
always in the midst of packing something. Even when they talk
about the weather" (Q, p. 9).

His fictional world partakes of Beckett's and of Simon's. The
material is at times, especially in his earlier works, similar to
that found in books by Marcel Aymé or Raymond Queneau,
but it is structured toward the achievement of effects like those
of a Beckett whose pessimism had been tempered with a
glimmer of faith. In one of his most widely read books,

L'Inquisitoire (1962), he has also experimented with a device of his own, the questioning voice. Here, the main character is a lonely, deaf old man who is forced to submit to a lengthy, persistent interrogation. Who does the interrogating is never made clear, although there is enough in the text to allow one's imagination to picture a woman stenographer taking everything down, while sheets of paper keep piling up (as they do in *Molloy*). That all questions must be written out, because of the man's deafness, adds a touch of implausibility that enhances the unreality of the fiction and, as often happens, its effectiveness. At the beginning one might have the impression that a detective or some sort of police or government official is asking the questions and that one should concern himself with the sudden disappearance of another individual. Long before the story is over, one begins to have doubts about the reality of the voice, or perhaps the whole affair could be taking place after death.

The old man complains that to relate his life in such fashion "is like dying a second time" (I, p. 408), and he speaks of "all these dead people around us" (p. 435). On the other hand, he has been asked if "his case is incurable" (p. 72), and he refers to the time he still has to live. Likewise, in *Passacaille*, it is unclear whether anyone has di̇ed and if so who it is, or whether someone might be imagining his future death or someone is dying—perhaps even the text is a sort of *mémoire d'outre-tombe*. Such uncertainties are similar to those involving the reality or identity of Beckett's characters. In asking these questions, one gives evidence of having succumbed to the realistic fallacy, which contemporary texts implicitly denounce more and more vigorously. In the case of both Beckett and Pinget, no satisfactory answers can be given, and that matters very little. It is like the paper that may (or may not) have been lost at the outset of *Quelqu'un*. As Northrop Frye remarked with reference to the ghost in *Hamlet*, a literary text presents one with an hypothesis or a postulate, which one accepts, and the imagination takes it from there—otherwise, one has "no business in literature."[2] The hypothesis in *L'Inquisitoire* is: let there be two voices, the one answering and the other questioning. Gradually the text, aided by the reader's imagination, causes the answering voice to materialize into a man of about sixty, who, although deaf, is generally sound of mind and body. His memory seems far from perfect at first, but one soon decides that he must be playing a game of sorts: actually, he has a phenomenal memory. His questioner is relentless, picking up every hesitation, every omission. In the end the old man is forced to reveal all, or nearly all.

The first half of the book is replete with people and places of Pinget country. Hundreds of characters appear fleetingly, many recurring out of earlier works, filling the countryside, the woods, the estates, the hotels, and the cafés in Fantoine, Sirancy, Agapa, and Douves. To date, it is the most comprehensive repertory of that imaginary world. The main character (the answering voice) has been employed as a servant on the large estate of two rich playboys, whose household includes a secretary, valet, maid, cook, and gardener. All his identifications of people, descriptions of places, and relation of events seem to have had one consequence, not perceptible to the reader until the second half of the book is under way: they have given him substance—created him, so to speak. He was mere emptiness, but he now begins to penetrate the book's substance, himself taking shape as it encloses what he reveals. When one refers, to his memory, to his descriptions, or even to his existence as a character, it is because one tends to forget the original postulate. There is no one there except an answering voice that, with the reader's help, creates itself and its surroundings as it answers. Still, for the sake of convenience, I shall keep on discussing him as a character who fully existed at the beginning of the book, rather than only at the end.

A melancholy meditation (I, pp. 219–222) on the vanity and solitude of his life marks the turning point (there are no formal subdivisions in the book). Soon afterwards, the reader learns that he has been married and has had a son. Both wife and son have died, under circumstances that lead him to suspect foul play, on the order of witchcraft. A number of things hidden during the first two hundred pages come to light, including a series of sadistic murders. The strangest revelation, though, has nothing to do with either crime or marriage. In spite of his having already given an extremely detailed description of his employers' estate, inside and out (he needs eleven pages to account for furniture in the salon alone), he is led to tell, because of a slip of the tongue as the book is about over, that the mansion also comprises an older section of historical interest, with official visiting hours. Furthermore, another slip makes him confess that a friend of his employers still lives there, a gentleman named Pierre, an amateur astronomer who peers at the heavens from the top floor of the dungeon. The old servant visited him as often as he could, for being with Pierre brought him peace. He even calls him a saint (p. 448). If one thinks of the answering voice as a character, the Freudian implications of such an oversight are obvious. Assuming that the hero-victim of *L'Inquisitoire* reveals more and more of his inner being as the interrogation progresses or that the answering voice, the narrator (and how close is he to the author?), has to explore further and further into the recesses of his imagination (or consciousness) in order to provide answers, the position of these last disclosures gives them added significance. The implicit reference to the keeper of the keys in the kingdom of heaven might well point to a transcendental faith that tempers the pessimism of the narrative. One might recall, in this connection, that an earlier book by Pinget, *Le Fiston*, was a selection of the *Club du Livre Chrétien*.

Pinget's universe was not created in a day. Its embryo may be found in his first published work, a collection of short stories, *Entre Fantoine et Agapa* (1951). These stand in relation to his later books very much as Nathalie Sarraute's *Tropismes* do

to hers. They are of course of a very different nature. To return
to analogies I suggested earlier, the fantasy of Pinget's brief
sketches first reminds one of Marcel Aymé; then important
differences come to light. Whereas Aymé draws out all the
consequences of his outlandish premises and exploits them for
all they are worth, Pinget merely suggests, then lets the reader
take over. Once Aymé has set the stage, a rigorous, albeit mad,
logic determines the outcome. In Pinget's imaginary world,
logic has little place. In this respect, he is more like Raymond
Queneau, who also comes to mind because of the strange names
given to characters. Somehow, Mahu, Blimbraz, and Polycarpe
de Lanslebourg seem related to Machut, Quéfasse, and Louis-
Philippe des Cigalles. In addition to the towns of the title, the
tales also introduce fictional place-names such as Sirancy-
la-Louve, the Grance forest, the Cygne bar, and Gou Street,
which reappear in subsequent books. They are not, however,
centered in fictional territory: places like Paris, Saint-Cloud,
London, and Murano are also used as settings. The same holds
true for Pinget's next three works.

In *Mahu ou le matériau* (1952), Fantoine and Agapa are
places one goes to. The former even needs to be identified:
"Fantoine, that's where I go on vacation" (p. 28) says one
character. They are constantly present, but on the fringes of the
narrative, which clearly takes place in Paris. In *Le Renard et
la boussole* (1953), the story begins in Paris, moves to Israel,
and returns to Fantoine as if to a new, mythical promised land.
One would expect Pinget's fiction to be anchored there from
then on, and he possibly intended it so. Nevertheless, *Graal
Flibuste* (1956) does not quite make it. Everything in that work
belongs in the domain of fantasy, and there is probably too
much reliance on the fantastic element. There are too many
literary reminiscences for the fictional world to acquire the
"reality" it later has. An early reference to a sultan and to palm
trees inevitably carries the reader's imagination to the Near
East. Subsequent references to Fantoine and Agapa do not

restore a balance. It is only with *Baga* (1958) that a coherent atmosphere is established. The setting is still mythical, but there are no false notes to lead the reader astray. Once myth has been removed, as in all later works, Pinget's universe can be said to be firmly established, consistent, and as credible as it is imaginary. There are, especially in *L'Inquisitoire*, no lack of allusions to the outside world—to Amsterdam, Switzerland, or America. But those places are almost invariably foreign. Life, in the narrative, is found in Agapa and in Fantoine as transpositions of French towns. Versailles is only an architectural style (and perhaps an inadvertence). What we know as reality lies beyond the borders. Contrary to what took place in *Mahu*, people no longer go to Fantoine; they have their roots there.

The metaphor of Pinget's fictional universe was possibly stated in the story from *Entre Fantoine et Agapa* entitled "Firenze Delle Nevi." This tells how Lorenzo de' Medici, towards the end of his life, tired of the frequent uprisings that threatened in Florence, decided to "compete with himself" (p. 73). Climbing the southern slopes of Mont Blanc, he found a spot on which to erect a rival to his own city, at an altitude of some 15,000 feet. It only required two years to build, and in 1491 Botticelli put the finishing touches to his frescoes for the Municipio. Brilliant festivities celebrated the rebirth of Florence in the snow—and there may be significance in this happening one year before the discovery of the New World. If you have never heard of Firenze Delle Nevi, it is because it was later destroyed in an avalanche. Pinget, as a new Lorenzo, somewhere in the heights of his mind has constructed a new world to rival the one in which he lives. If it does not have the beauty of Firenze Delle Nevi, it is that the world he knows is not as beautiful as Florence.

Basically, the texts of *Entre Fantoine et Agapa* are stories. Even the last section, entitled "Journal," could be viewed as a series of unrelated anecdotes, each one headed by an arbitrary date. That is an essential feature of Pinget's work. He and his characters have stories to tell; they must find a way to tell them and someone to tell them to. His esthetic problem is that he does not function in terms of one sustained major narrative: he would have been at home with the picaresque novel, and both *Le Renard et la boussole* and *Graal Filbuste* actually go far in that direction. That they were not as effective as later works follows not only from Pinget's failure to build a coherent world but also from another equally important fact: the anecdote matters less than the telling of it. Language and thought are one, and "one never thinks more than one says" (E, p. 56). Everyone, therefore, has a story to relate and that story is himself. "As I proceed with my story, I have the impression of being what I tell" (B, p. 126). Who, then, is that strange individual who calls himself an author and tells the story of others? Hence the tale of *Mahu*.

Mahu ou le matériau is narrated in the first person by Mahu himself, presumably as Pinget's surrogate. But "there is also Latirail, he writes novels" (M, p. 10), and a fellow named Sinture, the postmaster, who says, "I pull the strings, I pull the strings. I am the one who is writing the novel of your friend Latirail" (p. 21). To complicate matters, Mlle Lorpailleur, also a novelist, "is writing the story of Latirail, the novelist" (p. 42). Mahu, who thinks he, too, might be a character, wants to help Latirail, whose "novel" has hit a snag. He suggests a development, introducing two new characters into his friend's story and locating the incident in Agapa. Latirail, however, rejects the idea. At this point, neither Mahu nor Latirail realize that the new "characters" were conjured up by Sinture and sent to Agapa for the purpose of breaking into Latirail's novel. The next sequence displays them in Agapa, as "real" characters in Pinget's book, amused by their mission, but embarrassed at having to tell Sinture that they have been rejected. Later, one of them will be forced into Mlle Lorpailleur's novel. It is all a grotesque illustration of a remark made in the narrative about "a fellow who thinks one cannot write novels. He says one cannot put oneself in someone else's place" (M, p. 45). In other words, there are no characters; there are only parcels of an author's imagination, something critics have been saying for some time, or words in his text, as one prefers to think of them today.

At any rate, Pinget was obviously enjoying his fantasy when writing *Mahu*, and it is great fun while it lasts. Unfortunately, he cannot sustain the merry pace. Towards the end of the first part (subtitled "The Novelist") each chapter stands as a semi-independent unit, almost like the anecdotes of *Entre Fantoine et Agapa*. Logically, it leads up to the second part, "Mahu Splutters," in which the narrator attempts to give his story. Again, what one has is really a sequence of stories, related by someone who is either a participant or a witness; they do not add up to one unified major story. Here perhaps one should recall that passage from Sartre's *La Nausée*, to which I have alluded in earlier chapters, where Roquentin denies the possibility of what he calls "adventure"—something outstanding, with a beginning and an end, with an order in between. "When one lives, nothing happens. Settings change, people come in and go out, that's all. There are never any beginnings. Days are added to days without rhyme or reason, it's an endless, monotonous addition."[3] Adventures or unified stories can exist only in fiction, that is, as most contemporary commentators on that text would imply, in outdated forms of fiction. In a different context, one might been tempted to accuse Pinget of lacking imagination. What one should realize is that his activities are directed elsewhere. In harmony with a trend in twentieth-century fiction that antedates the concern with linguistic phenomena, his aim is more to create what André Malraux has termed "a universe, both particular and coherent."[4] It is also a necessary one, for, as Mahu says, "When someone has really invented something, he does not keep comparing it to the inventions of others, since his own has replaced everything else" (p. 88).

Mahu's "spluttering" refers to the disjointed nature of the events he relates; what gives coherence to the universe Pinget presents here is Mahu's voice. The narrated events are not important, and Mahu even suggests that they cannot truly be narrated, basing his arguments mainly on problems of spatial and chronological point of view. The significant ingredients of his tale are to be found outside the story proper, in language and in style. The latter, as Roland Barthes has described it, in part, "is the decorative voice of an unknown and secret flesh, it operates as a Necessity."[5] The uniqueness, solitude, and compulsion implied in Barthes' study are indeed a capital feature of Pinget's works, and again one is reminded of Beckett. The first step is to express one's authentic self, no matter what it is, and that is Mahu's concern: "What matters to me is not to sing well, but to hear my own voice without bronchitis, you know, bronchitis, it's full of small wheezes" (p. 212). The next step is to reach someone. A fairly obvious goal in the recent *Quelqu'un*, it was already expressed by the narrator of *Le Renard et la boussole*. "You at least know what I am thinking, and that is why we shall eventually meet. I have nothing to say to us, absolutely nothing, and you want to hear my voice, that's all" (p. 10). The prologue of *Graal Flibuste* pessimistically alludes to letters that never reach their destination; the king, in *Baga*, writes for his hypothetical nephews. Levert, in *Le Fiston*, pretends to write a letter to his son; Clope, in *Clope au dossier*, gathers evidence to prove his innocence, presumably for a judge; and the inability to communicate with other people on the estate is what made life misearble for the old man of *L'Inquisitoire*.

Before being able to express oneself, one should, from the standpoint of common sense, know who or what one is; actually, it is very hard to dissociate one process from the other. Mahu, toward the end of his narrative, seems to have found his voice. But he protests when he meets a black who claims that his name is also Mahu: "I have never been black. That I am sure of." When the man remarks that Mahu still has a long road to walk, "he has a long life ahead of him," and advises him to "Familiarize yourself with this black man that we are" (p. 204), the implication is that Mahu has not really found out who he was because he had not yet said everything he had to say. It is hardly surprising that Robert Pinget's fiction is permeated with the theme of an inner quest, sometimes metaphorically transposed to the level of the narrative.

The narrator in *Le Renard et la boussole* bears the rather preposterous name of John Tintouin Porridge. *Tintouin* is slightly archaic and colloquial for "worry." In addition to the amusing clash between French and English components of the name, this pulls existential *Angst* down to the comic level. Furthermore, the book is indeed a picaresque porridge or hodgepodge. A considerable amount of narrative confusion exists because, in part, the quest is conducted on a linguistic plane. One is not too far removed from the world of Raymond Roussel. Already in *Entre Fantoine et Agapa* Pinget had demonstrated his fondness for phonetic correspondences such as "Avec un zeste de citron / Avec un geste de siphon" (p. 7), which in English becomes nothing more than "with a twist of lemon" and "with a splash of soda," and for puns of all descriptions. In *Mahu* Mlle Lorpailleur's name, since an *orpailleur* is one who pans for gold, suggests the phrase *chercheurs d'or* to the novelist Latirail, who then decides to call his novel *Chercheurs de poux* (Lice Hunters), perhaps because one of his characters stumbles upon gold dishware at a flea market (he says lice can be trained the same as fleas)—but it is hard to figure out which came first!

Le Renard et la boussole begins with the narrator's name and a statement of his desire to write. A few chance encounters, such as the one with a Mary Stuart book in a store window, provoke a number of false starts, but when he recalls a Biblical verse, which he misquotes as "Beware of the foxes, the little foxes" (p. 21), it is as though he had hit upon a catalytic word. He accurately "takes" the fox, couples him with an old man who turns out to be the Wandering Jew, and packs them both off to Jerusalem. The Jew goes back to his origins, the fox, initially no more than a word out of the Bible, back to Biblical land. As each is a mere figment of Porridge's imagination, their trip is correlative to his own search for origins, a way of finding out who he is. Because the fox is referred to as Renard rather than *le renard*, thus suggesting Reynard the Fox, a medieval harmonic is added to the Biblical tone. This helps to undermine conventional chronology, establishing analogies between a postwar journey to Israel and the Crusades. As a result, the quest motif is also clearly stated. Porridge (or Pinget), who on occasion experiences some difficulty in distinguishing between himself and the characters he has invented, meditates, improvises, and describes innumerable events. The book is something of an illustrated essay on life, art, and reality—with the reader's imagination picturing the "illustrations." Boredom is avoided through the variety and implausibility of incidents. Suleiman the Magnificent, Don Quixote, and Mary Magdalene are thrown in with refugees from Nazi concentration camps and citizens of Agapa.

One's head swirls by the time Porridge, David (the Wandering Jew), and Renard decide to take advantage of Louis IX's return to France and come home on the same ship, "what does it matter if it is powered by oil or by oars" (R, p. 184). The fox and the Jew conveniently vanish, or rather they are absorbed back into the narrator's being. The picaresque aspect of the book is attenuated as Porridge comes back a changed man. Pinget expresses the transformation by having him show up not in the Paris he had left but in Fantoine, where he meets Sinture, Latirail, Mahu, and many others. Before his trip, he had been employed in a hat factory; now he takes care of the gas pump in a service station. The turning point seems to have come toward the end of the stay in Israel, when Renard exclaims, after Mary Magdalene accuses him of being too logical: "No, no, we are not French, relax . . . I am from Fantoine" (p. 176). Pinget himself exclaimed, during the course of a discussion, "I don't give a damn for logic!" Porridge's true self has roots somewhere between Fantoine and Agapa, just as Pinget's distinctive voice is that which catches the language of his inner world. It requires two more works, *Graal Flibuste* and *Baga*, to sweep out the dross that is not his—the wheeze of his bronchitis.

Inevitably, the narrator's solitude is re-emphasized. In *Baga*, the king speaks of "this prison in which I am" (p. 110), and the metaphor is extended, the prison materializes, complete with walls, iron bars, and a guard. In *Le Fiston* (1959), Monsieur Levert repeats the king's identical statement (for example, F, pp. 34, 36, 43), but maintains it at the metaphorical level. What was a fantasy is now an obsession, that is, a psychological reality. Indeed, the entire narrative takes place on that plane. The setting is the fictional town of Fantoine, but the "reality" of fictional events is often in doubt, most statements being metaphorical. The story appears to deal with a Monsieur Levert and his letter or letters to his son, or to himself, and because of it or them, one learns who he is and of his relationships with the town and its people. In the long run, what happened on this or that occasion matters less than Levert's having chosen to write about them. As is the case with all of Pinget's subsequent books, there are a number of pedestrian questions that cannot be answered with any degree of certainty. In this instance, the reader will never know if Levert was the real father of Marie, the cobbler's daughter, or where his son is (assuming that he does have a son, as the old man in *L'Inquisitoire* seems to believe), or the extent to which he himself actually exists. One probably should not even ask. A question, nevertheless, that surely haunts the reader is the one that was also put at the end of Butor's *Degrés*: "Who speaks?" There is throughout *Le Fiston* an uncertainty concerning the narrator similar to the one in *Clope au dossier*.

The narrative gets under way with what appears like an objective, flat, third-person account of Marie's funeral. It continues with a similar description of Monsieur Levert and his activities. Then there is a sudden switch to first-person narrative as Levert begins, "My dear son" (F, p. 34); the ten pages that follow are utterly subjective. Here, however, tension begins to manifest itself, for the narrative voice switches about half a dozen times from first to third person and back again—but without change of mood. Next, just as abruptly as before, the text becomes "objective" again and follows the actions of Marie's younger brother after the funeral. But as the young man begins to reminisce, illusions about the objectivity of this section begin to fade away. Much later, when similar reminiscences involving different characters are attributed to Levert himself, it becomes hard to reject the suspicion that the narrator, whoever he might be, is making up the whole thing. That, in a way, is rather obvious, since one knows that the narrator must eventually be recognized as Pinget's surrogate. The important point, nevertheless, is that those shenanigans result in a destruction of point of view. In other words, another literary convention is set aside, as it is later, in like fashion, in Jean Pierre Faye's fiction. Theoretically, *Mahu ou le matériau* contained similar implications, but the comic or fantastic nature of so many of its episodes helped to maintain literary definitions untouched as one was reluctant to take matters at their face value. More serious in tone, *Le Fiston* is naturally more disturbing. With *Mahu*, Pinget was very close to Aymé and Queneau; here, he is edging closer to Beckett's territory (one should not forget that it was Beckett's reading and appreciation of *Mahu* that led to a friendship between the two writers). When Levert, leaving no doubt as to the nature of his fiction, exclaims, "This lie bores me. Everything must be retold, and I don't feel like doing it. I go on, son" (F, p. 130), he seems to echo lines from the last page of *L'Innommable*: "you must go on, I can't go on, I'll go on."

As he "goes on" Monsieur Levert relates the events that constitute his being. The letters that he writes or pretends to write

to his son amount to an attempted justification of his own
existence. Part of the story may be that in giving an account of
himself (consisting of a particular vision of people and events
in the Fantoine area), he presents a mirror for his son to look at.
Recognizing himself, his son will perhaps return home where
he belongs. One knows, however, that "this letter will never
be sent" (F, pp. 93, 158, 166). Behind the mask of fiction,
Levert's justification must be intended for himself alone. Once
that is accepted, the choice of events acquires new significance:
death informs the narrative's entire structure.

    Levert is approaching old age. His wife has died some time
back; his housekeeper and his sister die between part one and
two. Marie, who may be his daughter and whose funeral opens
the book, is about the same age as his hypothetical son. Other
deaths are mentioned, and as he attempts to establish the fact
of his own existence, he is ironically led to present an eight-
page description of the tombs in the cemetery of Fantoine. It
seems as though a magnet were drawing him toward the inevitable end. Shortly after the cemetery scene, language itself,
which is the means of his justification, fails him and becomes
dislocated (pp. 88–89). Something has gone wrong. As the
second part begins Levert realizes that he may have jeop-
ardized his chance of success. He admits that those earlier
"objective" accounts might not have been quite accurate. He
proposes alternate or subsequent versions; he even transposes
events into a different setting. He becomes desperate as a sense
of failure overtakes him and he tries to put himself in his son's
place. He imagines his son writing to him, "But the father has
been dead for a long time" (p. 161). It is hopeless; even through
his son's eyes he cannot give himself substance. Possibly, he
does not really exist. Having reached that stage, he or it or
whatever produces the text can see no reason for going on.
Hence the last sentence in the book: "Aside from what is written down, there is only death" (p, 173). Matters may not be
quite as hopeless as they seem, for a fair amount has been written down, and in writing there lies salvation.

Clope au dossier (1961) also represents a justification, but it is directed outward. The third-person narrative form is sustained from the beginning to a few pages before the end, allowing shifts from one consciousness to the next without change in tonality or style, a traditional technique. Pinget nevertheless achieves a tension analogous to the one he built up in *Le Fiston,* and he does this in two ways, first, as in Alain Robbe-Grillet's *La Maison de rendez-vous,* by means of explicit statement. Referring to the activity of a woman, Simone, in her kitchen, he writes, "She fills it again with the hot water remaining in the pan, if none is left she puts some on the stove again or has already done so" (C, p. 51). There the reader has no way of knowing if there is any water in the pan or what Simone actually does. Second, through a shifting of tenses: as in the previous book, the reader is, at the beginning, lulled into taking the narrative for granted, shifts from present to past indefinite or imperfect being fairly commonplace in French fiction. But when a sequence in the conditional follows a matter-of-fact description in the present, he is alerted to the uncertain nature of the presentation (for example, pp. 60–61). In a later book, *Passacaille,* there are constant changes from present to past tense, to conditional, to future of probability. This again prompts the question, "Who speaks?", or, as Joyce phrased it in *Finnegans Wake,* "Who in hallhagal wrote the durn thing anyhow?"[6] The omniscient author is ruled out by definition. Since in order to be less than omniscient about his own creation he must pretend to be someone else, one searches for a surrogate. One might first be led to surmise that it is the writer's consciousness in *Passacaille,* Clope's consciousness in the earlier work, that are being spread out in the pages of the book, even though Clope, like Monsieur Levert, refers to himself in the third person and is able to describe (or imagine) the dreams of Simone. In the final analysis, however, it is probably best to forget such individual consciousness, whether a character's or the author's, and consider the text as an assemblage of words produced by a specific activity—the act of writing—which is governed as much by the laws of language as by the will of the writer. I shall return to that in my final chapters.

Like Levert, Clope is a solitary man. The book begins, "Being alone, that wasn't a position in life," and revolves about the conflict between the reality of each lone, isolated human being and the fables concocted by society. The rift is dramatized at the outset by Clope's unlawful shot that brings down a wild goose. In his supposed defense of himself, he keeps stumbling over that day "when everything might have begun" (C, p. 124). Is Clope actually guilty of something more serious; has he committed a crime? There is a strong temptation to suppose that there is, as in Robbe-Grillet's *Le Voyeur*, a void in the novel, a blank in Clope's mind: a murder might conveniently fill it. In both works, however, it is the reader who is trapped into imagining the crime, as stereotyped forms of reasoning, so-called common-sense logic, and more generally speaking the fables of his society naturally lead him in that direction. Clope has done no more than his *dossier* contains, for outside of the limits of the text he simply does not exist. The trivial shooting that reverberates throughout the book is a correlative to Clope's basic situation. He imagines himself indicted for antisocial behavior, and the reader unwittingly confirms this. Others consider him slightly mad when they speak as actors in the comedy of society. The narrative and its main character have been delivered to the reader in a malleable state, and in his interpretations the reader reveals himself.

A welcome quality, absent in *Le Fiston*, that has been restored in *Clope au dossier*, is Pinget's humor. Accounts of Simone's early morning activities, her unsuccessful efforts to keep her child and kitchen clean, and the sputtering reminiscences of two old-timers on the village bridge are delightful as they lack mean or bitter overtones. The combination of laughter and seriousness, already present in earlier works, is now more fully integrated, as it is in *Quelqu'un*. In these works Pinget's attitude resembles that of Pierrot at the conclusion of Queneau's

Pierrot mon ami, after all his efforts and hopes had come to naught. Thinking of what might have been and of what actually happened, he simply burst out laughing and walked away.

Humor and ambiguity, as well as the theme of death and the quest motif, are concentrated in *Le Libera* (1968). The title is taken from the response sung during the absolution of the dead in Roman Catholic liturgy: "Libera me, Domine, de morte æterna." A number of violent deaths, mostly of children, cast a pall over the narrative, and the description of a funeral constitutes its final episode. Again an unidentified voice is heard throughout, compulsively narrating, repeating, correcting, quoting, and surmising, alluding once more like *Baga's* king and Monsieur Levert to "this prison in which I am" (L, p. 216) and seeming to give testimony before some mysterious, unnamed judge—perhaps echoing the Lord's judgment anticipated in the third verse of the response: "Dum veneris judicare sæculum per ignem." He refers to many characters of the previous books, but he is not as all-inclusive as the old man of *L'Inquisitoire*, nor is he as much interested in objects and places. Perhaps for that reason, he does not really materialize into a character. The villain of the narrative is Mlle Lorpailleur, who was a novelist in *Mahu* and in *Le Renard et la boussole*. She now reappears as a school teacher, a position she had already assumed in *L'Inquisitoire*. Actually, the narrator's point appears to be that she still is a novelist of sorts, that is, a fabricator of tales. She has spread a story implicating him in the murder of a young boy, ten years earlier (as usual), and he naturally insists that it is pure fiction. As things turn out, nearly everything is. There are few incidents in the book that are not told twice or more with considerable variants. In some instances, one doubts that they ever took place. The general impression one derives is that knowledge of others and of past events is practically impossible, which was already suggested as far back as *Mahu*. The solitude of the narrator is again obvious, and there is little or nothing to enable one to detect intimate relationships between him and the characters he talks about. It is the problem of communication, stated in earlier works, but endowed with a new dimension. Possibly, an answer is implied to the question put in *Quelqu'un*: the answer is no, not in this world.

Among the few episodes in *Le Libera* that are not questioned, that of the children's gala performance stands out. Often hilarious, it is also an exercise in futility that subtly blends traditional humor with the negative theme of the work as a whole. There is something about it that is emblematic of all of Pinget's fiction. The woman who is given credit for writing the poems recited by the children is using someone else's material. She is complimented for verse that she had acknowledged to have been written by Lamartine. Some children read parts that had originally been assigned to others, and one girl makes mistakes that no one notices. Life is a bumbling comedy of errors in which no one really understands anyone else.

But death, too, is a comedy of errors in which no one understands what is going on. Grim humor has perhaps induced Pinget to give the name of a most civilized, formal dance, the *passacaglia*, to his next fiction, *Passacaille* (1969), a text that comes close to being a verbal *danse macabre*. Actually, the description of the *passacaglia* (or the related *chaconne*), with its lack of complete tune, the theme consisting of "a short succession of harmonies to be repeated over and over again without interruption," could apply to this book once "linear narrative" is substituted for "tune" and "descriptive fragment" for "harmony."[7] Among other things, the work features a procession of cadavers, perhaps led or conjured up by a scarecrow. There is the corpse of the main character, a solitary man referred to as *maître*, sometimes as *maître alchimiste*, who annotates a book and/or writes his memoirs and/or imagines the circumstances of his own death. Other corpses are of a retarded boy, who has been castrated by a farm implement, a mailman, who is also afflicted with a strange disease, a number of undetermined people, and, to add the indispensable element of the grotesque, a cow, a duck, and many dead animals in the woods. Many of the corpses end up on top of a pile of manure, to which there are some thirty references. In other words, "The whole country is in a state of decomposition, dead bodies are strewn over meadows and roads" (P, p. 93). Creation of present self, which I earlier suggested as being an object of Pinget's texts, becomes more and more questionable—partly because of the overwhelming threat of death, partly because the quest for identity appears hopeless (something one already suspected when reading *Le Fiston* and *Clope au dossier*). "Who speaks?" is once more a tantalizing question.

The narrative voice in *Passacaille* starts out in a very muted fashion. The first personal subject is "someone," tentatively governing a verb in the conditional, amid a number of verb-less phrases or impersonal statements. A "man" appears next, and only on the third page does the regular pronoun "he" assume its role. More than half-way through the book, the third-person narrator steps into the text, interjecting a "Don't interrupt me" (p. 86). One page later he produces the first "I," saying "I can still see it now," a statement that develops into a twenty-page first-person narrative (pp. 99–118), which reverts to isolated sentences, "I can still see him now" (p. 121), "I can still see the woman now" (p. 123), "I can still see the red piece of cloth" (p. 125), before dissolving completely. It appears again only in quotations from the *maître*'s last will, at the very end of the book.

To return to the very beginning: "Calm. Grayness. Not a sign of turbulence. Something must be broken in the machinery, but there is no outward sign of it. The clock is on the mantel, its hands show the time." One is reminded of the "something there that isn't working" in Beckett's *Comment c'est*. One also thinks of the moment of literary creation, the more so when reading the very hesitant paragraphs that follow, with their verbs in the conditional. What is broken in the machinery appears to be a major generator of incidents that, somehow, an anonymous narrator attempts, without success, to fit into a narrative line. He first hits upon the machinery of life, hence illness and especially death as the major presence in the text. Next, the clock is broken, and chronology is disturbed; then a farm tractor breaks down, requiring a mechanic to drive up in his pick-up truck. That truck, or another one, lands in a ditch; a scare-crow needs repairs. Something in mind and reason goes awry, producing the retarded boy, drunkenness, and belief in witchcraft. The fabric of society cracks, producing war, exodus, lawlessness, and corruption in governments. A break in friendship occurs, caused by death—and one is back where he started. To think that it was such a calm beginning, without turbulence. In the meantime, the narrative machinery has also broken down, a failure that produces a successful *passacaglia*, but the reader is left with a shattered text and a disembodied narrator— "Master alchemist of those trifles to which he owes his survival" (pp. 47, 59).

That Pinget consciously removed himself from the position of responsible author is indicated by the date line appearing at the end of the text: "Sirancy, 1968." *Passacaille* was not composed in Paris by the man with recognizable features known to many as Robert Pinget; it is a text that was generated in the imaginary country and ruled by the same language that has given shape to Pinget's mind, which he has been exploring since the days of *Mahu*. Call it a verbal country if you will, for *Passacaille* is a text that has been generated by a verbal context. One is within sight of Raymond Roussel, and life appears as a verbal whirlpool that sucks us into the sewers of death. As there is not much to be done about it, one might as well laugh.

NOTES TO CHAPTER EIGHT (Pinget)

[1] Robert Pinget, *Quelqu'un*, p. 11 *et passim*. Henceforth all references to Pinget's works appear in the body of the text with the following abbreviations: *Entre Fantoine et Agapa*, E; *Mahu ou le matériau*, M; *Le*

Renard et la boussole, R; *Graal Flibuste,* G; *Baga,* B; *Le Fiston,* F; *Clope au dossier,* C; *L'Inquisitoire,* I; *Quelqu'un,* Q; *Le Libera,* L; *Passacaille,* P. See Bibliography for complete references.

² Northrop Frye, *The Anatomy of Criticism* (Princeton: Princeton University Press, 1957), p. 76.

³ Jean-Paul Sartre, *La Nausée* (1938; rpt. Paris: Club du Meilleur Livre, 1954), p. 61.

⁴ Cf. Malraux's marginal annotation to Gaëtan Picon, *Malraux par lui-même* (Paris: Seuil, 1953), p. 38.

⁵ Roland Barthes, *Le Degré zéro de l'écriture* (Paris: Seuil, 1953), p. 20.

⁶ James Joyce, *Finnegans Wake* (1939; rpt. New York: Viking Press, 1965), pp. 107–108.

⁷ Willi Apel, *Harvard Dictionary of Music* (Cambridge: Harvard University Press, 1958).

CHAPTER NINE

Alain Robbe-Grillet

In 1895 Paul Valéry, then a young man in his twenties, as much interested in the visual arts as in the functioning of the intellect, published his now famous essay on Leonardo da Vinci. In a section dealing with the human tendency toward generalizations and preconceptions (at least in the Western world), he made an observation that is as pertinent to French fiction in the fifties as it may have been to the paintings of his day: "Most people see reality with their minds much oftener than with their eyes. Instead of sensing space and color, they conceptualize. A cubic shape, whitish in color, rising from the ground, and peppered with reflecting glass panes immediately becomes a house; for them, it is the House. A complex thought, a merging of abstract features."[1] That and several subsequent paragraphs, along with marginal comments Valéry added in 1930, now read like the theoretical text that could have inspired the elaboration of Alain Robbe-Grillet's first published work, *Les Gommes* (1953). (His first work of fiction, "Un Régicide," remains unpublished as of this date.) Robbe-Grillet's own statement, in a 1956 essay, concerning those shreds of our culture that keep clinging to objects and endowing them with a reassuring, human aspect, seems to echo Valéry's remark.[2] Whether or not there is influence is immaterial. The juxtaposition of texts separated by a sixty-year interval points to a deep-seated concern over men's relationship with the world about them.

There is a feeling that the accumulation of culture that is imposed upon succeeding generations has reached the point where people are being smothered by it and deprived of their conceptual freedom. Everything they see or hear is automatically related to something else, organized into preset patterns. That seems to happen periodically, whenever a culture becomes sclerosed. In the present instance at least, artists reacted early. Impressionism in painting, Schoenberg's musical revolution, and Flaubert's *Bouvard et Pécuchet* may be taken as preliminary witnesses to a growing challenge to the world as it has been represented for too long. Because that challenge has now been extended to nearly all political and social institutions and has assumed worldwide proportions, one must take care not to exaggerate the significance of changed literary attitudes, contributory as they might be. What matters is that they are not the gratuitous games of mandarins, the vocabulary of contemporary critics notwithstanding. They are necessary components of a broader picture. Related to Robbe-Grillet's early plea for a liberated vision are the concerns of Sarraute, Butor, and the writers of the *Tel Quel* group—more limited in the case of Nathalie Sarraute's struggle against characters and plots, broader with Michel Butor's indirect criticism of society, more radical in the activities of Philippe Sollers.

To the hurried reader *Les Gommes* resembles a mystery novel. But even a cursory perusal, aimed at discovering "what happened," uncovers some unusual features. A crime has been committed somewhere in the provinces. As the act appears to have important political ramifications, a detective is sent out from Paris to assist the obviously outclassed local police, and the customary search for a culprit is on. A slightly new twist is added as the reader, through a kind of dramatic irony, is given more vital information than the fumbling detective, and it is the local police official who finally solves the mystery—too late, however, to prevent the detective from committing an ultimate blunder. The poor sleuth does not know that the victim, a man named Dupont, has not really been killed but only slightly wounded and is hiding for the sake of his own safety. His final error is to kill the man whose murder he was supposed to investigate, mistaking him for a member of the gang he thinks is responsible for the crime. Such an ironic yarn, it is true, might have come to the minds of a number of writers and spun for the mere fun of it. Yet it contains too many disturbing elements; there are too few things that come out the way one expects them to; the reader is bound to be unsettled, or at the very least, intrigued. And the manner in which pieces of the puzzle are put together point to Robbe-Grillet's denunciation of the humanistic fallacy that Valéry had unmasked.

All the major characters in the book are mythomaniacs of one sort or another, and, when it comes to solving the problem, all of them are wrong—except the local police official, who keeps his feet firmly on the ground. Ironically, when the latter discovers that the victim is not dead the detective kills him, thus perfecting the crime that had been bungled twenty-four hours previously. But at that moment also, the reason for many of the fancies elaborated by other characters disappears. All the nonsense generated by the strange interlude can be erased (*gommes* are erasers); the local police is in charge; the detective is transferred to another division.

Events are presented by an omniscient narrator who writes as though he had selected a number of "takes," as a movie director might have done, and given them to us "objectively" (that is, without interference or explanation on his part), also adding impersonal statements on minor events or settings. The reader is thus shown what each of the major characters sees or imagines, as each one's subjectivity transforms reality and filters it through his mind, recalls it, or invents it to justify his actions. In addition, and independently of each character's consciousness, a number of hints have been inserted throughout the novel. Bruce Morrissette, who is Robbe-Grillet's leading exegete in this country, has carefully inventoried and analyzed the many references to the Oedipus myth and several to the Tarot pack.[3] The assumption is that after all these have been put together and added up, it will be easier for the reader to get at the significance of the book. Perhaps so, and perhaps not. *Les Gommes*, as I see it, turns out to be a rather misleading work. Serious critics, such as Roland Barthes and Morrissette, disagree on basic aspects.[4] My own view, which I have developed elsewhere[5] and in which I differ from Morrissette, is that the references to the Oedipus myth were inserted with the deliberate purpose of having the reader join the group of mythomaniacs in the text. The references constitute false clues that merely appere to fit together and point to an appropriate solution. But if one re-examines the evidence carefully, with both feet on the ground, like the police commissioner, he sees that the relevance of the myth is nothing but a myth, so far as the detective-story plot is concerned. In the words of Olga Bernal, "Robbe-Grillet has retraced, step by step, the itinerary of Oedipus. At the end of that minutely reconstructed itinerary, the Oedipus myth collapses."[6] If the myth does indeed collapse, something else remains: the architecture of the fiction is based on that of Sophocles' play, *Oedipus the King*, which acts as a vehicle for the reader's fancy. In contrast to Nathalie Sarraute's antagonistic attitude towards her readers, that constitutes a clever use of his tendency to appropriate the work in order to fit it into his own world view, which at the same time gives him all the evidence to show that it does not work—the detective simply is no modern Oedipus.

Looking at *Les Gommes* with a cold, rational eye, one is almost obliged to call it a wildly improbable fancy. Most mystery stories strain credibility to some extent, but this goes further than most in that direction. Unlikely events and strange coincidences abound, the most improbable being those about which the entire plot revolves. The detective's wristwatch stops unaccountably at seven-thirty in the evening, exactly when the victim is first shot and wounded, and starts anew twenty-four

hours later, again at seven-thirty, precisely when he unintentionally finishes the crime by killing the victim. That in
itself should be enough to indicate that Robbe-Grillet is not
interested in realism as it is commonly conceived. The major
portion of the narrative takes place outside the domain of
everyday reality, not only because everything one is told has
been distorted by individual subjectivities, but mainly because
ordinary time has been suspended. The twenty-four hours
during which the wristwatch has stopped are both mythical
hours, when characters' mythomania and readers' Oedipus myth
are on the rampage, and fictional hours, during which the narrator imagines a story.

In order to make the latter point clear, I shall posit two levels
of events within the novel, a realistic one and an imaginary one.
To the realistic side of the story belong two murders perpetrated either by a small gang or several accomplices against
two middle-class citizens in a small city; the two are killed on
successive days at the same time, early in the evening; the local
police investigate. To the imaginary side belongs the narrator's hypothesis. Let us suppose that something went awry
on the first day and the victim escaped with only a minor
wound—it matters little, as that first crime was a routine affair
that attracted no attention, acquired notoriety later only because of the repetition. Let us then imagine a set of circumstances that will enable someone to complete the first crime
at the time the second one is perpetrated. An immense political
plot involving a whole string of assassinations, shadowy connections between the two victims and high governmental circles
is made up to provide the background for the events that fill
those strange twenty-four hours separating the two crimes.
The man who completes the unfinished murder, supposedly
sent from Paris, does so as the narrator's agent, his wallah; he
is the detective, "Wallas. / 'Special agent' . . . " (G, p. 30). He
does not belong to the realistic world of the narrative. As the
police commissioner correctly but inadvertently says. "The

pistol shot that killed Daniel Dupont originated in another world!" (p. 62).

I have not given what I call "the narrator's hypothesis" as an attempted decipherment of what went on in Robbe-Grillet's mind when he wrote the book. Rather, it constitutes a rational way of accounting for what is in the text and emphasizes its unrealistic aspects, which are present from the very beginning. Now everyone assumes in the presence of fiction that he is reading something unreal, even though there may have existed a pretense on the part of traditional writers to pass off the fiction as reality. Thus Conrad's device of having a "real" person, Marlow, give the "true" account of his search for Kurtz in *Heart of Darkness.* In *Les Gommes,* exactly the opposite takes place: there is a double affirmation of fiction as fiction, and that is something Robbe-Grillet affirms more and more openly in his subsequent works. Wallas drops a few hints in that direction as he keeps inventing stories to justify his questions or actions—about the telegram when looking for a post office, about the erasers when entering the stationery store, and so forth. Going beyond the limits of this particular book, one could view such behavior as the fictional correlative of a person's need to integrate his actions, no matter how original or strange, into culturally acceptable pattern, that of a myth or fiction.

In *Le Voyeur* (1955), the fictitious elements emerge perhaps a bit more clearly. As Mathias is about to disembark on the island where he hopes to sell the watches he has in his case, several flashbacks (a term I use merely for the sake of convenience) help introduce him to the reader and prepare him for what is to follow. What happens is that the reader begins to construct a character that will fit the name "Mathias." He soon decides that this character has no distant memory, for the two stories from his childhood are each preceded by the sentence, "People had often told him this story" (V, pp. 9, 18). Mathias gradually takes shape. He was born on the island but remembers no one and no place. The day before coming, he has tried to learn as much as he could about topography and people, so that he could pretend to remember: "Success seemed especially, on this day, dependent upon imagination" (V, p. 32). The same is true of the book, and the statement could be interpreted as a clue to the unrealism of *Le Voyeur*. Firing that imagination, Mathias starts telling himself about his childhood games and wanderings with other children on the island, of which he plans to remind them in turn. "People don't have that much memory; he would manufacture childhoods for their benefit, and that would lead them straight to the purchase of a watch" (p. 32).

Getting off the steamer, he imagines his first sale, a successful one, of three watches to a lady and her two daughters; but after he has told the story to himself, he realizes that the scene has been ridiculously silent—not a sound was made, not a word exchanged. He tries again, starting this time with a resounding knock at the door. He is not very adept at dubbing the sound into his imaginary film and gets nowhere. His third try is off to a fumbling preamble as he makes up a connection with the lady's relatives. He gets out of it somehow, walks into the house, and opens his display case—but other images intrude, and the story dissolves into confusion (pp. 35–42). After he has begun his door-to-door canvass he tells a couple of erotico-sadistic stories, vaguer in outline than his watch-selling one. He tells the first as he sits on the rocks by the water's edge waiting for the bicycle he has rented and the second as he is forced to wait while a woman gives him boring details about her children— trapped as he is by having told her he was a friend of the family. Each one is inserted in an idle period, if one considers things from the standpoint of his intended activities on the island. One hour elapses between parts one and two of *Le Voyeur*, and in part two Mathias' story-telling role increases. He is seen as making attempts to account for the missing period of time. The reader, his imagination having been primed by the erotico-sadistic material he has read, soon suspects that Mathias is guilty of rape and murder, committed during that hour. The stories can now easily be interpreted as an effort to cover up the crime, an interpretation that helps them and the previous ones acquire psychological plausibility. In analogous fashion to the placing of Mathias' stories, the reader's erotico-sadistic vision inserts itself in the idle period not covered by the narrative. That interpretation of the book has been discussed at length and is only secondary in the present context, as it involves primarily the psychology of the reader.

Rhetorically speaking, there is no difference between the stories told by Mathias in the first part and those told in the second. They all correspond to the imaginary side of the narrative, as I defined it for *Les Gommes*, but more easily identifiable than in that earlier book. In both cases the story deals with an outsider who returns to a locale where he claims to have been before, and his actions have a superfluous quality about them. If Wallas belongs on the imaginary level of the story in which he appears, what that imaginary character does is clearly described in the text. What Mathias does during the missing hour, on the other hand, is left to the reader's imagination. Assuming the latter's suspicions to be correct for one moment, the "crime" either had been begun, perhaps even accomplished before he set foot on the island, or it would have been carried out anyway (Mathias' "victim" had a bad reputation, and when she disappeared another character says that, as most islanders see it, "It won't be much of a loss"—p. 188). Again, he is the narrator's agent, although he carries with him a much simpler fictional construct than Wallas did, a means to set fantasies in motion. At the end of *Le Voyeur*, he is able to leave the island as quietly as if nothing had happened. Actually nothing has, as far as verifiable textual elements are concerned.

Before the unaccounted-for hour that separates the two parts of the narrative, two of the stories he tells and many of the objects that attract his attention seem to presage the crime the reader thinks he will commit. While some critics have been inclined, in traditional fashion, to view such objects as symbols, Bruce Morrissette has more accurately referred to them as objective correlatives of the character's mental states. Perhaps a step further is indicated, for to the objects in *Le Voyeur* (cords, figure eights, chains, and the like) one must add premonitory stories and statements such as had also appeared in *Les Gommes*. Whatever their form, all such references might well be grouped under the heading of generative (rather than objective) correlatives because of their role in generating subsequent textual and extratextual fictional events. The principal domain of Robbe-Grillet's fiction is not the domain of material facts but more properly that of the imagination. Wallas' victim shows up wearing tinted glasses, one lens darker than the other, because the police commissioner had previously asked about such glasses. It is not because Mathias will commit rape that the author introduces suggestive references to such an act; rather it is as a consequence of his own fixations and of his relating them that he will either be led to his crime or be accused of it by the reader. Here, since there are no words to describe the crime on the realistic level of the narrative (or anywhere else for that matter), the only one who actually witnesses it is the reader, who thus becomes the voyeur of the title. What characterizes the missing hour, from his viewpoint, is no longer traditional ambiguity but tension, as his growing certainty vies with the text's refusal to give direct evidence.

Robbe-Grillet used basically the same narrative technique in *Les Gommes* and *Le Voyeur*. In the latter, the narrator presents his "takes" from the mind of a single character, and outside, impersonal statements are more numerous. *La Jalousie* (1957) represents a more rigorous, exclusive use of one aspect of that technique, the transcription of interior "takes," which also characterize his subsequent book, *Dans le labyrinthe*. The realistic level of the story has been all but eliminated, and nearly everything takes place on the imaginary level, a single character being involved. The "takes" are still offered objectively by the omniscient narrator, not distinguishing what the character sees from what he imagines or recalls; nor, in the latter case, is there any way of telling whether his memory is accurate or not, whether it is willfully or accidentally distorting things. If the main character no longer can be considered a complete outsider from the point of view of the realistic part of the story (he is a Frenchman in the French West Indies), he remains one from the psychological standpoint. He is nameless, although we soon understand that he is the husband of A. . ., he gives little direct evidence of speaking or being spoken to, and whatever goes on between his wife and their neighbor, Franck, he cannot fathom its nature— whether there is sexual involvement, friendship, or casual relationship. All he can do is tell or invent the story of what may have happened on several recent occasions. when Franck came for dinner, when he was invited for lunch but did not show up, when he drove A. . . to the neighboring town to do some shopping, or when the husband just sat watching A. . . or gazing at his plantation.

As everything one reads has been "taped," so to speak, from the husband's mind, questions as to precisely which incidents are real, imagined, or distorted, or as to how many times Franck actually came to dinner, are somewhat irrelevant. There may be some value in attaching stylistic significance to the adverb *maintenant* (now)that begins five of the book's nine unnumbered sections and appears elsewhere within the text and in seeing it as a signal for a factual "take." It may well be that the counting of banana trees is factual, representing a form of therapy, a means to rid the husband's mind of obsessive jealousy. It is quite likely that the flaming crash of Franck's car into a tree is imaginary. But the reader is not asked to sit in judgment on the husband's truthfulness. The thing that really matters is that the reader is made to participate in the husband's own story, exactly as it is, with all its subjective deformations. The reader is not given an analysis of jealousy; he is not even told that the husband is jealous. One must create that feeling out of the raw materials of sense perception and mental images and experience it as it arises. There is tension between a seemingly dislocated text and the reader's efforts to give it unity. The strength of such tension, hence the intensity of feeling, will then depend upon his sensitivity and imagination. It is even quite conceivable that some readers may stop short of jealousy, ascribing the images conjured up by the husband to excessive concern. In a way, each reader, through this and much other fiction, analyses himself. As Gérard Genette says, "All we see is a finicky, homely man, a fastidious observer."[7] The reader does the rest. In that light, the statement attributed to Franck, as he and A. . . play at changing the plot of a novel they are reading, seems ironic. "Things are what they are: one cannot change reality one bit" (J, p. 83). For the husband, reality is incomprehensible; as for the reader, he imagines his own.

Now basing my version of the work on the elements provided by the text, I shall suggest that, acting as catalyst for the husband's feelings, the incident of the centipede haunts him and the reader both. In killing the beast that proved so distasteful to A. . ., Franck has usurped the function of the husband. The manner in which references to the insect are developed in the text punctuates the rise of jealousy. It appears first as a blackish spot (p. 27), then as a trace (p. 50). Immediately after another mention of a "dark spot" there is a close-up, detailed description of the spot, which reveals the outline of the centipede with some remnants still clinging to the wall (p. 56). The image gradually grows in intensity, each time generated by references to Franck. Then, provoked by Franck's offer to drive A. . . to town (or the memory of it), the husband gives a three-page description of the crucial scene (pp. 61–64), during which, after A. . .'s horrified exclamation, Franck rises from the dinner table, swats and kills the two-inch long centipede with his rolled napkin. The next three passing references (pp. 69, 70, 90) are associated with A. . . rather than Franck, as if some of the feelings against him had now been transferred, as an unspoken reproach for her having given Franck the occasion to display his superiority. And indeed, after A. . . returns from town late and appears unwilling to give many details about the hotel where she spent the night, the dinner incident is presented again, although in a more condensed version, with many statements of the first one reproduced verbatim (pp. 96–98). Another repetition is caused by the image of Franck's exuberant telling of the car breakdown that forced him and A. . . to spend the night in town, followed by the husband's fascination with Franck's voracious appetite. This description is much briefer, and it is supplemented by an account of A. . .'s reactions (pp. 112–113).

The gradual concentration of the narrative is matched by the rising intensity of the verbs used to characterize Franck's getting up: *se lève* (p. 63), *se met debout* (p. 97), and *se dresse* (p. 112). As the husband remembers himself being alone, waiting for Franck and his wife, the pangs of jealousy appear to have banished the thoughts of anyone but himself. When he goes over the incident a fourth time, the centipede has grown in size, it appears on the wall and is killed without the mention of any human being (pp. 127–129). A spot on the tablecloth where Franck normally sits, reminder of his gusty eating habits, brings the reader back to a description of the evidence on the wall (p. 145). Later, there is another recollection of the dinner table incident, again without human beings, and this time the insect has become *gigantesque* (p. 163). Immediately afterwards, the final repetition is given. Completely crushed by jealousy and accepting A. . .'s unfaithfulness as a fact, the husband now pictures the scene as taking place not in his own dining room but in the hotel, where he imagines Franck and A. . . together in the same bedroom (pp. 165–166). It is then that he imagines the automobile crash, that is, he wishes they were dead. Upon the reality that one cannot change, the husband (or, more accurately, the reader) has superimposed an untold but present story of growing intimacy, adultery, and the deserved death of the culprits. The centipede is the major generative correlative of this piece of fiction, which develops in the mind of the reader much more than it does in the text; it is as unstated as the husband himself.

The liminary statement of *Dans le labyrinthe* (1959) openly warns the reader: *"The following narrative is a fiction."* This might be interpreted as being no more than the usual disclaimer of intentional similarities, as the story is told against the background of military defeat and foreign occupation of a city. More likely, it affirms the preponderence of the imaginary level of the fiction, as I have defined it earlier. As in *La Jalousie*, the "takes" are exclusively from the mind of a single character. This time, however, the narrator and main character are fused into one, and for the first time in Robbe-Grillet's fiction the narrator says "I"—although not often. His identity is not revealed; many have assumed he is a doctor, although he himself implies that he is not "a real doctor" (L, p. 212). Very little belongs to the realistic level: a room with its dusty furniture and drapes, a couple of objects on a dresser and a table, and an engraving on the wall. The narrator appears to be in the room, perhaps ill, or simply resting; perhaps he is even dying. One of the objects he sees is in the shape of a cross. In conjunction with the book's title, and remembering that some labyrinths were shaped like a cross (the allusion being to the inscrutable nature of the divinity), it suggests the idea that Robbe-Grillet is enjoying his role as inscrutable author. Be that as it may, another object, a box on the dresser and the engraving labeled "La Défaite de Reichenfels" are the generative correlatives that set the narrative in motion.

Rayner Heppenstall has suggested that of all the works of Raymond Roussel *La Vue* was probably the most influential where Robbe-Grillet was concerned.[8] Indeed, the original title for *Le Voyeur* had been *La Vue*, and as far as his fourth fictional work is concerned the creative analogy between the miniature photograph in Roussel's pen and the Reichenfels engraving is hard to dismiss. That engraving also functions as a metaphor of the text in which it appears. It represents neither a battle scene nor the remnants of an army fleeing in defeat but shows the interior of a café, crowded with customers—bourgeois, working men, a young boy, and three soldiers. For the picture's caption to make sense, one must imagine events that are not depicted and create relationships linking them to the café scene. That is apparently what the narrator does or attempts to do in mentally isolating the box wrapped in brown paper and imagining a story to explain its presence in the room, using characters from the engraving, mainly a soldier and the boy (who holds a box smaller to the one in the room), and assuming the contemporary reality of the defeat implied by the caption. This idea, the source of the story narrated in *Dans le labyrinthe*, is after all basic to the very concept of fiction or myth. It is an attempt to explain the existence or appearance of a phenomenon that the mind, at that moment, cannot rationally comprehend. Thus myths are born to account to primitive people for the sun's daily rising in the east, stories are told to children to explain how the leopard acquired its spots, and tales are elaborated to convince people that they must fight a war.

In this book, the reader is made to witness a mode of the creative process itself, of which the title also gives a representation. The writer is pictured as a man caught in the maze of a labyrinth and stubbornly attempting to find his way out. He tries one corridor, or one sentence, sees that it leads nowhere, discards it, tries another, and yet another, believes himself to be on the right path, then takes a wrong turn, is stuck again, experiments with several possibilities, stops to reflect every now and then, again finds himself making apparent progress for a while, runs smack into another dead end, and so on. Robbe-

Grillet is not the first to have linked the concept of the labyrinth with a book, and it may well be that he was intrigued by
one of Jorge Luis Borges' short stories, "El Jardín de Senderos
que se bifurcan" (1941). In that story, however, Ts'ui Pên has
written a book that is a labyrinth; that is, he has set forth and
explored all the possibilities that could come out of a given
situation. Obviously, Marguerite Duras, for instance, chose
to have the narrator of *Le Marin de Gibraltar* abandon his
mistress and follow Anna. Claude Simon chose to let the captain
be killed in *La Route des Flandres*. Both must then abide by
their choice, which determines what follows, but Ts'ui Pên refused to choose. He imagined that a man could both be killed
in a battle and come out of it alive, simultaneously, and his
fiction would examine both outcomes. Naturally, subsequent
actions were pregnant with a variety of consequences, all of
which needed to be explored. The ramifications are infinite.
The possibility of such a book's being in existence dazzles the
mind. A fiction to end all fiction, it might be thought of in terms
of an impossible ideal or of a temptation to be desperately
avoided. In Borges' story, the labyrinth was meant for the
reader; in Robbe-Grillet's fiction, it is something from which
the narrator must escape in order to make creation possible.

At the outset of *Dans le labyrinthe*, he tries several weather
settings: "Outside it is raining . . . outside it is cold, the wind
blows through black, leafless branches; the wind blows through
the leaves. . . . Outside the sun is shining . . ." (p. 9). None of
them seems adequate, and he muses a moment, letting his gaze
wander over the furniture in the room, particularly over the
dust that covers much of it (or the dust that he imagines) and
the imprints left by objects that have been displaced. He is
perhaps struck by the analogy between dust and snow, and he
essays another setting: "Outside it is snowing" (p. 11). That
seems better, the story is off on the right track, generated by a
speck of dust. Still, he is unsure of himself and allows the
imaginary narrative to dissolve into the realistic fiction of the

room once more. During this pause he realizes somehow that his narrative requires more snow than the beginning flurries he had envisioned: "Outside it is snowing. Outside it has been snowing, it was snowing, outside it is snowing. Thick flakes are coming down slowly, in a steady, uninterrupted fall" (p. 14). Gradually, the pieces fit into place: the soldier waits in the snow, the package under his arm; the picture comes to life, and the boy talks to the soldier; they both walk in the snow-covered streets, all seemingly identical, seeking their way in a city that resembles a labyrinth; the soldier walks alone, he knows he is supposed to deliver the box to someone, somewhere.

As the story takes shape in the narrator's mind, it is not always apparent to the reader which sequence replaces a previously discarded one, which should be inserted earlier in the series than where it appears, and which brings the narrative closer to its goal, that is, the appearance of the box in the narrator's room, thus closing the circle. Occasionally the writer is caught in a tighter maze and a number of false starts (for example, pp. 96–97), are punctuated by "No," but in most cases the reader is on his own and must use his imagination. Eventually, the soldier is wounded by machine-gun bullets fired by enemy patrols entering the city and is brought into a nearby building, where the narrator, unaccountably, gives some assistance. The soldier dies of his wounds, and the box is entrusted to the narrator, along with a bayonet that did not belong to the soldier, The narrator, perhaps, will see to having its contents delivered to the appropriate person: letters, an old watch with a chain, a ring, and another bayonet—that is, if one assumes that those objects are part of the ,realistic rather than the imaginary fiction, something the reader must decide for himself if he thinks it matters. Wherever it belongs, this is the third book in which a watch appears in a significant context, an interesting objective correlative to Robbe-Grillet's manipulation of chronology. (The watch comes with a chain, suggesting perhaps the way one's mind has become enslaved by clock time.) The book ends, in a manner reminiscent of Samuel Beckett's *Molloy*, with a denial of the fiction that has been elaborated, a reprise of a statement discarded on the first page: "Outside it is raining. Outside people are walking in the rain, heads bowed" (p. 219).

One begins to sense, in *Dans le labyrinthe*, a slight shift of emphasis in Robbe-Grillet's fiction. With the generative correlatives more openly displayed, the focus is now on the creative process (which is itself shown as being less "creative" than "generative") and consequently on the functioning of language. From now on, I no longer believe that metaphors and myths will be dismissed or used negatively. Instead of criticizing them for their failure to reveal any depth or truth (quite the contrary) concerning "human nature," Robbe-Grillet or his texts will present them for what they are—surface elements that play a role in our culture. It may be that the unexpected and misdirected critical success of *Dans le labyrinthe*,[9] the ease with which it was appropriated by middle-class culture, the metaphysical interpretations it allowed, all convinced him that a change was in order, hence accelerating the evolution. If readers would not realize that they were injecting their own phantasms into the fiction, as they were somewhat ironically invited to do, that meant that the text was not functioning properly. From implications pointing to a sclerosed culture, which seemed to preoccupy Robbe-Grillet at the time of *Les Gommes*, it is a short step to being concerned over the social and political consequences of such sclerosis of mind and imagination. It is of course hard to even dissociate the one from the other, ad I shall certainly draw no conclusions with respect to Robbe-Grillet's own political awareness.

Two liminary statements, on successive pages, confront the reader of *La Maison de rendez-vous* (1965). The first is much like the conventional disclaimer, denying any similarity between the fiction and actual life in Hong Kong. It corresponds to the realistic level. The second, claiming for the "author" a life-long acquaintance with Hong Kong, affirms authenticity and suggests that skeptical readers might have another look, for things change fast in such climates. Ironically, the affirmation of authenticity corresponds to the imaginary (which might now be called mythical) level, the same on which the statement, "Everyone knows Hong Kong" (M, pp. 13, 141) is made. Indeed, everyone today has "seen" Hong Kong and many other far-away places as well by means of photographs, films, essays, and reporting. What they have seen, of course, is a distorted representation, a series of myths, and that distortion is conveyed by the interplay of liminary statements. Even more than in *Dans le labyrinthe* the imaginary level predominates. The other level is glimpsed only through a few scattered references, the most extensive of which describes a visitor at the bed of a sick person, a Frenchwoman born in Belleville (a working-class section of Paris) who has never been to the Orient, but to whom stories about Hong Kong have been told—as they have been to all readers. While in the preceding work it was possible to establish a plausible link from one level of the fiction to the other, this is much more difficult here, and I doubt that it would be rewarding.

Again, there is a first-person narrator or there might possibly be three of them. The basic narrator, the one who says "I," is the visitor at the sick bed, and it is also he who, at first, seems to be telling the story that centers in the high-class brothel run by Lady Ava (or Bergmann) in Hong Kong and the incidents that occurred during one (or several) parties followed by peculiar theatrical performances, which involve drug smuggling, prostitution, and shady political intrigue—all things one likes to think of and enjoy, provided they take place at a considerable remove from one's own life. Also at the party, which is part of the imaginary aspect of the fiction and as such not subject to laws of contradiction and which might or might not have taken place in Hong Kong, there is a fat man who has lived in the British Crown Colony and talks about it a great deal. He is at one point called "the narrator" (p. 106) and at another the person I have designated as the basic narrator implies, in an aside, that he is merely transcribing the narration. "The fat man with a ruddy complexion expatiates with self-indulgent precision on excesses committed under those circumstances, then he continues his tale" (p. 168). He is apparently the "author" mentioned in the second liminary statement and also the one who has been telling stories to the sick woman.

Now things become a bit more complicated: the main character of the imaginary fiction could well be a man named Johnson (or is it Jonstone?), who is either Sir Ralph known as "the American" or the American known as "Sir Ralph" (every person or event is open to question). He has become infatuated with a girl named Loren or Loraine, who is either a prostitute or the fiancée of one Marchat or Marchand, whom she may or may not have abandoned in favor of Johnson or Jonstone. He is about to leave for Macao and wants to take Loren with him, but she will consent only in exchange for a large sum of money (everything today is a commodity) which he must put up before dawn, according to one version of the events, and the basic narrator appears to be describing his frantic efforts to do so. Soon after leaving Lady Ava's party he is stopped by the police because his behavior looks suspicious. Upon being asked to account for his actions that evening he explains, "I arrived at the Blue Villa by taxi at about ten after nine" (p. 96)—the identical words the basic narrator had used seventy-odd pages earlier (p. 23), and he repeats, verbatim, over half a page of that previous account, followed by "etc." Bruce Morrissette had, before *La Maison de rendez-vous* was written, brought up, in connection with *Les Gommes*, the ancient myth of Ouroboros, the dragon or serpent that bites its own tail. One is now confronted with a narrative that curls upon itself, bites its own tail, and even begins to swallow it. But who is the narrator?

After being questioned by police, Johnson and/or the narrator takes the ferry to Kowloon, stops at his hotel, goes to visit someone else, returns to the hotel, takes the ferry back to Hong

Kong, grabs a taxi, and arrives at Lady Ava's Blue Villa at 9:10, just in time for the party he had already left some time ago. It should be obvious that, from a standard critical viewpoint, the domain of *La Maison de rendez-vous* is not merely that of the imaginary but that of the fantastic. If one had previously witnessed the birth of fiction, he now is treated to the spectacle of fiction on the rampage. It might not be irrelevant to begin asking whether or not standard critical viewpoints are still relevant. Actually, what takes place in this text is not far removed from the uncensored workings of the inner mind and the peculiar logic of dreams. If Freud and Jacques Lacan are right, that is also the logic of language. The narrative of *La Maison de rendez-vous* is an avatar of surrealist texts—not automatic writing, but what one might call subconscious fiction, skillfully reorganized. One comes ever closer to the concept of fiction held by the writers of *Tel Quel*. As Philippe Sollers had said, in an essay on Robbe-Grillet written in 1962, that is, some time before *La Maison de rendez-vous* was published: "Only through composition does one avoid the absurd banality of description."[10] Representation of "reality" gives way before composition in language.

The Blue Villa is not the exclusive center of the fiction. It is the *maison de rendez-vous* of the title, a euphemism for brothel, but there is also a *maison du rendez-vous* (M, p. 69), the shift from partitive to definite article restoring the phrase's literal meaning, the house where the meeting took place. It is the house where Edouard Manneret lives—a name close enough to that of Edouard Manet to make one take note. Perhaps the oblique reference is intended as an hommage to the painter's style. A general resemblance of the scene on Lady Ava's amateur stage that shows Manneret lying dead on the floor (p. 73) to Manet's "Le Torero mort" lends some justification to the idea. (Robbe-Grillet has told me that it was Manet's portrait of Mallarmé that he had in mind, rather than "Le Torero mort." It might thus have generated some of the scenes in *la maison*

du rendez-vous instead of those of Lady Ava's stage. He further
pointed out that in using the name "Manneret," in which the
second syllable would normally be elided when spoken, he also
thought of the surrealist photographer Man Ray.) In general,
however, allusions to painting are few. Photographic and sculp-
tural correspondences are numerous, following a trend begun
with *Les Gommes* and *Le Voyeur*. Descriptions and actions in
Robbe-Grillet's imaginary fiction often dissolve into or emerge
from other representations. A magazine picked up by a street
cleaner bears pictures of Lady Ava's party that come alive in
the same manner the Reichenfels engraving did in *Dans le
labyrinthe*; sculptures on the grounds of the Blue Villa represent scenes that take place at the party and elsewhere. Such
scenes are apt to merge either with the garden sculptures or
with porcelain likenesses found in a show case in Lady Ava's
salon or even with baroque sculptures in the Tiger Balm Garden
of Hong Kong. Thanks to the stage in the Blue Villa, theatrical
references are plentiful; some scenes are so depicted as to make
it difficult to determine at once whether they take place on the
stage, in a store window, or as part of the imaginary narrative.
Clearly, Robbe-Grillet planned things that way, in order to lay
stress on the predominant role of imagination and myth—both
within the text and in life.

In spite of the shift in emphasis to which I have called attention, similarities with earlier works are numerous. The detective-story plot involving the murder of Manneret (he is
killed four separate times in at least four different fashions—
strangled by a dog, shot by Johnson, stabbed by a detective and
assassinated by communists) recalls *Les Gommes*. Marchat also
comes from *Les Gommes*. He had fled the city, fearing for his
life, and four books and many thousands of miles later he meets
with death in Hong Kong. He should have remembered the
tale of the appointment in Samara and stayed put. There are
several "frozen" scenes and a silent one like those in *Le Voyeur*.
The sadistic eroticism of the book is carried much further. In

addition to many sexually oriented images or descriptions, it culminates in the story of the young Japanese prostitute Kito, who is both a new recruit at Lady Ava's brothel and one who must have been there a long time (if one insists upon chronological reality). She is a guinea pig for the strange experiments of Manneret and others, during one of which she dies or is killed, ending up with her flesh served to amateurs of exotic sensations in one of the floating restaurants in Aberdeen—all of that being quite congruent with what the middle-class imagination often sees in the Orient. A small alarm clock, heir to the watches that were important in three other narratives, plays a part in one of the murders of Manneret. A couple of times, a scene is interrupted with an exclamation, *"Mais non!"* (M, pp. 143, 177), similar to the interruptions of *Dans le labyrinthe* (and also to the more explicit ones of Beckett's *Malone meurt*). During one of his attempts to raise money, Johnson is mistaken for a doctor, as the narrator of the preceding book had been by readers. To the ironic statement of *La Jalousie*, "Things are what they are," Robbe-Grillet now provides the necessary complement: "Things are never definitively straightened out" (p. 209). He joins the many other twentieth-century writers who keep affirming that reality is less important than the mythical order we impose upon it and, implicitly, that all of us have the power to change that order.

In *La Maison de rendez-vous*, above the apartment of the woman from Belleville, there lived a man, perhaps a madman, who was called King Boris and whose metal-studded cane could be heard through the ceiling. Those two people are the only remnants of the realistic side of the story. Toward the end of *Projet pour une révolution à New York* (1970), someone I shall call the narrator-interrogator asks concerning a rapping noise coming from above: "You are not really going to suggest that it is King Boris?" (p. 209)—thereby completely eradicating the realistic element. In *La Maison*, there is unresolved hesitation as to the identity of the narrator; in this one, there is hardly any doubt as to his nonexistence. If characters were ambiguous then, it has now become irrelevant to discuss them as such, Everything is being carried one step further, although ingredients and technique are very similar to those used in *La Maison de rendez-vous*.

Robbe-Grillet, on the surface, does not seem to have given up the narration. It would be possible to tell the story of *Projet pour une révolution à New York*—actually one could tell several stories—even though that might involve a number of contradictions or implausibilities, but it would not reveal too much about the book. Narration is important only because of Robbe-Grillet's concern for myths. Like the characters of *Les Gommes*, most people, if not all, are mythomaniacs of one sort or another. One more or less unconsciously accepts the myths of his society, of his class, the kind Roland Barthes examined in *Mythologies*,[11] those that constitute the stuff of one's daily life. While in his earlier fiction Robbe-Grillet had seemed more intent on showing the workings of myth, the evolution I mentioned previously is now complete, and in his most recent one he is simply working with myths. As in the case of Hong Kong, everyone knows New York, especially those who have never been there, through a series of stereotyped myths transmitted by means of consumer books and consumer movies. Robbe-Grillet uses them in a similar manner, adding some American myths to those accepted by outsiders, especially as they impose themselves on the minds of the middle class after the riots of the sixties in Watts, Detroit, and Newark. Those he has also supplemented with what appear to be his own obsessions. I refer to the erotico-sadism that I have already discussed in connection with previous works. While themes of such nature blend remarkably well with other elements of the book, I find them bothersome and unpleasant— thus probably revealing the extent to which taboos of Western middle-class culture can still control one's reactions. In any case, the book need not be reduced to a display of sadistic acts; they are part of the functioning of the text, and their links with reality are tenuous at best.

As in *L'Inquisitoire* by Robert Pinget, what I have called the narrator-interrogator has a purely grammatical function; their or its operation is even more problematic than in Pinget's book. Early in *Projet pour une révolution à New York* there appears to be a first-person narrative. A narrator is describing how he leaves his house pausing at the door to look back, contemplating the imitation wood-grain on the door, and beginning to imagine things. The process is a familiar one for the reader who is acquainted with the previous books. Various narratives follow. Eventually, the original narrator who walks along the street and then down a subway entrance, returns. Later, one is disconcerted to find the narrator referred to in the third person; then a narrative involving a girl called JR begins in the third person and switches to the first. In this instance the "I" is naturally feminine (the French rule for the agreement of past participles has some usefulness), but it suddenly becomes masculine again without any apparent change of character or locale. Finally, toward the end of the book, after many shifts in the narrative, the narrator is "identified" as one N. G. Brown, whom the reader remembers from his description as having been seen, on page 11, *by* the narrator as he looked at or through the door.

If the reader now thinks he can straighten that one out with a certain amount of careful rereading, he is in for another jolt. On the last page of the book, a character known as M, who was first shown as a hoodlum, then as a murderer who has been terrifying subway riders, and is now called "M the vampire," removes his rubber mask and is recognized as the narrator—whoever that is. In the meantime, some characters have been interrogating others, and soon enough an interrogative voice arises that challenges the text itself. Since the characters are no more amenable to positive identification than the narrator, it seems practical to refer to a narrator-interrogator as subject of the story, identifiable with whatever character each narrative segment deals with and serving to weld the text together.

As a magazine cover in *La Maison de rendez-vous* dissolved into a scene at Lady Ava's house, here the lurid paperback cover of a detective story, lighted in such a fashion as to deceive a man who is peeping through the keyhole, comes to life in the house behind the door. There are a number of such books lying around the house that is central to the story. There is also a girl named Laura (there may even be three of them) who is perhaps sequestered there. The assumption the narrator-interrogator makes about the way she reads those novels appears as a clue to the arrangement of narratives in the book, a metaphor of its fictional architecture: "Laura read all those books at the same time, thus mingling, as she moved from room to room, the detective adventures so meticulously calculated by the authors, therefore constantly modifying the composition of each volume, furthermore leaping a hundred times a day from one book to another, not fearing to go over the same passage several times, even though it be lacking in any apparent interest, while completely neglecting the essential chapter, the one containing the crux of an investigation and thus giving its meaning to the whole of the plot" (P, p. 85). It is "the labyrinth of her diseased mind" that organizes the fiction of which she is a part, and it in turn reflects the diseased state of a class in society that is tortured by its own fears.

At a subversive underground meeting—which actually is held underground—it is explained that the color "red" is the solution to the antagonism between "black" and "white". The three main variations on the theme are rape, fire, and murder. Later, however, the narrator-interrogator explains that these are "metaphorical acts" and, anyway, a revolution thus brought about through selective violence will be far less costly in human lives than the standard indiscriminate variety. The quoted phrase, followed by such a preposterous but amusing argument, again emphasizes that we are dealing with phantasms and myths rather than with reality. Abundant contradictions in the text confirm this. Typical is the one involving JR, who is presented as "a gorgeous white girl, endowed with abundant red hair that was most effective in bedroom scenes" (p. 57) and who proclaims, when the narrator-interrogator asks her if she is

Jewish, "No, not at all; I am a black woman from Puerto Rico" (p. 103). Robbe-Grillet is obviously enjoying himself.

In reading this book one becomes aware of a conflict between one's conventional reading habits (that is, one's tendency to view the text as a representation of reality, one's prejudice in favor of linear narrative) and the actual functioning of the text, of a language where signifiers play a part more important than that of the signified. The tension one feels is between comfortable appearances one hates to give up and a disturbing reality one is reluctant to face. The clash is also one between the "readable" and the "writable," to adopt Roland Barthes's terminology. Readable texts are those "caught within the Western system of closure, put together according to the aims of that system, slavishly conforming to the laws of the Signified"; those that are "writable" endeavor "to make of the reader no longer a consumer but a producer of the text."[12] Faced with *Projet pour une révolution à New York*, the consumer is likely to sit back, commenting on the preposterous nature of the fiction, secretly enjoying what he thinks of as sexy descriptions, and perhaps reflecting on Robbe-Grillet's lack of seriousness. The producer, while agreeing that Robbe-Grillet is not afflicted with what Sartre has sarcastically called *esprit de sérieux*, will work on the language of the text, especially on the signifiers, perhaps along the lines suggested by Ricardou in his essay on *Projet pour une révolution à New York*.[13] That in itself will bring no one closer to "revolution" in New York or elsewhere. It might contribute to a change in one's attitude towards language, hence perhaps one's perception of reality, a goal shared by many other contemporary writers.

NOTES TO CHAPTER NINE (Robbe-Grillet)

[1] Paul Valéry, "Introduction à la méthode de Léonard de Vinci," in *Œuvres*, Bibliothèque de la Pléiade (Paris: Gallimard, 1957), I, 1165.

[2] Alain Robbe-Grillet, "Une Voie pour le roman futur," in *Pour un nouveau roman*, pp. 15–23. Henceforth all references to works by Robbe-

232   FRENCH FICTION TODAY

Grillet appear in the body of the text with the following abbreviations: *Les Gommes*, G; *Le Voyeur*, V; *La Jalousie*, J; *Dans le labyrinthe*, L; *La Maison de rendez-vous*, M; *Projet pour une révolution à New York*, P. See Bibliography for complete references.

[3] Bruce Morrissette, "Œdipe ou le cercle fermé: *Les Gommes*," in *Les Romans d'Alain Robbe-Grillet* (Paris: Minuit, 1963), pp. 37–75.

[4] Their disagreement actually extends beyond *Les Gommes*. See Roland Barthes's preface to the book by Morrissette.

[5] Cf. my essay on "The Embattled Myths," in a volume edited by Frederic Will, *Hereditas* (Austin: University of Texas Press, 1964), pp. 77–94.

[6] Olga Bernal, *Alain Robbe-Grillet: le roman de l'absence* (Paris: Gallimard, 1964), p. 51.

[7] Gérard Genette, "Vertige fixé," in *Figures* (Paris: Seuil, 1966), p. 76.

[8] Rayner Heppenstall, *Raymond Roussel, A Critical Study* (Berkeley: University of California Press, 1967), p. 25.

[9] "*Dans le labyrinthe* then sold 15,000 copies the first year, and I was often much more taken aback by the praise bestowed on the *Labyrinthe* than by the objections to *La Jalousie*." Statement made by Robbe-Grillet in an interview with J. J. Brochier, "Robbe-Grillet: mes romans, mes films et mes ciné-romans," *Magazine Littéraire*, No. 6 (April 1967), p. 12.

[10] Philippe Sollers, "Sept Propositions sur Alain Robbe-Grillet," in *L'Intermédiaire* (Paris: Seuil, 1963), p. 149.

[11] Roland Barthes, *Mythologies* (Paris: Seuil, 1957).

[12] Roland Barthes, S/Z (Paris: Seuil, 1970), pp. 14, 10.

[13] Jean Ricardou, "La Fiction flamboyante," in *Pour une théorie du nouveau roman* (Paris: Seuil, 1971), pp. 211–233.

CHAPTER TEN

Claude Ollier

La Mise en scène (1958), Claude Ollier's first published fictional work, is set in the mountains of Morocco at a time when the French still ruled North Africa, in an area that has supposed not yet been mapped. An engineer named Lassalle has been sent to this remote section to determine the best location for a road that will lead to a mine. He proceeds to his destination, pitches a tent near a village in the sector called Imlil, does an apparently successful job, and returns. It is soon clear, however, that he has failed in something much more important than his overt assignment, for the outline I have just given reflects only one aspect of the book. Before he has read very far into the narrative, the reader experiences a tension between Lassalle's success story and the far less happy one of a geologist named Lessing, whose activities resulted in two deaths, probably two murders.

Contributing to the tension is Ollier's ability to create an atmosphere of anxiety and suspense, to infuse the narrative with a compelling aura of mystery. The opening chapter, related in the third person and in the present tense, describes a nameless man during a wakeful night alone in his room in what is obviously a tropical or subtropical country. He is bothered by the heat and by mosquitoes; he has slept some but has been awakened by the light of the moon entering his room. This must be his first night in the region, for he remembers and worries about the various animals against which he had been warned—many varieties of spiders, some poisonous, that might come down to his bed from the ceiling, all sorts of snakes, some harmless, others not, that might be wriggling up his bed sheet and whose presence he imagines. He actually sees a large insect, perhaps a spider, crawling fortunately on the outside of his window screen but ominously present nevertheless. Lighting his candle after hearing an unusual noise under the bed, he also sees and identifies a dangerous scorpion, which he chases but fails to kill. During the second chapter one learns that this man, whose name is just now given as Lassalle, is at a place called Assameur, which is practically the end of the line for Europeans, where there is a small contingent of officers and men of the French military administration. Through his conversation with the captain in charge of the area, his innocence is further emphasized. He does not know the language of the country. He is also not aware that Lessing has recently gone through Assameur, headed for the same region of Imlil.

Later in the day Lassalle becomes temporarily lost in the town when a dense crowd separates him from his guide. He is at a major intersection, called both *carrefour* and *rond-point* in the French text, and he calmly decides to wait until his guide, who will surely notice his absence, returns for him. But at that point something happens in the narrative, which had so far proceeded chronologically. One is told that this is the same intersection where the captain had previously brought Lassalle to meet his guide, an army sergeant. The scene is narrated briefly, and immediately it appears to be told a second time. That, however, is just a passing illusion; what has taken place is a replay of a scene earlier that morning when the captain greeted Lassalle outside his office before driving him to town. The captain's gait and gestures are identical in both instances—or better, since one is dealing with narrative rather than reality, the words used in each case are the same. Recalling those words apparently is what gives impetus to a section of the text that had been "censored": the account of the drive, during which the captain and Lassalle, attracted by a small crowd, stop at a first-aid station and see the body of Jamila, a young Moroccan girl, who has been fatally stabbed. The flashback ends when they arrive at the intersection in town, and the sergeant waves to the captain. In truth, he waves to Lassalle, not the captain, for the sergeant has indeed returned as soon as he had noticed that he was alone—just as he had been expected to do. Again, as at the beginning of the sub-narrative, the words used to describe the two scenes are identical. It seems almost as though the flashback had been inserted into a crack in the main narrative, lasting but a fraction of a second.

That same day, Lassalle is furnished military transportation to the next town, where the road actually stops and where he spends the night with a guard who is the last representative of the French administration. The latter tells about another engineer who had come through two years earlier, on the same assignment as Lassalle's and for the same concern, but who did not succeed in finding a satisfactory route. The main character's inexperience, the failure of his predecessor, the dangers that abound—everything confirms the reader in his feelings that some kind of catastrophe will ensue. He is kept off balance, nevertheless, for he becomes less and less sure of the form it will take. He first expects it to be directly related to Lassalle's assignment; then, as other factors are introduced into the narrative, he may think that Lassalle will meet with physical harm, or even death. Only gradually does he realize that his failure might be of a very different sort.

To the *rond-point* in Assameur corresponds a major turning point in the text. One becomes aware of the existence of two distinct narratives: the main (or surface) narrative and a secondary one that could be called latent, censored, or subconscious. The latent narrative is present in the introductory and concluding chapters of the book. Readers are most likely to notice it first in the flashback passage of Assameur, and it manifests itself a number of times throughout the book. Characteristically, Lassalle's name is invariably "censored" out of the text during the course of the latent narratives.

The immediate effect of the interplay between surface and latent narratives is to contribute to the tension experienced by the reader. It also introduces a textual operation that is even more important. The basis for that operation is the description of Jamila, which is given in the latent Assameur narrative. The position of the girl's head, her black braids, green eyes, and silver necklace are among the elements of a verbal set that is reinserted, with modifications, in subsequent latent narratives and applied either to the dead Jamila or to a live Yamina, whom Lassalle sees in Imlil. Some phrases also emerge into the surface narrative and are applied to younger girls. Other segments in the narrative function in similar fashion; their convergence is directed at a point where Jamila is identified with Yamina (who, in the meantime, had been linked to Lessing), Lassalle with Lessing; and the two stories merge into one.

It becomes clear as one progresses through the book that scenes that are recollections of the past, products of the imagination, or dreams are part of the latent narrative and correspond to periods of concern or anxiety. Matter-of-fact descriptions of the present belong to the surface narrative and represent periods of calm and indifference, only occasionally disturbed by the appearance of brief segments from the latent texts. From a rhetorical point of view, the handling of descriptions resemble that of Robbe-Grillet. In *La Jalousie*, however, the concern was readily interpreted as being of the nature of a pathological obsession. Lassalle's anxiety reflects an unspecified feeling of guilt, and his indifference is based on selfishness and ignorance—all of which can be found in the text as much as in the reader's imagination.

The appearance of the stabbed Moroccan girl early in the book represents not so much a threat against the innocent

engineer in his present assignment as it does an opportunity
to become aware of what is happening in the world, particularly
in a country subjugated by a foreign power. In the market
place at Assameur, he has watched a native use a club to kill
a dog that had come to lick blood drippings from a butcher's
stall. If Lassalle does not, perhaps the reader will recall that
Moslems in North Africa sometimes used the word "dog" as
an insulting epithet for Christians. In Morocco, Lassalle exists
only as a Christian, a representative of a foreign mining company, and as a protégé of the French military. Like Revel in
Michel Butor's *Emploi du temps*, he enters the locus of the
story out of an unspecified past and environment, returning
to the same unknown at the end. His experience might thus
be viewed as a microcosm of a man's life, in this instance a
man's life in a world dominated by colonialism. In the first
part of the book, comprising seven chapters, he is taken in
hand by the authorities: official French military ones at first,
then unofficial Moroccan ones in the person of one Ba Iken,
who speaks French because he has served in the French army
and could be viewed as a "collaborationist" of sorts. He meets
Lassalle on a mule path and is an indispensable unit in the
narrative as he knows everyone in the area, including *moqad-
dems* and *cheikhs*. The twenty-one chapters of the second part
see him through the completion of his engineering job, in
which he is assisted by a young native proposed by Ba Iken,
a twelve-year-old mute boy named Ichou. (Although there is
no formal subdivision, the three groups of seven chapters of
this central part serve to punctuate events of the narrative,
the crucial ones taking place in chapters VIII to XIV. This
also helps to call attention to the numbers 3 and 7, upon which
the architecture of the book is based.) A shorter third part,
of seven chapters like the first, takes the engineer back to
where he was on page one, although by a different route, which
suggests a circle—decidedly a common figure in contemporary
writing. Lassalle then experiences a metaphorical death.

The fate of the Moroccan girl arouses Lassalle's conscience

in an uncomfortable way, as evidenced by his momentary suppression of the first-aid station episode, for he is the intelligence of the text. He tries to find out the circumstances of her stabbing, but he can do so only indirectly. His contact with men, after he has left the small French outpost, is through Ba Iken. His isolation is further emphasized when he does not stay in the village at Imlil but must pitch his tent at some distance. Natives are generally fearful of him or openly hostile. Eventually, it is the mute Ichou who presents him with material evidence linking the stabbing of Jamila to the murder of the geologist and points to the probable culprit.

As the fatal journey of Lessing is clarified, however, textual transformations and latent narratives have been functioning as previously suggested. At the beginning of the book, Lessing's name sounded obviously German to Lassalle, hence typically foreign. As he progresses through his narrative, Lassalle must become increasingly aware of his own situation as a stranger (one might recall that Lassalle is the name of a German socialist of the nineteenth century), and, as parallels between his own story and that of Lessing increase in number, the phonetic resemblance between the two names becomes more significant. Lassalle comes to realize that he is as much responsible for the death of Jamila as Lessing was. Like Lessing, he, too, must die. His identification with the dead Lessing in the latent narrative at the end of the book signifies not only the end of his existence as a character in the narrative but the necessary death of a foreign presence in Morocco. He or the reader has come to this realization because the stage had already been set (*mise en scène*) by Lessing's dramatic journey—the latter was not named after a German playwright for nothing. The story operates as in Sartre's *Les Sequestrés d'Altona* (performed in the year following the publication of Ollier's book), where, through a representation of German behavior during the second World War, French audiences were led to an awareness of their own responsibilities for what was taking place in Algeria. In Ollier's book, however, the operation is far more subtle.

Curiously, *La Mise en scène* is told in the third person, but Lassalle is so constantly its central intelligence as to seem a narrator in disguise. Perhaps Claude Ollier needed to maintain a certain distance between himself and his main character, a certain indifference that is heightened by the impersonal style of much of the narrative. Perhaps, more objectively speaking, there is evidence here of the slow emergence of the text itself as subject at the same time as author and narrator lose their autonomous existence.

In *Le Maintien de l'ordre* the point of view seems at first to be identical. The reader then receives something of a jolt when he suddenly encounters the first-person pronoun "I" on page 28, at the end of the second chapter and realizes that he is dealing with a modified form of the first-person narrative. The pronoun does not appear again for the next ten pages and is used only about a dozen times throughout the book.

The locale and plot of this second work are very different, but theme and techniques are similar. Instead of out-of-the-way, uncharted territory, a large seaport, presumably Casablanca, constitutes the setting of *Le Maintien de l'ordre* (1961). The narrator, who is never identified, seems to be a minor official in the French civilian government of colonial Morocco. He has just uncovered some sort of torture chamber involving policemen as well as underworld extremists, but it seems that neither the underworld nor the authorities are eager to have a scandal break out openly. The former threaten, the latter mobilize the weights of inertia. The narrator is caught between his conscience and his fear, his duty and his security. This time, contrary to what happened in the previous book, the dilemma is not resolved. That evolution is again symptomatic of the gradual change in esthetics I have called attention to in other chapters. Ollier's concern in *La Mise en scène* for an externally polished architecture such as is reflected in the symmetrical order of chapters, for the perfect circular motion of the narrative, the concluding touch placed on the three actions (establishment of a route to the mine, the solution to the murders, Lassalle's unconscious and metaphorical identification with the dead Lessing)—all point toward an esthetics in which responsibility for the creative act is firmly centered in the author. The reader needs to play an active role, to be sure, but his is still a subordinate one. The author has clearly suggested his value judgments.

In *Le Maintien de l'ordre*, even though the author's hand was still too much in evidence for critics such as Jean Ricardou,[1] the burden is beginning to shift more toward the reader. There is no rigorous architecture to strike one at the outset, to suggest the striving for an accomplished masterpiece. A certain amount of symmetry is present (three numbered parts one comprising nine, the second seven, and the third nine unnumbered chapters), but its workings are more subtle. Also, the chronology of events is far less clear as the narrative swings back and forth between present and past, each time exploring a different level of the past. From that standpoint, the makings of a puzzle are certainly present, as they are in Robbe-Grillet's *La Jalousie*; but whereas Robbe-Grillet seems to have composed that work in such a way as to make a chronological reconstitution wellnigh impossible, Ollier gives the reader all the clues that are necessary for such a reconstitution. The reader must nevertheless take the initiative; he must make an effort that can be considered preliminary to, and also symbolic of, the true creative act. The first-person narrative enables him, in traditional fashion, to identify himself more closely with the nameless character and to re-create the ethical values of the story. He can feel the weight of the impersonal narrative segments as they establish the presence of the crooked former policemen and other events; all that tends to stifle the rare appearances of the personal "I". He can sense the shifting back and forth between the temptation to inaction and the weaker urge to moral action. The last word of the narrative is "tomorrow." While that might well allude to the impending liberation of Morocco from French rule, it is still up to the reader to decide what the narrator's tomorrow is made of—courage or indifference.

The oscillation also exists—one might even say that it is generated—on the textual level. First, one notices that verb tenses alternate between past and present (with a few refinements that need not be detailed here),[2] the latter corresponding to the more intense moments of fear. Second, there are, as in *La Mise en scène*, descriptive segments of text that are repeated with modifications. The very first paragraph of the book, while describing what can be seen from a window overlooking the port (it becomes clear, eventually, that this is the narrator's window), emphasizes the middle zone of the view, where it is hard to distinguish the sky from the sea, thus furnishing a correlative to the narrator's indecisive state of mind. It also establishes a kind of "vocabulary fund" to be drawn from in later descriptions, of which there are about seventeen. Two of these I am tempted to call focal points in the text. One is established when the narrator, who has been looking down toward the street to see if the two thugs (who have been shadowing him) are still there, jumps back to avoid being seen—and the open window then offers nothing but a "sudden vast glistening brightness."[3] The second is linked to his discovery of the torture chamber, when an outside door is opened, letting in "Raw, intense, blinding light" (O, p. 200). The first segment is correlative to the narrator's fear, the second to the scandal he has uncovered. There is also a second descriptive series that undergoes a metamorphosis, beginning with a passage in the second chapter that starts, "The lighthouse illuminated the room" (p. 27). It is taken up again about half a dozen times, ending with a mere flickering of the light. Here again the beams of light alternating with darkness represent the same psychological oscillation between fear (darkness) and scandal, that is, uncovering the truth (light). The two series, however, do not culminate in a specific message. The mere flickering of the light, in the last chapter, might seem pessimistic. On the other hand, the first series ends with "black" and "white" replacing the gray indistinctness of the initial paragraph, suggesting that a clear choice now exists.

Appropriately enough, considering the book's title, "staging" elements had played a dominant role in the narration of *La Mise en scène*. There was an abundance of both narrative and descriptive details, which were enhanced by two drawings inserted in the book (one is a map, the other a panoramic view of the Imlil sector). In *Le Maintien de l'ordre*, on the other hand, descriptions seem divorced from narration until one becomes aware of their textual role. One might perhaps say that the text begins to "speak" and to rival the narrator's voice. There is here a direct relationship between the style and changing vocabulary of the repeated descriptions on the one hand, and the meaning of the book on the other, while in Ollier's first fictional work meaning emerged more from thematic and narrative elements. The evolution continues with *Eté indien* (1963), accompanied by a return to the device of the third-person narrative, which allows the text to assume greater importance. Furthermore, there is no ethical problem to tug directly at the reader's conscience. He now begins to be more deeply involved in broader, essential questions involving meaning, language, and reality. From that standpoint, this book marks a turning point.

Generally speaking, the setting for *Eté indien* is a large city readily identifiable as New York. There is an introductory section that takes place in the tropics, presumably the Yucatan peninsula in Mexico, and a concluding one on a plane headed for those same tropics. The chief character, Morel, has been sent by a movie company to investigate the possibilities of making a film in Mexico, where it has some assets. He has planned a two-day stay in New York. On the level of the anec-

dote, the book deals with Morel's activities, part business, part
pleasure, in the city during the two days that become three
because he misses his plane. A reader who is familiar with
La Mise en scène clings to a repeated pattern. A man is sent
to a foreign country on a technical mission; he does not know
the language; before proceeding to a remote area, he is briefed
by an "expert" of sorts, a military man in the earlier book, a
professor of archaeology in this one. He then looks for hidden
elements to emerge on either side of the narrative. They do
not. Nor is Morel presented with a choice or threatened in
any way. He meets Cynthia, dates her, gets drunk, spends the
night with her, oversleeps, and has to postpone his departure.
That hardly upsets him; he just spends another day with Cynthia. The next thing one knows he is flying toward southern
Mexico, and the narrative ends as the plane comes down close
to its destination. Just before he had left New York it was
beginning to snow—the brief Indian summer was over.

One is puzzled and perhaps a bit disappointed. What happened? A more careful examination of the text is obviously
called for. As one goes over the introductory pages a second
time, they seem less "real" than before. Perhaps Morel, landing
at a New York airport, is projecting ahead to the event that
really matters—his arrival in the area of pre-Colombian pyramids. This seems all the more plausible as, later on, there are
several more flights of the imagination. One occurs as Morel's
subway emerges out of a tunnel and crosses the East River
on a bridge (E, pp. 81 ff.), with phrases and imagery strikingly
similar to that used in the introduction section. It is reassuring,
somehow, to feel that throughout the narrative one sees everything through Morel's consciousness—though not clearly. The
opening pages may also be a clue in suggesting that all of
Morel's subjective distortions are determined by his obsession
with scenarios to be set in Mexico. In other words, if the pattern of Ollier's first work still holds and the protagonist's stated
mission is only a pretext, one might look for significance in

those events that resist Morel's flights into the future. The only trouble is that almost everything encourages such flights: his exhaustion after the transatlantic plane flight, his tendency to get car sick, a low resistance to drink, a poor memory. And once all that has been stripped away from Morel, one discovers that Ollier's character is little more than absence of character. Here, again, the "void" that has haunted so much contemporary fiction is revealed as soon as the veneer of appearances has been peeled off. Actually, Morel is no more negative than the characters in his previous fiction. The concern that informed *La Mise en scène* and *Le Maintien de l'ordre* was communicated to the reader by the text much more than it was assumed by the characters. In the case of Morel, his emptiness invades the entire narrative as there is nothing to fill it, unless it be Cynthia.

Even his name does not ring true: it bears an aura of fiction, bringing to mind, in addition to a character out of Marcel Proust, the protagonists of Romain Gary's *Les Racines du ciel*, André Gorz's *Le Traître*, and Adolfo Bioy Casares' *The Invention of Morel*.[4] (Even the title of the book repeats that of an earlier work by Roger Vercel.) The people at the head office he seems responsible to are named Munch and Moritz. The identical initial letter recalls Samuel Beckett's parabolical naming of his personages. Moritz also rings another kind of bell: that was the name of the man who had gone to Imlil to make the initial survey two years before Lassalle, in *La Mise en scène*. This first clue to the unity of Ollier's fictional texts is given additional strength by Morel himself. When Cynthia shows him a number of snapshots either of herself or that she has taken, he can only show her two in exchange. On the first he is seen on a mule against the background of a rocky mountain terrain, and on the second he is walking along a narrow street with the sun beating against windowless white walls (pp. 190–191). The allusion to the earlier fiction is transparent; one begins to suspect that the same protagonist is involved in all three.

All this suggests that the "character" in Ollier's third fictional work has no more importance than the stories in which he is involved. The diminishing process has been a gradual one from Lassalle to Morel. One can reasonably argue that both plot and setting in *La Mise en scène* are closely connected with the anticolonial bias of the book, but in *Eté indien* plot, setting, and character are mere pretexts—decoys that attract the reader to the text itself. What happened to Lassalle between the beginning and the end of *La Mise en scène*, his identification with a dead Lessing, bore directly on the meaning. So little happens to Morel that one needs to look at the modifications of the text, not those of the character.

I have already indicated the role textual transformations play in the preceding fiction. Here the technique is the same, but it acquires greater significance as other elements lose theirs. The manner in which the introductory segment of the text undergoes a number of changes as it is disseminated through the pages of the book before being reassembled in different fashion in order to become its concluding section and a score of more or less distorted echoes that link other passages contribute to the assimilation of New York to the ruins of a pre-Colombian civilization in Mexico, just as Lassalle had previously been assimilated to Lessing. The difference is that now the reader is on his own. He may decide that the story presages the coming ruin of New York, of American capitalism, or of Western civilization; or he may simply enjoy a skillful linguistic performance. Above all, he should become more aware of the role of language and, more precisely, the textual development of a narrative in determining meaning.

L'Echec de Nolan (1967) relates the attempts an investigator makes at clarifying the circumstances surrounding the disappearance of a fellow investigator named Nolan, who was reported missing in a plane crash. He travels all the way up to a small village in Norway, within the Arctic Circle, to talk to the only known survivor of the catastrophe. What he learns or fails to learn leads him to seek out people who had been in contact with Nolan during some earlier episodes of his life. He goes to the Italian Alps, to Southern Spain, and finally to some Atlantic islands, but it seems that the deeper he probes the less he discovers. Finally, the narrative trails off on a note of ambiguity.

One common bond with his previous fiction stands out at once: the main character (unnamed, as in *Le Maintien de l'ordre*) is given an assignment in a foreign country (several countries in this instance), the language of which he does not know. He is given the assistance of guides or intercessors, but the amount of knowledge they impart is not in direct ratio to the apparent ease of communication—quite the contrary. In a more complex fashion, it recalls the pattern of *La Mise en scène*, in which Lassalle had learned nothing from the French army officer in Assameur, had been only partly enlightened by Ba Iken, whose native language was not French, and had glimpsed the truth thanks to Ichou, who was mute. The attitude toward language implied at this level is closely related to Maurice Blanchot's. Ollier makes it clear in *L'Echec de Nolan*, as the investigator describes the man he is questioning: "Groping for words, taking special care lest they go beyond the exact expression of his reawakening sensations, realizing in spite of everything that his words inveigle them, obliterate them, and strongly threaten, in substituting themselves for them, to abolish them forever" (p. 52). Negative properties of language, however, are not without positive values. As they black out external reality and confirm the difficulty there is in truly apprehending it, they create a new reality, which is not that of phenomena but of man's imagination. This should recall the myths Robbe-Grillet was concerned with, the "fantastic" aspects of his two most recent works of fiction, and also the *préciosité* of Giraudoux. As the narrator of *L'Echec de Nolan* describes the Norwegian peninsula where he has arrived, with the hamlet of Nö located at its tip, he places the name of that hamlet at the very end of his descriptive paragraph. He then adds, to emphasize the linguistic nature of the topography, as a separate paragraph, "Isolated at the end of a sentence" (p. 15). One is reminded of Giraudoux's sentence, which had been mistaken for a ship: "As I write these lines, we are off the coast of Timor Island. On an atoll, a Dutchman dressed in white stands at attention before what he thinks is a Dutch ship but is actually no more than a French sentence."[5]

Nolan, it appears, was on his way from New York to a tropical country when his plane crashed. As Jorgensen, the Norwegian survivor, recalls what he can of the last moments of the flight, the reader realizes he has seen those same words before. He discovers that words and phrases appearing on pages 59 and 60, for instance, come not from an earlier section of the same book but from the last two pages of *Eté indien*. Alerted by such echoes, he goes back over the previous pages and notices things that he had overlooked during the first reading. A photograph of Nolan that the investigator had brought, hoping Jorgensen would identify him turns out from its description (N, pp. 43–44) to be identical with the one Cynthia had taken of Morel in Battery Park (E, p. 93). The Statue of Liberty is in the background, and its torch is described as "what must be an object of worship," thus recalling the link between present-day New York and pre-Colombian temples that was established in *Eté indien*. Nolan's plane crashed on a trip identical with Morel's trip. Nolan reported missing the plane he had been scheduled to take, staying an extra day in New York, exactly as Morel did. Textual echoes reverberate again, as when words and phrases describing the road on which Jorgensen drives the investigator (N, p. 88) are the same as those used in the preliminary section of *Eté indien* (p. 10). When Jorgensen's daughter, Ingrid, drives him, the repetitions increase in length to include entire paragraphs from the previous work (N, p. 111; E, p. 203). The last phrase of the first part of *L'Echec de Nolan*, *A vau-vent*, is a distorted but unmistakable echo of the last one from *Eté indien*, *A vau-l'eau*—and the more carefully one goes back over the text, the more similarities one notices. All hesitations one might have had in identifying Morel with Nolan are swept aside when the investigator points out: "He never travelled under his real name. Each time there was a new one. A pseudonym" (N, p. 104).

Correspondences occurring at the level of the signified are not as interesting as those taking place at the level of signifier. The latter are an indication of Ollier's increasing interest in the textual aspect of the writing process, and they call attention to the composition of *L'Echec de Nolan*. In using the word "composition" I have in mind both its musical connotation and the strict, literal denotation given by Webster, namely, "The arranging of words to form sentences, paragraphs, verse, or other parts of any literary work or discourse." To this I should add, by way of emphasis, that words are considered in their totality, including signifier, signified, and what Roman Jakobson calls "the internal form," meaning by that "the semantic load of [their] constituents."[6]

I shall give one example of a musical type of composition. *L'Echec de Nolan* opens with what reads like a descriptive paragraph. It is followed by a scene during which the investigator waits for Jorgensen while Mrs. Jorgensen putters in her garden, and he rehearses the questions he will ask when her husband arrives. Some forty pages later, after the interview has proceeded without positive results and Jorgensen asks, "What more can I add without repeating what I already have said?" (p. 39), an embarrassing silence ensues. As the scene freezes, one's attention is called to the three faces seen by the investigator—Jorgensen's, his wife's, and his daughter's—and their relative positions with respect to the room he is in. Three points define a circle and the combination of circle and points bring to mind musical signs indicating that a piece is to be repeated from the beginning. After the phrase, "Repeating *da capo*" the initial descriptive paragraph is repeated, followed by a variation on the early scene, which eventually gets the interview going again, although in a different spirit.

Seen from a textual standpoint, *L'Echec de Nolan* no longer appears as the fourth link in a chain of fictional works where similar patterns and themes are repeated. It represents a systematic reworking of the basic ingredients of the preceding ones, in a spirit analogous to the one that prompted Jean Pierre Faye to rework elements of his first three books into *Analogues*. Obviously for work number 4 to function properly, the reader needs to be acquainted with numbers 1, 2, and 3. The text that is elaborated, or the story that is suggested by the fourth book (so far Ollier has always allowed the reader to extract a narratable anecdote from his fiction) will necessarily be affected by those elements taken from the other texts. Conversely, the latest text will also have a retroactive effect on the earlier ones. This is the process known as "intertextuality," which, like many things, has been with us for a long time, but only recently has begun to be systematically studied and practiced. Julia Kristeva has credited Mikhail Bakhtine with being the first to formulate the proposition that "Every text is built as a mosaic of quotations, every text is absorption and transformation of another text."[7] The broadest implications of that statement concerns one here only to the extent that contemporary writers have been prompted to do consciously what had previously been left, in large part, to chance. That is what Ollier does, "absorbing and transforming" his own texts into a new one. Instances of a more obvious and also somewhat traditional type of intertextual practice (its simplest form being the quotation, of which oustanding examples are in *Moby Dick*), as when André Breton absorbs a common French saying (*Tant va la cruche à l'eau . . .*) into the first sentence of the surrealist manifesto (*Tant va la croyance à la vie . . .*), are also found in Ollier. Ricardou, for instance, has noticed the transformation of a sentence from Flaubert's *Bouvard et Pécuchet* (*Comme il faisait une chaleur de 33 degrés, le boulevard Bourdon se trouvait absolument désert*) into the first sentence of Chapter IV in *La Mise en scène* (*Comme il fait une chaleur de quarante-cinq degrés, la grande rue d'Assameur se trouve absolument déserte*).[8]

L'Echec de Nolan can now be seen as working, in the parts entitled "First Report," "Second Report," and "Third Report," on the texts of Ollier's three previous works, but in reverse chronological order. The new text makes clear that Nolan is not only Morel, but, as was suggested in *Eté indien*, he is therefore also Lassalle and the anonymous narrator of *Le Maintien de l'ordre*. This raises the problem of the identity of the investigator in *L'Echec de Nolan*. The failure indicated by the title is his even more than Nolan's, for he sheds, on the level of the anecdote, little light on the latter's disappearance. It hardly makes sense, however, to suppose that Nolan has come back from the dead in order to investigate the circumstances of his own demise. And yet there are curious resemblances between the investigator and Nolan(s). Both have a poor memory, especially where names are concerned. Of his New York guide, all Morel remembers is that his initials are "J. J." Suddenly it comes back to him, the name must be Jurdle (E, p. 52). But that does not satisfy him, and he now decides the initials must be wrong. Between pages 121 and 131 he goes through most of the possibilities from Burdle to Wurdle and settles for the last one. In *L'Echec de Nolan* the investigator, on his Norwegian visit, designates his host's daughter as Astrid (p. 14), Sigrid (p. 21), and Rägnfrid (p. 22), before realizing that her name is Ingrid. Both the investigator and Nolan apparently require sexual diversion wherever they go. Morel has an affair with Cynthia. There are fairly transparent allusions to the investigator's having one with Ingrid; he clearly has one with Isa in Italy; and there is a curious interlude with Ida and Inez in Spain. Both men, of course, work for the same agency. Finally, there is a dream sequence during which the investigator relives an incident and rehears statements that are reproduced verbatim from *Eté indien*, in which the name Morel is replaced with Nolan and Jurdle with Jorgensen. In order to dream such a dream, the investigator would have to be Nolan, one would think. It would also follow that Jorgensen and J. J. are one and the same—but the problems ensuing from such

an identification are insolvable. Similar although lesser difficulties arise in the case of Jager, who could be the man the
narrator of *Le Maintien de l'ordre* referred to as "L," and in
the case of Jimenez, who is probably Ba Iken.

What these observations point to is that the problem cannot
be solved on the so-called realistic plane, where characters are
imagined as real flesh-and-blood people. One important clue
furnished in *L'Echec de Nolan* has yet to be mentioned: three
persons are listed as missing from the plane, and one of these
is Nolan. In other words, three Nolans have disappeared. More
important, they are not dead, they are missing. They have
always been "missing," for that matter. This is one instance
of the retroactive effect of this work on an earlier one, as it
deprives Lassalle of whatever "flesh" the reader gave him when
La Mise en scène stood alone. His metaphorical death at the
end of the narrative now acquires even greater dimensions.
He not only died as a character in that piece of fiction but his
death becomes correlative to the death of the concept of character in fiction. The catastrophe that was vaguely suggested
at the conclusion of *Eté indien* and affirmed in *L'Echec de
Nolan* has a double effect, establishing the "missing" or "absent"
nature of fictional characters, a trait already noticed in Morel,
and signifying that the only deaths connected with it were
those either of real people or of the realistic aspect of characters. What follows in *L'Echec de Nolan* is quite logical.
When a fourth Nolan emerges as the investigator, he is also the
nonexistent, impersonal narrator, having been absorbed by the
text to the extent of being deprived of every last vestige of
individuality, including the subject pronoun "he." The narrator
has given way to the text.

It would prove tedious to go into all the precise details of
the intertextual process as it develops between the "Second
Report" and *Le Maintien de l'ordre*, the "Third Report" and
La Mise en scène. Suffice it to say that the pattern outlined
for the "First Report" is developed to an even greater degree.
So far, however, I have ignored the investigator's visit to those

tropical islands in the Atlantic, supposedly the scene of Nolan's first mission. It is a baffling episode if the pattern of "reincarnations" is accepted, for it does not correspond to any of Ollier's published fiction. Chronologically, it should have referred to his first book, but *La Mise en scène* is the first work he published. One notes that at the time of that early assignment Nolan was possibly working for another company (N, p. 220) and that the name "Nolan" is not original with Ollier, who discovered it in a text by Jorge Luis Borges (Nav, pp. 151 ff.). Three explanations suggest themselves. The reference might be to Borges; or it acknowledges the debt Ollier owes another writer (the other company), perhaps Robbe-Grillet, since the tropical setting suggests *La Jalousie*; or it alludes to some early, unpublished work of his own. Although the latter seems less intriguing, it actually comes closest to the truth. As Ollier himself has told me, the fourth section of *L'Echec de Nolan* refers to the texts of the first section of *Navettes*, which were written before *La Mise en scène* but not published in book form until 1967—and the tropical island setting was intended as a tribute to R. L. Stevenson, whom Ollier was reading at that time.

If one moves for a moment to Borges' short story, "Theme of the Traitor and Hero," whence the character Nolan emerged, he may perhaps see things a little less darkly. An historian named Ryan, investigating the circumstances of an Irish patriot's assassination in the 1820s, unearths the fact that Nolan, a friend of the patriot, while himself investigating the failure of a number of uprisings, had found out that the patriot was a traitor. The latter is condemned to die, but the execution of the sentence is camouflaged in order to preserve the hero's image and indirectly serve the revolution.

What had struck Ryan in the first place were the similarities between the patriot's death and the deaths of Caesar and Macbeth: "These facets are of cyclic character; they seem to repeat or combine phenomena from remote regions, from re-

mote ages."⁹ That fits in very nicely with the idea of Ollier's
Nolan being an echo of his previous creations—until one
recalls that Borges' Nolan, a translator of Shakespeare into
Gaelic, had engineered the fictitious plot and assassination,
being undoubtedly inspired by the tragedies of *Macbeth* and
Julius Caesar. A final twist provides yet another jolt: the
traitor-hero was assassinated in a theater, prefiguring the
murder of Abraham Lincoln. Ryan also realizes that Nolan
had inserted in his plot a sufficient number of clues to enable
an investigator such as himself to uncover its mechanism, thus
including the historian in the plot. As a consequence, he decides
to perpetuate the patriotic legend. As Ollier sees it, in his
commentary on Borges' text, "Everyday reality, initially postu-
lated as existing, finds itself gradually diluted, caught in a
more and more perfect system of relationships that, finding
support in one another, end up by constituting not a possible
reality but *the only true reality*" (Nav, p. 157). In such manner myths are born, as I suggested earlier. In a more limited
fashion, that is how Ollier's Nolan imposes a new reality on
Morel and Lassalle, not just his but the true reality of all four
(if we include the anonymous narrator of *Le Maintien de
l'ordre*). Or, to quote the text of *La Vie sur Epsilon*: "Each one
of his avatars is false, taken by itself. Taken together, they are
true" (p. 392; see note 3). What Ollier has been doing is to
suggest, as J. J. did to Morel, that the elements of reality can
always be rearranged: "Beautiful setting, don't you think? . . .
Glimpses into the wilderness . . . Backdrop of ruins . . . The
story hardly matters, in the end" (E, p. 58).

His first four works of fiction having been reorganized and
revitalized, Ollier began planning the next four. None of those,
obviously, could stand independently now that intertextuality
was consciously assumed. Numbers 5, 6, and 7 are to be related
to 1, 2, and 3; number 8 will be related both to number 4 and,
presumably, to 5, 6, and 7. The course is thus charted for *La
Vie sur Epsilon, Enigma No. 1, Enigma No. 2,* and *Vingt Ans*

après. Texts of the new series had already been adumbrated in the "Fourth Report" of *L'Echec de Nolan.* That report ended with a textual reprise of the last line of "Nocturne," the first item of *Navettes.* Immediately preceding it, one first finds a reference to a "homologue on a distant system" (N, p. 228), suggesting at the same time the homologous relationship binding the two groups of fiction, the chronological distance separating the one from the other, and the location of the new one in a distant, hence different, (planetary) system—in other words, the introduction on the level of the anecdote of the realm of science fiction. Next, there is a paragraph describing someone setting out one morning on red earth, then progressing through sand and snow, anticipating a departure that takes place in *La Vie sur Epsilon* (to be published in 1972).

The anecdote covers a period of seven days, earth time, on a planet named Epsilon located in a different solar system, where four suns make earth-time reckoning inapplicable. It involves four astronauts who have made a successful landing, after which an unspecified interference incapacitated all their machinery and communications equipment. Two of the men decided to go on an expedition. Weeks later, a third undertook to find out what had happened to them. When the reader opens the book, the commander is alone in the silent space ship. Soon, he, too, sets out in search of the other crew members. He finds them, one by one, and one by one they return to the ship as the interferences cease and communication is re-established with their base. Such a brief outline brings out a pattern that I have identified in earlier fiction: a man is sent to a distant land, he has an assignment to carry out (here the commander gives himself the assignment), he carries it out successfully in spite of many difficulties, and he returns safely to his point of departure. *La Mise en scène* fits that pattern best.

When Lassalle, spending his first night in a strange country, thinks of the danger that might possibly threaten him, he remarks, "And yet he had been warned, in several instances" (S,

p. 11) of some of those dangers. In *La Vie sur Epsilon*, at the very outset, the commander, thinking of the awesome phenomena that are manifested on the planet, recalls that "He had been instructed at length, during his training years" (V, p. 2) about such phenomena. Other textual echoes soon reverberate. For instance, "the line of demarcation between light and darkness" (S, p. 10) brings forth "a fluctuating state of relationships between light and darkness" (V, p. 2). The "slats" and "hinges" of shutters in the room at Assameur (S, p. 11) produce "slats" that are "hinged" (V, pp. 3 *et passim*; 22) in descriptions of a peculiar atmospheric disturbance, which, like shutters in the room, produce darkness when it engulfs the spaceship (V, pp. 94 ff.). The "slats" are seen as "sliding, crisscrossing, and permuting" (V, p. 3), while on the wall of his room Lassalle sees threadlike shadows "undulating . . . interweaving, unravelling" (S, p. 13). He soon realizes that the shadows are caused by leaves on a palm tree; in French, except for the initial letter, *lame* (slat) is an anagram of *(p)alme*. Thematic details also reappear, like the moving geometric visions in both the introductory and the closing sections of *La Mise en scène* that become "natural" visions of the strange slats or images on television screens. The memory of crouching behind a bush of mountain laurel (V, p. 260) suggests the ravine where Lassalle hid from Idder (S, p. 138), near the spot where there were also bushes of mountain laurel (S, p. 146). The last image on the screen of the spaceship is a five-pointed star (V, p. 394), which is also the emblem on the Moroccan flag, and *La Mise en scène* was set in Morrocco. Many more examples could be given.

Heretofore, protagonists of Ollier's fiction did not know the languages of the countries to which they were sent, nor did they bother to learn once they arrived there. At first, that would seem to set *La Vie sur Epsilon* in a category of its own. On that far away planet there is no animal or plant life; there are no human beings. Even the four astronauts hardly qualify. In their case, we can readily discard the "living" or "human" attributes of traditional fictional characters. They are successors to Ollier's previous ones, in alphabetical order. After L(assalle), (. . .), M(orel), and N(olan) we now have O., P(erros), Q(uilby), and R(ossen). The extraordinary phenomena that are found on Epsilon, of which the enveloping "slats" constitute only one of three, cause those who are caught in them to lose present consciousness and to relive other episodes—not necessarily of their own lives. Furthermore, two different "individuals" may relive exactly the same episode. That, on the level of the anecdote, thoroughly destroys the individuality of the characters.

In order to designate them, initial letters would have been enough for a definite advantage in emphasizing that the commander in the anecdote, protagonist in the fiction, amounts to a mere zero in the text. But here is where the analogy with the earlier fiction is reaffirmed to some degree. Rather than O., it is the text that is being given the assignment on Epsilon, and it is linguistic in nature. Its task is to explore Epsilon·as a foreign text, for almost anything can be considered as a text or hieroglyphics to be deciphered. Such an enterprise is rather clearly stated within *La Vie sur Epsilon*, as a result of the now familiar process of inscribing key segments of relatively short length into the narrative and then repeating them with significant variations. Here there are three such segments, which are given in close succession as the book opens. The one that immediately concerns the reader is the first. Its initial sentence reads: "At the beginning, he does not attach essential importance to such metamorphoses: it is an attribute of this land, he says to himself, of this sand, of this land of snow and sand, an aspect of its climate, perhaps seasonal, a fluctuating state of relationships between light and darkness." In one of its early repetitions, the word "metamorphoses" is replaced with "metaphors" V, p. 20) and "land" with "language." When all the instances of the repeated segment are compared, it is easy to form two clusters of words that may be said to be in a dialectical situation: light, source of light, sun, image, space, and lines on the one hand; darkness, materials, shadows, words, narrative, and colors on the other.

While the text, or the language, of Epsilon is unknown, Ollier's text must use known words in its exploration of it— just as the reader constantly does, using words that apply to a past experience (not even one's own) to account for the new situations he finds himself in. A difficult task, seldom met with success. At one point, Ollier's text admonishes, "One must describe everything, even at the risk of inventing everything" (V, p. 106). Words are obviously inadequate, but "It is better to say 'sand' and 'snow' for the while. Keep on saying: air, light and water, lavender, yellow, and white" (p. 142), even though the items they designate do not correspond to what they commonly stand for. It is perhaps not possible to see things as they really are. One might as well accept "as a practical compromise and basis for future calculations that everything actually happened as he imagines that it did" (p. 172). That may be the failure that undermines the seemingly successful mission of O., one that is implied in the final pages of the book, when the five-pointed star appears on the screen and Rossen admits he does not know what the symbol stands for: "It does not figure in the code!" (V, p. 395).

La Vie sur Epsilon is indeed to be read as a study in and on language, but its science-fiction anecdote (where there is far more fiction than science) allows one to enjoy it as an adventure in language. One awaits the publication of the remainder of the series with considerable curiosity.

NOTES TO CHAPTER TEN (Ollier)

[1] Jean Ricardou, "Aventures et mésaventures de la description," *Critique*, No. 174 (November 1961), pp. 937–949.

[2] I have detailed a number of textual operations effected in Ollier's first three works of fiction in a paper entitled "Le Jeu du texte et du récit chez Claude Ollier" read in 1971 at the Centre Culturel International in

258   FRENCH FICTION TODAY

Cerisy. It appears in *Le Nouveau Roman: hier, aujourd'hui* (Paris: 10/18, 1972).

3 Claude Ollier, *Le Maintien de l'ordre*, p. 49. Henceforth all references to Ollier's work appear in the body of the text with the following abbreviations: *La Mise en scène*, S; *Le Maintien de l'ordre*, O; *Eté indien*, E; *L'Echec de Nolan*, N; *Navettes*, Nav; *La Vie sur Epsilon*, V. For the latter, references are to the manuscript, as it was not available in book form at the time of this writing. See Bibliography for complete references.

4 In the order the titles are listed, these books were published as follows, Paris: Gallimard, 1956; Paris: Seuil, 1958; Austin: University of Texas Press, 1964. Vercel's *Eté indien* was brought out by Albin Michel in Paris in 1956. Bioy Casares' Morel invented a machine analogous to some of these described by Raymond Roussel in *Locus solus*. It "films" the totality of a person, and when reprojected he or she appears in three-dimensional totality; but the person dies after the film has been taken. Morel, on a tropical island with friends, decides to relive forever a seven-day sequence. They die and the "film" is replayed again and again, Morel, as I see it, having become like an actor in a continuously performed play or a fictional character in the minds of readers who read and reread the book where his name is inscribed. Originally issued in Buenos Aires in 1940, it was available in French translation in 1955 (published by Laffont).

5 Jean Giraudoux, *Choix des élues* (Paris: Grasset, 1939), p. 155.

6 Roman Jakobson, "Closing Statement: Linguistics and Poetics," in the volume edited by T. A. Sebeok, *Style in Language* (Cambridge: Technology Press of M.I.T., 1960), p. 376.

7 As paraphrased by Julia Kristeva, "Le Mot, le dialogue et le roman," in *Recherches pour une sémanalyse* (Paris: Seuil, 1969), p. 146.

8 Ricardou, "L'Enigme dérivée," in *Pour une théorie du nouveau roman* (Paris: Seuil, 1971), p. 168.

9 Jorge Luis Borges, "Theme of the Traitor and Hero," in *Ficciones* (New York: Grove Press, 1962), p. 124.

CHAPTER ELEVEN

Marc Saporta

In an essay published in 1956, Michel Butor called for experimentation in fictional forms. Since the nature of fiction in any given society discloses the appearance that reality assumes for its members—that, at least, is the premise on which he predicated his observations—it follows quite logically that "new forms will reveal new aspects of reality and new relationships."[1] Almost as if he had been waiting for the call, Marc Saporta, three years later, began publishing a series of works, the most striking characteristic of which is experimentation. By now, he may well have decided to write no more fiction. Whether he does or not, the five samples of his reconnoitering in the field should be of interest to anyone studying techniques of fiction writing.

The title of *Le Furet* (1959) refers to the French variety of the game known to English children as hunt-the-slipper, in which an object is passed from child to child around a circle, while the one standing at the center tries to guess where it is. Paradoxically, the main character of *Le Furet* is the elusive "object." Nameless and invisible to the reader, he might be called a narrator, except that he never says *je*. That, as examples from other writers demonstrate, is not necessarily a hindrance. As in the case of Claude Ollier, one is reminded of Robbe-Grillet's *La Jalousie*, which had appeared in 1957. In that book, as it should now be clear, the reader shares the visual impressions of a man who mixes imagination and reality and seems to brood over several incidents without respect for normal chronology—in short, a highly distorted vision of an elusive reality that the reader must then re-create. There is, on the other hand, little doubt as to the reality of events and setting in *Le Furet*. The locale is anything but exotic: it is in Paris among businessmen and office workers. The description of the building where the action begins is such as to tempt the reader to identify it with a precise structure on the Champs-Elysées. All objects, as a matter of fact, are familiar ones; they are clearly described and easily recognizable. The events are also commonplace, of the sort one often reads or hears about, and they are accounted for in conventional chronological sequence. Exceptions tend to conform with standard fictional procedure, and the reader is seldom confused. In such fashion, the narrator attempts to reconstruct an episode to which he had not paid attention at the time, or, after his mistress breaks off the affair, he goes over various aspects of the intrigue in his mind. As to people, all but one are standard types—the dynamic boss, the competent young assistant, the plain-looking, efficient secretary, and so forth. What is unusual in the narrative is that all such ordinary ingredients are pushed into the background, while emphasis is placed on a number of selected objects that appear to determine the course of the narrative. The features of human beings, for instance, are described cursorily, while objects that identify them are accorded far greater attention. We know more about the hat, handbag, and coat of an old lady who shares an elevator with the narrator than we do about her face or size. Two persons who work in the same office with him eventually become obliterated by the garments they wear: "The coat in imitation leather and the duffel coat have gone out for lunch."[2] Occasional use of such a device may be found in many works of fiction; in this one, it is systematic. Nevertheless, there is one privileged character, the narrator's temporary mistress, Michèle V. . . .

A simple narrative sequence can be extracted from *Le Furet*

without the slightest difficulty. The narrator falls in love with
and seduces the beautiful secretary of a company his own firm
has business dealings with. After a few months, the girl has
had enough; deeply affected, he proposes marriage to a less
glamorous woman he had been seeing off and on. He cannot go
through with it and commits suicide—but the various developments of that plot are controlled by objects. The story is
presented, not from the point of view of the narrator, but
through his eyes. Actually, it might be more accurate to say
that it is presented by means of an omniscient narrator, whose
eyes are synchronized with those of the main character and
who can read his mind, for in several instances we have the
impression of being outside that character. The opening pages
are very much like a movie sequence, in which the camera,
with the cameraman (or audience) taking the place of a character, enters an office suite, takes in the furnishings of the
reception room, goes down a hallway, making a visual note of
the number of doors, enters through one of these, and so on.
The narrator has brought a file, entrusts it to the blonde secretary, is entranced by her smile, makes a note of her name, and
leaves. The feelings she arouses in him are mentioned or suggested, after a first reference to a smile "that is extremely
pleasing and even a bit moving" (F, p. 15), in objective fashion: "The feelings that she arouses are perhaps due to the
contrast between her dark eyes and her blond hair." The sight
of a wedding ring brings forth the comment that all men
undoubtedly notice it, and that leads to the general statement:
"It is always disappointing to notice a detail of that kind in
a woman that is as young and as pretty as this one." Objectal
considerations are involved in both instances, but the ring has
symbolic value, pointing to the category of objects that will
be most active in the story. In the next chapter, in the narrator's
own office, his infatuation is made clear by such details as
notes stuck on the wall with the reminder to call Michèle V. . . ,
similar jottings on his calendar pad, and the contrast that is

noted between her voice and that of the telephone operator. The narrative moves on toward the seduction scene, which takes place within the period of time that separates the sixth chapter from the fifth. Each chapter represents a continuous sequence of images or thoughts and gaps of varying lengths of time occur between each chapter. The existence of intervals is not directly stated but needs to be inferred either from events or from oblique references. That reinforces the impression, received at the outset, that the book is an objective "recording" of outer reality. In Robbe-Grillet's *La Jalousie*, on the contrary, a similar impression is soon destroyed.

From one important standpoint, *La Jalousie* and *Le Furet* may be considered as offering contradictory statements. In the former the husband is transformed by the reader into a victim of his own pathological jealousy; Saporta's man is being manipulated by his surroundings. Both writers deny the humanistic view that ascribes to man a central, deminating position in the universe, but where Robbe-Grillet tends to see men and their surroundings in a contingent relationship, Saporta opts for a more primitive outlook that fills matter with mysterious forces. A clue is given in the latter part of *Le Furet*: "In life, objects play hunt-the-slipper with men" (p. 170). Man is dependent upon "the whim of objects." Emphasizing that point, each of the twenty chapters bears as its title the name of the object that acts like a magnetic pole, orienting lines of forces that affect events.

The office into which the narrator penetrates at the beginning of the book is silent and nearly empty, like a sanctuary. Looking for the president of the company, he enters the only room from which a sound emanates—it is the noise of a typewriter, the god that presides over the destinies of all businesses. Michèle is the priestess who serves this power and casts a spell over her visitor. What brought him to her was nothing personal or even human. It was another object, the file, full of papers, themselves emanating from a typewriter. Other items enter the stage with a part to play. A telephone ties the narrator to Michèle; a crowded elevator enables him to make the first advances. Later, a red carnation dominates their first dinner in a restaurant predominantly decorated in red—the color of pulsing blood and surging emotions; then, an abandoned hairpin signifies the end of the affair. Finally, a vial in a medicine cabinet orients the narration in the direction of suicide, and a rope renders the action possible. The narrator hangs himself in his kitchen and dies with his mind full of images of Michèle. The fatal rope is connected with the title, for in Saporta's version of the game the children, forming a circle, hold a rope along which the hidden object circulates: "In the final analysis, it is always the rope that has the last word" (F, p. 172).

The experiment of Le Furet consists in taking a trite love story, whose protagonists are nonentities set in a banal decor and imposing upon it a rigorous technique. The text exudes a pessimistic attitude as to man's freedom. Its narrator has been the toy of forces over which he has no control. Sex, chance, and the mysterious working of objects have precipitated his end. A different setting and anecdote could have been used to the same purpose, and it is quite conceivable that the same title and chapter headings could have been selected. Those headings, along with the technique, are a source of meaning. The narration contributes almost nothing. One might say that there is a double vacuum at the center, the story and the story teller. The metaphor of this work is stated within the text, as the narrator and Michèle look at a poster for an exhibit of art from India. The poster reproduces an early miniature representing Buddha on horseback; the horse and an umbrella are shown in realistic detail, but in between the two there is nothing. Buddha is invisible, but "His presence is noticeable, even though he does not figure in the miniature, and the more so as he does not figure in it" (F, p. 59). The faithful surely must have put a lot into that void; into the center of Saporta's

novel the reader places himself as he would in the middle of
the children's circle, and he attempts to give flesh to the invisible narrator.

La Quête (1961) contrasts with *Le Furet* in that the story
has some originality. Also, partly as a consequence, it is more
topical. There are two antagonistic narrators instead of one,
but this hardly affects narrative technique. The major change
is that objects have lost their role: those mysterious extrahuman
forces are now embodied in collectivities. It is a clash between
two such masses, a student protest and the so-called forces of
law and order, that sets things in motion.

One of the narrators is a soldier who remains anonymous
except for his army identification number. His unit has been
assigned to riot control duty. It has taken up a position in the
path of demonstrating students, rifles have been loaded, and
the order to fire is expected momentarily. The students draw
extremely close, tossing rocks and bottles at the troops, but
just before the bugle sounds, as expected, the soldiers are
warned to fire into the air. All the muzzles slowly move upward,
all but one—the narrator's. The order to shoot is given, and
he aims at a girl. The second narrator is a student who is
fully identified, with a family, a background, and the name
Alain. He is with the column of demonstrators, and so is his
sister, Anne; he is in the middle of the column and believes
his sister is up front. When the soldiers fire, the students retreat
in disorder, and the police charge after them, making arrests.
Alain tries to find out what happened to his sister amid rumors
that she has been hit.

It has soon become obvious to the reader that Anne was
the girl the soldier aimed at and that she has probably been
killed. From then on, a double quest is under way, that of the
soldier for the girl he has shot and that of Alain for the soldier.
Their alternating narratives form the substance of *La Quête*.
On the surface, both quests fail, although Saporta sustains
reader interest by twice bringing the hunters extremely close

to their quarries. But the main interest lies elsewhere, in the solution of a psychological problem, what led the soldier to disobey orders? Finding an answer is not simplified by the soldier's attempt to find his victim, for it is not clear what his motives are in doing so. Perhaps he, too, is trying to discover what made him fire at Anne. The soldier, as befits his anonymity, is thus the big question mark in the first half of *La Quête*. Even Alain, at first, seems impelled by a desire for truth more than for justice. He explains to a minor character that the soldier "is perhaps a poor bastard who became scared, who let his rifle go off at random, who pulled the trigger without knowing why . . . that soldier is perhaps a student too, led to his assignment by chance, transformed into a war machine by circumstance" (p. 78).

As he continues his search, however, his tolerant attitude gradually changes. After a soldier who has been hit by a rock makes disparaging remarks about the students, Alain wishes the stone had done him greater damage. Later, when he thinks he has located the soldier's barracks, he wonders how difficult it might be "to take over the garrison by surprise, with a group of friends, and to plunge into the throat or the olive drab chest of these anonymous men the long dagger that those on watch carry in their belts" (pp. 135–136). He, too, has been transformed into a machine by circumstance—an instrument of revenge. Nevertheless, there is no explicit condemnation of Alain because of that change, and at the end of the book he stands watching the troops leave their barracks for another assignment. He is described in purely objective terms, without any emotion. The case of the soldier is more complex. By the time he marches out of the barracks, enough data have been gathered to enable the reader to adopt a definite attitude toward him, but there are chances that it will vary considerably according to each reader. It is also hard to predict with which narrator a given reader might identify himself in the end.

Another character complicates this matter, for he plays an

ambiguous role—not in the story itself but in the meaning generated by the text. In two successive interludes, he faces, in turn, Alain and the soldier. He is a lieutenant, and Alain has traced the soldier to his unit. Their interview adds depth to one character and confirms the hardening attitude of the other. It is the second interview that is disturbing. Obviously, in relating Alain's visit to the soldier, the lieutenant wants to give the latter the opportunity either to clear himself or to admit his guilt. The soldier remains silent, and the lieutenant, suspecting his guilt, assumes full responsibility and volunteers himself and his unit for overseas duty. Before they leave, the soldier goes to a brothel and makes love to a prostitute who resembles Anne. As they get dressed and he tells her his story, she concludes, "If you had given her as much pleasure as you have given me, you wouldn't have had to kill her" (p. 174). It seems evident that Saporta intended the soldier to rise in the reader's estimation, compensating for the downfall of Alain.

As the narration is concluded, the soldier appears more as a victim than as a criminal. He has fallen prey to two different forces over which he has no control: first, that of sex, which, like objects in *Le Furet*, is endowed with a primitive power beyond the comprehension of rational man; second, that of society, equally powerful and mysterious, which has placed him in a revolting position where he might be called upon to fire upon his fellow man. It is the convergence of those two forces that causes Anne's death. Alain, in his downward path, is shown as belonging to that class of society that has placed the soldier in such a position; he should, therefore, assume a share of responsibility in his sister's death. The lieutenant seems to understand all this, and he realizes the extent of his own responsibility. It is probably with him that the reader is meant to identify himself in the end, for, more than likely, he also belongs to that group in society that would maintain "order" at all cost.

La Distribution (1961), published the same year as *La Quête*, constitutes a different kind of experiment involving the nature of the reader's participation. The title refers to the cast of a play; the book is about a writer who thinks in broad outlines about a play he has conceived and, as he elaborates on the details of the casting, finds that he has produced a work of fiction. The writer, as creator of the play, becomes the omniscient narrator of the work of fiction—and the "reality" of the fiction is the fiction of the play. He gives no intimation of what he thinks he has done or even of his existence. The volume has a double title page: that of Saporta's *La Distribution*, with the usual indications as to author and publisher, and that of "La Pinède / A Play in Three Acts and a Prologue," with no mention of author or publisher. The clash between the words "play" on the fictitious title page and "novel" on the cover is the initial clue to what has taken place. The setting of both *La Distribution* and "La Pinède" is in a seaside resort hotel with an atmosphere of petty intrigues and jealousies. The plot of the play centers in the machinations of several characters to compromise a wealthy eighteen-year-old redhead with a waiter at the hotel. The plan succeeds beyond the schemers' expectations, for it leads to the girl's suicide.

The fictitious playwright has set down, act by act, considerations about his characters in the order of their appearance on stage. As he comes to the less important ones, he is naturally led, since their role is to support the leading characters, to return to those he has already discussed and elaborate on their backgrounds and actions. As he does this, he thinks about the future cast of his play, how the actors will interpret their parts, and how his meaning will be transmitted to an audience. Such lengthy considerations are in marked contrast to the simple gestures and sounds into which they are eventually translated. On the stage, the spectator will see for himself what characters do and how they do it: "In the theater the physical presence of actors and the immediate perception of their behavior in the end always get the best of the reasoning of the person sitting in his seat" (D, p. 144). The reader of a book can interrupt his reading any time he wishes, allowing his imagination to take hold of the material the writer has presented and carry it further or letting his critical intelligence question the same material. That, the spectator normally cannot do. Saporta's playwright insists that author and actors are to contrive things in order that "the audience gradually loses its critical sense" (p. 144). Thus, a spectator, seeing the evidence in front of him, "will accept on the stage what he would not have been willing to tolerate in fiction or in life" (p. 145). In life, presumably, the action is not concentrated artificially, and one has a greater opportunity to exercise judgment. Also he can intervene and modify the course of events.

Such observations, incidentally, along with the blurring of distinctions between traditional genres, suggest that new and more fruitful categories might be established, based on the viewpoint of the participant. Different devices of rhetoric (in the broadest sense of the word) are involved when the author's opus is to be performed with the collaboration of a single individual (the lone reader in his living room) or with that of a group (a theater audience, for instance); when that performance is to be completed within one uninterrupted interval of time, or in several stated intervals, or at random; when symbols are the direct link from author to participant (as in the case of linguistic signs in a book); or when one or several interpreters act as intermediaries.

Saporta's narrator does not indulge in theoretical consideration of that sort. He limits himself to emphasizing one distinction between book and play: for the theater audience, characters have the qualities of objects, while for the reader of fiction they are more fluid, malleable (Marguerite Duras' clay mistress comes to mind). The experiment Saporta has undertaken here appears devised to find out if he could write fiction in which characters had the solidity of those in a play. To the argument that the experiment, if successful, cannot be convincing, because his characters are by definition those of a play, there is a reasonable answer: it is only on stage that they are objectified, because of the actors' solid flesh. In a book, characters come into being through a statement or combination of statements that provide fuel for the readers' imagination. An analysis of those made in *La Distribution* would provide a clue to the operation and practicality of the device. While such a minute examination would be out of place in the context of this essay, two devices are readily identifiable. First, Saporta constantly refers to the characters by means of their physical traits, costumes, or functions. Thus there is the "tall blond girl," or the "short red-head." A woman who looks like an old hag is "the old witch." A harsh, obtuse, masculine-looking governess is "the SS woman." In something close to *commedia dell'arte* style, a male character is simply known as "the confederate." Second, the reader is frequently warned against reaching any conclusions other than those that are specifically stated. As everything cannot be stated at once, he is warned that his first impressions may be false, that present ambiguities will be resolved, and that it is not really up to him to create characters. All that, of course, under the guise of recommendations for the use of eventual interpreters of the play. Like Nathalie Sarraute, Saporta struggles against his readers, not because he wishes to keep them from constructing a standard character, but to impose upon them a character of his own design. Still, if characterization has been taken care of in great detail, the narrative sequence has been left rather vague. The reader's creative imagination is needed to fill in the particulars of the characters' interaction. In a back-cover notice Saporta compares the situation to that existing at the beginning of a chess game, with all the pieces identified as to nature and capacities. The game can then proceed according to the participants' imagination and skill in a practically limitless variety of manners.

Composition No. 1 (1962) is a loose-leaf book comprising 149 unnumbered pages. Its physical aspect was enough to throw conservative critics into a tailspin, with the more naïve asking which of the astronomical number of possible combinations of pages he was supposed to "judge." Actually, the experiment in this case is far less radical than it might seem, for it serves mainly to dramatize in an almost tangible way two generally accepted points. The first one is that the reader, with the author's indispensable collaboration, always writes his own fiction and there are, theoretically, as many versions of any given piece of fiction as there are readers. The second point is that the order in which events take place and the time when they occur have greater significance than the events themselves. The latter consideration emphasizes order and relationship, and a demonstration of the importance of such factors no longer needs to be given. Recognition of it lies at the basis of classical harmony as well as of modern collage. *Composition No. 1* transposes the opportunities presented in *La Distribution*: instead of characters being given, events are. The metaphor of the chess game no longer holds, for the order in which events are assembled is determined purely by chance. Of course, once the pages are arranged in the desired sequence, the work has attained the condition of any bound book, with the path still open for the reader's imagination to compose his own version of that particular sequence. When he has completed his reading, he may wish to read yet another narrative. He can reshuffle the pages and start reading again.

In all probability, however, he will find that this is impossible, and he will still be reading the same narrative. Picking up a conventionally bound work of fiction one has already read and rereading its chapters in haphazard fashion will not change the experience either. Events naturally fall back into the slot the first reading had put them in. The experience is different from that produced by Raymond Queneau's *Cent mille milliards de poèmes*,[3] for the combinatory units are much longer (a page instead of a line of verse), each one constituting a narrative unit, and the total work does not allow for additions or exclusions. Queneau had supplied 140 lines capable of making ten sonnets. Subsequent variations could be made by replacing a given line with the equivalent line from another sonnet, never by internal rearrangement. In that manner, additional sonnets could really be called new and different. Saporta could have achieved a similar effect, but with fewer possibilities, only by providing an additional stack of pages containing different events, which might then have been used to replace pages of the original pile. Of course, nothing prevents a reader from dividing the pages of Saporta's book into two sets; for instance, by deciding that the first set constitutes the original story and then using the second set to provide substitute pages and therefore substitute events for those of the original set. And there are surely other possibilities. At any rate, the perhaps unintended limitations of *Composition No. 1* as originally conceived call attention to the importance of the first reading of any composition. It is often at that moment that the work is created. With linear narratives, the creative experience can seldom be renewed, only recalled and possibly enriched.

A necessary feature of *Composition No. 1* is that each page forms a complete unit, narrative or thematic. As a consequence of that, the pages in a number of instances read like prose poems after the manner of Baudelaire's poems. After reading them, one wonders if what was done as a matter of necessity here might not be extended to bound books as well. Rather than let the contents of a page depend upon the printer's choice of type size and spacing between lines, an author might find it more effective to maintain control of what should go on any given page. A sentence beginning at the bottom of one page and continuing at the top of the next may not have the same affective value if placed at the center of a page. The page fortuitously left blank at the end of the first part of Robbe-Grillet's *Le Voyeur* and the critical interpretations that followed provide one obvious example of the importance of typography, even in conventional page-setting. In a far from conventional work, Mallarmé has shown what could be done with arrangements of lines on a page in his *Un Coup de dés jamais n'abolira le hasard*. In our own time, Michel Butor has been concerned with that very problem, and in several texts, such as *Où*, he has used the page as a unit.

Marc Saporta's most recent work to date is *Les Invités* (1964). The title describes both the narration and the techniques. All the characters are guests at a party, and the narrative styles are borrowed from a number of other writers. The epigraph acknowledges the debt: "This book is intended as a ceremonious tribute to the masters [who have influenced] contemporary literature, Herman Melville, James Joyce, e. e. cummings, Marcel Proust, Franz Kafka, John Dos Passos, William Faulkner, and DOSTOIEVSKY." To that list of guest-authors should be added the various facets of Saporta's own writing personality responsible for producing his earlier works. Due allowance being made for Gide's stature compared with Saporta's, the relationship between those works and *Les Invités* resembles the one linking the Gidian *récits* to *Les Faux-monnayeurs*. Also, it illustrates Bakhtine's postulate about all texts being absorption and transformation of other texts.[4]

Events of the narration cover a bit more than twelve hours, with the usual background references to the past. Within that time span, the party given by Luc, a journalist, has run its course. Within the party, a game is played, inspired partly by Kafka, partly by group therapy, partly perhaps by Friedrich Dürrenmatt's short work of fiction, *Die Panne*,[5] of which a French translation had appeared in 1958. Three guests assume the role of judges, taking the names of the three judges in Hades, Aeacus, Minos, and Rhadamanthus. Other guests appear before them, the purpose of the game being to discover, since everyone is assumed to be guilty of something, what each one shall be accused of. Out of twenty people present at the

party, only eleven are put on mock trial, among them, predict-
ably, all the major characters. As in *La Quête*, there are two
main characters, each one handling portions of the narrative.
Unlike their earlier counterparts, they give their accounts in
the first person. Furthermore, their narratives do not make up
the entire book. There are at least eight different kinds of
statements in *Les Invités*: first-person narratives in the form
of sustained interior monologues; brief alternating interior monologues in the form of duets (from which Claude Mauriac's
concept of interior dialogue is absent); third-person biographical narratives; transcribed dialogues; apologues; quotations
from reference works; objective descriptions; poetry; and finally
experimental prose. That last group could be subdivided even
further, but matters are complicated enough as they stand.

The book opens and closes with narrative statements, one by
each of the two main characters. The first one is by Ty, a
Vietnamese doctor, who gives a fairly comprehensive exposi-
tion, enabling the reader to grasp the situation at the outset
of Luc's party. He has two preoccupations weighing on his
mind. As Luc's doctor, he has recently had to tell him that he
has cancer; he has given Luc about three months to live. As
a disenchanted husband, he is obsessed with a girl named
Isabelle, who will be at the party, and who has so far turned
down his advances. It is perhaps he who suggests the game,
but he is not sure; perhaps it is Luc. At any rate, he pursues
it in the hopes of winning Isabelle. Ty is given two other narratives, one during a pause in the game at a moment when
victory seems at hand, the second one at the end of the game
when he gives an account of his defeat. His monologues are
unpunctuated, in stream-of-consciousness style. The closing
statement is made by Luc. As in *La Quête*, but in much clearer
fashion, the two characters' evolution is symmetrical. Ty dominates the situation at the beginning, apparently calling the tune
and condemning Luc to death, while at the end he in turn has
been condemned and rejected. Luc starts out as a condemned

man and, in his monologue, seems close to being overpowered
by the thought of death, nearly committing suicide, but he pulls
himself together (his normal, punctuated prose perhaps led us
to anticipate such a development) and closes both his statement and the book with a quotation from Paul Valéry's *Cimetière marin*: "The wind is rising, we must endeavor to live."

Ty's second statement divides *Les Invités* into two parts. The
core of the first part is constituted by the biographical narratives, seven profiles of as many characters and one mock profile
of the dog a guest has brought along. The meat of the second
part is in the dialogue transcriptions of the eleven "trials."
Together, they communicate a large part of what the book is
about, but the atmosphere or context is missing. That is supplied by all the other elements, interspersed among the profiles
and the various trials. There is dancing at the party, to music
that is alternately recorded and live, the live portion being
supplied by three volunteers, younger guests who can handle
drums, the trumpet, and the saxophone. The kind of music they
play is suggested by fifteen quotations dealing with jazz mu-
sicians (Duke Ellington, Artie Shaw, Miles Davis, and others)
or jazz forms (scat, swing, blues, and so forth). Three additional quotations describe spaniels and Irish setters—as incongruous as the dog at the party and the reason for its being
there. The architecture and decor of Luc's studio apartment,
the behavior, moods, and attitudes of the guests are expressed
by means of forty-four miscellaneous pieces. Some are simple,
objective descriptions of the studio, the record-player, the
stairs, and other physical features; some are poems (haikai composed by Ty), experimental texts either in the manner of
Apollinaire's *Calligrammes* or in that of e. e. cummings' poetry;
others are brief snapshots of people taken at intervals during
the evening. Two duets made up of contrasting interior monologues, "recorded" while the couples involved are dancing
together, and three symbolic apologues, the latter all in the
second part, complete the picture.

Except for duets and apologues, all but one of the other elements constitute brief statements that fit into a single page— perhaps as a result of the experience of *Composition No. 1*. The excerpts from reference works, reminding one in capsule form of Melville's treatment of the whale, are not a new device with Saporta. In *Le Furet*, the vial in the medicine cabinet brought forth several factual pages on the nature, handling, and sale of poisonous drugs and their effects, and one of the pages of *Composition No. 1* is a transcription of articles 379, 381, and 384 of the French penal code. One page of *Les Invités* is headed "La Distribution" and contains a list of the book's twenty characters, their professions and their family relationships, suggesting the cast of a play and the previous book of fiction by that name. There is indeed an effort made to objectify a number of the characters. Several minor ones have been deprived of their names and appear as "The Hunter," "The Spaniel," "The Kid," and so forth. Ty's wife, "The Otter," is thus completely eclipsed by Isabelle, who has both her name and a nickname, "The Poney." Some of the characters are themselves linked to earlier fiction. An architect is disturbed by memories of a war-time incident, identical with the one described on a page of *Composition No. 1* and presumably experienced by that work's problematic protagonist.

Paul, now a successful executive, feels guilty because of an act committed during his military training period when assigned to riot duty. He seems identical with the anonymous soldier of *La Quête*. Ty, Luc, and Paul himself refer to the incident separately, and all in all many details are provided. Paul clarifies his attitude at the time of the riot, and the episode, as stated in *Les Invités*, appears as Saporta's justification of his intentions when writing *La Quête*. It also reads like an ironic commentary on the ability of the middle class to salvage individuals and absorb them into its system of values. The shooting of the blond student is now shown to have been no more than an unfortunate accident that has not prevented

Paul from enjoying material success in his life. Nevertheless, the incident gnaws at his conscience. All such matters are related to "intertextuality." At first, an unconscious victim of the realistic fallacy, one is reluctant to accept the modification of one text by a subsequent one—and this, ironically, out of respect for the text as it stands. The fiction of *La Quête* stands as it is, one in inclined to say, with all its ambiguities. Paul's story represents another version of the events—a variation on *La Quête*, not a correction nor an explanation of it. And yet, such an argument implies the reality of something that exists mainly in one's imagination. An organized sequence of words having determined that "reality," one should accept the possibility, even the likelihood, of its being modified by an ulterior sequence. That is exactly what happens when some pages of *Les Invités* are brought to interact with the fiction of *La Quête*.

The different backgrounds revealed in the seven biographies, the presence of one Oriental and two blacks among the guests, do much to expand the scope of *Les Invités* when contrasted with previous works by Saporta. Restricted though it is to the upper middle class, it nevertheless communicates a comprehensive picture of contemporary culture and anxieties. The forms and techniques that Saporta uses, which must be experienced rather than read about, are indispensable to such a communication. The very aspect of the book is fragmented, even chaotic, odd, intriguing, and challenging, but no more so than a number of works that have appeared during the sixties—and certainly no more than the times. The material that is presented constitutes a mixture of fact and fancy, objectivity and distortion, indifference and neurosis—for which there are also many echoes. Saporta's earlier experiments would seem vindicated by this more ambitious volume, even if it is not a total success. I believe it is too intricate to be as fruitful as it might be, even on its own terms, which are to deal almost exclusively with thematic, narrative, and anecdotal elements, hardly at all with linguistic ones. The reader is manipulated as much as he is challenged, and his share is reduced to nearly what it used to be in the conventional type of fiction. What might be needed is a further step in the direction of those "mobile structures" that Michel Butor has delineated.[6]

NOTES TO CHAPTER ELEVEN (Saporta)

[1] Michel Butor, "Le Roman comme recherche," in *Répertoire* (Paris: Minuit, 1960), p. 9. (Written in 1955; first published in *Cahiers du Sud* in April, 1956.)

[2] Marc Saporta, *Le Furet*, p. 86. Henceforth all references to works by Marc Saporta appear in the body of the text with the following abbreviations: *Le Furet*, F; *La Quête*, Q; *La Distribution*, D. See Bibliography for complete references.

[3] Paris: Gallimard, 1961.

[4] See page 249 above.

[5] Zürich: Die Arche, 1956.

[6] Butor, "Recherches sur la technique du roman," in *Répertoire II* (Paris: Minuit, 1964), pp. 98–99.

CHAPTER TWELVE

Michel Butor

In Michel Butor's first work of fiction, *Passage de Milan* (1954), there lies a wealth of signs pointing in several directions: into the past, into the future, and into the author—as writer rather than as ordinary person. Keeping strictly to the literary domain, one encounters ironic allusions to older writers such as André Gide and François Mauriac as well as specific references to Charles-Bernard Renouvier's *Uchronie*, all remnants of the past. Foreshadowing future works, a certain amount of fire imagery prefigures the conflagrations of *L'Emploi du temps* (1956) while a burning piece of paper damages Martin de Vere's painting, which had previously been compared to an "emploi du temps" and was divided into twelve squares, just as the city of Bleston, whose map Revel later burns, comprises twelve precincts. The apostasy of Father Jean Ralon has its counterpart in *La Modification* (1957) through the figure of Julian the Apostate, a correlative of Léon Delmont's interior change. The transformation in relationship that takes place between Louis Lécuyer and his first cousin, Father Alexis Ralon, the one a student, the other a chaplain in the same *lycée*, and the fiction one of the characters is writing, in which he seeks to "put the simplest human relationships to a test, and, with that in mind, he modifies family ties,"[1] both adumbrate a major theme of *Degrés* (1960). The attention given to the dreams of Félix, Jean, and Alexis anticipates the role dreams play in *Histoire extraordinaire* (1961), *Mobile*

(1962), and others. From the standpoint of technique, the discontinuous architecture of this first book, in which the reader is confronted with a very large number of juxtaposed sequences, each dealing with a different set of characters or actions, points, beyond the narrative continuity stressed in *L'Emploi du temps* and *La Modification*, to the more deliberate rhetoric of discontinuity that characterizes *Degrés* and is fully developed in *Mobile* and several of the works that follow.

As to the third area of resonance in *Passage de Milan*, it emerges most clearly from a confrontation with one of Butor's more recent works, *Portrait de l'artiste en jeune singe* (1967). Called a "capriccio," this "portrait" might well be termed autobiographical fiction, if all fiction were not, to some extent, autobiographical and all autobiography fictional.[2] The salience of patently biographical elements is due, in part at least, to the shift in rhetoric that I have just alluded to. Such a change is related to the realization that the elements of a work of art are less important in themselves than the order in which they are assembled. Recognizable bits of "reality" need not be disguised or transfigured in order to become significant parts of a "fiction"—although they might be distorted in the process. Georges Raillard has noted, in speaking of Michel Butor's family home during the thirties, "Its atmosphere is that which is described in *Passage de Milan* (the Mognes)."[3] One might have guessed as much, and the fact deserves no more importance than Raillard's incidental reference. The relation the Mogne household bears to reality plays no role whatsoever in the emergence of meaning. What matters is the internal order that family assumes and the way it and its components are related to other elements in the book.

The central feminine figure in *Passage de Milan* is Angèle Vertigues, whose name suggests "angel of the heights," for whom a party is given. Among those dizzied by her charms is Louis Lécuyer. She is also one of the queens of the standard pack of cards, of which Martin de Vere is trying to give a representation in the twelve areas of his painting. The characters are manipulated as by the player of a game of solitaire or as by the painter in his complex construction. When the corresponding queen is accidentally destroyed by fire on De Vere's canvas, Angèle dies because of Louis' well-meant but clumsy interference. The link between the two events was established earlier in *Passage* when the narrator warned that Angèle might be displaying seductiveness in vain: "Into pitiful ashes might you find your fine flames resolved" (p. 215). In the end Louis is about to leave for Egypt, where he could well experience a spiritual rebirth.

Portrait de l'artiste en jeune singe is narrated on two separate levels—dream and reality—in alternating chapters. The realistic side gives an account of the visit paid by the narrator (specifically identified with a youthful Butor) to a German nobleman shortly after the end of the second World War, during which he explores his host's priceless library and teaches him new games of solitaire. To the other side of *Portrait* belong his nights. He imagines a serialized dream that is adapted from the tale of the second Kalandar, begun by Scheherazade on the twelfth of her thousand and one nights. In that tale, the Kalandar, who has been changed into an ape, is unwittingly responsible for the death of not one but two women—and the second one is literally turned into those ashes that were metaphorically introduced in *Passage de Milan*. In *Portrait*, the Kalandar becomes a visitor to the German castle narrating a dream. While its basic features have been retained, the Arabian story has been shortened and modified in several respects. Particularly pertinent here is the episode in which the dreamer, still in the guise of an ape, engages the King in a contest. As Scheherazade told it, they matched their skills in games of chess, which the King loses, but in Butor's dream the King is bested in his knowledge of solitaire. That there may be a connection between card games and chess in its ancient form is less relevant than the emphasis on solitaire, which expresses the prophetic properties of card playing. Although there is no mention of solitaire as such in the text of *Passage de Milan* (the previous reference was my own metaphor), cards play a similar prophetic role in De Vere's painting.

In both stories a young man's future is at stake, and chance is instrumental in shaping it. A propitious outcome is intimated by the recurrent number twelve, a symbol of salvation. Chance, however, is normally surrounded with an aura of mystery and obscurity. Father Jean Ralon muses at the outset of *Passage de Milan,* "Wasn't there a path opening there, the path into night-fall, which, invariably too soon, one ceased pursuing, which one would never find the courage to follow down to its major turning points?" (p. 9). Ralon is an Egyptologist, and Egypt, one of the main sources of gnostic lore, is also thought by some to have been the birthplace of playing cards. While Angèle's party, which bears the earmarks of a modern initiation, moves on toward its fatal climax, Jean Ralon has an extraordinary dream, resembling a more arcane initiation, inspired by the Egyptian *Book of the Dead,*[4] which confirms his estrangement from the Church. In *Portrait de l'artiste en jeune singe* the narrator is intellectually initiated to the writings of Athanasius Kircher, who, as the first serious student of Egyptian hiero-glyphics, might be called a prototype of Father Ralon, of alchemists like Nicholas Flamel and Basil Valentine, of the Protestant mystic Jacob Boehme, and of others, even more obscure. Note that I said "writings" rather than "thought." What matters here is the language of the texts, particularly those pertaining to alchemy, its array of symbols, which illumine areas of consciousness that have been darkened by rationalism.

As Butor explained in an essay written about the same time as *Passage de Milan,* "The language of alchemy is an instrument of considerable pliability that allows one to describe a process with precision, relating it to a general concept of reality."[5] In *Portrait de l'artiste en jeune singe,* the narrator does not discuss those writers (who are not all alchemists); he quotes them.

That explains why the playing cards of neither book can be assimilated to the Tarot pack. Butor needs to remain outside of its closed system of symbolism as much as he must stay at one remove from alchemy and gnosticism. His viewpoint recalls that of André Breton toward the dark, subsurface forces in the mind: "It is of the utmost interest that we gather them, gather them first, and later submit them, if need be, to the control of our reason."[6] As objective correlatives of such depths, the German castle contains a collection of precious stones, rare minerals extracted from the bowels of the earth (one recalls that Mogne, in *Passage de Milan*, had shown much interest in a newspaper article on mines). After the relation of his trip to Germany has come to an end, the narrator concludes, "How could I not, after that, at the earliest opportunity that presented itself, how could I not have sailed for Egypt?" (A, p. 231)—echoing the outcome of *Passage de Milan*.

The selection for the dream sequence of *Portrait de l'artiste en jeune singe* of a passage from *The Book of a Thousand Nights and a Night* is extremely suggestive. In the central chapters of *Passage de Milan* (and on the central floor of the apartment building as well), concurrently with other events, a group of intellectuals discuss a work on which they might possibly collaborate and other works that they have individually written. One of them, who has published a book called "Les Faubourgs de Trieste," is quoted as having said, in answer to a question pertaining to his writing method, "I imagine myself after my own death . . . attempting to see what is going on in those places where I have lived" (P, p. 138). That statement, also referred to by Georges Charbonnier in the course of an interview with Butor, transforms the removal of the writer from his creation and his topic into a distance between the writer and the world expressed through the metaphor of death. During the same Charbonnier interview, Butor himself developed it into a myth, that of the writer as Scheherazade. Ill at ease in a society that he cannot accept, in a universe that he does not fully understand or approve of, dissatisfied with his own being, the writer, at the same time as he removes himself from the stage, re-enters the world by means of his literary work. In so doing, he transforms the outside world for his own use; he also provides others with a vision of reality that can help them effect a transformation of their own. In related fashion, Scheherazade, through the telling of her tales, managed to postpone her own death and also to remove the threat of death that was hanging over the women of Bagdad. "Every writer is Scheherazade, every writer harbors within himself a threat of death . . . both within himself and about himself. The threat that lies outside of him corrodes him, so to speak, internally. . . . The writer, in speaking, will at once remove the threat of death that weighs upon him, and, of course, also weighs on the entire future of society."[7] It is probably no more than a coincidence that Butor's name is a near-anagram of Burton's, the translator of the Arabian tales, which is also the name of the mystery story writer in *L'Emploi du temps*. But the coincidence could not be more suggestive.

1. EARLY FICTION

Scheherazade's role is congruent with the impression one derives from the main characters of Butor's first four works of fiction, who are also the author's surrogates. Louis Lécuyer, Jacques Revel, Léon Delmont, and Pierre Vernier are strangers who appear out of nowhere to disappear into the unknown at the end of each book. That impression is greater than in the works of several other writers I have discussed, Robbe-Grillet for instance, because of the weight given to linear narrative in this group of novels. Where there is similar stress, as in Ollier's *La Mise en scène*, the same effect prevails. The protagonist's alien status is clearly stated in *L'Emploi du temps*, where it is an integral part of the anecdote. It is implied elsewhere by various means that isolate the character from his family and his environment. Louis Lécuyer does not belong in the apartment house of *Passage de Milan* in the same manner as others of his generation, who all live with their parents (even Henriette lives with her father, although she does not know it). The only one in a situation vaguely resembling that of Louis is Ahmed, the Egyptian boy, who is literally a stranger. Nor has Louis been invited to the party in his own right: it is Henriette who is invited and who had asked him to escort her. He is in love with Angèle, but she does not even know his name. His aunt, who has practically adopted him, implies that because his father had died and his mother was worthless he has had no real upbringing: "We nicknamed him Puss the evening he landed in our home . . . he looked like a wet kitten" (P, p. 28).

Louis bears a large part of the text's burden of significance, but to think of him as a main character in the usual sense of the term is to betray the work of which he is a part. *Passage de Milan* stands halfway between the next two books, where there is greater emphasis on the principal character (even though in each succeeding one the traditional concept of character tends to disintegrate further),[8] and the following ones, where the emphasis lies elsewhere. All are related, and a key to the concern that informs the aggregate of Butor's works can perhaps be found in the final chapter of his first book: "Every apartment building is a warehouse . . . / As every mind is a warehouse . . . of which an inventory is never taken" (P, p. 281). The reader has been presented with a partial inventory of the building and the minds of individuals as incomplete as the map of Bleston or as the list of objects and cities in *Mobile*. It is one possible view of a Paris apartment, but even though it is a distorted one it makes a significant statement about its values. As Jacques Revel exclaims in *L'Emploi du temps*, "How precious was such a distortion!" (p. 122). That selective process serves to emphasize human solitude, within and in spite of certain social structures, because of certain others. The two brothers of the second floor, who are pointedly brothers in Christ since both are priests, are complete strangers to each other. The numerous members of the Mogne family who are crowded into the third-floor apartment are solitary human beings, avoiding one another as much as possible. The intellectuals gathered on the fourth floor fail to respond to their host's call for collaboration. The party that is given on the fifth floor is the very symbol of separation and failure. When Virginie Ralon opens the door to her son, Father Alexis Ralon, as he returns from his *lycée*, he goes into his room without speaking a word. When Frédéric Mogne gets home from a day at the office, opening the door to his apartment with his key, no one bothers to greet him, and he goes alone into his room to put on his slippers. Mogne's father and mother-in-law, who also live in the apartment, are even more isolated that he is, having been cast aside by those who are younger. Young people also bear the heavy weight of solitude, and theirs is essential to the meaning of *Passage de Milan*, but detailed expression of isolation among older people tends to remain in the reader's mind because of an imagistic link with the theme of deterioration that also runs through Butor's work.

Decay is quite naturally associated with death; solitude fits the idea of an inventory of discrete things or beings. All four are stated in the opening pages of *Passage de Milan*. The lonely priest contemplates a vacant lot in which a complement of discarded, useless objects slowly deteriorate while a bird of prey ominously hovers above. Those are correlatives of the evils of the world, against which the writer battles. Paradoxically, he must make common cause with evil in order to vanquish it—remove himself from life in order to sustain it, represent reality in order to change it, choose solitude in order to communicate, produce a series of functioning texts that are in constant danger of becoming mummified. It is a paradox that was already present in the legend of Scheherazade, who, in order to live, had condemned herself to a form of death, existing only through the stories she told.

The writer's situation is more ambiguous than hers, for he agrees with King Shahryar, who cried out, "Only in utter solitude can man be safe from the doings of this vile world! By Allah, life is naught but one great wrong."⁹ In essence, that is similar to the remark made by Albert Camus' Caligula, "Men die and they are not happy"—and in both instances the reaction led to additional wrong-doings and deaths. In the end, the King praises Scheherazade for having been "the means of my repentance from slaying the daughters of folk,"¹⁰ and Caligula is forced to admit: "I did not follow the right path, I have come to nothing." Both, out of different forms of despair, like those responsible for the Santa Barbara bombing I mention in the third section of this chapter, were driven to violent action. Scheherazade, on the contrary, was moved by compassion, and her means was to change the King's outlook. So the writer, knowing he cannot change the world through direct action or even propaganda, attempts to change his reader's conception of the world.

Such a change, if effected in one's reading the fiction of Michel Butor, may be the cumulative result of statements and images, none of which is shocking by itself. In that, he differs from those writers who, instead of relying on the scandal caused by conflicting representations, seek to dismantle, so to speak, the very process of linguistic representation in order to show how one such process (that of bourgeois society) can produce a "great wrong." Butor accepts the means of representation of his society, but he keeps changing his angle. What he has said of Raymond Roussel could, with a slight alteration, be applied to himself: he wonders, in the presence of any sort of event, if it could not be represented in a different light or from a different standpoint. In his four early pieces of fiction that difference is insidiously suggested to the reader in statements such as Jenkins makes to Revel concerning the city of Bleston in *L'Emploi du temps.* "You have mainly seen the fine sections until now, those avenues and gardens where the trees protect us, but some day you will necessarily go forth into those nearly deserted streets where one gets lost" (p. 91). Just as the theme of solitude and the imagery of decay oriented the reader of *Passage de Milan* toward a rejection, or at least a questioning, of a behavior that he, as a Frenchman, recognizes as his own, the same factors, intensified in *L'Emploi du temps*, imply a broader challenge of urban life in western Europe.

Images of decay and disease are supplemented by others that suggest basic structural flaws. Typical of such is the fissure that has long existed in the tower of the Old Cathedral, preventing the bells, of which the city was proud, from being rung on festive occasions. The correlation is obvious between that image and the writer's inability to find happiness because life is "one great wrong." In this book, everything crumbles except the written text itself. Even fire, of which there are many manifestations, loses part of its dual symbolism, and its purifying and regenerative virtues give way before a vision of annihilation. Tinged with a kind of death-wish, apprehension rather than hope dominates the narrative. When Jacques Revel, the narrator, who has already lost Rose, learns of Ann's engagement, he pictures himself as thoroughly vanquished, with no hope of revenge, "As if I were already dead" (E, p. 252), and during his last few days in Bleston he behaves like a specter: "Ghostlike, Saturday, in the house of All Saints Garden . . . Ghostlike during the afternoon, on Sunday . . . Ghostlike each evening . . ." (p. 296). When Jenkins expresses his own anxiety, telling Revel that "the desire swells in me more and more to see all those calamities break out, in order to bring the suspense to an end"—that part of the statement is more likely to remain in the reader's mind than its less discouraging sequel: "and enable us to walk at last, speak at last, breathe" (p. 92). Jenkins, of course, whose family is from Bleston and who himself has never left the city, is close to being the warden of established order that Burton, the mystery-novel writer, talks about. As such, he has reasons for being fearful of the future.

Revel, on the other hand, resembles the detective whose aim is to "shake up, disturb, ransack, lay bare, and change" (p. 147). He does little of that in Bleston, but he is only the author's agent and his presence is that of a passive consciousness, which, as it acquires deeper awareness, tends to prod the reader into active consciousness. Bleston is eventually a representation of the reader's reality, and what Revel does not do in his fictional existence, the author may well effect within the reader.

If *La Modification*, which also carries forward the same themes and imagery, is the instance of the greatest emphasis on a single character, who is this time pointedly assimilated to the reader by means of the second-person narrative, *Degrés* marks a return to the multiplicity of characters and stress on relationships that distinguished *Passage de Milan*. *Degrés* also relies less on relatively conventional plot and fictional continuity than *L'Emploi du temps* and *La Modification* and points in the direction of Butor's more recent works with its emphasis on discrete textual elements. The unsettling effect of *Passage de Milan*, both within the text and within the reader, was obtained by confronting sixty-odd solitary characters with one another within two separate frameworks—a family unit and a social event. Basically, the same holds true for *Degrés*, with the *lycée*, "that building for dreary initiations" (D, p. 241), taking the place of Angèle's party. In addition, outside factors are given a greater role. I refer not only to the presence of a stranger, Maurice Tangala, who expands the part of Ahmed (as Horace Buck had done in *L'Emploi du temps*) or to family events that are allowed to intrude upon the activities of the *lycée* but also to the quotations. These, although an integral component of the teacher-student complex, represent an intervention from outside the time-space limits of this book and manifest a conscious intertextuality that reinforces its functioning and significance.

Even more than previously, all components of the fiction are commonplace. This applies to the realistic elements and to the imaginary ones as well. It includes characters' impressions, dreams, and fantasies, although the latter are far less frequent than in the previous fiction. To French readers who have had a secondary education (Butor himself admits that under present conditions that is the only audience he can hope for), every detail of the book is a familiar one: the behavior of students in and out of the classroom, their teachers' appearances and attitudes, family life with its concomitant pleasures and sorrows, the various courses in the curriculum, the types of homework, recitations, classroom procedures, tests, and the authors that are read. The scene will remain familiar to such readers at least until members of the generation that began school in the mid-sixties start graduating. Of course, not everyone has experienced within his own family the complete assortment of adultery, divorce, and deaths that plague families in *Degrés*, nor has everyone taken Greek, Latin, Italian, and English in school; but even though some of the experiences may have been vicarious, they are all related to commonplace events. All those who have attended a *lycée* have undoubtedly read selections from Clément Marot, Rabelais, Montaigne, Bossuet, Boileau, Racine, Saint-Simon, and other French writers, usually those precise texts that are quoted. Likewise, those who took Greek read Homer; those who took Latin studied Vergil and Livy; those who selected Italian read Dante; and the many who enrolled in English courses know *Macbeth, Julius Caesar*, Keats, and Coleridge. They have been confronted with the same experiments in physics, the same exercises in algebra, the same illustrations of the way the earth's surface is projected on a map. But no one, surely, has had anything comparable to the experience provoked by a reading of *Degrés*. The order in which the elements of the text are put together is what matters (Marc Saporta's demonstration of that proposition, *Composition No. 1*, was published two years later). Within such an order, interactions between contiguous elements acquire importance as chronology and ordinary time intervals are eliminated.

During an interview given in Buffalo in 1964, Karlheinz

Stockhausen said that to compose was to relate. That is essentially what Michel Butor has done in *Degrés*. The originality of this work, when contrasted with *L'Emploi du temps* and *La Modification*, lies in the importance given to the newly created relationships and in their direct contribution to meaning. The story line is important, but it is less a means to signify than a framework within which signifying elements are located. In *La Modification*, the contiguity in Delmont's wallet of an expired membership card in the Louvre museum and a valid one for the Dante Society has meaning only as a correlative to the complex feelings he has toward Paris, Rome, his wife, and his mistress. In *Degrés*, the teacher of Italian returns home to his wife, who is critically ill. When she asks what happened in class, he answers, "Well, it was the usual routine stuff" (p. 51). Before he can finish, his sister brings the routine afternoon tea. The next sequence shows a student watching his physics teacher "go through the same gestures he had made one year ago, at the same moment of the solar cycle" (p. 51). That page conveys much concerning death and its inability to disturb the habits of life and, conversely, the failure of dull, deadly teaching to spark intellectual life. That is closely related to the narrative thread along which Pierre Vernier proceeds, but it reaches the reader independently of it. The story line is so intimately fused with the architecture of the novel that it tends to recede into the background while one reads, coming to the fore again during reflective periods after the book has been finished and helping to unify its many components.

Degrés is about relationships or, as the title suggests in part, about degrees and qualities in relationships; it also effects a removal of masks. The twenty-one characters who are introduced in the first part of the book are presented in seven groups of triads, ranging from the very tight to the extremely loose. The tightest is formed by the three main characters, narrators or pseudonarrators: Pierre Vernier, his nephew Pierre Eller, and the latter's other uncle, Henri Jouret. The loosest is comprised of the black student, Tangala, the physical education instructor and the Catholic chaplain; within the historical past, there is no possible way in which they could be related. For his closely related triad, Butor might have chosen a tighter although less plausible group than a nephew and his two uncles. A son and his two parents would have been hard to fit into the context of a *lycée*; but perhaps the main reason for rejecting such a group was its naturalness rather than its implausibility, the more social aspects of an uncle-nephew relationship being better suited to the book's scheme. As they stand, the triads might be seen as ranging from the social (or contrived) to the purely human (or true). In this instance, the most human triad is also the loosest. The initiation at the *lycée* consists in introducing its participants into the basic community of people, and the process is made possible by the complex web of relationships Butor has devised, that is, by the book's architecture. That initiation is what a *lycée* should provide in actual life but does not. By presenting, as a backdrop to the drama that unfolds, the reality of the *lycée*, its failure to educate truly, Butor leads the reader through a more effective form of education or initiation. But, as in all such ceremonies, his active participation is required if the process is to be fruitful.

While one focus of *Degrés* is on relationships, a second lies in the courses that are taught, especially what is called the pivotal lesson on Columbus' discovery of America (pivotal both in the book and in history) and others on aspects of the Renaissance. They were obviously chosen because they correspond to an age when so many things were being seen in a new light. As one of the students expresses it in class, it was a time when "people have been obliged to admit that the world was not what it had been thought to be" (p. 34). They were also chosen because of a number of parallels that could be suggested between the Renaissance and present times. To the physical discovery of America would perhaps correspond a spiritual one, that of a new concept of the brotherhood of men, to which America is not completely foreign and which is symbolized by the group formed by Tangala, the priest, and the instructor. It is signified in negative fashion by the interest Tangala shows in "everything that can take away from Europe, from Whites . . . that exclusiveness of civilization they continue to claim for themselves, in spite of all the evidence they have themselves unearthed, which they themselves continue to search for and bring forth, fostering that contradiction, that great cleavage, that great lie that undermines them" (D, p. 91). The fissure of Bleston's Old Cathedral reappears, running through the length of Europe.

The Renaissance is linked not only to a general attitude present in this century but more specifically to the *lycée* as well when the students are asked to read what Rabelais and Montaigne wrote concerning education. Explaining that a changed view of the world entailed a corresponding change in the educational system, the narrator adds, "an educational reform that took a long time getting under way, that is perhaps no more than roughed out even today" (p. 3). Pierre Eller has been undergoing the inadequate initiation provided by the *lycée* when he is suddenly confronted with his uncle Henri wearing the mask of a teacher: "You didn't get over that tremendous change . . . for the man who was so gentle, so whimsical, so playful, whom you knew so well . . . suddenly has become someone else, tough, curt, somewhat sarcastic" (p. 23). As a result, both the former mask of uncle and the present one of teacher are destroyed, leaving Pierre Eller with the sense of a new relationship that he does not quite understand, the strangeness of which causes him to blush. A similar doffing of masks, although for different reasons, occurs when the teacher of Italian, after the death of his wife, can no longer hold back his tears in front of his class.

Pierre Vernier undertakes to write his book for his nephew and, indirectly, for all those who, like him, have been through the grades in a *lycée*, in order to correct the "great wrong" that is embodied in the present system. The compelling force that drives him and Butor even more so is implicitly mentioned when students are translating *The Rhyme of the Ancient Mariner*, and he quotes one of Coleridge's marginal commentaries, "And ever and anon throughout his future life an agony constraineth him to travel from land to land." This calls attention to the unquoted lines, "And till my ghastly tale is told / This heart within me burns"—a perfect example of the workings of intertextuality, as unwritten words are nevertheless inscribed in the text. His is a dangerous project, and as his friend Micheline warns, "You will lose your own life at this" (p. 320). He is willing to risk death in order to save his nephew and countless others, just as Scheherazade was willing to face the same danger when she asked her father to take her to the King, and she persisted in spite of his warnings. "I shall never desist, O my father."[11] Pierre Vernier's answer to Micheline is that of a lover: "Fortunately you are with me." She remains with him to the last paragraph of the book, when he lies on a hospital bed, long since unable to continue his work. The narrative has managed to progress without his help. That is one indication that *Degrés* does not represent a step backwards (in the direction of *Passage de Milan*) from the standpoint of narrative technique. Vernier's withdrawal does not merely reveal the failure and death of a character, it signifies the death of the narrator as the subject of fiction. It is true that Revel and Delmont tend to disintegrate, but it is left for Vernier to demonstrate that the narrative can continue even though he, the narrator, remains silent. "Who speaks?" is the anguished question that closes the book.

2. NONLINEAR WORKS

If *Degrés* develops and perfects fictional concepts present in the series of four early works of fiction that Jean Roudaut has grouped under the heading "Romanesque I,"[12] the books of

"Romanesque II," particularly *Mobile* (1962), further expand on a fictional device present in *Degrés* and *Passage de Milan*. The narrator, having been exposed as a dispensable device, no longer needs to be present. Yet it is characteristic of Butor that he does not allow himself to be constricted by any rhetorical principle. In works that follow *Degrés* the narrator is either present or absent, textual matters are dominant or subordinate, according to the specific needs of a particular book. In *Mobile* the narrator has vanished and, as in the first and fourth works, commonplace elements are carefully rearranged in order to produce an uncommon impression, more valuable, nevertheless, than the conventional one. The rhetorical shift already in evidence in *Degrés* is now fully effected. Plot and the narrative continuity one associates with it, which had made a comeback of sorts in *L'Emploi du temps* and *La Modification* only to decline again in *Degrés*, have now been discarded and are thus no longer available as a vehicle for meaning. Intertextual operations, already present in *Degrés* in the shape of allusions, references, or quoted texts, are given considerable emphasis. One is tempted to say that fictional elements have, like plot, completely disappeared, but the statement would be meaningless here. Representational fiction, after all, is no more than a rearrangement of "reality"; every minute element in the wildest of fantasies possesses a specific referent in that "reality."

In *Mobile*, textual elements are not fused into a narrative having the continuity one is conditioned to impose upon events. They have been welded into an architectural continuum that is esthetically unfamiliar, thus giving the impression of discontinuity. The process could be more effective in disturbing the reader's prejudices to the extent that he is aware of its arbitrariness. This sensitivity determines meaning more freely than within a narrative sequence. In *L'Emploi du temps*, when Revel fails to note Horace Buck's address at the time of his first visit, making it impossible for him to return as he promised, even though he makes a foredoomed effort to do so, the reader is almost inevitably led to pass judgment on his character. When in *Mobile* a mention of the Southern Ute Reservation is placed alongside a quotation from Dodge and Zim's *The American Southwest* describing Indian culture of about 400 A.D., the reader is free to consider the juxtaposition as irrelevant, or interesting, or shocking.

One is again reminded of surrealist images created by bringing together signifiers that refer to unrelated concepts. The spark touched off within the reader's imagination is the greater as the referents are less closely connected. The rhetoric of Michel Butor is, in this second series of works, distinguished by emphasis on the device of juxtaposing either references to extra-textual elements or small fictional components that are too limited to acquire much meaning by themselves. Unlike surrealist metaphors, however, the potency of the association is not expended at once, and elements are brought together several times in a kind of permutation. In *Degrés*, a number of brief quotations are repeated: Banquo's question, "What, can the devil speak true?" a couple of lines from Keats' "On First Looking into Chapman's Homer," and a phrase from Montaigne's essays. But in the main the excerpts are sequential, reflecting the students' progress in the texts they studied. Repetitions are equally plausible, given the triple narrative architecture. In *Mobile*, as there is neither narrator nor narrative, matters of plausibility become irrelevant. Effectiveness is the sole criterion.

By selecting a relatively long quotation, provided it is unified by a strong theme or subject-matter and, after breaking it up in such a way as to preserve the theme in each fragment and distributing it throughout the book, Butor eschews the dullness of repetition and contributes to architectural cohesiveness. Since there is, within the quoted text, narrative progression from one fragment to the next, that contributes to the motion or "mobility" of the whole. Using a number of quotations taken from a variety of outside texts enhances such results. To anyone interested in the United States, and it is hard to imagine *Mobile* as being read by someone who is not, the quotations do not offer new knowledge. The basic referents of the text, being theoretically factual, are also familiar to those living in the United States and to many who have read about it. The small fictional components, such as "An apricot-colored Nash driven by an old black" (p. 83), are little more than accentuations (rather than distortions) of factual elements. In short, with the possible exception of a few dream sequences, every detail of *Mobile* is a familiar one, in most cases with a factual referent, but the aggregate is fictional because of the unconventional view that is conveyed.

The United States has been subjected to an interpretation similar to the one applied to the *lycée* in *Degrés*. In the process, both shortcomings in the present and opportunities for the future have been disclosed. In both instances, the revelation has come out of the reader's experience with the text rather than because of a demonstration by the author. When Sartre, in *Le Sursis*, confronts the situation of Mathieu in Southern France with that of Milan Hlinka in Central Europe, he explains: "At three-thirty in the afternoon, Mathieu was still waiting, on the threshold of a frightful future; at the same instant, at four-thirty, Milan had no more future."[13] In *La Peste*, before describing Paneloux's first sermon, Camus warns: "Long before that sermon, people were already talking about it in town, and it constituted, in its own way, an important date in the history of that period."[14] Interpretation in traditional fiction is often added to the narration as an integral part of the text. Interpretative statements were present in *Degrés*, as when Pierre Vernier pretends to read Tangala's thoughts but actually gives Butor's own indictment of Western civilization. Nor are they totally absent from *Mobile*. Toward the end of the forty-ninth chapter ("Wisconsin") the exclamation, "How eagerly we await you, America!" along with several others in that and in the final chapter are attributable to Butor, thus testifying to the difficulty authors have in leaving the reader alone. Such statements, however, are relatively rare. They also retain their share of ambiguity. One reader might accept the statement just quoted with the understanding that expectations will eventually be fulfilled; another might take it as an ironic or pathetic expression of a forlorn hope.

Before the typography of *Mobile* is discussed, a brief examination of *Description de San Marco* (1963) will be useful at this juncture. Though it reminds one of *Mobile* in several respects, it signals the reappearance of the narrator. That is less a reversal of a rhetorical trend than a necessity brought about by the nature of the text. In addition to the quoted texts, the architecture of *Mobile* was based on alphabetical listings (of states, colors, flavors, and so forth) and on echoes reverberating from state to state because of the many cities with identical names (Cordova, in Alabama and Alaska; Douglas, in Alaska and Arizona; Florence, in Arizona and Arkansas; and so on). Clearly, neither the alphabet nor homonymy could provide a satisfactory basis for an interpretation of San Marco. Quotations remained a possibility, and Butor might well have used works by Ruskin, Proust, and many others. But the basilica provided its own text, the numerous inscriptions taken from the Latin Vulgate translation of the Bible serving as captions to the mosaics in the church. Mosaics and captions provided the means to translate spatial architecture into the sequential features of a book. Since San Marco is one of the major tourist attractions in Venice, a distinction that tends to eclipse its existence as a place of worship, the narrative account of a visit, esthetic rather than touristic, is a logical device to give effective unity. It could also be one through which a form of irony is introduced, for had not the basilica been degraded from its original state, its true narrator would have been an officiating priest. Also, because of the fixed, monumental nature of its object, as opposed to the motion that characterized so many referents in *Mobile*, the narrative line adds an indispensable minimum of movement to the text. The result is a work of fiction, for clearly a description of San Marco either narrated by a priest or centered in the consciousness of a person attending Mass would have been an utterly different one, as it would have been had Butor chosen to emphasize statuary and architectural lines rather than mosaics. To paraphrase Jean Ricardou,[15] the most objective description of the basilica would be limited to those two words, San Marco.

Detailed description, because it is both incomplete and linear, marks the birth of fiction. Rather than a true description, it at once becomes a "precious distortion," to adapt a phrase from *L'Emploi du temps*—provided the author is able to endow it with that quality. Here, it is inevitably a worldly representation; the visit begins on the *piazza* in the midst of tourists from all nations, buying souvenirs and consuming coffee, fruit juices, and *gelati*. They are present throughout the visit, as indispensable to San Marco today as were the merchants, butchers, *condottieri*, and pillaging crusaders of earlier times. Tourists' conversations, echoes from the past, descriptions of mosaics, and Latin inscriptions are the basic elements that are played against one another as others were in *Mobile*. All are familiar to anyone who has visited Venice; most of them are familiar even to those who have merely read about that city. As in previous works, their selection and ordering determine the meaning that a reader will extract from the text, although Butor's own suggestions appear stronger than before.

Format and typographical disposition distinguish *Mobile* and *Description de San Marco* as much if not more than anything else. It could be argued that such physical features are not absolutely indispensable. It could also more convincingly be shown that they go hand and glove with the concept of a discontinuous rhetoric and enhance the effect of the two works. They represent an effort, on Butor's part, to make better use of the physical characteristics of a book along lines once explored by Mallarmé. Full success cannot yet be claimed, for some of

the breaks between one page and the next are esthetically somewhat awkward. The ideal solution, as I have suggested in an
earlier chapter, would involve treating each page as a complete
unit, but in 1963 Michel Butor had not yet reached that point.
Of the two, *Mobile* is the more remarkable achievement in that
respect. After an initial period of disorientation, the reader soon
realizes that the unusual typography actually constitutes a
guide, once its correlations have been understood. The use of
capital letters for towns, cities, and states makes them stand
out; the book is divided into chapters according to states, and
homonymous cities and towns afford a link between the states.
Within each chapter, one is not solely concerned with the
features, problems, or activities of a single state, since, depending on their location and importance, states have cultural or
economic effects on their neighbors. At a glance, a reader can
tell "where" he is: in the state the chapter deals with, in a
neighboring one, or in one slightly more removed, according
to the distance separating the text from the left-hand margin.
Each city generates a small textual unit, the core of which is
printed in italics and the surrounding matter in roman type.
Italic statements convey what might be termed the coat of arms
of each state, expressed either by means of quotations or direct
mention. Quotations are reproduced in conventional fashion,
while other references are set in emblematic patterns. Three
themes, for instance, fill North Carolina's coat of arms: the sea,
Cherokee Indians, and the Blacks. The Cherokees appear in a
series of quotations, the Blacks by means of the single, isolated
word *Noir* or *Noire* pushed against the left-hand margin, and
the sea is translated into a rhythmic typographical disposition:

La mer,   *Sea,*
           les vagues,   *waves,*
le sel,   *salt,*
           le sable,   *sand,*
l'écume,   *foam,*
           les algues.   *seaweed.*

As the theme recurs, words describing other, more detailed or precise aspects of the sea, its life and action, replace the original ones. Birds, a portion of Florida's coat of arms, appear in flight formation:

Geais de Floride,	*Florida jays,*
cailles colombes de Key West,	*Key West quail doves,*
gobes-mouches à queue fourchue,	*fork-tailed fly-catchers*
coucous de Maynard,	*Maynard cuckoos,*
oiseaux royaux gris.	*gray kingbirds.*

The flora is depicted in freer form:

Bananiers,	*Banana plants,*
orangers de Valence,	*Valencia orange trees,*
orangers de Jaffa,	*Jaffa orange trees,*
feuilles de cuivre,	*copper-colored leaves,*
plantes chenilles,	*caterpillar plants,*
agaves.	*American aloes.*

Rules of punctuation are scrupulously respected, enabling readers to find their way through the strange disposition, avoiding confusion between neighboring emblematic representations. That, incidentally, is an indication that Butor does not advocate innovations for the sake of novelty. Even though his desire may be to unsettle his audience, there is no deliberate attempt at obfuscation. The functional purpose of typographic design is clearly in evidence when one compares the pages of *Mobile* to those of *Description de San Marco.* In the latter work, as I have pointed out, the discontinuous aspect of the rhetoric is mitigated by the presence of a narrative line that enables the reader to keep his bearings. Composition of the page is modified only to distinguish tourists' conversations (against the left-hand margin), narrative and commentary (one inch from the left), and description of the church and its mosaics (two inches from the left); italics are used to transcribe tourist talk, large capitals to reproduce the inscriptions in San Marco. Since no other device is needed, none is used.

The two other items Jean Roudaut included under the heading of "Romanesque II," *Réseau aérien* (1962) and *6 810 000 litres d'eau par seconde* (1965), had been originally designed for radio broadcast. When published in printed form, however, and this is especially true of the latter work, both take into consideration the reader's specific requirements, as distinguished from those of the listener. (A stage adaptation of *6 810 000 litres d'eau par seconde* was also performed by La Comédie des Alpes in February, 1968, at the mobile theater in Grenoble's Maison de la Culture, in conjunction with the 1968 Winter Olympics.) The esthetics of a work designed to be heard by individual listeners sitting in their own homes is closer to that of a volume designed for an evening of solitary reading than, say, the esthetics of the theater where live actors combine their performance with visual, sound, and dynamic effects to convey an experience to a group audience. Obviously, the rhetoric of audio communication is markedly different from that of sight communication, especially when language is involved. In *Réseau aérien*, concern for the medium appears to have been less developed than in subsequent works. It features no narrator and develops along a slender story line. A man and woman, both teachers, board a plane for Noumea, where they have accepted positions, and during their flight brief snatches of dialogue convey their anxiety, dreams, and hopes. At the same time, passengers in the same plane and those in nine others exchange words that supplement those of the principal couple. Everyday realism is not sought for, as only ten different voices are used in order to speak the various dialogues. Because all exchanges are roughly of the same length, because of their conciseness and the suggestivity of the vocabulary, *Réseau aérien* possesses definite lyrical qualities. Anonymity and the use of the same voice to transmit words of different characters, both help to universalize the links between couples. The process is related to, although distinct from, what took place in *Degrés*. The relationship existing between two distinct persons, man and woman, forming a well-defined unit unlike any other, is destroyed only in its uniqueness; its essential qualities remain. Compared with other works by Butor, it reads like a limited experiment, with interesting possibilities yet to be developed.

Examining *6 810 000 litres d'eau par seconde*, a work centered in Niagara Falls, one is in more familiar surroundings. Typography and format recall those of *Mobile* and *Description de San Marco*. Two texts from Chateaubriand's works, depicting the Falls, play a role similar to that of biblical inscriptions in *Description de San Marco* or to the varied quotations in *Mobile*. The motifs of tourists visiting a famous monument and of the interaction between visitors and monument are taken up again with different emphases. The technique of using a multiplicity of couples, here better integrated because of the honeymoon tradition associated with Niagara Falls, to express the recurring interests or obsessions of a few and thus broadening them, recalls *Réseau aérien*. Disintegrating relationships make one think of *Degrés*. A complex architecture based on numbers and units of time is common to nearly all other previous works. That, while probably not exhausting the list, again emphasizes the unity of Butor's fiction. The differences, also quite noticeable, exist on account of his seeking more effective means of conveying his dissatisfied view of the world, a vision partially contained in each of his compositions.

6 810 000 litres d'eau par seconde is divided into twelve sections corresponding to months of the year, from April to March. On another level, the book encompasses a continuous time sequence of some seventy-six hours. Those, however, are not evenly spaced out among the twelve sections. As the waters of the Niagara seem to increase their speed on approaching the precipice before the final, downward rush, the time of individual life appears to accelerate with the approach of death. In Butor's text, too, hours slip by faster and faster, their number being regularly augmented until the final section includes twelve. Throughout the book, an announcer, who recalls in a depersonalized fashion the narrator of *Description de San*

Marco, whose voice predominates, provides a descriptive and thematic narrative. A second voice, not quite so strong in intensity, reads Chateaubriand's prose. At first there are two fairly continuous short excerpts that are soon broken up into isolated sentences and gradually rearranged so that words from one sentence are exchanged with words from another, with both old and new sentences, along with single words or phrases, inserted in a carefully chosen context, which adds a suggestive touch of surrealism to the words of the nineteenth-century writer. Those two voices are meant to originate at center stage, so to speak (a stereophonic broadcast is assumed). The remaining voices—newlyweds, older married couples, unwed couples, divorcées, widows, widowers, and solitary persons—are divided between right and left loud speakers for purposes of contrast and balance. A number of accompanying noises (in addition to chimes, always "centered," which mark the passage of time) are also divided between the two speakers. With the broadcast performance in mind, Butor has provided what he elsewhere called "mobile structures":[16] the broadcaster may choose among ten possible versions varying in length, and the listener, playing with his channel controls, "will be able to change seats within the architecture that is being broadcast" (N, p. 20). The reader, too, has the necessary instructions in order to select the version he deems most suitable, and furthermore, "mobility of reading being greater than that of any kind of hearing situation," he will be able to, "book in hands, dream of all sorts of listening possibilities" (p. 20). The announcer's text, because of its intensity, appears in bold-face type; Chateaubriand's text is in italics; time indications are in small capitals; conversations, thoughts, and dreams are in roman type; different margins approximate the separation between broadcast channels.

After the first section introducing Niagara Falls, mostly by means of Chateaubriand's words, two couples arrive at the site. One shares their expectations, their hopes, their reactions, and their memories, among the profusion of flowers in the park and baubles in souvenir shops. The hint of deterioration heard in the initial section ("It goes without saying that the sight has changed considerably"—p. 14) becomes a major theme in the third, its correlative being the appearance of a black couple and reference to the isolation into which blacks are driven. Afterwards, it gradually permeates all relationships. At the core of the volume, a "Bachelor's Invocation" expresses the lament of the contemporary individual, alienated from so many things, especially from love. The theme of love (which a mere mention of Niagara Falls is bound to evoke), that of its decline, and the pageant of seasons from spring to winter conjure up in the mind ancient myths of death and resurrection. Intimation of rebirth, however, such as could be detected in *Passage de Milan* or *Mobile*, is lacking here. The mood is more in keeping with that of *L'Emploi du temps*. The time of the final section is March, but there is no spring, nor does Adonis come to life again. Toward the end, the announcer speaks of tears and blood: the newlyweds fail to communicate; the older couple echo the words of the opening section, "We have changed." The text closes with Chateaubriand's description of badgers attempting to fish out of the whirlpool the broken remains of other animals. The very last words are taken from the subtitle of *Atala*: "The Loves of Two Savages in the Desert."

Once more, one has witnessed the same process in its operation. Niagara Falls does not belong to the American folklore alone; it is as internationally famous in its own way as San Marco is. All the details presented in *6 810 000 litres d'eau par seconde*, with the probable exception of such precise data as are given in the title or here and there in the text, are familiar to Europeans and Americans alike, but the total impression is unlike anything the words "Niagara Falls" could have suggested before. Once more the writer has seen that life was "one great wrong" and, like Scheherazade, has described it in his tale, hoping to change the reader-king before he does additional wrong.

The folklore that surrounds Niagara Falls and San Marco is basically no different from that which misrepresents Hong Kong or New York City. While one might say that Butor's ultimate aim is similar to Robbe-Grillet's, the difference in their approach to myth are quite evident in spite of Robbe-Grillet's evolution after *Les Gommes*, a change that tends to reduce the contrast. With the latter, signs inscribing the myth in the text are liable to proliferate on the textual plane, leaving the referents far in the distance, nearly forgotten. Butor's point of departure lies with the referent, to which he endeavors to give a new representation.

3. Textual Production

Portrait de l'artiste en jeune singe, with its undisguised autobiographical elements and interplay of two series of fragmented narratives, heralds a third period in Butor's fiction. It is one in which intertextuality plays a dominant function. He has been conscious of the process before, as I have shown, and as a 1964 text suggests: "A book must be a mobile awakening the mobility of other books, a flame rekindling their fire."[17] As with Jean Pierre Faye's *Analogues* and Claude Ollier's *L'Echec de Nolan*, the primary, purposeful work is done with his own previous texts, but the process is altogether different. As of this writing, two major works give evidence of that phenomenon, *Illustrations II* (1969) and *Où* (1971).[18] Each one in its textual genesis, evidences distinctive characteristics. I should stress again that Butor's interests are seldom exclusive. During this same period he has published other quite different works, including the one in which he pays tribute to Charles Fourier, *La Rose des vents* (1970), which is linear in its development.

At the source of *Illustrations II* lie nine texts that had originally been generated by photographs, engravings, watercolors, paintings, music, and "logograms," the latter being a special form of poetry invented by Christian Dotremont—one might also say, a special form of painting with words. Dotrement's presence here furnishes a key, as it implies that his work and, say, André Masson's are basically of the same nature. In other words, Butor's concept of "text" is a very broad one. To him, paintings and other works in the plastic arts are texts; landscapes are texts; the city of Bleston, in *L'Emploi du temps*, is a text that Revel needs to decipher. Seen in that light, those nine elements are themselves conscious absorptions, transformations, and representations of other texts. They are then transformed a second time, recast into a new shape.

Sometimes an intermediate step is involved. To elucidate this, a specific example should prove helpful. Out of the nine texts that eventually produced *Illustrations II*, I have chosen the one based on engravings by Jacques Hérold. First, fifteen plates were published under the title *Dialogue des régnes* (1967), each one displaying an embossed engraving by Hérold and a text by Butor. The plates are boxed but neither bound nor numbered so no definite sequence has been imposed upon the series. On each plate, arrangement and length of text differs according to the shape and mass of the engraved surface. Sometimes the text appears to rush in and fill all available nonengraved space; sometimes there is a mirrorlike effect between engraving and text. In all cases, perhaps because of the contagious effect of the title, a dialogue seems to develop between the free, rather dynamic abstract shapes and colors of Hérold's work on the one hand, and Butor's verbal inscriptions on the other. Lesser masses of text, usually vertical in shape, tend to be enumerative and devoid of syntax. Larger masses, often but not always horizontal, are made up of one or more complete sentences. In nearly all instances, each textual mass begins and ends with one of a series of key words: *sommeil, murmure, poussière, brume,* and *ombre*. On each plate, the word that ends one mass usually begins the next one. Days of the week, months, and seasons also provide recurrent words for the texts, as do names of countries and continents. The reigns of the title are those of the animal, vegetal, and mineral kingdoms. From the actual dialogues that have been imagined within the texts, there arise familiar themes, common to much of Butor's fiction and none the less serious for being stated by lesser creatures. Those dialogues merge into a lament conveying feelings of solitude and separation, exile and imprisonment. One is reminded of Revel's exile and imprisonment in Bleston, the bachelor's solitude as expressed at Niagara Falls, or the separation between Vernier and his nephew.

The intermediate step was taken when Butor's text alone was published in a conventionally bound book.[19] As a first consequence of that, an unchangeable order for the text had to be established. It turns out that the bound version begins with what was the ninth plate of the original collection as it came from the publisher: "Shadows of pine trees stretch out over the water on a Monday dawn." The selection may have been made because the references to dawn and to the beginning of the week seemed logical in such a position. What was originally the first plate now constitutes the last sequence, with references to sleep, November, night and midnight. To avoid the too obvious coming together of identical words at the end of one paragraph and the beginning of the next, more noticeable now that masses of text have been changed into linear sequences, one or several of the original series of key words have been inserted as separate paragraphs. Later, a full phrase or sentence, containing one of the same words, is placed in a similar position. So that there would not be too great a difference in length between sequences (several of Hérold's engravings left little room for the text), the total number has been reduced from fifteen to ten. While the mobility of the original plates has been lost, Butor has tried to prevent the order from becoming too rigid by separating them with the phrases *Ou bien* and *Ou encore*; both imply the possibility of permutation.

The final transformation occurs when the text of *Dialogue des règnes* is absorbed, along with others, into *Illustrations II*.

A number of changes were made in preparation for the insertion. For instance, some of the longer run-in paragraphs have been pruned of many phrases or clauses that accented their lyrical quality. They are now set in lines of unequal length, and the resulting general appearance of "verse" compensates for the loss of a more obvious lyrical effect. Key words, groups of words, or statements that served as articulations between paragraphs have generally disappeared, since the linear nature of sequences, which gave them birth, has also vanished. The text is now composed to function on the page, each page existing as a unit, with the size and shape of the masses of print again being taken into consideration. On occasion, the former articulations have been replaced with vertical series of words taken from a larger vocabulary store in the text; the series play the part of thematic echoes.

Since the text has been inserted into *Illustrations II* among others emanating from different sources, intertextuality properly speaking begins to function. What preceded is not very different from what an author might do when preparing previously published short pieces for inclusion in a collective volume. It would clearly be impossible to go into all the details of actual and possible interactions between the nine texts (or seven texts and two vignettes, as Butor refers to them) inasmuch as they depend in large part on qualities of the reader's imagination. I shall therefore only attempt to give a general idea of the placing of sequences from *Dialogue des règnes*. The ten have been reduced to five groups. Disjunctive phrases like *Ou bien* have been maintained, but the unity of the ten earlier sequences has been abolished. The table of contents of *Illustrations II* permits one to identify precisely the page on which each group begins and where it ends, but what happens in between is less obvious. Yet one perceives at once that since the text of *Dialogue des règnes* is disseminated between pages 40 and 157 of a 262-page book, it will interact more strongly with some texts, less with others. Since those having their source in a painting by Irving Petlin or in photographs by Bill Brandt do not appear before pages 184 and 226, respectively they will, presumably, have only a secondary effect (which a textual analysis might nevertheless be able to trace). On the contrary, the presence of texts based on watercolors by Ruth Franken, *Dans les flammes*, and on music by Henri Pousseur, *Paysage de répons*, will be felt at once; the more so, I believe, because of the contrasts that exist between these three. As befits the title, there is something allegorical and archaic about *Paysage de répons*, and that in itself acts as a setoff. *Dans les flammes*, on the other hand, has its original source in Ruth Franken's reaction to the self-immolation of Buddhist monks in Vietnam. Butor's accompanying text is entitled "Song of the Monk, addressed to Mme Nhu" (Mme Ngo Dinh Nhu, the sister-in-law of Ngo Dinh Diem, who died in the 1963 coup). Its opening lines, appearing on a left-hand page, "Lips of fire./Nostrils of black fire/ in a castle of balks" (I2, p. 50), confront a segment from *Dialogue des règnes* on the right. "February sleep in Piedmont at dawn,/ come, beautiful still waters, said the spark,/ come into this modest hearth, come and glow,/ slowly burn in the center of this core of fervent porphyry" (I2, p. 51). The corresponding nouns "fire" and "spark" serve as catalysts for the interaction, also recalling and revitalizing an earlier association between "spark," "burning," and "blood" within the the text of *Dialogue des règnes* (I2, p. 42).

It is in this book (actually in its predecessor, *Illustrations*, which falls outside the scope of my topic) that Butor, rather than the printer, becomes the master of his own page. That not only allows him tighter control over his conscious intertextual operations, but it also permits him to select thematic running heads that at the same time identify sources of the text. For instance, "Song—Mist—Song" at the top of page 66 indicates that there are two different texts on that page, one from *Dans les flammes*, the other from *Dialogue des règnes*. "Mist" (*brume*) was one of the five key words I noted in connection with the text as it appeared on Hérold's plates. Their presence remains as significant as it was in the source, along with that of other recurrent words. Their role is not only thematic but generative, like that of a rhyme in conventional poetry, since the necessity to end a textual mass with one of five available words determines part of the movement and meaning of its sentences. Also, phrases such as *le murmure des merles* or *la brume du Brésil* most certainly came into existence drafted, so to speak, by the near-homophony of the nouns' first syllables. The second phrase, through the initial consonants of *brume*, may well have called forth *branches des hêtres*. To *maison de cristal*, probably generated by the engraving, corresponds *cristal de mercure*. *Parfum* is often connected with the East, the association being a literary cliché at least since Baudelaire (the word *Asie* actually figured on the original plate), and the word is linked to *pêches* both on account of the alliteration and because peaches originated in the East. *Pêches*, in turn, since that fruit has a pit, brings forth *amande* (I2, pp. 41–42). In other words, this is a book distinguished by textual as well as intertextual operations. One effect of the latter that I can merely suggest, because of its complexity, is to bring together Jacques Hérold's engravings and Ruth Franken's watercolors against a background of music by Henri Pousseur.

The death of a watchman in Santa Barbara, following the explosion of a bomb at a university faculty club, in *Où*, corresponds thematically to the fiery suicide of an Indo-Chinese monk in *Illustrations II*. In *Où* there are seven texts (or, in the same manner as before, five and two, the latter called poles rather than vignettes).[20] Their "autobiographical" nature is what one notices at first, out of habit, I suppose, and a bad one at that. Indeed, those of *Illustrations II* are just as "autobiographical," for they represent the result of a writer's personal confrontation with a newly discovered "text" in the plastic arts. The basic sequences of *Où* are the outcome of the same writer's confrontation with another kind of "text": a place or event to which he has come or which he has experienced for the first time. In either case, the problem is to find a linguistic text that will adequately account for the experience, and I do not see that there is any essential difference either in the experience or in the process of representing it. Actually stressing the similarity, there is mention very early in the book of "the rectangle of my window" (p. 11), by means of which the scenery is framed very much as a painting is (the very word "rectangle" is disseminated throughout the text). The possessive in that quoted phrase pinpoints the one major distinction between *Où* and *Illustrations II*: here a narrator reappears, as he did in *Description de San Marco* following the more "textual" *Mobile*.

The presence of a narrator constitutes one of two unifying factors, the other being a thematic use of climatic phenomena in the five texts: "La Boue à Seoul," "La Pluie à Angkor," "La Brume à Santa Barbara," "La Neige entre Bloomfield et Bernalillo," "Le froid à Zuni." The two "poles" about which those texts revolve are Paris and Sandia Mountain in New Mexico. "J'ai fui Paris" opens the book; its corollary "Je hais Paris" is near the center. Both reverberate throughout the book while on the two closing pages are statements such as "I am coming back," "I shall have to flee again," and "But I shall come back" (O, pp. 391–392). Sandia Mountain also gives birth to two sequences, "35 vues du mont Sandia le soir l'hiver" and "Neuf autres vues du mont Sandia" that are similarly fragmented. Bringing the two together—thirty-five and nine views of Sandia Mountain—calls attention to another intertextual operation, in addition to the sort that was found in *Illustrations II* and for which my previous discussion should provide the pattern. In *Répertoire III*, Butor had entitled "Trente-six et dix vues du Fuji" his commentary on Hokusai's prints, *The Thirty-six Views of Mount Fuji*.[21] That suggests an analogy between Sandia Mountain and Fuji-san, the sacred mountain of Japan, the diminished number of "views" implying a hierarchy between the two. But Sandia is no sacred mountain. The sacred abode of the Taos Pueblo Indians, in the Blue Lake area, lies to the north. Sandia's first syllable repeats Fuji's honorific suffix, emphasizing that it is sacred only as a textual echo; it is a sacred word in the text.

In his essay on Hokusai Butor also drew an analogy between the Japanese artist and Claude Monet, who, in 1862, painted twenty views of the Rouen cathedral as seen from the same window (Hokusai's prints each show Mount Fuji from a different vantage point). That, in turn, permits me to propose a further analogy, this time between Monet looking at his cathedral, always from the same spot, and Michel Butor observing Sandia through the rectangle of his window always from the same angle, bemused by changing shapes and light patterns as the sun goes down. I intimated earlier that for Butor a painting was a text; the equivalence is now complete as his text becomes a counterpart of Monet's paintings. Still, in the same essay he pointed out that "for Monet, the cathedral in Rouen is a pretext."[22] The word "pretext" is perhaps a bit strong where Butor's use of Sandia is concerned, but with that qualification it helps in understanding what is involved in his "representation" of reality. His work is, without question, a textual representation, as the subtitle of *Mobile*, "Study for a Representation of the United States," already indicated; and I noted earlier that even the "description" of San Marco constituted a distortion of the basilica. His concept of "representation" will be further clarified if one recalls that the French phrase *représentation théâtrale* corresponds to our *theatrical performance*. In the word "performance" the idea of mimesis is no longer present. Putting it differently, in a "representation" the process is more important than its object—which has almost become a mere pretext. As if to justify such an interpretation, Butor himself has written: "I feel more and more like organizing visual images, sounds, with words. In that respect, anyway, one can view a book as a small 'theater.' "[23] The narrator of *Où* also casts

some doubt on the appropriateness of the word "description"—
"My description (is it a description?)" (p. 390).

Motion is an important theme in *Où*. The notion of travel
is implied in the five basic component texts. The manner in
which Paris penetrates the text suggests both an attraction and
a repulsion, translated into references to flight from and return
to the city. Sandia Mountain, seemingly the most stationary
landmark in the book, is itself constantly changing as sunlight
hits it at different angles, bringing out its different facets. The
presence of a narrative also contributes to the feeling of movement. An even more eloquent manifestation of that theme is
the way in which the act of writing has maintained its dy-
namism on the printed page. Far from becoming frozen into a
rigid text, it preserves an atmosphere of constant struggle as
the narrator attempts to give a textual representation of what
he experiences. "I endeavor to cast my very small net over
that enormous prey" (p. 15). He frequently explains that he
might have written or should have written something else, that
he is tempted to erase or strike out what he has written or that
he has just torn up a page. In the end, he is forced to admit that
what he has written is not what he thought he was going to
write. In the meantime, the reader has been prompted to share
in the performance.

One of Michel Butor's most bountiful works, *Où* calls for a
far lengthier analysis than this one. It will receive its due, in
time, for it belongs *par excellence* in Barthes's category of
"writable" works. As I reluctantly (and temporarily) abandon
it, however, I would call attention to the evidence it gives of
the writer's sharing with King Shahryar a revulsion at the "great
wrong" that permeates the world. Here it is the wrong perpetrated against the Indians by the Whites who came to America
(the book is dedicated "to all the Indians of New Mexico); the
wrong done by idealists, driven to despair, who resort to bomb-
ings; finally, the ever present wrong of war. "*A pool of blood*

from distant not so distant wars present and close spatters you" (O, p. 252). And everyone else.

NOTES TO CHAPTER TWELVE (Butor)

[1] Michel Butor, *Passage de Milan*, p. 152. Henceforth all references to works of fiction by Michel Butor appear in the body of the text with the following abbreviations: *Passage de Milan*, P; *L'Emploi du temps*, E; *Degrés*, D; *Mobile*, M; *6 810 000 litres d'eau par seconde*, N; *Portrait de l'artiste en jeune singe*, A; *Illustrations II*, I2; *Où*, O. See Bibliography for complete references.

[2] Butor himself has written that Beethoven's "Variations on a Theme by Diabelli" was also an autobiography. Cf. *Dialogue avec 33 variations de Ludwig van Beethoven sur une valse de Diabelli* (Paris: Gallimard, 1971), p. 237.

[3] Georges Raillard, *Michel Butor* (Paris: Gallimard, 1968), p. 14.

[4] See Jennifer Walters' essay, "Symbolism in *Passage de Milan*," *French Review*, XLII, 2 (December 1968), pp. 223–232.

[5] Butor, "L'Alchimie et son langage," in *Répertoire* (Paris: Minuit, 1960), p. 19.

[6] André Breton, *Manifeste du Surréalisme* (1924; rpt. Paris: Pauvert, 1962), p. 23.

[7] Georges Charbonnier, *Entretiens avec Michel Butor* (Paris: Gallimard, 1967), pp. 41–42.

[8] I have developed this point in an essay entitled "The Problem of Point of View in the Early Fiction of Michel Butor," *Kentucky Romance Quarterly*, XVIII, 2 (1971), 145–159.

[9] Richard F. Burton, trans., *The Book of the Thousand Nights and a Night*, Medina Edition (Printed by The Burton Club, n.d.), I, 9.

[10] *Ibid.*, X, 55.

[11] *Ibid.*, I, 23.

[12] Jean Roudaut, "Parenthèse sur la place occupée par l'étude intitulée '6 810 000 litres d'eau par seconde' parmi les autres ouvrages de Michel Butor," *Nouvelle Revue Française*, No. 165 (September 1966), pp. 498–509.

[13] Jean-Paul Sartre, *Le Sursis* (Paris: Gallimard, 1945), p. 7.

[14] Albert Camus, *La Peste* (Paris: Gallimard, 1947), p. 109.

[15] Jean Ricardou, *Problèmes du nouveau roman* (Paris: Seuil, 1967), pp. 18–19.

[16] Butor, "Recherches sur la technique du roman," in *Répertoire II* (Paris: Minuit, 1964), pp. 98–99.

[17] Butor, "Victor Hugo romancier," in *Répertoire II*, p. 240.

[18] *Illustrations* (1964), in my opinion, does not quite belong to this group. It does share with *Illustrations II* a similar origin, and changes in the original texts were made when they were collected in a volume. They were not fused together, however, and their individuality remained intact. The intertextuality involved is of a more common kind.

[19] Butor, *Paysage de répons suivi de Dialogue des règnes* (Paris: Castella, 1968).

[20] Cf. also Butor, "Comment se sont écrits certains de mes livres," in *Le Nouveau Roman: hier, aujourd'hui* (Paris: 10/18, 1972).

[21] Honolulu: East-West Center Press, 1966.

[22] Butor, "Trente-six et dix vues du Fuji," in *Répertoire III* (Paris: Minuit, 1968), p. 163.

[23] Butor, "Réponses à *Tel Quel*," in *Répertoire II*, p. 297.

CHAPTER THIRTEEN

Jean Pierre Faye

The first book by Faye, *Entre les rues*, made a rather quiet appearance in 1958, at a time when the notorious special issue of the review *Esprit* was publicizing the fact that something was astir in the world of fiction.[1] Belonging to the same generation as Robbe-Grillet and Butor, he waited longer than they did before writing his first work of fiction. A poet like Butor, he published poetry when he was twenty—much earlier than the latter. Indeed, strands of poetry run through Faye's early work, and he often daubs objects with an aura of significance quite different from the correlative status to which they appeared limited in Robbe-Grillet's early prose.

Entre les rues exhibits neither the rigorous architecture of Ollier's *La Mise en scène*, for instance, nor the technical and theoretical preoccupations of Robbe-Grillet's *Les Gommes*. At first glance, the formal divisions of the book seem haphazard: there are two parts numbering 71 and 136 pages, with seven unnumbered chapters in the first part and eleven in the second. Chapters are of uneven length, and four chapters in the second part, not always the longer ones, are subdivided into two or three sections. It would also appear that the world of appearances is respected. The events of the narration follow in conventional chronology, taking place in easily identifiable locations. Of course it does not take long to discover a simple pattern in the organization. The shorter chapters describe actions or events, the longer ones are made up of reflections or discussions of those events and are located close to the beginning and end of each part. Two short chapters precede the first long one (obviously something must happen before it can be discussed), two short ones follow the last long one—and they suggest the consequences of a failure. While chronology is respected, not a single date is given, nor is it possible to determine precisely how much time elapses between the beginning and end of the narration—certainly several weeks, perhaps a number of months. A geographical reference to Cicero on the third page unmistakably places the setting in Chicago, and later the scene shifts to Nevada and to Los Angeles. Chicago, however, is not mentioned by name. I assume the presence of Las Vegas because it is a gambling town reached while driving, with the Mojave Mountains visible in the rear vision mirror, and I take Los Angeles for granted because there is little else west of Las Vegas that might fit Faye's description. The French reader, for whom the book was intended, could probably not reach such conclusions, and it hardly matters. The point is that Faye is not concerned with reproducing everyday reality; he suggests it, as a matter of course, or even plays with it, something that is quite evident in his treatment of detail.

Occasionally, one is reminded of Giraudoux—a Giraudoux who would have read Henry George, the nineteenth-century journalist and social reformer, rather than La Motte Fouqué. There are in *Entre les rues* narrative ellipses of a sort that Giraudoux might have committed, as when the narrator, who is guiding a Chicago policeman to the body of a dead man at the end of one chapter, appears on a Nevada highway at the beginning of the next. Sometimes the ellipsis takes place within one sentence: "We were riding along without a word, and she was waving to me from the car window as she drove away."[2] What has clearly been left out, immediately following the comma, is something like "and then she let me off in front of my place; I watched her leave." Faye's statement manages to convey more effectively the narrator's impression and state of mind. *Entre les rues* also contains Giraudoux-like images, those resulting from an unexpected and suggestive association of words that carry the statement far beyond what the immediate context could have suggested. The opening paragraph of the novel presents an expressionist description of a barber shop, with a row of customers facing a row of containers of shaving cream, hair lotions, and the like on a shelf along the mirror. "One must read them differently, objects from left to right, men from right to left from professional to conjugal hand." Giraudoux's tone was different, and he was much more verbose, but the stylistic approach was very similar. "She had written to Houbigant, to the tailor, to *Old England* for sweaters, to the other tradesmen for socks, to all such addresses as Jérôme had imposed upon her like holy scriptures and which were now the frightful tags of Bardini's life."[3] When Faye comments, still in that same first paragraph, "The ivory object . . . encloses this empty section of the mirror where a face was nodding; he was sleeping ironically, but it was no longer true, because faces are stated in the imperfect amidst things in the present," he reminds one of Giraudoux's remark about the Germans "Who have invented, in order to pass away life and time, beer, war, the ocarina, and such a large number of irregular verbs."[4] None of this is meant to imply that Jean Pierre Faye was influenced by Giraudoux; rather it suggests a more general kinship analogous to that which allowed Claude-Edmonde Magny to draw a parallel or two between Giraudoux and Maurice Blanchot. It also identifies one of the poetic strands I have referred to.

A European immigrant or visitor, Verdier, stumbles upon two seemingly unrelated events one evening in Chicago: a conversation overhead in a cafeteria and the floor plan of an apartment inadvertently left on the table on the one hand, and on the other an unidentified dead man lying in the apartment of a girl named Mona, where Verdier was supposed to obtain an address. Partly by chance and partly because he is curious by nature, he finds himself trapped in a series of interlocking circles, all circumscribing the victim whose body he had discovered. They include militants of the left, intellectuals, blacks, labor union groups, artists, and a few who have made a political switch to the right. In his stumbling fashion, he comes close to solving the murder, which, with the uncertainty common in this work, appears to have been both political and fortuitous—unless a woman was the pretext. At any rate, someone decides that Verdier has become too inquisitive. As he walks along a quiet street a car stops beside him, three men jump out and push him inside. He is driven out of town to an abandoned quarry or tunnel or perhaps a cave, and the reader is left in doubt as to his ultimate fate.

Olivier de Magny has said that "*Entre les rues* makes us participate in the obstinate, hesitant walk of a man trying to orient himself."[5] Verdier, who tells his story in the first person, does wander a great deal, but his obstinacy also makes one think of a quest and brings to mind some of the other quest-oriented fiction of contemporary French literature. Comparisons and contrasts, enlightening as they might be, would take one too far afield. I shall simply mention a few analogies, which may be no more than coincidental, with Céline's *Voyage au bout de la nuit*. Like Bardamu, the narrator of *Entre les rues* turns out to be a former medical student; like him, he has undergone brain surgery and appears recurrently afflicted by it. In both instances there is a wandering that is brought into focus through an agency that is independent of the narrator—the existence of Robinson and his determined presence in Céline's book, a murder in Faye's. Both protagonists go to America, one briefly holding a job at the Ford plant in Detroit, the other working in a steel mill in Gary, and both fail in their undertakings. In both instances, the text ends with a lyrical statement conveying at least pessimism and perhaps despair. The effect of each work is very different of course, and Faye's ellipses contrast most obviously with Céline's dynamic profusion. But lest such analogies with Giraudoux or Céline lead one to the wrong conclusions, Olivier de Magny's initial reaction is worth remembering: "[It is] the most unusual, most baffling, and perhaps most original novel that has been published in a long time."[6]

Entre les rues is told exclusively from the point of view of a first-person narrator, even though, from the standpoint of the reader, some uncertainty on that score pervades the first few pages. In effect, the text conveys a discontinuous series of immediate sense perceptions. In his second work of fiction, *La Cassure* (1961), Faye exploits the ambiguity of the narrative point of view, thus pointing to what is surely his major pre-occupation as a writer: the meaning of narrative. As in the previous work, the main character appears to be drifting among members of several circles, but this time the locale is France. The book derives its unity not from a murder but from something more intrinsic to that character's being—it is not something he stumbles upon by chance, it is something within himself that produces a break with his wife. To the previous question, can the murder be solved? now corresponds a new one, can the marriage be repaired? There is tighter integration of the various components of the book when the medical problem, for again there is one, affecting the main character, is used as a correlative of much of what takes place. It is also reflected in the book's title.

Simon Roncal, the protagonist of *La Cassure*, wanders from woman to woman (his wife, Guiza, walks out on him several timès), and is more or less loosely tied to three separate social or political groups. At one point he briefly attends an informal lecture and discussion on the subject of *hébéphrénie* (C, p. 81). This refers to a specific form of schizophrenia; important as the reference is, however, I do not believe we need be concerned with precise clinical manifestations of such a psychosis. The allusion helps to enlarge upon the meaning of the title and to structure a number of features or events in the direction of a single center. Justification for tying hebephrenia to Simon is provided in the text, when he is introduced to those attending the lecture: "He is interested in what you are doing now" (p. 78). Many things then fall into place. When Simon is asked if he is married, he answers, "Partly" (p. 34). He is an elementary school teacher conducting a series of examinations in the north of France when the book opens, but although the month is June (not yet summer vacation in France) the text gives no sign of any pupils, and when he is asked about his friends he replies, "Here I don't have so many friends" (p. 29). In the fall is is transferred to Paris, without a regular teaching assignment—he says he is *détaché*, and that appropriate administrative term acquires suggestive connotations (p. 133). His situation is similar to that before: "Do you have any friends here?—Hardly anybody" (pp. 73–74). Having drawn on the wall of a phone booth a symbolic design (a diamond inscribed in a rectangle) that clarifies for himself his relationship with other characters in the fiction, he feels he cannot relate his discovery to anyone else, that is, transform a spatial network into linear, narrative terms. "What in space constitutes a single chord . . . cannot be translated into a sequence without falling to pieces" (p. 172). The narrative is linear, of course, but flashbacks begin to undermine it, and the sort of ellipses already noted in *Entre les rues* acquire greater relevance here. In that earlier work I tended to think of Giraudoux rather than mental illness. When the latter was noticed it seemed an isolated character's illness, one which did not affect the core of the work. In *La Cassure*, such ellipses echo the break between Simon and Guiza, as well as the disturbances that affect each one individually, the gap that separates the groups (teachers and labor unions) that Simon is working with, and finally the split within France that nearly exploded in full-fledged revolution— the narrative ends in May 1958, when the Fourth Republic collapsed under the pressure of French army generals in Algeria.

Actually, to speak of discontinuity in the narrative line is not enough. There are six different narrative lines in this work, each one being identified by the person of the subject-pronouns. The third-person narrative accounts for an overwhelming majority of the statements in the text. On the second page, however, one encounters the first of nearly a dozen shifts to the second person singular, generally of short duration. At the outset of the second chapter, there are shifts to the first person singular as well as less frequent instances of the first person plural. That plural person varies in designation and must therefore be considered as making up two separate narrative lines. In chapter II, *nous* designates Simon and his wife Guiza; in chapter VIII, Simon and Liana, the woman who looms more and more importantly in his life. Finally, there are two instances, one in chapter III and one in chapter IV, where the first-person pronoun quite obviously refers to Liana and not to Simon. With the latter two exceptions, one might be tempted to assume that it is Simon who is speaking throughout, whether he speaks of himself in the third person, or whether he uses the first and directs his words at Guiza as *tu* (this invariably happens in her absence). In a different context Emile Benveniste, taking Arab grammarians as a point of departure, has said that the third-person pronoun is used to designate the one who is absent; it represents "a nonpersonal invariant and nothing else." He is led to the observation that "the statement 'I is another' in Rimbaud furnishes a typical expression of what is, properly speaking, mental 'alienation,' in which the 'I' is deprived of its essential identity."[7]

One might say that when Simon refers to himself in the third person he proclaims a distance between his two selves, mirroring his schizophrenic condition. A clue to that, as well as to the likelihood that the first-person narrative corresponds to a higher degree of consciousness, occurs when Simon settles down for the night in an armchair: "He touched the arm of the chair, and he searched beyond as he turned on his side; the distance would awaken him, again he was saying I" (C, p.

160). The split within Simon goes far back, and he tells a personal myth to explain it. Born on the French side of the Pyrenees, he bears the name of a small town, Roncal, that lies on the Spanish side—perhaps because of the indiscreet behavior of one of his female ancestors who returned pregnant from a festive trip across the border. Nevertheless, one should keep in mind that Simon is the focus of the narration, whatever complexity might have been engendered by a multiplicity of pronouns. He is the intelligence through which nearly all that happens is conveyed to the reader. It is not so much that he is mentally ill, rather, conditions are such as to be amenable to significant statment only in terms of mental illness and its linguistic correlatives. If the blurb on the back cover of the book is any indication of Faye's intentions, the *cassure* is to be found first in Guiza and not at all in Simon. Apparently his correlatives got out of hand; or, perhaps, the statement should be taken ironically (which implies a more subtle form of *cassure*). The initial break that exists within Guiza, although a minor one, enables both characters and readers to become fully conscious of the more important ones that exist within themselves and within their society.

Seemingly casual references to the town of Cicero, to Henry George, and others in *Entre les rues* are echoed in *La Cassure* by the mention of Guernica, Jules Guesde, La Bourse du Travail, La Libre Pensée. They should serve to establish within the reader's consciousness the network of a canvas upon which a meta-text can be woven—one that possesses a definite political orientation. For a number of readers, however, this did not happen. French reviewers of those two works made no mention of any political overtones. This seems hard to account for, even if one grants that the American setting of the first text might have made political references more obscure. One possible explanation is that those who read Faye in 1958 and 1961 were prejudiced by the label of poetry pasted on his previous publications and by the affinity they detected with other young writers whose absence of overt political statements in their fiction they had misinterpreted. Be that as it may, it became impossible to ignore the political context of *Battement* (1962).

At this point, the extent to which basic patterns are repeated becomes particularly striking. Again the main character is alienated; he is a stranger, as was Verdier in *Entre les rues*, and is designated by the same initial letter as that of the earlier protagonist, V. It appears that he worked in a pharmaceutical laboratory in France, but the job has become unbearable. He has been given a temporary position, selling medical encyclopedias. As the book opens, he is in Munich, where he is to spend a few months. His wife has stayed behind, in Paris, thus completing his estrangement. Actually she believes he has come to Munich because a former mistress, who has since married, lives there—but he does not even know her married name. As with the earlier Verdier, much happens to V. by chance, and he soon stumbles upon the woman, now married to a Bulgarian doctor. That is important, as much because of the stumbling as of the actual meeting. It suggests, beyond the nature of the role of reality that I have already mentioned, the role anecdote plays in Faye's fiction—something I shall make clear presently.

The word of the title, *battement*, refers to a beat or a pulsation, which is translated into every aspect of the text. Thematically, it imposes itself in the very first pages, as sounds and lights from the city break like waves, rhythmically, into the hotel room where the main character is staying. The rhythm is not only temporal but spatial, for zones of light and darkness hit him from several directions, creating stripe-like patterns on the walls (also providing a title for the first of the book's three sections—*Bandes*). Such thematic manifestations are present throughout. In addition, some of the correlatives of the constantly present pulsations are linked, imagistically, to narrated events. For instance, the pulsating sound that emanates from crowds in the city is, on several occasions, translated as *abois* or *aboiements* (barkings), which echo the sound of barking dogs V. remembers hearing outside the mental hospital where he had been treated earlier (his symptoms are similar to those of Verdier and Roncal). Another sort of oscillation develops, mental rather than physical, between city and hospital. But the phenomenon also takes place on the level of the narration. At this point it will be helpful to remember that, during a symposium held under the aegis of *Tel Quel* and presided over by Michel Foucault, Jean Pierre Faye stated his conception of the present moment as divided between an actual present and an immediate past, as a person is both receptive to impressions from the outside and productive of verbal statements (interior or spoken).[8] At any given moment, one of the two usually predominates. It constitutes the person's actual present, and the other is relegated to the immediate past. Sometimes inner consciousness pushes the outer world aside, sometimes outer consciousness obliterates thought. Faye expresses such alternations, in the text of *Battement*, through shifts from present to past imperfect tense and, seemingly to add a further disruptive element, from first to third-person subject. Consequently, what according to Benveniste is the "absent" subject commands a verb in the present while the first person (expressed or implied) is tied to the (immediate) past. The text might be said to be throbbing internally as its verbs oscillate. Each succeeding brief chapter, of which there are about a hundred and twenty, some of them flashbacks, alternately presents the main character from the inside (*je*) and from the outside (*il*). Yet in spite of that there remains the impression of a single narrator—a word used by such a knowledgeable reviewer as Philippe Sollers.[9] Obviously there is no one else, aside from the author, to whom the sections written in the third person could be ascribed. One is allowed to penetrate no other consciousness, and since V. is continually present throughout, one might say that everything, regardless of pronouns, is described from his point of view.

In the early sixties it had not yet become the practice to

speak of the text as a somewhat autonomous, generative assemblage of signs. Books like *Battement* soon made a new terminology indispensable. As in the case of some of Ollier's protagonists, calling V. a "narrator" raises a number of irrelevant questions having to do with realism and plausibility (that was not so obviously the case in *Entre les rues*). Referring to V. as the central intelligence is not particularly adequate, for there is nothing to be filtered through his consciousness aside from the events that affect him directly, and, on the other hand, the impersonal style of much of the text often conveys the impression that he is not really involved. He seems as much detached from the events in Munich as personal pronouns referring to him are scarce, whether *il* or *je*. There are chapters where the first-person pronoun is avoided throughout, even though, according to the pattern of alternations, those pages should present a first-person narrative with verbs in the imperfect. Personal pronouns appear more frequently when V.'s individual problems come to the fore. That might be considered to conform with the behavior of a schizophrenic person, who has difficulty in maintaining an interest in the world. Yet I do not see *Battement*, any more than the two preceding books, as a study in mental illness.

As the plague in Maurice Blanchot's *Le Très-haut* was metaphorical, schizophrenia in Faye's fiction appears to correlate to the plight of the uncommitted. V. seems as much lacking in political or social awareness as he is incapable of true emotional involvement. He goes to Munich for purely selfish reasons. Once there, he makes some half-hearted attempts to locate his former mistress, Merie. But everything that happens to him is accidental. It simply turns out that the woman who occupies the room next to his and with whom he strikes up an acquaintance is connected with the F.L.N. (the National Liberation Front of Algeria). It is by sheer coincidence that he meets Merie again, who is also working for the F.L.N. and gives him a copy of a book directed against French colonialism

—which he does not refuse. It is merely by accident that he later drops the book in the street, thus allowing it to be identified by members of *La Main Rouge*, the rightist group, who are following him because of his meetings with F.L.N. sympathizers. The rightists quite logically conclude that his encyclopedia business is merely a cover for his distributing F.L.N. propaganda, and, on the last page of the book, they kill him. There is, however, no overt statement in the text that specifically justifies any of the points I have just made, nor is it even stated that the action takes place in Munich. Rather, the work is so structured as to make such conclusions, in my opinion, inescapable.

The story in *Battement* functions as a kind of lens through which verbal and thematic elements are refracted, converging on its focal point, which is the meaning of the narrative. The protagonist of Camus' *L'Etranger* has no socially accepted scale of values and had also been, by chance, trapped by a series of events that eventually led, after he killed a man, to his execution. It was accordingly quite appropriate for Philippe Sollers to entitle his review of Faye's book, "Un Nouvel Etranger." But while Camus could not hide a certain amount of feeling for Meursault and endowed him with a peculiar aura of innocence, V. benefits from no such treatment. He is not innocent but ill, and to Meursault's moment of happiness correspond V.'s moments of suffering. Meursault's innocence might be said to signify either his estrangement from a society in which a man may be condemned to death because he failed to cry at his mother's funeral or a refusal to accept the guilt of colonialism. In the final analysis, as all elements in *Battement* converge, they point to V.'s illness being not so much schizophrenia as alienation. It is a total alienation, beginning with the Marxist connotations of the word (and that is probably why Verdier, Roncal, and V. reveal so little of professional activities that are, in such a sense, alien to them) and broadening to include the self. As V. says, after he remembers seeing the faces of the two men who followed him reflected in a store window, "As if I had seen them without knowing it, as if they had been seen without my being involved by the one who watches everything without thinking about it" (p. 64). Such a person, in the presence of a danger he does not comprehend, can only behave like a trapped animal: "This might precisely be, perhaps, the time to recognize that an animal has fallen precipitously and flutters or stays trapped indefinitely, or remains petrified in a show case in an unspecified location" (p. 111).

Those three works of fiction have displayed the growing involvement of Jean Pierre Faye with narrative technique, not so much on account of the techniques themselves, but because of the meanings the various forms of narrative can generate. I have alluded to the interplay between the several pronouns, *je*, *il*, and *nous* and also between verb tenses and to the assault made on narrative linearity. I have also mentioned a similarity in the pattern of events, which mirror the narrative techniques. The question now raised by *Analogues* (1964) is whether those fragmentary narratives are truly independent or constitute fragments of a larger narrative.

Labelled *Récit autocritique*, implying, as did *L'Echec de Nolan* by Claude Ollier, a reworking of the former narratives, *Analogues* begins with an *Hors-texte*, which might have been called a "preface," in which Faye brings up the issue of the narratable and the nature of the narration. Putting aside all questions related to ethics, the question of what is esthetically narratable has received varying answers over the centuries, and concern over the effect of narrative on narration has probably increased of late, concomitantly with that of point of view. That there might be a correlation with the historical evolution of musical composition is also suggested: "It cannot be purely a matter of chance if the first romances in prose are contemporary with *Ars antiqua* and the first examples of polyphony; and if so-called classical narration is an outgrowth of the Renaissance as much as Florentine and Venetian recitatives" (A, p. 12). The evolution from tonal to serial composition has a counterpart in the development of contemporary narrative techniques. (Faye's interest in music was already in evidence in *La Cassure*, where he compared spatial representation to a musical chord.) If broadening the concept of the narratable and multiplying points of view actually enrich the narrative, increasing its significant possibilities, an author might achieve similar results by filling in gaps, so to speak, and having earlier narrative segments proliferate. And that is precisely the function of *Analogues*.

As I understand it, the title refers to the relationships between events in narration and the narratives (when there is more than one point of view) and between different characters and events in separate narratives. At first sight, the book would seem to presuppose the reality of the characters in the three earlier works of fiction, the author now deciding to reveal details, antecedents, or developments that he could not, for one reason or another, mention before—somewhat as François Mauriac revealed what happened to Thérèse after she disappeared into the crowd in Paris at the end of *Thérèse Desqueyroux*. But that is the kind of realistic fallacy that needs to be guarded against. There are indeed "characters" in Faye's fiction, and they are "credible" to the extent that a French critic, in reviewing *Battement*, found himself puzzling over what could have made the narrator's former mistress so attractive to him.[10] There are also, as I have pointed out, recognizable settings. In either case, however, belief and recognition are subjective and incidental, taking place in the reader's mind rather than in the text. There is such a place as Roncal, in the Spanish Pyrenees, but had Faye invented it the effect in *La Cassure* would have been the same. There is a girl named Dow-Jones in *Entre les rues*, who says she is the grandniece of the corporation's founder, and it matters little that the actual founders, Charles H. Dow and Edward D. Jones, were separate persons, for the name is needed for its suggestive value; it gives rise to the burlesque incident in which she marries a stranger in order to get rid of such a compromising surname.

The setting of *Battement* is clearly Munich, but all it needs to be is a large foreign city. More important than links with commonplace reality is the interplay between pronouns, verbs, places, and circumstances, for what this ultimately involves are fundamental relationships between human beings, both as individuals and as groups. Hence, in large part, the inevitable political overtones of Faye's fiction.

The main setting for *Analogues* is the city of Basel, through which the Rhine flows, describing a curve in the reverse image of the one traced by the Seine in Paris and dividing the city into unequal parts. The correspondence recalls the title of Faye's collection of poems, *Fleuve renversé.*[11] The mirror image could suggest the distortion imposed upon a narration by a new narrative. The city stands at the intersection of three countries, France, Germany, and Switzerland. It is thus analogous to the book, which is born out of the confrontation and proliferation of three earlier works of fiction. It is a multilingual city, just as the book is written in a number of narrative styles.

There are two parts to *Analogues*. One might say that these parts are articulated by means of *La Cassure*, the "break" having become a hinge. The name of Guiza is used in section headings exclusively in the first, that of Simon almost exclusively in the second. The section concluding part one is indeed like a hinge that allows the second part to unfold. The major domain of Mona, a name from *Entre les rues*, is part two; and El., from *Battement*, while dominating part one, cannot be ignored in part two. For me, at least, El. dominates *Analogues*—poetic justice after having been practically suppressed by the main character of *Battement*. Each part, in turn, is divided into "Genesis," where the emphasis is on narrative, and "Counterpoint," where it is on characters, all of which are now described in the third person. The effect is one of a gigantic collage (there actually is a sequence entitled "Collages" with excerpts taken from texts ranging from the *Iliad* to *Finnegans Wake*) and held together in the reader's mind by the very analogies that exist between *Entre les rues*, *La Cassure*, and *Battement*. A new character, Imra, who acts as a sort of mirror, is introduced to provide an anecdotal link with Mona, Guiza, and El., feminine characters of previous works. What she reflects is not reality, for she operates within the fiction only, serving to generate analogies. The male characters are obviously linked through their mental illnesses and surgery and additionally through the new connections established between feminine characters. Another new character, this one male, an Algerian who remains nameless, emerges in order to give El. the possibility of engaging in a self-searching dialogue that runs through a large portion of *Analogues.*

As narratives, dialogues, and statements are played against one another, as characters grope their ways often in languages not their own, one gets the impression that all this is a struggle to become integrated in a universal human Narrative that transcends the various languages that men speak and that, if attained, would speak the truth about the human condition. There seems to be a vague mystical aura about *Analogues.*

In the same year as *Analogues* and two years after *Battement,* *L'Ecluse* (1964) brought Faye general recognition, as the result of a literary prize. Many elements in this fourth work of fiction (placing *Analogues* on a separate plane, as a sort of meta-fiction) are similar to those of the previous ones, which Faye had earlier described as a trilogy. Perhaps, even though the blurb for this one speaks of *le carré du récit,* they could be viewed as constituting something like a tripod, a base from which this new work has been launched. *L'Ecluse,* while it does not enter into the narrative complex of *Analogues,* shows the same allusive treatment of reality and plot. It presents an estranged main character, handles the narrative line by means of shifts from first to second and third-person pronouns, and develops the theme of illness—just as the previous works did.

The initial letter of the main character's name is again V. But this time it is a woman, and that letter links her to the protagonists of *Entre les rues* and *Battement* only through an artifice: her name was Jane, but an Italian friend changed it to Gianna and later to Vanna. That is the phonetic equivalent of the French word *vanne*, meaning a sluice, which makes of her a correlative of the book's title. Verbal echoes then reverberate in several directions. Most of the setting for *L'Ecluse* (three out of four parts) is Berlin, and that city's network of canals brings to mind the necessary sluice gates. The same word, sluice, is used to refer to a checkpoint between East and West Berlin, where currencies and languages are commuted (p. 118). Vanna herself, at one point, because she cannot, on account of special circumstances, outwardly express thoughts or emotions, is described as being imprisoned within herself—a condition linked to the title by way of the book's epigraph, *exclusa aqua, eau enfermée*. Many other references might be adduced, but the last one mentioned reinforces the analogy between Vanna and earlier characters. I should emphasize, however, that Vanna differs from them in one important respect: in spite of her being manipulated by powerful forces, she appears much more aware and concerned than they were.

Cleavages similar to those affecting Roncal and V. are shown to be present in Vanna. Her mother was English, her father was a French general. She still loves a man, Alexandre (known to some as Alé, to others as Sandro), who has left her to marry another woman and possibly sleep with a third, but she has successive affairs with two other men. She resides in the divided city of Berlin (a character in *Entre les rues* says, "When I hear people talk about leucotomy I think of Berlin"— p. 75). Though she works in the West she is much intrigued by what goes on in the East. She fantasizes a great deal, but not all her day-dreams are exclusively self-centered. In the end she survives, and it is Alé who is killed, presumably by the mysterious organization whose presence is felt throughout most of the book.

Vanna herself is not pictured as being ill, although she does become so at the end of the second part. Indirectly, her sickness results in her inability to return to East Berlin, and that could well be symbolic. Other characters are ill or they have head scars similar to those of Liane in *La Cassure*. All that should be familiar material to a reader acquainted with Faye's previous books, especially as the most significant use of illness transcends individual instances. Vanna recalls that, earlier, she had to explain the Berlin situation to Alé by equating Nazism to a disease: "The city had suffered a long and violent illness, and no one had known how to treat it; and by chance, or for want of something better, not knowing anything better to do, they had cut it in half" (E, pp. 38–39). That, in fact, is the only specific reference to a generalized pathological state, a presentation quite in keeping with Faye's allusive technique. It suffices nevertheless to raise the significance of illness as symbol beyond what it had previously seemed to imply. At times *L'Ecluse* comes close to being hallucinatory. A member of the international subversive organization to whom Vanna has been introduced describes to her a developing situation that may possible lead, and therefore will lead, inevitably and by chance, to the destruction of Jerusalem (a divided city when Faye was writing and therefore similar to Berlin), without anyone's being able to blame anyone else for it—the perfect international crime. One implication is that it could only be conceived by madmen. A subtle basis for one's acceptance of that wild scheme is established by suggesting an analogy between the present and the early Middle Ages, when Christianity was supposedly united in a holy war against the "infidels." Vanna's fantasies, in which she imagines first Alé and then others as Ogier the Dane, a reference to Galahad, and the introduction of a character named Gavin, which, to a French reader's ear, might suggest Gawain, all help to create an atmosphere that is congenial to the spirit of a modern, paranoid crusade.

Les Troyens (1970) is subtitled *Hexagramme ou roman*. Allusion is thus made to the existence of six narratives—the six books of fiction published by Faye, including the present one—and to the manner in which they are related. Early in the book there are descriptions of cloud patterns over a city and light patterns on the ceiling of a room, both gradually changing shape, into which the word "hexagram" is inserted. Within the last twenty-five pages of *Les Troyens* there are five instances of diagrams and *calligrammes* that either suggest or clearly depict a specific geometric figure. Examining their design and further prodded by medieval allusions similar to those just noted in *L'Ecluse*, one might easily think of the *hexagrammum mysticum* of medieval times, later systematically studied by Pascal. But I am less impressed with the hexagram's geometric properties as demonstrated by Pascal than with its "mystic" modifier, since it confirms the impression made by *Analogues* concerning the direction Faye's narratives appear to be taking. I have already noted the extent to which, from the very beginning, links between narration and reality or between signs and their referents were unessential to the significance of the narrative. At best, reality was a prop for the narration.

Already in *L'Ecluse* there were hints of its being pushed even farther into the background, some passages making me wonder if Faye was not about to plunge into a form of science fiction. "To this purpose, powerful reflectors have been set up and, in effect, turned back inward and aimed at the city; they register an image of the city; they emit a violent radiation that takes the city's cast, so to speak, removing it completely, and then they flash in order to reflect it several times before it is finally sent back by transmitters, and finally stabilized and condensed in a special way (particles of light penetrate into a stabilized zone—an expanse of stationary waves clothed in a kind of skin or wrapping: they penetrate into it, and that is where each shining particle is changed into a couple of particles of matter with opposite electrical charges, and into an output of darkness)" (pp. 129–130). In that book, there was perhaps a hiatus between such statements and those that clearly referred to the actual city of Berlin, with its dividing wall, its canals, subways, and airport. In *Les Troyens*, on the other hand, there is greater homogeneity in the narrative; reality is mainly in the text itself. Not only is the reader drawn into its verbal functioning, but even the "characters" are engaged in linguistic activities. One could possibly say that the author is, for the reader's benefit, attempting to create or to convey the experience of a mystical awareness, no longer of God, but of human reality as language—as a web of narratives.

A noticeable architecture, which I had found lacking in *Entre les rues*, has gradually been asserting itself through the interplay of narratives, beginning with the alternating *je* and *il* of *Battement*. Now the figure six presides over the organization of *Les Troyens*. There are six chapters, entitled "Walls," "Night," "Sea," "Wave," "Siege," and "Body". There are six "characters" or functions, three of them male, often referred to as narrator, witness, and participant (*interlocuteur*), and the three others female. There is, of course, the hexagram. In one of its diagrammatic representations the thread linking the six chapters is exposed to the reader's imagination. In conventional linear form and put into English it may be unraveled as follows: "Greenness or death/ and winding garland/ of life, unavailing/ when it comes to open/ the sluice gate to the ebb and/ flow of what dismembers them/ will it . . . them" (T, p. 351). That probably seems quite hermetic, but the connection between each line (or side of the hexagram) and the narratives is clarified when that diagram is confronted with one appearing a few pages later. This I have kept in the original French; the italics are my own:

1. *verd*eur ou *m*ort   *verd*ier ou *m*ona
2. et *g*uirlande *s*inueuse   *g*uiza et *s*imon
3. de *v*ie, *v*aine   *v*. comme *v*anini
4. lorsqu'*elle* vient ouvrir   et elle: *el.* ou *ell*a
5. *vann*e au flux et   alle gio*vann*a: ou *vann*e
6. reflux de ce qui *les* écartèle   et celle qu'écartèle le nom
                                              lé-lin ou lin lee

x. *va*-t-*elle les*   *vann*a *el. lé*

       (T, p. 351)   (T, p. 355)

In case anyone wonders why a hexagram appears to have seven sides, Pascal showed that in the mystic hexagram the points of intersection of three pairs of sides were located on a straight line. Faye's seventh line is obtained in such manner, and it provides the interrogative meaning in the narratives—a choice between the putrefaction of death and the greening of life.

As in previous fiction, the setting of *Les Troyens* is an unnamed city; in this case, its inhabitants are known as *Troyens*. Now there is a French city named Troyes in Champagne, and it played a role in *Battement*. It has been laid siege to many times in history (a useful correlative for chapter five, "Siege"); it is divided into high and low sections (a feature mentioned in the text—and any such division is important to Faye), and produces hosiery, glassware, and textiles. Glass, as used in picture frames, doors, windows, and store-fronts, is important in the text. Hosiery is related both to textiles and to the erotic theme, much more developed than before. The analogy between weaving cloth and "weaving" narrative lines needs no elaboration. In other words, Troyes is a good city for Faye's purposes. Still, I do not think that it looms as large in the consciousness of someone reading *Les Troyens* as did, for readers of previous books, the other cities he had then selected: Chicago, Paris, Munich, Zurich, and Berlin. The cultural presence of Homer's Troy is quite strong, especially when assisted by a statement such as, "No longer the Trojans, *but Hector is being pursued*" (p. 241), preventing an unquestioned identification with the French city. One might recall that the number six has long been a symbol of ambiguity.

The narrative function itself is ambiguous, as it had been in *L'Ecluse*, for instance, but more so. The subject of the narrative is not given a name until page 79; it is Nar, and the word seems strangely incomplete—or else unnecessary. It could be a short form for "narrator" (who, as Faye remarked at an intellectual colloquium held in the abbey of Cluny in 1970, is also *narus*, in Latin, the one who knows),[12] but it could also mark the beginning of the German *Narr* (madman) or the Spanish *naranja* (orange). The latter brings to mind the House of Orange, whose princes often bore the hyphenated name of Orange-Nassau, a cognominal correlative of schizophrenia. As to the former, while schizophrenics are not exactly "mad," the connotation is a possible one. Be that as it may, there is no other reference to the mental state of any of the six main characters (or functions). The pronominal subject of the narrative, both before and after a name is introduced, oscillates between *il* and *je* but without the regularity that accompany such changes in *Battement*. The articulation between the *il* and the *je* series is often provided by phrases like "The one who said I" or "The one who says I," thereby calling attention to the shift. This is part of a more visible emphasis placed on the linguistic process. On a different level, it is analogous to El.'s asking Nar, "What language is your country?" (T, p. 79).

The narrator has come to the city in search of a lost narrative continuity. In a series of leather-bound volumes, presumably the complete works of an author whose name is missing, a ribald narrative is suddenly, at the beginning of a subsequent volume, replaced with a prudish one, while nothing in the appearance or presentation of the volumes has changed. In a manner slightly reminiscent of Kafka, he seems to depend for his subsistence and also his assignment to the city upon a vast, mysterious bureaucracy. Thinking that he has come to the wrong place to search for his lost narrative he asks for a transfer, but the delays involved make it seem hopeless. When he is asked about his job, he does not immediately talk about the books; he answers that he works in textiles (*je travaille dans le fil*, p. 48). If there is again ambiguity there is no real contradiction, for, as I have suggested above, cotton thread and narrative thread are analogous for the purpose of this text. In addition, and perhaps in opposition, to the bureaucracy upon which the narrator depends, there is another vast, secret organization with which he comes into contact. There are

amusing references to specialists in romance philology and to
the Old-French mafia. It is clear that, like Faye and others,
this worldwide subversive association knows the power of
language.

Nar, especially in his dialogues with El., plays a role that
is similar to that of the nameless Algerian in *Analogues*, who
had made El.'s acquaintance because of a cinder in her eye.
In *Les Troyens*, Nar meets El. on account of an injured kitten (p. 39). Much later, over the phone, she makes the connection: "It's true, I answer anybody's call. Even if all he does
is bring me a tuft of cat fur, or a speck of dust in the eye" (p.
312). Even more than functioning as a narrator, Nar seems
to act as prompter for narratives, and that explains statements
such as these: "a mute narrator" (p. 164), "on his part, he
questions; he is a narrator who tells no story" (p. 178), or "the
narrator without words" (p. 72). As a surrogate for the contemporary author who needs a reader in order to complete his
work and give it meaning, the often silent narrator utters his
call for assistance. In correlative fashion, within the text, someone issues a call of distress. An Algerian in *Analogues*, a Puerto
Rican in *Les Troyens* (Nar says he was born in Guayama), in
either case a member of a nonwhite population, appeals to a
Western conscience. (As this is the first time Faye's text openly
suggests such a specific interpretation, I might note that the
number six was also considered as a symbol of the human soul.)

The general pattern is not new. In each instance, as in Maurice Blanchot's narratives, beginning with Verdier and Mona,
the call has gone from man to woman. Before *Analogues* the
nature and purpose of that call were not clear. As they are made
explicit in the sixth book they also become involved in the
other set of analogies I have just alluded to—that pertaining
to the relationship between author, reader, and text. As implied
in Blanchot's interpretation of the Orpheus myth and also
affirmed by Philippe Sollers, the relationship between a writer
and his writing can be interpreted in erotic terms; so can the

interaction of text and reader. In Faye's fiction the appeal made from man to woman becomes more and more patently erotic. The narrator experiences intense desire for three women— the three female functions of the text. One he knows only through her picture. She is Vanna or Joanina, and he writes to her presumably in Berlin, although he associates her name with the besieged city of Ioannina, Ali Pasha's stronghold in Greek Epirus. The other, El., is directly linked to the hexagram in that the geometric design the narrator sees on his ceiling comes from her room across the courtyard. To him, she seems a figure that can be drawn within the framework of her window, and it is his drawing her that arouses his desire. The third is Linda Lee or Lé Lin, depending on where she happens to be. The split that existed in earlier characters shows up again, but it is first expressed in linguistic terms on the level of signifier rather than in mental terms on the level of the signified. The duality of her name, that is, her being endowed with two signifiers, is translated to the level of the signified in physical terms: she often dreams of violence and blood, and at the end she is seriously wounded, dismembered (*écartelée*) as had been the woman of her dreams, under circumstances that are left to the reader's imagination. On the last page, the narrator purposely breaks the glass pane of a door behind which Lé Lin is lying and repeatedly slashes his hand.

There is more sexuality and also more violence in *Les Troyens* than in the previous works of fiction. There is a riot, which reminds one of the student riots of 1968 but prompted Faye to specify that the book was completely written by February of 1968. Actually, as the description of the riot is interspersed with many brief quotations from what might be *La Chevalerie Ogier de Dannemarche*, it is relatively easy not to succumb to the realistic fallacy. The generalized violence, nevertheless, might be interpreted as a sign of Faye's moving in the direction of a deeper realism that, as opposed to the superficial realism of verisimilitude, reflects the dangerous and potentially violent conditions of human relations today. Seen from that standpoint, *Les Troyens* is a disturbing text and certainly the most challenging one he has written so far.

NOTES TO CHAPTER THIRTEEN (Faye)

[1] "Le 'Nouveau Roman,'" *Esprit*, No. 7–8 (July–August 1958), pp. 1–111.

[2] Jean Pierre Faye, *Entre les rues*, p. 171. Henceforth all references to works by Jean Pierre Faye will appear in the body of the text, the following abbreviations being used: *Entre les rues*, R; *La Cassure*, C; *Battements*, B; *Analogues*, A; *L'Ecluse*, E; *Les Troyens*, T. See Bibliography for complete references.

[3] Jean Giraudoux, *Les Aventures de Jérôme Bardini* (Paris: Emile-Paul, 1930), pp. 27–28.

[4] Jean Giraudoux, *Siegfried et le Limousin* (Paris: Grasset, 1922), p. 83.

[5] Olivier de Magny, "*Entre les murs,* par Jean Pierre Faye," *Les Lettres Nouvelles*, No. 65 (November 1958), p. 607.

[6] *Ibid.*, p. 605.

[7] Emile Benveniste, "Structure des relations de personne dans le verbe," in *Problèmes de linguistique générale* (Paris: Gallimard, 1966), pp. 231, 230.

[8] "Débat sur le roman," *Tel Quel*, No. 17 (Spring 1964), p. 23.

[9] Philippe Sollers, "Un Nouvel Etranger," *Nouvelle Revue Française*, No. 121 (January 1963), p. 115.

[10] André Marrissel, "Jean Pierre Faye: *Battements*," *Esprit*, No. 59 (December 1962), p. 1068.

[11] Paris: GLM, 1960.

[12] Faye, "L'Idéologie littéraire (changement matériel et changement de forme)," in *Littérature et idéologies* (Paris: Editions de la Nouvelle Critique, 1971), p. 191.

CHAPTER FOURTEEN

Philippe Sollers

Philippe Sollers today is the driving force that has made the review *Tel Quel* and the group associated with it one of the most challenging and controversial enterprises in recent French intellectual history. He and his friends question most concepts previously associated with literature, belles-lettres, humanism, and the like. He was a different young man when he founded the review in the spring of 1960. The title brings to mind that of a work by Paul Valéry, and indeed in his presentation of the new quarterly Sollers quoted approvingly Valéry's image assimilating the work of art to an "enchanted structure". He implicitly rejected *littérature engagée*, denounced the sway of ideology over literature, and placed poetry, "in the broadest sense of the term," on the highest plane.[1] The five other members of the editorial committee of *Tel Quel* were little known, with the possible exception of Jean-René Huguenin, who shortly afterwards was killed in an automobile accident. None remains with the review today. Sollers himself had published two works of fiction, *Le Défi* and *Une Curieuse Solitude*, the first of which was less than forty pages in length.

1.

If any evidence were needed to point to the vitality of surrealism after the Second World War, those two texts by Sollers, who was born twelve years after the publication of the surrealist manifesto, would provide convincing pieces. *Le Défi*, written in 1956 when he was barely twenty and published the following year, carries an epigraph taken from André Breton's *Nadja*: "A few very exceptional human beings, who can expect and fear everything from each other, will always recognize each other thanks to their extreme capability to challenge." A self-centered tale of love and death, told in the setting of a seaside resort town, its mood and style bring Julien Gracq to mind. Occasionally, a touch of youthful cynicism reminds one of Radiguet—"Youth is the art of wasting time within the family circle."[2] Affirmations couched in a sort of abstract lyricism are evocative of Camus—"The insoluble and the contradictory were indeed my kingdoms" (D, p. 7). There is one sentence in *Le Défi* that reads almost as if it had been lifted out of a text by Breton, which it evokes even in its syntactic pattern: "And what can we expect, anyway, out of life, if not, on the occasion of an apparently commonplace event, furtive glimpses of the supernatural (*merveilleux*)?" (p. 9). Sollers has also confessed to having been influenced by Chateaubriand. Imitation and pastiche are natural in a young man's first writings. Echoes from Camus and Radiguet, even those of Gracq, soon fade away. Surrealism, although it is not a tradition one would detect in Sollers' texts today, cannot be so easily dismissed.

When his first full-length work of fiction, *Une Curieuse Solitude*, appeared in 1958, one could see that it did not betray the "literary promise" evidenced by *Le Défi*. Influences are still noticeable, that of Radiguet in particular, and, to me at least, overtones from Stendhal are more in evidence than those from Chateaubriand. It is the story of a young man's experiences in sexual desire, told in the first person (as had been *Le Défi*), full of innocent cruelty and deceit with a concomitant mixture of suffering and joy. The narrator is as egocentric as before, but as he discovers himself he also becomes conscious of the world and his role in it. In *Le Défi*, the girl who gets involved

with the narrator and whose suicide he is responsible for was
hardly more than a phantasm ("I relished my own self under
the name of Claire"— p. 12). Now, the Spanish girl, Concha,
is clearly the Other. Actually it is he, not she, who tends toward nonexistence. Concha calls him Felipe, and since he is
French his name can only be Philippe, the same as the author's,
but nowhere is that name mentioned. The situation is that of
the narrator's accepting the mask imposed upon him by the
Other, just as the author seemed to accept his role of writer
within a given cultural tradition and adopted what Roland
Barthes called the scription (*écriture*) of the French twentieth-
century "novel." Written in an impeccably controlled style,
Une Curieuse Solitude was welcomed into the bosom of belles-
lettres by Aragon (*Le Défi* had been highly praised by
François Mauriac)—but it was no revelation. Sollers recently
dismissed that work as having been written not so much by
himself as "by a specific social group (the bourgeoisie), whose
spokesman I happened to be at a given moment because of my
class origins."[3]

Still, with the benefit of hindsight, it is possible to detect several signs pointing to his more recent works. Perhaps that book
was indeed written by a young bourgeois eager to adopt the
esthetics of his class, but he also happened to be Philippe Sollers
—that is, a person who received a specific intellectual formation and was developing a given awareness. While *Le Défi* contained the seed of a well-rounded plot, *Une Curieuse Solitude*
shifts the emphasis to the narrator's interpreting a problematic
relationship, for which no resolution is provided. His words
matter more than what they describe. Even in the case of
Concha her name is as important as her being: "The woman
whose name it was seemed to me so perfectly wedded to it that
I could not separate the one from the other, and I only possessed
her through its intermediary" (S, pp. 69–70). Along similar
lines, an awareness of the determining role of language crops
up in a number of instances. Some of these merely reflect tra-

ditional attitudes, such as this distant echo from La Roche-
foucauld: "But desire consists mainly in the vocabulary of desire" (S, p. 38). A few others give a more compelling ring:
"There might, moreover, be something quite healthy . . . for
those who, at times, get tired of language to an extreme degree, in suddenly changing it, speaking only in borrowed
phrases, creating for themselves a new, restricted world, without connections with that of their childhood and their weari-
ness" (p. 24). One might even suggest that the sexual encounter
between Felipe and Concha constitutes but an extended
metaphor for the erotic experience Philippe, as narrator, has
with language as he gives shape to the text. The role her name
plays in Felipe's possession of her would then be correlative
to the role language plays for the narrator in coming to terms
with the world. Such remarks, however, to which I might add
an interesting mirror metaphor—"that mirror of my awakening,
capable of ordering the strangest elements that become caught
in it" (S, p. 83)—acquire significance solely in retrospect.

In his next work, *Le Parc*, it could be said that Sollers had
come into his own. With the publication of that work, a new
writer was born. A very different influence now appears to be
at work. Even more than in the early fiction of Claude Ollier,
it seems to develop along the pattern of a work by Robbe-
Grillet. A narrator transcribes a series of visual impressions,
first provoked by "reality" and then by memory and imagination, all blending in such fashion as to make it difficult to distinguish the one from the other. He lives in a corner apartment with a balcony on the sixth floor of a building in a large
city. The location affords a privileged view in several directions,
enabling him, for instance, to look into a number of apartments
across the way, peer back into his own room, or watch the
street scene below. The reader is with him from dusk to dawn
on a night when he can hardly sleep, partly because of asthma,
partly because of a sequence of obsessive thoughts, and again
throughout a day that may or may not be the following one.

A man and a woman, who are strangers to him and are seen to move about in the living room of another apartment he had been watching, gradually fade away, being replaced by acute remembrances of a different man and woman. Later, the figure of a child is woven in. The child is probably himself and he may have had a love affair with the woman. The man, whose friend he was and with whom he occasionally identifies, is now dead.

That much I think we can reasonably be sure of, although the web of relationships that link those three roles to the narrator is not clearly defined. Reminiscent of Robbe-Grillet's handling of the engraving in *Dans le labyrinthe* is Sollers' introduction of a painting in the apartment bedroom. It represents a fishing port teeming with the activities of sailing vessels, while on land, "right here, two men and a woman, all three impassive, appear to pursue a conversation or to make parallel statements without connection with what is taking place behind them" (P, p. 16). These could be the three main characters of *Le Parc*, whose involvements are equally ambiguous or enigmatic. But in contrast to what happens in Robbe-Grillet's book, the characters (if the word is still appropriate; Jean Ricardou calls them "pronominal characters," and I have suggested the phrase "grammatical functions" in another chapter of this study) do not emerge out of the painting in order to participate in the narrator's phantasms. Rather, the painting seems to draw them like a magnet to the other side of visible reality. Very near the end of the text, the narrator describes himself and the woman in a setting that is precisely that of the painting—one implication being that they have removed themselves from the "reality" of the fiction. In other words they are no longer characters in the traditional sense of the word.

A public park serves as the setting for some of the incidents and gives the book its title. Also, as defined in the epigraph by means of a quotation from Rousseau, it provides the text with its own metaphor (which recalls the mirror image in *Une Curieuse Solitude*). "It is a mixture of sites that are very

beautiful and picturesque, whose contributing parts have been
chosen in different countries, and where everything appears
natural except the aggregate." Slightly transposed, that could
also have been applied to those works by Claude Simon in
which every detail seems realistic but the entire work does not.
To the various spots in Sollers' park correspond, in one set of
analogies, the separate elements of the narrative, and in another,
the several pronominal characters involved. Robbe-Grillet, in
the final analysis, may well have been more of a challenge than
an influence, and Sollers' ties to surrealism remain unbroken at
this stage. As he himself explains on the back cover its sentences and paragraphs proceed "like the imagination," by means
of analogies. The epigraph also suggests a bringing together of
several distant elements of reality. It is out of similar confrontations that, according to André Breton, surrealist images are
born. One might thus go to the surrealist manifesto to find an
esthetic justification for the enigmatic quality of *Le Parc*: "The
two parts of the image have not been deduced from each other
by the mind *with the intent* of producing a given spark";[4] rather,
the elements are placed in juxtaposition, and then one records
and appreciates the "luminous phenomenon." Such a phenomenon can only take place in the reader's imagination.

In addition to exhibiting a tension between reality and
imagination, between persons seen and persons imagined, the
narrative gravitates about different texts. Various colors of ink
and kinds of paper distinguish those written by the child, the
woman, the man, and finally the narrator himself. Eventually,
just as the "characters" were drafted away from reality, the
whole narrative is drawn to the words of one text. The last
sentence of the volume refers to "the orange-colored notebook,
patiently filled, overladen with an even handwriting that has
been led to this page, this sentence, this period, by the old
fountain pen often and automatically dipped into blue-black
ink" (p. 155). Again it turns out that what the narrator has
been writing becomes the book one is reading. The time has
perhaps come, however, to ask whether such a statement of the

process, culminating with the book and its implication of finality, is the most fruitful one. It might indeed be better to reverse the terms and think of the book's being read as a text that is being written. In addition to placing emphasis on its generative aspects, that further suggests that the book the author proposes is still lacking something essential when purchased by a prospective reader. "A book exists in itself only as a virtuality, and its actualization (or its production) depends on its being read and on the moments when such reading is performed."[5]

Le Parc appears to represent a quest for meaning in which the author can point the way toward the grail but cannot reach it alone. What is sought for is the meaning of self, and he can obviously not impose an answer on his readers. Enlightenment, if it comes to them, will derive from the "luminous phenomenon" Breton has spoken of. The role played by elements of the narrative should now become more apparent. Little need be said about the part assigned to the woman and the man in developing themes such as love and friendship or of the contributions those concepts make toward an understanding of oneself. The balcony enables the narrator not only to see his room as an outsider might (or, symbolically, to see himself in the same fashion), it places it (and his existence) at a spatial distance from himself. A temporal distance is then provided by childhood memories (the distance is increased by the use of words like *l'enfant* instead of first-person pronouns). That, along with illness and preoccupation with mirrors, which Pierre Mabille called "the most commonplace and at the same time the most extraordinary of magical devices,"[6] a statement with which any reader of Lewis Carroll would agree, insinuates the theme of death. Its presence can be felt long before the death of the narrator's friend is recorded on the last page of the first part of the book, without any appearance of the word "death." As the narrator, early in the book, begins to suffer an attack of asthma, he watches the mirror for signs of his own deterioration. "Yet in the mirror, above the mantelpiece, the face remains the same

at the conclusion of those minute transformations that have
led him to this evening" (P, p. 24). Mirrors emphasize or even
multiply a woman's body; they also accentuate visual reality
and its limitations. A close, detailed examination of his own
eyes in a mirror leads only to unproductive statements such
as, "I see, now, what causes me to see" (p. 54), or else he notes
a possibly false likeness to the woman's eyes. Later, thinking
about the letters of his dead friend, about which he can no
longer ask for precisions or elaborations, he looks into the mirror
in vain. "And it isn't that face in the mirror that can give me the
answer, the final expression that could not reach it" (p. 100).

The connection with death is further emphasized in the attempt to reproduce his friend's facial expression when he was
killed. "That face is mine, my eyes are looking at me. Mouth
open, muscles taut, I gradually compose the expression: the
last moment, the end, the bursting, the torture" (p. 121). But
all that gets him nowhere. The hint of a possible solution is
given near the end of the book as the narrator, once more, faces
his mirror. This time he concentrates less on the material self
that confronts his gaze than on some intangible, imperceptible
gap that might be detected between existence and its reflection.
That enables the reader, I believe, to point to a preoccupation
that affirms itself more and more in Sollers' texts—the fusion of
problems of meaning and existence with those of writing—or,
as that word is inadequate for conveying the special connotations that today accompany the word *écriture*, meaning both
the work with language performed by a writer and the interplay
of signifiers in the text, I shall use the term "scription."

Jacques Derrida, in his attempt to define the science of
"scription," which he calls "grammatology" and in which he
would include word as well as script, is led to generalize from
a concept introduced by Ferdinand de Saussure—that of the
"difference" (with other words) that enables one to distinguish
any one particular word. At the source, "the concept of script
(*graphie*) implies, as a possibility common to all systems of
meaning, the process of *instituted marking* (*trace instituée*),"[7]

meaning an unmotivated but distinctive marking, a reference by means of which a "difference appears *as such.*" The conceptual and purely hypothetical "arch-marking" is then defined, in order to express the notion of movement implicitly contained in the idea of difference: *"The (pure) marking is a deferring."*[8] Hence the preoccupation with the gap that separates the markings in the mirror from what they designate and the difference it refers to—himself. There is also a suggestion of a world beyond the mirror in which characters and events bear the same relationship to the "real" world of the book as those of the previously mentioned painting. They constitute a structure of signs that tends to absorb everything else into it. Something similar has been implied on another occasion when the narrator opened the door of a dark closet in his room. He had the impression of being in the presence of the world's other side, of what he termed its "unthinkable wrapping" (P, p. 122). The episode of the mirror is perhaps more satisfactory, as it affirms the presence of both the "real" world and of another, from which it cannot easily be distinguished and for which the reflection in the mirror is the metaphor. As to the link between the two, "It comes and goes like a breeze from the tree to the window and, going through the pane, from my breast to the tree, to the trees, to the houses" (p. 149). After that epiphany, the narrative is brought to a rapid conclusion, not because of any resolution in the "plot," but because whoever is writing has reached the last page of the orange-colored notebook he was using.

To those looking for realistic, linear narrative, Sollers' third full-length work of fiction, *Drame* (1965), will seem even more esoteric than the second. It might be useful to recall that he himself suggested the phrase *poème romanesque* in connection with *Le Parc.* That puts him at an equal distance from traditional fiction and from Claude Mauriac's concept of *essais romanesques.* What removes *Drame* from convention is that, even more than in *Le Parc,* anecdotal elements have faded far into the background. What distinguishes it from an essay is that the quality of "abstract lyricism" detectable in Sollers' earlier narratives has been transformed into a more concrete kind of poetry. In *Drame*, one is constantly confronted with particulars, with tangible aspects of reality, even when they are molded into rather unusual images and metaphors. The title itself owes something to Mallarmé. In a talk given in 1965 (the same year as *Drame* appeared) and first published in *Tel Quel* the following year, Sollers remarked that, for Mallarmé's writing the great Book, "the fundamental problem is . . . the theater, that is, the three-dimensional book."[9] He then added, after several developments, "We must therefore realize the possibility of the text as theater at the same time as that of theater and life as text."[10] References to the stage abound in *Drame*, but the link between the idea of theater and the action of the text on the reader is more organically integrated into Sollers' next book.

In *Drame* he is again attempting to explore an individual consciousness—his own, naturally. But he generalizes the experience by projecting it in two directions: first, that of a community of beings, thereby enabling the reader to participate in the exploration; second, that of the writer, again bringing in the reader, this time by means of the concept of double creation—which we are now familiar with. The text itself oscillates between two points of view, that of a seemingly omniscient narrator who describes the quest and that of someone or something writing about his or its quest—the latter sections (or cantos) readily identifiable by being set within quotation marks and preceded by the statement, "He writes." There are also other pronouns or grammatical functions, a feminine one with whom the subject is involved but who does not ever become a subject, and a second-person pronoun whose referent may vary. A child makes a most fleeting appearance. It would be as difficult and as pointless to attempt a summary of the narrative sequence of *Drame* as it would have been to paraphrase Blanchot's *L'Attente l'oubli* or Beckett's *L'Innommable*. There are two settings, each appearing to correspond to one of the projections I have mentioned: a large city by the ocean, with its port, streets, buildings, and beaches, and a library, perhaps a private one, with its world of books. Giving the fiction unity, one is clearly the correlative of the other. Travel is alluded to a number of times, by car, by train, or by plane (only once by ship), but no destination is involved. There is an accident or two, perhaps even three, but no possibility of establishing realistic logical links or anecdotal continuity. The "story" has a beginning of sorts that is established by the words "At the outset," "first," and "beginning"—all on the initial page. The brief second sentence, "Swiftly, he conducts the investigation," evidently proposes a quest, but of what? A few pages before the end, at first reading, one is hard put to imagine why or how the narrative would come to a close. Indeed the first-person subject explains in the final paragraph: "One might as well imagine that the book founders (*échoue*) here" (D, p. 159). A situation similar to that in *Le Parc*, where the text ended because the last page of a notebook had been reached. In French, *échouer* commonly means to fail; basically it means, when speaking of ships, to run aground. The main ship in the book is the book itself, which now lies on the beaches of the reader's mind.

In large part, again, we are dealing with the account of a book being written in the active presence of the reader. Such an account might be termed ironic in that it also describes the failure attendant upon the conventional process of (successful) fiction-writing, based on the assumption that once an author has a story to tell, he will readily find the words needed to relate it—"He thought that at the required moment [the French phrase *au moment voulu* recalls the title of Blanchot's fiction] the true story would allow itself to be told" (D, p. 11) —and eventually results in a novel sort of text that draws its strength from its inability to become a "novel." Toward the beginning, the word *manqué* (missed) signals a few false starts, recalling Beckett's "what tedium" in *Malone meurt* as well as Robbe-Grillet's "No" in *Dans le labyrinthe*. Irony and that sort of reminiscence soon fade away before a more positive textual experience.

The two settings, city and library, correspond to the two aspects of reality one experiences—matter and language, the authentic woof and warp of experience. Emphasizing the elemental nature of such constituents, images of earth, water, air, and fire are frequently introduced, fire being apparently associated with language (this would fit the transforming role that Sollers connects with writing). The narrative of *Drame* begins with the affirmation of both language and matter as areas to be investigated. Parts of the body have stored memories of sense impressions, and what may be a dream has whoever says "I" penetrate into the library through one of the books on its shelves. Body and dream are significant because they have been for so long the suppressed elements in Western culture. In the present instance, not only is the dream presumably experienced at night, but the events of the dream also take place during the night. Night has considerable value for Sollers. Its connotations strike a familiar chord in contemporary fiction and thought, and in the text of one of his essays Sollers links his concept of darkness to Joyce's: "Into the night where Joyce entered by means of his writings, tongues loosen and come to life, they uncover their ambiguity, their multiplicity, of which we are the daytime reflections, reflections or images that believe themselves protected and plain."[11] By means of that statement he dismantles language of its function. No longer a convenient tool for conveying thoughts, a means by which to express onself, it becomes a reality that is a constitutive element of our consciousness. In *Drame*, a book is opened in the hope that it might prove of assistance in writing the text, the drama of which unfolds. That book, however, was not written by a Proust, or a Joyce, or a Blanchot, and it is of no avail. It is replete with characters who indulge in much activity without realizing that they accomplish nothing. Of them we are told that they sleep, eat, read, write, and so forth, "Without realizing that they have not progressed beyond a single page, a single word, they are still and ever on the same side." In other words, they have not taken that step through the looking glass. Furthermore, "They have not for a single moment experienced the night when they talk about night"(D, p. 92).

Mirrors had seemed significant in *Le Parc*. Their presence, by implication at least, in the statement in the essay concerning Joyce and their continuing role in *Drame* is an indication that they belong to Sollers' store of fundamental imagery. In *Drame*, however, the nature of mirrors varies. They can be like a looking glass; they can gain transparency and become an ordinary pane of glass; or they can lose all but their reflective qualities, and the reflection then is synesthetically transformed into an echo. In all three cases, there is some form of interference between the object perceived and the perceiver, and it is hardly surprising at this point of the analysis to discover that in many of those images words are the tenor. They are the looking glass through which the writer attempts to lead the reader. If the latter persists in considering them as signs that point to referents in "reality," he is apt to remain mired on the near side, where meanings are imposed on him and creativity is lacking. In one instance, the writer appears to be luring the reader, as he imagines him on the other side. "I sometimes imagine your being beyond the line that the sky reaches by means of a single black curtain riddled with stars: there, again close by, you come and go in a boundless land . . . I wonder if you know that power" (p. 33). He sees him on the other side of words, on another shore. That statement, in the same passage, suggests to him the image of a wall at the far end of an estate (again the idea of interference), with games being played on the near side and only silence on the far one. Silence has evocative powers similar to those of darkness; it is a word "toward which other words proceed and vibrate" (p. 65). In an essay on fiction and, more specifically, the act of writing, Sollers has stated that "One writes in order to speak less and less, to reach the written silence of memory that, paradoxically, gives us back the world in its coded operation, the world of which each one of us is the hidden, irreducible cipher."[12] Beyond the wall of *Drame* lies authentic matter (as distinct from "reality"), here specifically the earth with its hills, vegetation, rocks, animals, and so forth. All these, in the aggregate, make up "the necessary coating for the mirror of words" (D, p. 34). It is the same mirror, in the very next sentence, that turns words back into silence.

A strictly rational analysis of the imagery of that section would lead only to confusion. Yet Sollers has been able to communicate something important about language that cannot be expressed in any other way than the one he used. This has to do with the powers and limitations of language, with written language conceived as a negation of common speech, and hence as a form of silence. If it could all be translated into a conventional organization of words, such a translation might actually undermine Sollers' statement. What happens when one reads the text is that clusters of images gradually form, with meaning emerging out of the interplay of images within each cluster and also out of the juxtaposition of clusters. This may be due only to my desire to see a similarity, but such a distribution into clusters appears related to the more analytical description of texts proposed by Julia Kristeva, in which she uses the mathematical concept of sets. Window panes, mirrors, echoes, walls, words (a printed page is described as "Wall and mirror"—D, p. 89) would be part of one group. The four basic elements, various combinations of matter such as the human body, forests, mountains, or lakes would constitute another. A third brings together significant human activities, like the theater, fiction writing, and game playing.

In the latter set or cluster, one game dominates, chess. At the end of the initial statement produced by the first-person subject, bodily existence is likened to a "moving chessboard" (p. 21), where all the given elements of the problem are located, beginning with the board itself, which represents time (p. 24).

Sollers, in a statement on the book's back cover, suggests that the sixty-four cantos of the work, made up of the alternating narratives by what he calls chorus and individual, bear a resemblance to the sixty-four squares of the chess board. "It is well known that, for the player, such a division [of the board into squares] figures time projected into space. Likewise, the fragments that are linked here by means of scription aim to reveal an immediate projection of thought into language, which nevertheless includes thought." For Jean Pierre Faye, the sixty-four alternating cantos suggested the sixty-four hexagrams of the *I Ching* and its alternating principles of yin and yang, an analogy someone might fruitfully pursue. In the final analysis, language is the main topic of this book. That is what links its three main image clusters. A product of the human body, it is a system of signs corresponding, through a complex of "mirrors," to other signs or markings in the universe, and it is the major constituent of men's ritualistic activities. The plot is linguistic. If what were first thought to be a narrator and characters are nameless, it is not for any reason that might bring Nathalie Sarraute to mind. It is rather because they are words, like the ship seen by Giraudoux's Dutchman and like some of Blanchot's "characters": "The two of us together constitute a dark, oscillating sentence that perceives and returns the slightest signal" (D, p. 75). *Drame* is, like any fiction or poem, an assemblage of words. Hyperconscious of that fact, its author does not, however, allow it to degenerate into a mere rhetorical exercise. From the epigraph, "The blood that permeates the heart is thought," to the final sentence, "Thought . . . that is nimblest and swiftest of all and rests upon the heart," it is firmly rooted in materiality.

2.

In the fall of 1960, Sollers recalled the enthusiasm with which, at eighteen, he had read E. M. Cioran's *Précis de décomposition*, in large part because of its appeal to what he called the "corrupting exuberance of life". He was also struck by a statement "that seemed to me, that seems to me still one of the most appropriate maxims, almost a slogan, of the new spirit: 'One does not discuss the universe, one expresses it.' Wonderful, I thought. We have come a long way. All we need do is begin."[13] He has travelled yet a longer way to reach those concepts that underlie the composition of *Nombres* (1968), as they underlie, though to a lesser degree, *Le Parc* and *Drame*.

"I imagine," he wrote in 1962, "the beginning of a book; its sentences, asserting their presence in an unusual way, surprise the most sophisticated reader."[14] That reader, he continued, vainly seeks the writer's usual qualities, his themes, his obsessions, nor does he discover references to fiction passed off as reality. Instead of entering a kind of different world, organized by someone else, instead of confronting a specific object existing outside of himself, "he is, on the contrary, thrown back to his own personal situation."[15] Rather than a representation that he could appreciate, accept, or reject, the text facing him "has both the opaqueness of a façade and the limpidity of a mirror."[16] The image is the same as that which I have already noted in Sollers' fiction. The rejection it implies is not only that of literature conceived as a representation of reality—he has called that an absurdly naive preconception[17]—but also literature as an expression of an individual thought or feelings. As in the case of several other contemporary writers, his point of departure seems to lie in the works of Mallarmé. The idea of considering the outside world as a text (I also noted this where Butor is concerned), of asking oneself how it can be written, of a writer's removing his presence from the text—those now familiar notions are stressed again. "In short, a book is the locus of a double process: suppression of the author (a book is often compared to a *tomb* by Mallarmé) who abandons word in favor of script, thus allowing time to become transformed into space . . . [and] enhancement of the reader"[18]

The matter of the author's disappearance needs some elaboration. There is no question that a specific writer is involved in the making of a text. The common error, according to Sollers, and I believe he is right, has been to view the author as the source of the text. "An author is not really the cause of what he writes, quite the contrary, he is its product."[19] Roland Barthes, in an essay written in 1960, had previously come to the conclusion that the traditional view of the relationship between the author and the work seemed "less and less defensible". He also asked, "What if the work were precisely what the author does not know, what he does not live?"[20] It remained for Sollers to give the statement a rigorous justification based on contemporary linguistic theory.

According to Emile Benveniste, "the possibility of thought is tied to the properties of language, for language is a structure endowed with significance, and to think is to handle the signs of language."[21] One should not deduce from such an affirmation that a specific language might prevent a given intellectual development from taking place. To use Benveniste's own example, the structure of Chinese was no obstacle to the assimilation in China of dialectical materialism. What it does suggest is that language structure can determine the direction one's thought will take, unless one is actively aware of that structure and of its operation. To deal with specific points, French society today "needs the myth of the 'novel'" (as undoubtedly American society does, too), the reason being that "The novel is the manner in which that society speaks of itself, the manner in which the individual must think his life in order to be accepted in it."[22] Fiction in literature reproduces whatever myths are imposed on a people, and people then reproduce the myths (and the characters) of literature. When art imitates "reality", reality in turn imitates "art"—and neither is true. What we know as "reality" is no more than a convention. "What is called real, under given historical circumstances, is what the majority, through those who hold power and for precise economic reasons, are forced to accept as real. Such a

358   FRENCH FICTION TODAY

reality, furthermore, is revealed nowhere else but in language, and the language of a society, its myths, is what that society has chosen as constituting its reality."²³ Each person's options are either to accept what society guarantees as real, at the same time forgoing the possibility of making any fundamental challenge or change, or else dismantle the myth from the inside, that is, within the functioning of language. The process begins with "the realization that we are signs among other signs, signs that produce signs."²⁴ Precisely because his fiction no longer resembles the traditional novel, Sollers maintains the word *roman* on the cover of his books, thereby attempting to dismantle the literary concept of genre, again from the inside. His definition, "We shall call *novel* the unceasing, unconscious, mythic discourse of people,"²⁵ aims at debunking the notions of "creative genius" and "originality." "Authors" and their "masterpieces" or "works of art" give way before scription and reading.

The writer, or, as Sollers sometimes calls him, the scriptor, is no longer concerned with "telling a story with varying degrees of effectiveness or art, expressing this or that, imagining (phantasmagorizing) or producing this or that."²⁶ His purpose is to upset the perspectives of the world in which he lives. When the reader enters the picture, he does not, "as people too often put it, turn his reading into the making of a book." He should, on the other hand "become at every moment his own scription—that is, destroy within himself the speech that is spoken by preconceptions, so that he may decide for himself on the basis of relevant evidence, and succeed in *generating* himself."²⁷ He needs to brush aside the childlike desire to listen to a story. Instead, he should "open [his] eyes, at the risk of blinding [himself], to the source of all stories, knowing that such an activity is and must be considered delinquent from the standpoint of the reigning stories and myths."²⁸

In conjunction with his evolving concept of literature, Sollers' attitude toward surrealism also underwent a modification. The problems he faced were, on the surface, not unlike André Breton's, whose iconoclastic views on the myths of French society together with a considerable interest in Hegel and Marx brought him at one time close to the French communist party. When the chips were down, however, Breton decided to pursue his own course, refusing to submit poetry or art to any ideology. As Sollers kept edging closer and closer to a Marxist-Leninist position and felt the need to bring his literary, social, political principles into harmony, he was probably led to take a closer look at the surrealist adventure from a philosophical and political standpoint. In doing that, he detected in Breton's writings strong strands of old-fashioned idealism. In a commentary on the vocabulary of the 1925 *Lettre aux recteurs des universités européennes,* he wrote, "Petty bourgeois anarchism has found its phraseology."[29] I do not believe Sollers has rejected Breton completely, although it would probably be difficult to draw a line between what he might consider as having been positive aspects of surrealist thought and negative ones. "The surrealist movement has, as a matter of fact, both set and misappreciated all the problems that necessarily beset a Western avant-garde whose 'literary' activity is no more than a borrowed term belonging to the realm of an extinct knowledge."[30] Breton's major sins spring evidently from his choice of Fourier over Marx, of Jung over Freud.

While he was elaborating a literary theory, Sollers continued working in fiction. His activities in that domain so far have culminated in *Nombres* (1968). The reader, perhaps a bit awed by the essays, may well approach this book with fear and trembling, wondering what he is supposed to do. The answer is simple—read. *Nombres* is not a difficult book once one has discarded a few bad reading habits. It should be read deliberately, as one might read poetry, absorbing each word, allowing connotations and resonances to develop. One should not, of course, try to extract characters and anecdotes from the text. At the end, the reader will emerge a changed person.

Architecturally, the book is made up of twenty-five sections of four sequences each for a total of one hundred sequences—which amounts to the square of the sum of the first four numbers (the title defines the architecture). Each sequence is numbered in the margin, identifying its place both in the book as a whole and within a given section. Opening the book at page 81, for instance, and seeing the figure 4.64, we know that it signals the sixty-fourth sequence, the fourth one in the sixteenth section. Within each section, the first three sequences are written in the imperfect tense, the fourth in the present; all are written in the first person (singular or plural), but the fourth sequences show a preponderance of second-person pronouns, a means of drawing the reader into the text. Diagrams printed in the book suggest that sequences one, two, and three may be thought of as developing on the three surfaces of something that vaguely resembles a stage. This is drawn from the top and appears as an inverted "U." The fourth side, directed towards an assumed audience, is where the fourth sequence takes shape —a sequence more openly directed at the reader. The surface is made of thin air, or seems to be, but that is merely an illusion: it is a "distorting panel," an "invisible, opaque veil," a "mirror or reflector" (N, p. 22)—whence arise a number of illusions for the spectator. The reader should not be taken in, for the page on which the text is printed is seen as "wrapped" around both stage and house, and it gives the only truthful account. One is reminded of the world's "unthinkable wrapping" that appeared in *Le Parc*.

If pressed to say what *Nombres* is about, I could not answer that it deals with any one topic or that it is specifically one thing or another. It refuses to become the subject of "literary" chitchat. Yet it is possible to enumerate several domains one is conscious of exploring when reading the book. There is the writer's own experience in and through language; there is the situation of the reader with reference to the language of his culture; there is the functioning of the text itself, correlated with sexual acts; there is the existence of a world-wide revolutionary situation; there is the confrontation between the two diametrically opposed cultures of east and west; and there is the increasingly encompassing manifestation of Marxist thought. All of these take place successively and concurrently, separately and homogeneously. Jacques Derrida, in a seventy-five-page essay (Sollers' text is 112 pages long),[31] has attempted to convey that complex process, and he has succeeded to a degree made possible only by the intricacies of his own scription, more baffling in some ways than the text it describes. Far less ambitiously, I shall try, without ossifying that text, to demonstrate some of its operations in a few specific sequences—mindful of the warning that "what is coming toward you . . . can neither be reduced nor translated" (N, p. 90).

Nombres begins with a denial of formal beginnings (only stories have a beginning), with three dots and a lower-case initial letter: ". . . the paper was burning, and it involved all the things drawn and projected there in regularly distorted fashion, while a sentence was speaking: 'this is the exterior side'" (N, p. 11). At once a connection is established with the last page of *Drame*, "One might well imagine that the book founders here—(burns) (disappears)" (D, p. 159), and with a statement made by Sollers in an essay: "The novel must therefore burn and consume all traces of a novel or else resign itself to being nothing but a novel."[32] In more ways than one, *Nombres* germinates at the point where *Drame* died, foundered, and succeeded. The destruction of the book where reality is represented ("drawn and painted"), transformed by the author's art ("in regularly distorted fashion"). The "exterior side" is a reference to the near side of the mirror, where referents are located. Further in that first paragraph we read: "Large expanse already beyond measurement. . . . it's a matter of a departure that left us without a past." Fifty sequences later, those sentences are recalled: ". . . and in short, the ordeal was to withstand the first expanse, the one that continued to transform itself and to disintegrate, instead of ceaselessly remaining in the volume that opened with the murder of words without past . . ." (N, p. 67). Feelings of awesome immensity, change, infinite connections and complexities arise at that point. The notion of "ordeal" is supplemented a half-dozen lines later by that of the "continuity of armed struggle." Comparing the last phrase of the two statements, it is clear that an analogy is set up between "us" and "words," bringing to mind the already quoted "We are signs among signs."

I have just noted the thread that runs through the words "book," " words," "consume," and "burn". To the ancient symbolism of fire as a transmitting agent, a "mediator between forms that vanish and forms in creation,"[33] one can add the association between fire and violence, particularly revolution. The connotation is confirmed not only by the "armed struggle" but by such references as the one to a "red narrative" (N, p. 57), which orients it in the direction of a Marxist revolution. Returning to the initial paragraph of the first sequence, one sees that as the paper burns it curls up, forming what might look like a cylinder or a column. Neither word is in the first paragraph, but each one appears later, retroactively charging it with meaning. Derrida has suggested that they provide a connection with texts of the cabala, particularly with the thirteenth-century *Zohar* and with the Tower of Babel, and that it also constitutes a phallic symbol. In French as in English, the word "column" for numbers and for texts provide yet another homogenizing element. Finally, the rolled paper brings to mind the appearance of sacred Oriental texts. Moving ahead in such fashion from that first paragraph is not as artificial as it may seem, for the paragraph itself is repeated three times in the text, verbatim or with variations, maintaining its presence throughout the length of the narrative and receiving added semantic charge as it recurs. As one almost inevitably is led to refer to the initial statement, that one, in turn, also benefits from the additional connotations.

As one continues to read, a familiar image crops up: that of the mirror, which appears as a "black mirror" (p. 39) and hence presents an interference. Later, the very idea of going through the looking glass is specifically stated—*cette traversée du miroir* (N, p. 65); one of its final mentions is in a quotation, "The mirror is not a source" (N, p. 117). Those three selected instances offer suggestions for the imagination parallel to the ones I have previously discussed in *Le Parc*. At this point, however, I am loath to generalize. As has been seen already, fixity is not a characteristic of Sollers' texts. Now more than ever the context is essential and generalizations dangerous. In my opinion, a conventional study of literary imagery in his fiction would not be fruitful.

The specific connection made with *Drame* implies that intertextuality plays a role in *Nombres*. Confirmation comes with an intensity and form different from those in works by Ollier or Butor. Its simplest and most obvious manifestations are when first sentences of both previous works are quoted. The quotation from *Le Parc* is accompanied by a short comment: " 'The sky, above the long, glossy avenues, is dark blue': that, in short, is the sentence from which I started—" (N, p. 30). As I noted earlier, that indeed marked the emergence of a new writer. Soon one notices an increasing number of short quotations, given without indication or suggestion of source and, except for the quotation marks, well integrated (absorbed, transformed) into Sollers' text. For the first ten pages they appear at a rate of slightly fewer than one per page; there are ten quotations in the last two pages of the book, all within one sequence and adding up to more than a third of its length. In *Drame* the first-person function quoted from books in the library, but the number of citations was not great. Here they are numerous and their fields coincide with the various topics I have tentatively enumerated; they are more or less identifiable according to one's familiarity with the field—or unfamiliarity, as the case may be. The idea, however, is not to engage in a sterile hunting game for precise references. The quotations function, as I see it, in two different fashions. First, they serve to invest a given ideology in the text. Tracing, for instance, a quotation on page 97 of *Nombres* to page 149 of Maurice Granet's *La Pensée chinoise* does little good unless one is acquainted with Granet's overall view of Chinese culture. Second, they become part of the text and as such a productive element in it. Textual production, it should always be stressed, takes place on the level of the signifier rather than on that of the signified.

The first activity of the quotations belongs to what Julia Kristeva, in an essay even more useful than Derrida's for a comprehension of the processes that are involved in *Nombres*, calls the geno-text, the second belongs to the pheno-text.[34] In her theory, the geno-text produces not so much a sentence or a sequence of sentences as it does a string of complex signifiers, which she calls "numberers" because of the multiple possibilities of significations they afford. To choose a very simple example, the brief quotation, "We were dancing on a volcano" (*Nous dansions sur un volcan*—N, p. 44), refers to an aristocratic ball given just before the French Revolution of 1789. It reinforces the revolutionary presence previously introduced by such elements as three mentions of severed heads and one of a king's execution, adding the suggestion of imminence. It also inscribes the word *dansions* into the text. It now acts as a "numberer," generating the word "measure," which appears a couple of lines later in the phrase "measure of time." That easily leads one to the notion of dancing on a stage, which turns up later (p. 78), and the two combined revive a sentence in Sollers' essay on Mallarmé: "The light thrown on the world reveals it as scription at the intersection of Theater and Book, and that intersection is Dance."[35] The word "measure" suggests "counting," which shows up in similar position in the next sequence, and is repeated three times. "Not counting for the white inhabitants of the world, who believe.in another world ... Not counting for the machines that go faster than sound, carrying the message of the creator . . . Not counting for the mountains that now witness a revolution without fear—" (N, p. 45). The second "numberer," *volcan* generates the first sentence of that next sequence, ". . . as if we suffered the consequences of an explosion" (N, p. 44), with its accompaniment of fire and violence, together with a rhythm that gives the sequence the atmosphere of a dance of death. Finally, if one takes into consideration the "literality" of the words involved, one notices a lexical thread running through *voile, volcan, voilà vivants, convulsés*—words that appear on pages 44 and 45. *Volcan* might bring to mind its *cratère*, and that gives us *créateur* on page 45, out of whom the world was spewed forth. The series also suggests *viol* (rape) and *violence*, among other things, and both are implied on page 45; *volcan* is also phonetically related to the German word *Volk* (why limit the possibilities of the imagination?) suggesting an explosion of the people.

Probably the most striking intertextual operation, noticed even when one merely flips through the pages of *Nombres*, is that produced by over twoscore Chinese ideograms disseminated through the text. Obviously, they mean nothing to the majority of readers, who can do no more than identify them as elements of Chinese writing. They produce a certain amount of tension on the pages where they appear, but as far as immediate effect goes, Sollers could have tossed in ideograms culled at random from Chinese prints. Nevertheless, he chose them carefully, for their meaning is always relevant to the context—sometimes simply translating a preceding word or phrase, sometimes summing up a statement. For instance, the quotation from Lao Tzu, "To produce without acquiring, to act without gaining self-assurance, to help develop without imposing one's will," (N, p. 95) is followed by the symbol transliterated as *Tsu*, meaning "sufficiency."[36] For one who understands the Chinese elements, their role is purely thematic. Yet I suspect Sollers put them there less as thematic symbols than as indications of the growing presence of an alien thought and culture, that of the Orient. He himself, when asked why he had used them, answered that they were there in order to stress, "1) that we use a conventional, arbitrary system of writing that seems natural to us although it probably has unconscious, determining effects on our thought, 2) that the meanings of one system could be grasped in unique fashion in the context of another system."[37] Before they have those effects, however, they are likely to provoke reactions based on fear, hatred, simple curiosity, or enthusiasm within the reader, depending on his ideological position. A certain element of provocation may have prompted their insertion, at the beginning at least, as a means of separating friends from foes. Their emergence on the pages of *Nombres* helps to increase the effect of the many references to China and quotations from the works of Mao Tse-Tung.

Presumably, Sollers' next book will be called *Lois*. An excerpt was published in the summer, 1971, issue of *Tel Quel*. It confirms the direction taken by *Nombres*, Chinese ideograms included, perhaps accentuating something Sollers had said with reference to Sade. Paraphrasing what Georges Bataille had written concerning philosophy, "However much men might shudder because of it, philosophy must say everything," he claimed that literature, too, must say everything.[38] The fragment is nevertheless too short to enable one to say anything about the shape *Lois* may eventually assume.

Similarly it is too soon to draw any final conclusions concerning the work of a writer still in his thirties.

NOTES TO CHAPTER FOURTEEN (Sollers)

[1] "Présentation," *Tel Quel*, No. 1 (Spring 1960), p. 3.
[2] Philippe Sollers, *Le Défi*, in *Ecrire 3*, p. 5. Henceforth all references to the fiction of Sollers appear in the body of the text with the following abbreviations: *Le Défi*, D; *Une Curieuse Solitude*, S; *Le Parc*, P; *Drame*, D; *Nombres*, N. See Bibliography for complete references.

[3] Sollers, "Réponses," *Tel Quel,* No. 43 (Fall 1970), p. 71.

[4] André Breton, *Manifeste du surréalisme* (1924; rpt. Paris: Pauvert, 1962), p. 53.

[5] Sollers, "Le Roman et l'expérience des limites" (1965), in *Logiques* (Paris: Seuil, 1968), p. 235.

[6] Pierre Mabille, *Le Miroir du merveilleux* (1940; rpt. Paris: Minuit, 1962), p. 22.

[7] Jacques Derrida, *De la grammatologie* (Paris: Seuil, 1967), p. 68.

[8] Derrida, p. 92.

[9] Sollers, "Littérature et totalité" (1966), in *Logiques,* p. 112.

[10] *Ibid.,* p. 115.

[11] Sollers, "Le Roman," p. 240.

[12] *Ibid.,* p. 238.

[13] Sollers, "Choisir son style," *Tel Quel,* No. 3 (Fall 1960), p. 43.

[14] Sollers, "Logique de la fiction" (1962), in *Logiques,* p. 15.

[15] *Ibid.,* p. 16.

[16] *Ibid.,* p. 16.

[17] Sollers, "Le Roman," p. 244.

[18] Sollers, "Littérature," pp. 108–109.

[19] Sollers, "Le Roman," p. 235.

[20] Roland Barthes, "Histoire ou littérature" (1960), in *Sur Racine* (Paris: Seuil, 1963), pp. 157, 164.

[21] Emile Benveniste, "Catégories de pensée et catégories de langue" (1958), in *Problèmes de linguistique générale* (Paris: Gallimard, 1966), p. 74.

[22] Sollers, "Le Roman," p. 228.

[23] *Ibid.,* p. 236.

[24] *Ibid.,* p. 237.

[25] *Ibid.,* p. 232.

[26] *Ibid.,* p. 242.

[27] *Ibid.,* p. 243.

[28] *Ibid.,* p. 249.

[29] Sollers, "La Grande Méthode," *Tel Quel,* No. 34 (Summer 1968), p. 22.

[30] Sollers, "La Lutte idéologique dans l'écriture d'avant-garde," in *Littérature et idéologies* (Paris: Nouvelle Critique, 1971), p. 74.

[31] Jacques Derrida, "La Dissémination," *Critique,* No. 261 (February 1969), pp. 99–139; No. 262 (March 1969), pp. 215–249.

[32] Sollers, "Le Roman," p. 244.

[33] J. E. Cirlot, *A Dictionary of Symbols* (New York: Philosophical Library, 1962), p. 100. Nearly all other references to symbols in this and other chapters have been checked in Cirlot as well as in Sigmund Freud, *The Interpretation of Dreams* (New York: Modern Library, 1950).

[34] Julia Kristeva, "L'Engendrement de la formule," in *Recherches pour*

une sémanalyse (Paris: Seuil, 1969), pp. 278–371. Especially p. 280: "The text is not a linguistic *phenomenon* . . . It is its *engenderment*; an engenderment that is inscribed in the linguistic 'phenomenon,' that *pheno-text* constituted by the printed text—the later being readable only when one retraces his way *vertically* through the genesis a) of its linguistic categories, and b) of the topology of the signifying process. . . . What opens up that vertical dimension is the (linguistic) operation of the pheno-text's generation. We shall call this operation a *geno-text*, thus dividing the concept of text in two, pheno-text and geno-text (surface and depth, signified structure and signifying productivity)."

[35] Sollers, "Littérature," p. 114.

[36] Thanks are due Professor Goren Malmquist of the University of Stockholm, who was visiting professor at Columbia during the summer of 1968 when I was reading *Nombres* and who translated the ideograms for me.

[37] Jean Gaugeard, "Philippe Sollers: écriture et révolution," *La Quinzaine Littéraire*, No. 49 (15–30 April 1968), p. 4.

[38] Sollers, "Le Roman," pp. 233–234.

CHAPTER FIFTEEN

Jean Ricardou
and
French Writing Today

In July, 1971, at the *Centre Culturel International* in Cerisy, a ten-day colloquium brought together fiction writers, critics, and a number of interested bystanders. The object was to examine the state of such fiction as had been heralded as "new" about a dozen years earlier and attempt to determine where it was now headed. All the writers who came to speak or sent a paper to be read (Sarraute, Simon, Robbe-Grillet, Butor, Pinget, and Ollier) had once been included in the so-called *Nouveau Roman* confederation; the turn their fiction was taking led people to talk of a *Nouveau Nouveau Roman*. Forgetting the label, if possible, the truth remains that what prompted its coinage was the most significant conclusion to be drawn from the meetings of that Cerisy decade. Indeed, it was possible to detect a break in the work of almost all writers who were discussed after which the fiction they publish shows a different orientation. What may be even more significant, no matter how uniquely distinctive the fiction of each writer might have been before the change, the orientation it assumes afterwards is similar—although it retains distinguishing traits. Invariably, their work is now directed toward a subversion of literary and social structures by means of textual procedures. One exception is Nathalie Sarraute, who keeps on doing the same sort of thing with ever increasing skill. My own examination, in the foregoing chapters, of twice as many writers leads to the same conclusion: something happened during the sixties that made it difficult for them to write as they had before. I hope I have also shown that the seed of discontent was present earlier and that the change was not due to sudden illumination. Perhaps what happened is that they discovered a better way to deal with social responsibility and relationship to readers.

The "discovery" of Raymond Roussel in the fifties is an omen of things to come—certainly not a cause. Actually, a truer predecessor was Blanchot, who quietly effected his own break in 1948 with *L'Arrêt de mort*. Beckett's *Comment c'est* and Sollers' *Le Parc*, both in 1961, register the new mode, although Beckett's presence in French fiction will never again be what it was in the fifties. Butor's *Mobile*, early in 1962, was not only a break but a scandal, leading some to question the author's sanity. A few months later, *Battement*, by Faye, accentuated a development already visible in his work. Then came Duras' *Le Ravissement de Lol V. Stein* (1964), Robbe-Grillet's *La Maison de rendez-vous* (1965), and Ollier's *L'Echec de Nolan* (1967); those were followed, almost simultaneously, by Pinget's *Passacaille* and Simon's *La Bataille de Pharsale* in 1969. Mauriac and Saporta may well have been driven to silence.

One might always point out, of course, that the sixties were the logical years for changes in writing to take place. After all, nearly everything else has been shaken. Those were the years of worldwide student upheavals, of the rise to consciousness and militancy of blacks, Algerians, and other oppressed groups, of the Chinese cultural revolution, of the "conquest" of space, of war in the Middle East, of the sex and drug "revolutions," of the Russian-American confrontation over Cuba, of the Czech revolt, and of the spectacle of the most powerful nation on earth showering a record tonnage of bombs over one of the weakest in a vain attempt to subdue it. In such times, a revolution in writing is plausible—but why this particular one? There must have been a connection, but I am not sure those events alone could have been determining.

Some of those present at Cerisy in 1971 may have suspected a lesser cause and identified it with Jean Ricardou, one of the organizers of the colloquium, who chaired many of its sessions. They were mistaken, of course; and yet, here, too, there is a connection. An investigation, I think, will prove more fruitful in this case than in immediate sociopolitical causes.

Although Ricardou's critical essays have recently attracted considerable attention, he prefers to think of fiction as being the locus of his major activity. He has four volumes of fiction to his credit and two collections of critical essays. The many references to the latter throughout the chapters of this study are an indication of the esteem in which I hold his essays. Most noteworthy in the present context is that his first published work of fiction, *L'Observatoire de Cannes* (1961), is roughly contemporary with those books marking the new direction taken by the writings of Sollers and Butor and that its course is a parallel one. (Actually, it preceded Sollers by six and Butor by ten months.) Ricardou's work has no main character, no narrator, no definite point of view. The concept of "omniscient author" is hardly relevant, for there is no concealed information to impart either as thoughts or as secreted material, and the text seems to have an independent existence of its own. There are four "settings" involved: a compartment in a train moving along the French Mediterranean coast, an observation tower overloking the city of Cannes, a section of the beach at Cannes together with an adjoining part of the city, and a series of photographs in a book.

Although there is no plot in the accepted sense of the term, one might venture to say that the book exhibits a new concept of "plot" consisting in the manner statements about the settings and a half dozen names (characters) are combined in order to produce a given effect on the reader. In other words, the structure of the fiction is also its plot. *L'Observatoire de Cannes* is made up of thirty-one sections, the first and the last two being set in the train compartment, as are three others spaced out in between. As the text shifts to tower, beach, and city with photographs providing an articulation, one notices that most of the words and phrases of the initial compartment setting are used again, with or without variations. That recalls the process used by Ollier in *La Mise en scène* several years earlier, but in Ollier's text, descriptions are repeated, while Ricardou reuses words, in many cases concerning himself with signifiers alone. The description of the compartment provides a vocabulary store, and its eight seats inscribe that number in the text for recurrent use. The observation tower then provides the correlative on the basis of which the text develops. As the cable-car goes up the hill toward the tower more and more of the scenery is unveiled at a gradually increasing distance from the hill, and at the top of the tower one enjoys an unrestricted view of the entire region. Likewise, there is a gradual, imaginary unveiling of a young woman's body. Finally, what is also unveiled is the manner in which language functions in order to create an impression of the surrounding reality.

Even such a summary account should demonstrate that from the start Ricardou was ahead of almost everyone else in his emphasis on textual matters. In *La Prise de Constantinople* (1965) he goes even further in establishing the text's independence from signified and referent. The book has no other source than the book itself and its situation in a continuum of language and literature; it generates its sentences in the same fashion as in *L'Observatoire de Cannes*. There had been a few basic referents in that work (the city of Cannes, the train, and so on). Perhaps no more than a few specks of dust generated Robbe-Grillet's *Dans le labyrinthe*, but those tiny referents were still something. Now there is nothing, and the source of the book lies in the necessary elements of its cover, that is, the author's name, that of the publishing house he is tied to by contract, the publisher's emblem (the five-pointed star attached to an "m" of *Les Editions de Minuit*). That already provides numbers (so many letters in each name), a topic (the m[ysterious] star, which eventually becomes the setting for a science-fiction story), names (*Editions* produces Ed, Edith, and Sion—which is the French spelling for Zion), and initial time setting (*minuit*). The coincidence that gives a common series of five letters to the names of both Ricardou and Villehardouin, a chronicler of the Crusades, adds the parallel topic of the Crusades to that of space science fiction. The Fourth Crusade is selected for several precise reasons—one of them is that once the common letters have been removed from "Villehardouin" there remains "ville" and "in," suggesting the idea of penetration into a city, and that is what the soldiers of the Fourth Crusade did in Constantinople.

As the book started from nothing, *rien* becomes the first word of the text; in conjunction with other elements, it suggests a statement from Mallarmé's *Un Coup de dés jamais n'abolira le hasard* that begins with the same word, and thus introduces intertextuality. As a means of working against people's linear reading habits, pages, chapters, and parts are unnumbered. Since the back cover could traditionally be conceived as a sort of exit out of the linear narrative, a "left-hand" title page replaces it, on which *La Prose de Constantinople* is substituted for *La Prise de Constantinople*, thus also pointing to the textual nature of the book (within the narrative, naming a character Ed Word further emphasizes it). Where the signs "star" and "crusade" are concerned, the referents are not, of course, the real star in space or the actual crusade; they are respectively a marking on a book's cover and the words of another book. The referents of signs in this instance are other signs. As with several of the works of fiction of the other writers I have examined, it all amounts to a "Singular Book in which the hero will be invited to read the story of his own adventures . . . and of his entire life, henceforth a fictitious one." The statement occurs about one fourth of the way into the text. Replacing the word "hero" with "reader" will bring it in line with what Sollers has said concerning readers being "signs" and needing to think of themselves as characters in fiction.

I could go on in the same manner, describing the main body of *La Prise de Constantinople* (not in so many details, since much of what I have said was provided by Ricardou himself at Cerisy) and eventually account for the existence of the entire text, but that would require many more words than the book itself contains. It might actually be the only truthful way of dealing with it. Along with Sollers' *Nombres*, for instance, and in spite of the many differences between the two books they have this in common, that one cannot "talk" about either one at a cocktail party. One can experience Ricardou's fiction, and one can give a rigorous description of one aspect of its textual functioning. But try as one may, Ed Word will never resemble anybody's uncle Edward. While *Les Lieux-dits* (1969) and *Révolutions minuscules* (1971) are far less "extreme" in appearance, they are based on similar principles and must likewise be read and experienced rather than talked about. I might, as Ricardou himself has done for fiction by Robbe-Grillet and Simon, analyze one of their operations, but that is beyond the scope of an introductory study such as mine. The main point is that, as in true with several other contemporary writers, Ricardou's aim is to dismantle (*déconstruire*) and subvert categories of literature and patterns of culture that most readers tend to accept unquestioningly.

Jean Ricardou seems then to occupy a leading position in the development of textual fiction and the concept of generative scription. There remains, however, one important fact to be mentioned: Ricardou was for nine years on the editorial board of *Tel Quel*, from the spring of 1962 to the fall of 1971, and a contributor beginning with its second issue (summer 1960). In my opinion, whatever influence he may have had is inseparable from that of the review and of the group to which he belonged in the sixties. Perhaps the question I asked earlier can receive at least a partial answer through a brief examination of *Tel Quel* between 1962, when it can be described as having assumed its identity, and the fall of 1971, when it was rocked by a political crisis still unresolved at the time of this writing. Not that I consider *Tel Quel*, any more than either Ricardou or Sollers alone, as the exclusive cause of the change in fiction writing or in writing in general during the sixties. What I am suggesting is that a scanning of the texts (theoretical, fictional, analytical, political) published either in the review itself or under the group's aegis (in a special series at the publishing house of Le Seuil) between 1962 and 1971 might permit one to identify what lines of thought have converged toward textuality. As such a scrutiny could easily form the matter of a thick volume, I shall obviously have to limit myself to a brief outline.

As I see it, *Tel Quel* (which I shall now use as an emblem of what is "textual" and hence revolutionary in French writing today) is at the point of convergence of specific intellectual activities occurring in six areas: esthetics, politics, psychoanalysis, philosophy, linguistics, and culture.

Important though it is, esthetics is perhaps not the most important field in this context, for this is the one in which writers work. A change as radical as the one we are witnessing, in that it challenges the very concepts of literature and esthetics, had to come mainly from without. True, the ground had been prepared. Intricate plots, "real flesh-and-blood" characters, and so-called psychological analyses had gradually ceased to serve as significant elements of the structure. A reading of Dostoevsky had led writers like André Gide and François Mauriac to cast doubt on the notion of personality, but neither was willing to translate those doubts into writing as Sarraute did. For some time, too, French literature had been evidencing an irresistible aspiration towards poetry (if not yet toward music). When Mallarmé praised novelists like Flaubert, Goncourt, or Zola, it was for those works that, to him, read very much like poems. In the first half of this century, Valery Larbaud and Jean Giraudoux were exemplary in bringing fiction and poetry closer together, although here again it led nowhere. Larbaud soon became discouraged and silent, and Giraudoux, while continuing to write, was not able to make his *préciosité* mean enough. Others had effected a breakthrough of sorts, and there were the works of Lautréamont and Artaud (those of Sade, too, if one goes further back in time)—also those by Raymond Roussel. The point is that very few people read them. The contribution made by the trinity of writers so often mentioned with reference to postwar fiction, Proust, Joyce, and Kafka, is far from negligible, but it required perhaps the advent of the generation of writers (and critics) I am concerned with before the full "scription" of the productive texts of these three could be read.

The interest in Mallarmé displayed by Butor, Sollers, and others, and that in Valéry evidenced by Ricardou point to the contributions Mallarmé and Valéry were making toward a new esthetics, but there was a general impression in literary circles that they, especially Mallarmé, had reached a dead end. Since the end of the nineteenth century, music and the plastic arts have been going through esthetic revolutions only belatedly followed in literature. Perhaps in the case of Michel Butor alone, who has joined neither *Tel Quel* nor any other group, can one say that his formal break with the past, *Mobile*, was as much the result of esthetic preoccupations as of extra-artistic ones. His understanding of the arts, especially music and painting, might well have been an important factor. Roland Barthes, in analyzing *Mobile* and explaining what he termed its "rhetoric of modulation" (*translation*),[1] made reference to Webern and Mondrian.   If one returns to *Tel Quel*, one esthetic movement that needs to be taken into consideration is Russian formalism. Although it started nearly half a century before *Tel Quel* did, it is doubtful if Sollers or Ricardou received an initial impulse from those Russian theorists who, in spite of a few publications by scholars (and the translation of a book by Troubetzkoy on phonology in 1948), were not too well known in France until the sixties. Rather, the writers of *Tel Quel* and others discovered them as they proceeded along paths parallel to those previously explored by the formalists. In 1965, Tzvetan Todorov translated and published a number of essays by Russian formalists such as O. M. Brik, Viktor Shklovski, Boris Eichenbaum, Roman Jakobson, V. Propp, B. V. Tomashevski, J. Tynianov, and V. V. Vinogradov in a volume entitled *Théorie de la littérature*, which *Tel Quel* sponsored. Their emphasis is on the text itself. They show a tendency to consider art as a "process" rather than the perfectly accomplished and mysterious result of "inspiration," and they conduct their investigations in the texts in a scientific manner, rigorously and empirically. All that struck a responsive chord within members of the group. More recently, Julia Kristeva has contributed her direct acquaintance with the texts of Russian criticism to the group's information (I have already mentioned her readings in Bakhtine).[2] What is interesting in terms of other elements of the convergence I shall mention presently is that formalist activities lie on a borderline between esthetics (or poetics) and linguistics. It all began with the founding of the Linguistic Circle of Moscow in 1914, which eventually sired the Linguistic Circle of Prague in 1926, where one theory of structural linguistics originated.

Surrealism, especially at the beginning, sought to be more than an esthetic movement, although many people think of it mostly in terms of painting and sometimes of literature. Whatever opinion one may have of its various activities between the First World War and the present, it is beyond question the one force that made much of contemporary literature what it is. Above all, it has been a liberating force. Now as ever, it is a center of controversy. From the point of view of *Tel Quel* (and I touched upon this when discussing Soller's fiction), surrealism recognized the problems of current society, but when it came to offering solutions it either failed to ask the right questions or to follow through from its premises. In other words, *Tel Quel* views surrealism in the same light as Breton viewed Dada in the twenties: the *Tel Quel* group considers it negative and non-productive.

In the area of politics, the names of Marx and Engels identify the theory that permeates the thinking at *Tel Quel*. That is admittedly a very vague identification, for there are perhaps as many varieties of Marxists as there are of Christians. One needs therefore to add the name of Lenin, not only for his own contributions but in order to restore the balance between Marx and Engels. As Sollers explains it, "If, obviously, the fundamental book, the scientific basis on which Lenin rests his thought is Marx's *Capital*, his philosophical references are, insistently so, to Engels. One does not generally give Engels the decisive place he deserves."[3] Presumably neither Marx, Engels, nor Lenin were approached without intercessors, and among these Louis Althusser deserves the front rank.[4] In practical terms, in addition to the rejection of all idealism or transcendence and of mechanistic materialism in favor of dialectical materialism, the presence of a Marxist-Leninist current signifies condemnation of the bourgeois, humanistic concept of literature, especially in its degraded form—literature as an art designed to give satisfaction (Malraux would say satiation) during moments of leisure, a consumer product, in which imagery and style are pretty, decorative elements. This general area provides one of the touchstones that separate Butor from Sollers, the same that prompted Sollers to part company from surrealism: Butor, like Breton, admires Charles Fourier more than he does Karl Marx.

In the area of psychoanalysis, one naturally expects the presence of Freud. But it is Freud with a vengeance, as interpreted by Jacques Lacan, and as opposed, for instance, to the psychoanalysis of C. G. Jung. Here one might contrast Sollers' belief that literature must "say everything" with Jung's reported reluctance to discuss improper topics with his patients or to take Freud's ideas on sexuality literally. Lacan, on the contrary, insists that Freud's writings need to be interpreted literally. Speaking on the necessity for psychoanalists to go back to Freud's teaching, he proclaimed that "the meaning of a return to Freud is a return to the meaning of Freud." Obviously, this implies a lifting of taboos in literary texts. But what constitutes the most noteworthy aspect of Lacan's writings where *Tel Quel* is concerned, aside from his emphasis on psychoanalysis as a science, is the connection he makes between language and the unconscious: "It is the complete structure of language that psychoanalytical experience discovers in the unconscious." Of even greater interest in this context is Lacan's primary concern with the signifier rather than with the signified or the referent. He speaks of "the illusion of believing that the signifier responds to the function of representing the signified." Meaning is found in the sequence of signifiers, "but one of its elements is constituted by the meaning of which it is capable at that moment." While that is analogous to the statement that a word within a (literary) context has a meaning different from the one it has out of context, it goes much farther. The sequence Lacan refers to, which might be termed the structure of signifiers, does not coincide with the linear, grammatical structure of the text; it is independent to the point that "it enables one to use it in order to signify something completely different from what it says."[5] The link with Julia Kristeva's concept of "numberers" and with Ricardou's essays on Simon and Robbe-Grillet seems clear. As in the case of Russian formalism, one is again encroaching upon linguistics.

In the area of philosophy (epistemology might be a more precise term), one encounters the ideas of Michel Foucault, who, as the *Times Literary Supplement* put it, "at a time when there is a crisis of confidence in philosophy . . . has re-launched philosophy in France single-handed."[6] In his book *Les Mots et les choses* he posited the existence of a specific "order of things" (which is the more appropriate title of the English translation, a title he originally had favored over the one chosen by his French publisher).[7] This is the order that a given culture at a given time instinctively or unconsciously assumes corresponds to the real, fundamental organization of the universe: "In any culture, at an intermediary level between the habits determined by what one might call programming codes and theorizations on order, there lies a bare experience of order and of its modes of existence." To that direct experience Foucault gives the name of *epistémè*—let us say, epistemic experience. Next, he detects in the history of Western Europe two breaks in that epistemic experience. The first one came at the outset of the French neoclassical period in the middle of the seventeenth century. Its effect was to destroy the universal harmony based on a complex system of nearly limitless correspondences, analogies, similitudes, and sympathies constituting, in Foucault's phrase, the "prose of the world." In the sixteenth century, such correspondences enabled men to decipher the world as a text. Language was not an independent system of signs, but "rather an opaque, mysterious entity closed in upon itself . . . which here and there is mixed in with the symbols of the world, is tangled up in them: to such an extent that, all together, they constitute a network of markings in which each can play . . . the part of content or of sign, that of secret or of clue." Words and things were similar and interchangeable. With the end of the Renaissance, however, the edifice crumbles; "things and words are going to part company," and language, instead of being intimately combined with the rest of the world, "will be no more than a particular instance of the process of representation," or, to use contemporary terminology, of signification.

The second break occurs in the nineteenth century, when the theory of representation ceases to form the basis for epistemic experience. "A far-reaching historicity penetrates into the heart of things, isolating them and defining them within their own coherence, imposing on them such forms of order as are implied by the continuity of time." That break coincides with the birth of disciplines like philology, which dominates the approach to language. Also emerging in the same century are "the chimeras of new humanisms and the facileness of an 'anthropology' understood as a general study of man, semi-positive and semi-philosophical in nature." While literature, in general, reflected that new vision of the world, Foucault detects an important strand of literary activities that implicitly refuses the corresponding epistemic experience. Going against both the trend of its own time and that of the preceding period, it approaches a concept of language similar to the one that existed before the advent of neoclassicism. That strand can be traced throughout the works of Hölderlin, Mallarmé, and Artaud, and it is characterized by a denial of the representative or significative function of language. Such a literature is "pure and simple manifestation of a language whose only law is to affirm —as opposed to all other forms of discourse—its own craggy existence." Language once more has become a structure of things or of signs among signs. As to the situation of the individual in all this, Foucault sees him caught in the network of his cultural structure: "The fundamental codes of a culture . . . establish from the outset and for each man the empirical orders which he will have to face and within which he will find his identity."[8] Lacan, in related fashion, had placed him within the structure of language: "The subject indeed, if he may appear to be a slave to language, is even more a slave to a discourse within the universal movement in which his position is already inscribed at birth, even if only in the guise of his own name."[9]

In the area of linguistics proper, everything of course begins with Ferdinand de Saussure. Yet for my purpose here, the qualifications or corrections added to one aspect of Saussure's theory by Jacques Derrida are crucial. I have in mind mainly the first part of his treatise *De la grammatologie*, in which he emphasizes what he calls the ethnocentricity of scholars, particularly the logocentricity of Western linguisticians. His main criticism of Saussure is that, as far as writing is concerned, he appeared to endorse the ancient definitions put forward by Plato and Aristotle. Quoting Aristotle's definition, "Sounds uttered by the voice are symbols of the state of the soul and written words symbols of those uttered by the voice," he compares it with Saussure's: "Language and writing are two distinct systems of signs; the only justification for the existence of the latter is that it represents the former."[10] According to Derrida, the similarity between the two statements may be traced to the same flaw: both Aristotle and Saussure postulate either the superiority or the universality of phonetic writing. He then argues that since phonetic writing is only one among several modes of writing, no definition based on its specific characteristics can account for the nature of writing in general. Furthermore, such logocentric definitions, claiming anteriority and superiority for the spoken language, also imply that it possesses a sacred attribute. For Greek thinkers, the *logos* was closer to the soul and therefore to the truth in reality, which only the soul could sense. Later, the Word of God, then natural law, vouches for the authenticity of the *logos*. By rejecting logocentric definitions of writing, whether formulated by Aristotle or Saussure, Derrida undermines not only the accepted hierarchy between spoken and written language, but he also takes away the guarantee of truth they presupposed. Actually, he claims anteriority for "writing," although he gives that word a meaning somewhat different from the one it has in everyday usage. His science of scription has very broad claims, including the spoken language within its domain, and I have already given a brief description of his concept of "markings."[11] Concerning the guarantee that has been withdrawn, it is easy to see how that might invalidate the notion of literature as *mimesis* or as the authentic expression of a particular human being.

In the cultural area, two factors need to be mentioned. First, there is the growing awareness of Oriental presence, which has surprised, concerned, frightened, and finally interested the Western mind. Its origin, as far as any general consciousness of the phenomenon is concerned, can perhaps be traced to the tremors that were sent through European capitals in 1905 by the news of Japan's victory over Russia, especially because of the virtual annihilation of the Russian fleet. What was distressing to many was that a culture so alien, so unfathomable (therefore, implicitly, so inferior) could rise to challenge and defeat a power then considered as Western. What, on the other hand, was eventually deemed interesting was precisely the opportunity to study, compare, and contrast two different or even opposed cultures, examining each one in the light of the other. Writers were naturally interested in examining the possibilities of a nonphonetic system of writing. Paul Claudel, among others, was fascinated, as his *Cent phrases pour éventails* testifies—but apparently not enough to follow through. Sollers' interest is well known; he has even gone to the trouble of learning Chinese and has published translations of poems by Mao Tse-Tung.[12] The *Tel Quel* writers, however, are concerned not merely with contemporary Chinese writing but with the entire gamut of that country's thought, beginning with such texts as the *I Ching* and the *Tao-te Ching*. Out of a confrontation between Oriental and Western cultures, they believe there could result a dismantling of Western structures— just as, perhaps, a confrontation between Oriental political structures and Western Marxist thought resulted in a subversion of the old Chinese empire.

The second cultural factor worth mentioning has been the re-evaluation of the mind of the so-called primitive people and the ensuing realization that there were other modes of thought than that of the rational mind, and that they are just as valid. Here, the name of Claude Lévi-Strauss naturally comes to the fore, especially because of his 1962 book *La Pensée sauvage*, where he explained the concept of *bricolage*, which, in the textual practice of several writers, merges with intertextuality. I might recall, by way of stressing the extent to which the study of other modes has led to a distrust of rational thought, Lévi-Strauss' long-standing admiration for the Orient and the wistful thought expressed in the concluding pages of *Tristes tropiques,* that if only East and West had come together a few centuries ago, "that slow osmosis with Buddhism would have Christianized us more, in a manner that would have been as much more Christian as we would have risen beyond Christianity itself."

Now, at the heart of the field of convergence of lines of thought developing in the six areas mentioned above lies the concept of scription, which I have defined earlier.[13] With the added insight provided by those writers whose thought I have just surveyed, it can be called the inscription and interplay of signs in the text of a book, within the framework of a given linguistic structure. In "scriptional" activity, the author is a product as much as a cause. The signs in the text do not necessarily represent reality, nor do they express either the author's personality or the truth. Within signs, signifiers are as important as signified concepts, and sometimes as independent of them as signs are of their referents. Scription aims to subvert, through its textual operations, the literary, political, social, and moral structures of Western culture.

As I have suggested, the ground for the basic textual activities of *Tel Quel* was prepared in the fifties by other writers, especially the so-called *nouveaux romanciers.* These, in turn, or at least a number of them, appear to have been stimulated and given a sense of direction by *Tel Quel.* It is important that Philippe Sollers and the members of his group (which in December, 1971, included Jean-Louis Baudry, Marc Devade, Julia Kristeva, Marcelin Pleynet, Jacqueline Risset, Denis Roche, and Pierre Rottenberg) are not the only ones to practice textual activity with a subversive purpose in mind. Whether or not the group has any future (political or "literary"), whether or not French writers in the 1980s become reconciled with their society or despair of any attempts to change it, its present influence, on the threshold of the seventies, is undeniable. We must leave aside Michel Butor, who has on several occasions expressed interest in the activities of *Tel Quel* but who is allergic to groups and goes on in his independent way, absorbing various cultures of the world, and intending to subvert his own culture and society in the process. His purposes, sometimes even his theories, are similar, as witness his affirmation that "political activity becomes truly efficient only when it is enlightened by theory, when it shows us texts to go by,"[15] but where he parts company with the group is in his belief that one can change society by painstakingly unveiling what it is really like, thus forcing it to become different. On the other hand, Robbe-Grillet, Ollier, and Simon, who have no official connection with *Tel Quel*, have been engaging more and more in similar textual activities with the same subversive intent.

Jean Pierre Faye has broken with *Tel Quel* to establish what he terms a "collective" with his publication *Change*, which also sponsors a series of books. Polemics with *Tel Quel* have been violent and textual activity differs to some extent (probably no more than among individual writers of *Tel Quel*), but subversion is still the professed aim. Two other reviews, *Poétique* and *Littérature*, founded respectively in 1970 and 1971, claim no subversive intent but affirm a new approach to literature. Both, in their initial statement of purpose, used the phrase *production de texte*, and it is unlikely that they would have done so without the stimulus of *Tel Quel*. Furthermore, the influence of *Tel Quel* is being relayed through other reviews outside Paris that have expressed solidarity with its principles and practice. For instance, *Promesse*, edited in Poitiers, stated editorially in 1971, "As everyone knows, we have been working with the *Tel Quel* group for several years; that collaboration is based on a solidarity arising from a common theoretical and practical activity, which we insist on reaffirming strongly."[15] Similarly, in

Marseilles, the editors of *Manteia* expressed their approval: they "consider as fundamental the theoretical propositions formulated in *Tel Quel* and recognize as their own the scientific and political activities that it has openly undertaken."[15]

In short, what *Tel Quel* may well have brought writers outside its tightly knit group is a justification for their existence when they were faced with the worldwide upheavals of the sixties. Jean-Paul Sartre had rendered a similar service a couple of decades earlier with his theory of *littérature engagée.* After a while, however, he had to confess that nothing writers had done could prevent the Algerian war, stop the tortures, or prevent the killing; when Algeria became free, they could claim no credit— merely report that they had been on the side of the angels. Sartre's famous statement, "Scaled against a child that is dying, *La Nausée* does not carry enough weight," provoked a public debate in Paris in 1964. The theme was stated as, "What can literature do?" Jean Ricardou, who in the 1960s often seemed to be acting as *Tel Quel's* ambassador-at-large, was present. His argument, in rebuttal of Sartre, was that the writer, through his work in language, creates a structure that is antagonistic to that of society, thus challenging it. He also suggested that the very existence of literature was what turned men's suffering into a scandal.[17] Encouraging (or consoling) as that might have been to other writers, it probably was not as satisfying as would be the feeling of actively contributing to a specific undertaking. Development of the concept of dismantling from within, by means of language, of subverting literary forms and structures of thought, could well have furnished such satisfaction—convincing writers that literature was not yet obsolete. I do not mean that the concept was ever intended to give them a sense of potential accomplishment. I merely offer that interpretation as a possible explanation for the influence *Tel Quel* has wielded during the sixties, especially when backed by the persuasive argumentation of Ricardou, while he stood with the group, and of Sollers, based on theoretical texts by Marx, Engels, Lenin,

Althusser, Freud, Lacan, Foucault, Derrida, Lévi-Strauss, and, more recently, Julia Kristeva. Will it work? If it does, and Western European culture is indeed dismantled, will the new structures be any better? And anyway, how long will it take?

No one can honestly presume to answer such questions. But considering the present state of society, it is hardly surprising to find some of the leading French writers willing to give the venture a chance. In Roland Barthes's words, *"Tel Quel* is a group committed to a difficult struggle and one in which I am deeply interested. . . . They must not give up, for their disappearance would be felt as a serious regression."[18] Sollers has warned that it might become a necessity to engage in the sort of writing activity that implies a thorough commitment to the textual functions of language and their transforming possibilities, for *"He who will not write shall be written."*[19]

NOTES TO CHAPTER FIFTEEN

[1] Roland Barthes, "Littérature et discontinuité," in *Essais critiques* (Paris: Seuil, 1964), p. 185.

[2] See above, p. 249; the first chapter of Todorov's *Poétique de la prose* (Paris: Seuil, 1971) sums up the heritage of the formalists.

[3] Philippe Sollers, "Lénine et le matérialisme philosophique," *Tel Quel*, No. 43 (Fall 1970), p. 8.

[4] Cf. Louis Althusser, *Pour Marx* (Paris: Maspéro, 1965); *Lénine et la philosophie* (Paris: Maspéro, 1968); with Etienne Balibar, *Lire le Capital* (Paris: Maspéro, 1968).

[5] Jacques Lacan, "L'Instance de la lettre dans l'inconscient ou la raison depuis Freud," in *Ecrits* (Paris: Seuil, 1966), pp. 495, 498, 502, 505.

[6] "The Contented Positivist," *Times Literary Supplement*, July 2, 1970, p. 698.

[7] Cf. letter by John Harvard-Watts to the editor of the *Times Literary Supplement*, July 31, 1970, p. 855.

[8] Michel Foucault, *Les Mots et les choses* (Paris: Gallimard, 1966), pp. 13, 49, 58, 14, 15, 313, 11.

[9] Lacan, *Ecrits*, p. 495.

[10] Quoted by Jacques Derrida, *De la grammatologie* (Paris: Minuit, 1967), p. 46.

[11] See above, pp. 348–49.

[12] "Dix poèmes de Mao Tsé-toung, lus et traduits par Philippe Sollers," *Tel Quel,* No. 40 (Winter 1970), pp. 38–57.

[13] See above, p. 348.

[14] Michel Butor, "Propos sur le livre, aujourd'hui," *Les Cahiers du Chemin,* No. 12 (April 1971), pp. 47–48.

[15] "Jalons," *Promesse,* No. 29 (Spring 1971), p. 12.

[16] "Etat," *Mantela,* No. XI (1971), p. 63.

[17] Simone de Beauvoir *et al., Que peut la littérature?* (Paris: 10/18, 1965), pp. 57, 60.

[18] Barthes, as quoted by Gilles Lapouge, "Voyage autour de Roland Barthes," *Quinzaine Littéraire,* No. 130 (December 1–15, 1971), p. 4.

[19] Sollers, "Le Roman et l'expérience des limites," in *Logiques* (Paris: Seuil, 1968), p. 242.

Selective Bibliography

I. GENERAL WORKS

In French

a) In whole or in part about contemporary French fiction.

Barthes, Roland. *Essais critiques*. Paris: Seuil, 1964.

Blanchot, Maurice. *La Part du feu*. Paris: Gallimard, 1949.

———. *L'Espace littéraire*. Paris: Gallimard, 1955.

———. *Le Livre à venir*. Paris: Gallimard, 1959.

Butor, Michel. *Répertoire*. Paris: Minuit, 1960.

———. *Répertoire II*. Paris: Minuit, 1964.

———. *Répertoire III*. Paris: Minuit, 1968.

Faye, Jean Pierre. *Le Récit hunique*. Paris: Seuil, 1967.

Genette, Gérard. *Figures*. Paris: Seuil, 1966.

———. *Figures II*. Paris: Seuil, 1969.

Goldmann, Lucien. *Pour une sociologie du roman*. Paris: Gillimard, 1964.

Janvier, Ludovic. *Une Parole exigeante*. Paris: Minuit, 1964.

Ricardou, Jean. *Problèmes du nouveau roman*. Paris: Seuil, 1967.

———. *Pour une théorie du nouveau roman*. Paris: Seuil, 1971.

Robbe-Grillet, Alain. *Pour un nouveau roman*. Paris: Minuit, 1963.

Sarraute, Nathalie, *L'Ere du soupçon*. Paris: Gallimard, 1956.

Sollers, Philippe. *Logiques*. Paris: Seuil, 1968.

Zeltner, Gerda. *La Grande Aventure du roman français au XXe siècle*. Paris: Gonthier, 1967. Originally published in Germany as *Das Wagnis der Französischen Gegenwartromans*. Hamburg: Rowohlt Verlag, 1960.

b) Theoretical background

Barthes, Roland. *Le Degré zéro de l'écriture* suivi de *Eléments de sémiologie*. Paris: Gonthier, 1968. Originally published in 1953 and 1964 respectively.

Beauvoir, Simone de, *et al. Que peut la littérature?* Paris: 10/18, 1965.

Benveniste, Emile. *Problèmes de linguistique générale.* Paris: Gallimard, 1966.

Derrida, Jacques. *De la grammatologie.* Paris: Minuit, 1967.

Doubrovsky, Serge, and Todorov, Tzvetan. Eds. *L'Enseignement de la littérature.* Paris: Plon, 1971.

Eco, Umberto. *L'Œuvre ouverte.* Paris: Seuil, 1965. Originally published in Italy as *Opera aperta.* Milano: Bompiani, 1962.

Foucault, Michel. *Les Mots et les choses.* Paris: Gallimard, 1966.

Jakobson, Roman. *Essais de linguistique générale.* Paris: Minuit, 1963.

Kristeva, Julia. *Recherches pour une sémanalyse.* Paris: Seuil, 1969.
———. *Le Texte du roman.* Paris: Mouton, 1970.

Lacan, Jacques. *Ecrits.* Paris: Seuil, 1966.

Lévi-Strauss, Claude. *La Pensée sauvage.* Paris: Plon, 1962.

Poulet, Georges, *et al. Les Chemins actuels de la critique.* Paris: Plon, 1967.

Ricardou, Jean, *et al. Le Nouveau Roman: hier, aujourd'hui.* Paris: 10/18 [scheduled for 1972].

Riffaterre, Michael. *Essais de stylistique structurale.* Paris: Flammarion, 1970.

Saussure, Ferdinand de. *Cours de linguistique générale.* Paris: Payot, 1967. Originally published in 1916.

Tel Quel. *Théorie d'ensemble.* Paris: Seuil, 1968.

Todorov, Tzvetan. *Littérature et signification.* Paris: Larousse, 1967.
———. *Poétique de la prose.* Paris: Seuil, 1971.
———. Ed. *Théorie de la littérature.* Paris: Seuil, 1965.

In English

Frohock, W. M. *Style and Temper.* Cambridge: Harvard University Press, 1967.

Grossvogel, David I. *Limits of the Novel. Evolution of a Form from Chaucer to Robbe-Grillet.* Ithaca, N. Y.: Cornell University Press, 1968.

Mercier, Vivian. *The New Novel from Queneau to Pinget.* New York: Farrar, Straus & Giroux, 1971.

Peyre, Henri. *French Novelists of Today.* New York: Oxford University Press, 1967.

Sturrock, John. *The French New Novel.* New York: Oxford University Press, 1969.

Zants, Emily. *The Aesthetics of the New Novel in France*. Boulder, Col.: University of Colorado Press, 1968.

II. INDIVIDUAL WRITERS

1. RAYMOND ROUSSEL

a) Works of fiction by Roussel

La Doublure (1896). Paris: Pauvert, 1963.

La Vue (1902). Paris Pauvert, 1963. This volume includes *Le Concert* (1903) and *La Source* (1904).

Impressions d'Afrique (1910). Paris: Pauvert, 1963.

Locus solus (1914). Paris: Pauvert, 1965.

Nouvelles Impressions d'Afrique (1928). Paris: Pauvert, 1963.

Comment j'ai écrit certains de mes livres. Paris: Pauvert, 1963.

English translations

Impressions of Africa. Berkeley: University of California Press, 1967.

Locus Solus. Berkeley: University of California Press, 1970.

b) Works about Roussel

In French

Caburet, Bernard. *Raymond Roussel*. Paris: Seghers, 1968.

Ferry, Jean. *Une Etude sur Raymond Roussel*. Paris: Arcane, 1953. Preface by André Breton.

———. *Une Autre Etude sur Raymond Roussel*. Paris: Collège de Pataphysique, 1967.

———. Ed. Special issue of *Bizarre*, No. 34–35 (1964).

Foucault, Michel. *Raymond Roussel*. Paris: Gallimard, 1963.

In English

Heppenstall, Rayner. *Raymond Roussel*. Berkeley: University of California Press, 1967.

2. NATHALIE SARRAUTE

a) Works of fiction by Sarraute

Tropismes. Paris: Denoël, 1939. (Consulted in Minuit edition of 1957.)

Portrait d'un inconnu. Paris: Robert Marin, 1947. (Consulted in Gallimard edition of 1956.)

Martereau. Paris: Gallimard, 1953.

Le Planétarium. Paris: Gallimard, 1959.

Les Fruits d'or. Paris: Gallimard, 1963.
Entre la vie la mort. Paris: Gallimard, 1968.
Vous les entendez? Paris: Gallimard, 1972. (Not seen.)

English translations
Tropisms. New York: Braziller, 1967.
Portrait of a Man Unknown. New York: Braziller, 1958.
Martereau. New York: Braziller, 1959.
Planetarium. New York: Braziller, 1960.
Golden Fruits. New York: Braziller, 1964.
Between Life and Death. New York: Braziller, 1969.

    b) Works about Sarraute

In French

Cranaki, Mimica & Yvon Belaval. *Nathalie Sarraute.* Bibliothèque
    Idéale. Paris: Gallimard, 1965.
Micha, René. *Nathalie Sarraute.* Classiques du XXe Siècle. Paris:
    Editions Universitaires, 1966.
Tison Braun, Micheline. *Nathalie Sarraute ou la recherche de*
    l'authenticité. Paris: Gallimard, 1971.

In English

Temple, Ruth Z. *Nathalie Sarraute.* Columbia Essays on Modern
    Writers. New York: Columbia University Press, 1968.

3. MAURICE BLANCHOT
    a) Works of fiction by Blanchot
Thomas l'obscur. Paris: Gallimard, 1941.
Aminadab. Paris: Gallimard, 1942.
Le Très-haut. Paris: Gallimard, 1948.
L'Arrêt de mort. Paris: Gallimard, 1948.
Thomas l'obscur. Nouvelle version. Paris: Gallimard, 1950.
Au moment voulu. Paris: Gallimard, 1951.
Celui qui ne m'accompagnait pas. Paris: Gallimard, 1953.
Le Dernier Homme. Paris: Gallimard, 1957.
L'Attente l'oubli. Paris: Gallimard, 1962.

    b) Works about Blanchot
Special issue of *Critique,* No. 229 (June 1966).
Collin, Françoise. *Maurice Blanchot et la question de l'écriture.*
    Paris: Gallimard, 1971.

4. SAMUEL BECKETT
    a) Works of fiction written in French by Beckett

Molloy. Paris: Minuit, 1951.

Malone meurt. Paris: Minuit, 1951.

L'Innommable. Paris: Minuit, 1953.

Nouvelles et textes pour rien. Paris: Minuit, 1955.

Comment c'est. Paris: Minuit, 1961.

Imagination morte imaginez. Paris: Minuit, 1965.

Assez. Paris: Minuit, 1966.

Bing. Paris: Minuit, 1966.

Mercier et Camier (1946). Paris: Minuit, 1970.

Le Dépeupleur. Paris: Minuit, 1971.

Note: *Murphy*, first published in London by Routledge in 1938, appeared in a French translation by Beckett in Paris in 1947, published first by Bordas, then by Minuit.

b) Works about Beckett

Criticism of Beckett's work is so abundant that I shall simply refer those interested in a complete listing to the bibliography compiled by Raymond Federman and John Fletcher, *Samuel Beckett: His Work and His Critics* (Berkeley: University of California Press, 1970). As a token of gratitude, however, I shall list those books I happen to have benefitted from:

In French

Bernal, Olga. *Langage et fiction dans le roman de Beckett*. Paris: Gallimard, 1969.

In English

Cohn, Ruby. *Samuel Beckett: The Comic Gamut*. New Brunswick: Rutgers University Press, 1962.

Fletcher, John. *The Novels of Samuel Beckett*. London: Chatto and Windus, 1964.

Kenner, Hugh. *Samuel Beckett: A Critical Study*. New York: Grove Press, 1961. (A revised edition was published by the University of California Press in 1968.)

Tindall, William York. *Samuel Beckett*. Columbia Essays on Modern Writers. New York: Columbia University Press, 1964.

5. MARGUERITE DURAS

a) Works of fiction by Duras

Les Impudents. Paris: Plon, 1943.

La Vie tranquille. Paris: Gallimard, 1944.

Un Barrage contre le Pacifique. Paris: Gallimard, 1950.

Le Marin de Gibraltar. Paris: Gallimard, 1952.

Les Petits Chevaux de Tarquinia. Paris: Gallimard, 1953.
Des Journées entières dans les arbres. Paris: Gallimard, 1954.
Le Square. Paris: Gallimard, 1955.
Moderato cantabile. Paris: Minuit, 1958.
Dix heures et demie du soir en été. Paris: Gallimard, 1960.
L'Après-midi de Monsieur Andesmas. Paris: Gallimard, 1962.
Le Ravissement de Lol V. Stein. Paris: Gallimard, 1964.
L'Amante anglaise. Paris: Gallimard, 1967.
Détruire dit-elle. Paris: Minuit, 1969.
Abahn Sabana David. Paris: Gallimard, 1970.
L'Amour. Paris: Gallimard, 1972. (Not seen.)

English translations
Sea Wall. New York: Farrar, Straus & Giroux, 1952.
Little Horses of Tarquinia. London: Calder, 1960.
The Square. New York: Grove Press, 1959.
Moderato Cantabile. New York: Grove Press, 1960.
Four Novels by Marguerite Duras. New York: Grove Press, 1965.
    (In addition to the two preceding items, this volume includes
    10:30 on a Summer Night and *The Afternoon of Mr. Andesmas.*)
The Ravishing of Lol V. Stein. New York: Grove Press, 1966.
English Lover. New York: Grove Press, 1968.

   b) Works about Duras
Seylaz, Jean-Luc. *Les Romans de Marguerite Duras.* Paris: Lettres
    Modernes, 1963.

6. CLAUDE MAURIAC
   a) Works of fiction by Claude Mauriac
Toutes les femmes sont fatales. Paris: Albin Michel, 1957.
Le Dîner en ville. Paris: Albin Michel, 1959.
La Marquise sortit à cinq heures. Paris: Albin Michel, 1961.
L'Agrandissement. Paris: Albin Michel, 1963.
L'Oubli. Paris: Grasset, 1966.

English translations
All Women Are Fatal. New York: Braziller, 1964.
The Dinner Party. New York: Braziller, 1960.
The Marquise Went Out at Five. New York: Braziller, 1962.

   b) Works about Claude Mauriac
Mercier, Vivian. *The New Novel from Queneau to Pinget,* New
    York: Farrar, Straus & Giroux, 1971.

7. CLAUDE SIMON
   a) Works of fiction by Simon
Le Tricheur. Paris: Sagittaire, 1945.
Gulliver. Paris: Calmann-Lévy, 1952.
Le Sacre du printemps. Paris: Calmann-Lévy, 1954.
Le Vent. Paris: Minuit, 1957.
L'Herbe. Paris: Minuit, 1958.
La Route des Flandres. Paris: Minuit, 1960.
Le Palace. Paris: Minuit, 1962.
Histoire. Paris: Minuit, 1967.
La Bataille de Pharsale. Paris: Minuit, 1969.
Orion aveugle. Paris: Skira, 1970.
Les Corps conducteurs. Paris: Minuit, 1971.

English translations
The Wind. New York: Braziller, 1959.
The Grass. New York: Braziller, 1960.
The Flanders Road. New York: Braziller, 1961.
The Palace. New York: Braziller: 1964.
Histoire. New York: Braziller, 1968.
The Battle of Pharsalus. New York: Braziller, 1971.

   b) Works about Simon
Mercier, Vivian. *The New Novel from Queneau to Pinget.* New
    York: Farrar, Straus & Giroux, 1971.
Sturrock, John. *The French New Novel.* New York: Oxford Uni-
    versity Press, 1969.

8. ROBERT PINGET
   a) Works of fiction by Pinget
Entre Fantoine et Agapa. Jarnac: La Tour de feu, 1951. (Consulted
    in the Minuit edition of 1966)
Mahu ou le matériau. Paris: Robert Laffont, 1952. (Re-issued by
    Minuit.)
Le Renard et la boussole. Paris: Gallimard, 1953.
Graal Flibuste. Paris: Minuit, 1956.
Baga. Paris: Minuit, 1958.
Le Fiston. Paris: Minuit, 1959.
Clope au dossier. Paris: Minuit, 1961.
L'Inquisitoire. Paris: Minuit, 1962.
Quelqu'un. Paris: Minuit, 1965.
Le Libera. Paris: Minuit, 1968.

Passacaille. Paris: Minuit, 1969.
Fable. Paris: Minuit, 1971.

English translations
Monsieur Levert. New York: Grove Press, 1962.
Mahu or the Material. London: Calder & Boyars, 1966.
Baga. London: Calder & Boyars, 1967.
Inquisitory. New York: Grove Press, 1967.

    b) Works about Pinget
Mercier, Vivian. *The New Novel from Queneau to Pinget,* New
    York: Farrar, Straus & Giroux, 1971.

9. ALAIN ROBBE-GRILLET
    a) Works of fiction by Robbe-Grillet
Les Gommes. Paris: Minuit, 1953.
Le Voyeur. Paris: Minuit, 1955.
La Jalousie. Paris: Minuit, 1957.
Dans le labyrinthe. Paris: Minuit, 1959.
Instantanés. Paris: Minuit, 1962.
La Maison de rendez-vous. Paris: Minuit, 1965.
Projet pour une révolution à New York. Paris: Minuit, 1970.

English translations
The Erasers. New York: Grove Press, 1964.
The Voyeur. New York: Grove Press, 1958.
Two Novels. New York: Grove Press, 1965. (Includes *Jealousy* and
    In the Labyrinth.)
Snapshots. New York: Grove Press, 1968.
La Maison de rendez-vous. New York: Grove Press, 1966.

    b) Works about Robbe-Grillet

In French
Alter, Jean. *La Vision du monde d'Alain Robbe-Grillet.* Geneva:
    Droz, 1966.
Bernal, Olga. *Alain Robbe-Grillet ou le roman de l'absence.* Paris:
    Gallimard, 1964.
Jaffe-Freem, Elly. *Alain Robbe-Grollet et la peinture cubiste.* Amster-
    dam: Meulenhoff, 1966.
Miesch, Jean. *Robbe-Grillet.* Classiques de XXe Siècle. Paris:
    Editions Universitaires, 1965.
Morrissette, Bruce. *Les Romans d'Alain Robbe-Grillet.* Paris:
    Minuit, 1963.

In English

Morrissette, Bruce. *Alain Robbe-Grillet*. Columbia Essays on Modern Writers. New York: Columbia University Press, 1965.

Stoltzfus, Ben. *Alain Robbe-Grillet and the New French Novel*. Carbondale: Southern Illinois University Press, 1964.

10. CLAUDE OLLIER
a) Works of fiction by Ollier

La Mise en scène. Paris: Minuit, 1958.

La Maintien de l'ordre. Paris: Gallimard, 1961.

Eté indien. Paris: Minuit, 1963.

L'Echec de Nolan. Paris: Gallimard, 1967.

Navettes. Paris: Gallimard, 1967.

La Vie sur Epsilon. (Scheduled for 1972 publication. My references are to the manuscript.)

Enigma No. 1. (In manuscript.)

Enigma No. 2. (In manuscript.)

Vingt ans après. (In preparation.)

English translations

Law and Order. New York: Red Dust, 1971.

11. MARC SAPORTA
a) Works of fiction by Saporta

Le Furet. Paris: Seuil, 1959.

La Quête. Paris: Seuil, 1961.

La Distribution. Paris: Gallimard, 1961.

Composition No. 1. Paris: Seuil, 1962.

Les Invités. Paris: Seuil, 1964.

English translation

Composition Number 1. New York: Simon & Schuster, 1963.

12. MICHEL BUTOR
a) Works of fiction by Butor

Passage de Milan. Paris: Minuit, 1954.

L'Emploi du temps. Paris: Minuit, 1956.

La Modification. Paris: Minuit, 1957.

Degrés. Paris: Gallimard, 1960.

Mobile. Paris: Gallimard, 1962.

Réseau aérien. Paris: Gallimard, 1962.

Description de San Marco. Paris: Gallimard, 1963.

Illustrations. Paris: Gallimard, 1964.

6 810 000 litres d'eau par seconde. Paris: Gallimard, 1965.
Portrait de l'artiste en jeune singe. Paris: Gallimard, 1967.
Paysage de répons suivi de Dialogue des règnes. Paris: Castella, 1968.
Illustrations II. Paris: Gallimard, 1969.
La Rose des vents. Paris: Gallimard, 1970.
Où. Paris: Gallimard, 1971.

English translations
Passing Time. New York: Simon & Schuster, 1960.
A Change of Heart. New York: Simon & Schuster, 1959.
Degrees. New York: Simon & Schuster, 1962.
Mobile. New York: Simon & Schuster, 1963.
Niagara. Chicago: Regnery, 1969.

b) Works about Butor

In French
Albérès, R.-M. *Michel Butor.* Classiques du XXe siècle. Paris: Editions Universitaires, 1964.
Charbonnier, Georges. *Enttretiens avec Michel Butor.* Paris: Gallimard, 1967.
Raillard, Georges. *Michel Butor.* Bibliothèque Idéale. Paris: Gallimard, 1968.
Roudaut, Jean. *Michel Butor ou le livre futur.* Paris: Gallimard, 1964.
Van Rossum-Guyon, Françoise. *Critique du roman. Essai sur 'La Modification' de Michel Butor.* Paris: Gallimard, 1970.
Special issue of *L'Arc*, No. 39 (1969).

In English
Roudiez, Leon S. *Michel Butor.* Columbia Essays on Modern Writers. New York: Columbia University Press, 1965.

13. JEAN PIERRE FAYE
Works of fiction by Faye
Entre les rues. Paris: Seuil, 1958.
La Cassure. Paris: Seuil, 1961.
Battement. Paris: Seuil, 1962.
Analogues. Paris: Seuil, 1964.
L'Ecluse. Paris: Seuil, 1964.
Les Troyens. Paris: Seuil, 1970.

14. PHILIPPE SOLLERS
Works of fiction by Sollers

Le Défi. In *Ecrire 3.* Paris: Seuil, 1957.
Une Curieuse Solitude. Paris: Seuil, 1958.
Le Parc. Paris: Seuil, 1961.
Drame. Paris: Seuil, 1965.
Nombres. Paris: Seuil, 1968.
Lois. [Scheduled for 1972 publication]

English translations
A Strange Solitude. London: Eyre & Spottiswoode, 1961.
The Park. New York: Red Dust, 1969.

15. JEAN RICARDOU
   Works of fiction by Jean Ricardou
L'Observatoire de Cannes. Paris: Minuit, 1961.
La Prise de Constantinople. Paris: Minuit, 1965.
Les Lieux-dits. Paris: Gallimard, 1969.
Révolutions minuscules. Paris: Gallimard, 1971.

Index

402

402 INDEX

ditional, 97 ff.; communication, zones of, 90 ff.; circularity, 89; humor, 81, 102; influences on, 101; love, 102; material possessions, irrationality and, 91; Ollier and, 100, 244; Pinget and, 185–86, 193, 197, 203; Queneau and, 81, 83; quest, 83–84; Robbe-Grillet and, 91, 222, 227; Sollers and, 352

Belacqua (Beckett character), 98, 99

Belaval, Yvon, 38, 40

Benda, Julien, 148

Benveniste, Emile, 322, 325, 357–58

Bernal, Olga, 209

Bernard (in Simon's *Le Sacre du printemps*), 163

Bioy Casares, Adolfo, 244

Blanchot, Maurice, 55–79, 350, 370; Beckett and, 55, 67, 75, 79, 92, 100; Breton and, 65–67, 71, 72, 77; Butor and, 78; characterization, 55, 76–79; Duras and, 113; existence, experience of, 77–79; Faye and, 326, 338; Giraudoux and, 62–63, 318; human condition theme, 71; Kafka and, 59, 66–67; language, 55 ff., 100; Mallarmé and, 55–56, 58; C. Mauriac and, 146; narrator role, 72–73, 75–77; Ollier and, 246; Orpheus myth, 71–72, 77, 338; reader relationship, 72 ff.; Robbe-Grillet and, 62; Roussel and, 55; Sarraute and, 33, 39, 55, 78; Sartre and, 68–69; silence concept, 26, 79; Simon and, 179; Social unrest theme, 71; Sollers and, 75, 351, 355; surrealism, 55–56, 61 ff., 77; "warning signal," 60–61, 62

Blum (in Simon's *La Route des Flandres*), 167–68

Boehme, Jacob, 281

Bonini (in Butor's *Degrés*), 142

Borges, Jorge Luis, 220, 252–53

Bourget, Paul, 158

Bouvard et Pécuchet (Flaubert), 207, 249

Brandt, Bill, 309

Brée, Germaine, 108

Breton, André: Blanchot and, 65–67, 71, 72, 77; Butor and, 282; Dada, 378; politics, 359, 378; Roussel and, 12–13; Sollers and, 342, 356, 359, 363; surrealism, 15, 26, 61, 77, 146, 249, 346–47; on unconscious, 71

bricolage, 175, 383–84

Brik, O. M., 377

Buck, Horace (in Butor's *L'Emploi du temps*), 288, 294

Burton (in Butor's *L'Emploi du temps*), 283, 287

Burton, Sir Richard, 283

Butor, Michel, 259, 278–314, 369–70, 376; Beckett and, 82; Blanchot and, 78; Breton and, 282; catalogues, 25; composition, 290; deterioration theme, 285 ff.; dreams, 278 ff.; Faye and, 305, 316; history sense, 153, 291–93; imagery, 278 ff.; independence, 376, 385; intertextuality, 140, 294–98, 305 ff., 363; Mallarmé and, 376; C. Mauriac and, 140–42, 144–45; motion theme, 313; narrator role, 141–42, 293, 294; nonlinear works, 293–305; Ollier and, 237, 283, 305; order, internal, 279 ff.; Pinget and, 183, 184, 196; plot and narrative, 294; politics, 207, 286–87, 378; radio works, 301–5; reader relationship, 23, 288–89, 296–97; relationships concept, 144–45, 279, 290–93; Robbe-Grillet and, 207, 283, 305; Roussel and, 13, 21, 23, 286; Saporta and, 259, 277; Sartre and, 296; Scheherazade, writer as, and death, 282 ff., 293, 304; Simon and, 171, 178; solitude theme, 285 ff.; Sollers and, 371, 378; structures, mobile, 277, 303; symbolism, 279–82; technique, 279; textual works, 305–14; typography and format, 272, 298–300, 302–3, 306–8

Caldwell, Erskine, 107

Camus, Albert, 69, 70, 92; Butor and, 286, 296; Faye and, 327; Sollers and, 342

About the Author

Leon S. Roudiez has two bachelor degrees from the University of Paris and an M.A. and a Ph.D. from Columbia University. He has taught at Columbia College, Pennsylvania State University, and since 1959 at Columbia University, where he is Chairman of the Department of French. He is the author of *Maurras jusqu'à l'Action française* (1957) and *Michel Butor* (1965), and has contributed to the *French Review, Romanic Review, Saturday Review, New York Times Book Review, Symposium, Yale French Studies,* and *Critique.*

*The text of this book was set in Caledonia Lino-
type and printed by Offset on P & S Special Book
manufactured by P. H. Glatfelter Co., Spring Grove,
Pa. Composed and printed by Rae Publishing Co.,
Cedar Grove, N. J. Bound by A. Horowitz & Son,
Clifton, N. J.*